Out of the Wilderness

Out of the Wilderness
1780–1980

The Brethren and Two Centuries of Life
in Central Pennsylvania

Earl C. Kaylor, Jr.

Cornwall Books
NEW YORK • LONDON

Cornwall Books
4 Cornwall Drive
East Brunswick, New Jersey 08816

Cornwall Books
69 Fleet Street
London EC4Y 1EU, England

Cornwall Books
Toronto M5E 1A7, Canada

Library of Congress Catologing in Publication Data

Kaylor, Earl C.
 Out of the wilderness, 1780–1980.

 Bibliography: p.
 Includes indexes.
 1. Church of the Brethren. Middle Pennsylvania
District. I. Title.
BX7820.M52K39   289.7'3   80-69861
ISBN 0-8453-4716-0   AACR2

Printed in the United States of America

This book is dedicated to the memory of two men,
both of whom, though different in how they lived their Brethrenism,
were very special to me:
My father—EARL CLIFFORD KAYLOR *(1905–1973)*
and
My father-in-law—WILLIAM MCKINLEY BEAHM *(1896–1964)*

Contents

Special financial support for this history was generously provided by the following persons:

James and Lucille Baker
Samuel and Wilma Baker
Arlan and Delores Barkman
Harold B. Brumbaugh
Milton Burgess
Ronald and Betty Ann Cherry
Gale and Ruth Crumrine
John and Minnie Dean
Dale and Virginia Detwiler
Emmert and Ruby Detwiler
Ardie and Jane Dillen
Charles and Pat Dillen
Calvert and Elizabeth Ellis
George and Mary Etzweiler
A. Emmert Frederick
Barry and Marlene Halbritter
James and Doris Hershberger
Rex and Dorothy Hershberger
Sara E. Hoover
Earl and Harriet Kaylor
George and Dona Kensinger
Leon and Eleanor Kensinger
Wesley and Shirley Lingenfelter
Ross and Miriam Miller
Eugene and Allegra Morrall
Ralph and Mary Over
Robert and Mildred Over
John and Dorothy Patterson
Clayton and Judy Pheasant
Ray G. Replogle
John and Ruth Risser
Lloyd and Lura Sollenberger
John and Jane Swigart
Ben and Maxine Van Horn
Kenneth and Gladys Weaver
Roy and Mildred Wilson
Virgil and Lillian Wineland
Luther and Hazel Yoder

Promotional Patrons:

Altoona First	Mr. C. R. Dillen
Altoona 28th Street	Mrs. Janet Zook
Bedford	The Reverend D. Howard Keiper
Carson Valley	The Reverend R. Eugene Miller
Upper Claar	Miss Mary S. Claar
Lower Claar	Mrs. Robert Mock
Clover Creek	Miss Mary Ellen Kensinger
Curryville	Mrs. Grace Nicodemus
Dunnings Creek	Mrs. Virgil Felix
Fairview	Mr. James K. Loose, Jr.
Hollidaysburg	The Reverend Harry Spaeth
Holsinger	Mrs. Donald Miller
Huntingdon	Miss Alberta Haught
Juniata	Mr. Bruce Poorman
Koontz	Mrs. Dorothy M. Steele
Lewistown	The Reverend Walter E. Coldren
Maitland	The Reverend Wilbur E. Fether
Martinsburg	Mrs. Minnie Dean
New Enterprise	Dr. Ben F. Van Horn
Pine Glen	Mrs. Gladys Hesser
Roaring Spring	Mr. John M. Patterson
Spring Run	Mr. Roy D. Wilson
Stonerstown	The Reverend Daniel M. Brumbaugh
Williamsburg	Mrs. Hazel A. Weaver
Woodbury	The Reverend Raymond Boose

Preface

This history has been long in coming forth—nigh unto fourteen years. I was commissioned to write it in January 1967, a task taken on, as I indicated then, as a "labor of love" and not for compensation. A combination of circumstances contributed to the delay. First, it was my discovery, early in this project, that the 1925 history of Middle District, which I was counting on to be the major source for material on the District's formative period, would not serve my purpose. I found it to be both sketchy and error-riddled, a situation that changed my whole approach. It was now necessary for me, in order to construct a full and accurate account of events up to 1925, to research fully on my own the span of time covered by the former history. Only after that could I begin to give thought to the decades since. Enlarged responsibilities at the College and time out to prepare its centennial history caused further holdup. Nevertheless, I have devoted the better part of two sabbatical leaves since 1967 to preparing this volume.

The reader needs to understand that I completed this history under two constraints, one of them self-imposed. The first constraint was dictated by the terms of my commission itself—"to write an interpretative history of the Church of the Brethren in this geographical area." That means that I was expected to develop the history of Middle District in the context of the times: what was happening in the Brotherhood or, less often, what the world, national, or local scene was like. This is in contrast to the 1925 history, which tends to be discursive, narrowly regional in perspective, a work of reference—in terms of dates, names, statistics—and primarily, as its preface states, a "history of the several churches of the Middle District." This is not meant to discredit the earlier work. Quite the contrary; its purpose was simply different, and I found it to be an invaluable guide, despite the frequency of factual slips.

The second constraint, of my own exaction, had to do with the congregational sketches. These were not eliminated by the charge given me, but I inferred that, though updating them was part of my task, they should not be overstressed. Consequently, the cameos of local churches, particularly for the time since 1925, are deliberately condensed, dwelling more upon building programs than people.

This is unfortunate and not what I would have preferred. But limitations of space and the impossible dilemma of deciding which individuals deserved mentioning mandated this policy. In other chapters, however, I have tried to build my story around people as much as possible. Moreover, my own research has enabled me to bring fresh information into the recital of congregational origins and growth.

The invitation to me from the District Historical Committee also asked that this work be "written for popular appeal." That I have tried to do, aiming for a middle-level style, neither too academic nor too informal. And often, especially in those chapters on earlier times and people, I have resorted to anecdotal narration to bring events to life. One further comment: my commission specified that this history "will be based on thorough research." As I have intimated above, the most time-consuming aspect of my assignment was fulfilling this charge. In my first draft I documented sources copiously. But, upon later reflection and to avoid being tedious, I decided to reduce the number of citations drastically, only including enough to preserve my professional credibility and integrity.

Significantly, at no time did the original Historical Committee so much as hint that my manuscript must be cleared by some examining body before it went to press. As a longtime college teacher, I appreciate this respect for academic freedom. Among other things, this admirable attitude on the first Committee's part has allowed me to be genuine in the praise of individuals and congregations. For, as is observed in a line from the opera *The Marriage of Figaro:* "If censorship reigns, there cannot be sincere flattery."

Two other matters of lesser import. First, I have consistently used the term *conference* when referring to the stated annual congresses of both the Brotherhood and the District. In the former case, the word *meeting* began dropping out of currency around the time of World War I, while Middle Pennsylvania's constitution of 1933 gave the official stamp to the designation *District Conference.* Second, when I make comparative references, or give the "most recent" congregational tallies—as in chapters 4 and 5 and the conclusion—I have drawn upon the *Church of the Brethren: 1976 Statistical Report,* which is the latest compilation of Brotherhood data available.

Finally, this has been a "labor of love" in much more than a figurative sense. On and off for a long while now, I have lived—in my imagination—in other times, among people of simpler ways and of a different outlook on life. I came to feel very much "at home" with them. But above all, I gained a new appreciation of what they did and what they stood for. Each of us with rootage in Central

Pennsylvania can truly say with the Psalmist, "Yea, I have a goodly heritage." That is why I think the lead title of this history aptly describes this District's role in the Church of the Brethren's past. It brings to mind three symbols: pioneering, prophetic mission, learning. Each represents progress, each means deliverance from a "wilderness" condition, whether it be terrestrial, spiritual, or cultural.

Juniata College
Huntingdon, Pennsylvania

Acknowledgments

Many people have gone to great lengths to help me in this project. Initially, of course, Clarence H. Rosenberger and the original District Historical Committee, whose members are named in the introduction, were of inestimable assistance. Under the Reverend Rosenberger, who was then Director of Church Relations at Juniata College and later took a church in Eastern Pennsylvania, the Committee worked diligently to create a separate archival collection of Middle District historical materials in the L. A. Beeghly Library at Juniata and to secure the appointment of congregational historians to update the post-1925 record of local churches.

Others who have served on the Committee, some of whom read portions of the manuscript in its earliest stages and made helpful comments, were Calvert N. Ellis, Kenneth W. Crosby, and Elaine Sollenberger. The present members, Harold B. Brumbaugh and Alberta Haught, were ministering spirits in seeing the history into print. Indeed, Dr. Brumbaugh, an active layman whose name for the past forty-four years has been all but synonymous with Juniata College as a result of his duties with the alumni and development offices and the Trustee Board, gave untiringly of his time and talents to get this book published.

Others besides those who have served on the District Historical Committee also merit thanks. The information provided by each of the local church historians, whom it is not possible here to recognize individually, proved very useful and spared me, in most cases, considerable research time. The staff of the L. A. Beeghly Library was unfailingly accommodating, as was Dr. Joseph Mason while District Executive. Daniel M. Brumbaugh, Harold B. Brumbaugh, Minnie G. Dean, Dale W. Detwiler, Calvert N. Ellis, George A. Etzweiler, Monroe C. Good, Alberta Haught, Rex W. Hershberger, George E. Kensinger, John D. Keiper, Richard L. Landrum, Lloyd E. Sollenberger, John W. Swigart, Benjamin F. Van Horn, and Roy D. Wilson graciously proffered sound guidance on promotional and marketing techniques. I am very grateful to the administration of Juniata College, which granted me two sabbatical leaves in the last thirteen years to work on this history.

I owe a special debt of gratitude to Miriam Williamson and June Peters, both of the District Office, who collaborated in typing the manuscript. Their patience, skills, and helpful suggestions were much appreciated.

Happily, my wife, Harriet, though herself immersed in completing a doctoral program while teaching full time, was always most understanding and supportive through all stages of this study. She contributed much toward making my writing a delightful experience.

When all is said and done, of course, the author must bear final responsibility for any mistakes that may remain in the pages that follow.

Introduction
The Brethren Begin
to Tell Their Story

Martin G. Brumbaugh Publishes First Historical Study of the Church

The Brethren did not have much of a mind for history until the late nineteenth century. Until then they were generally negligent about keeping records and, for the most part, indifferent about their origins. It was not until 1914, for example, that Standing Committee of Annual Conference acquiesced in minuting their proceedings.

There were exceptions, of course. Alexander Mack, Jr., gathered information from the papers of his father and Peter Becker on Brethren beginnings, which he published as a prefatory statement in the second edition of Mack senior's doctrinal booklet, *Basic Questions.* Before 1854 ex-Lutheran Henry Kurtz, founder of the *Gospel Visitor,* began to collect historical material "for the benefit of our children." But he never completed the work. Middle District's own Henry Holsinger led the fight to transcribe and print the debates at Annual Conference in the 1870s, which included identifying the speakers. His *Brethren Family Almanac* frequently featured historical and biographical sketches, usually penned by the famous antiquarian Abraham H. Cassel from Eastern Pennsylvania.

The historical climate of the Brotherhood began to change in 1895 when Annual Conference gave permission "for some brother to compile and publish in book form a history of the ecclesiastical world, that made the inception of the Brethren Church a necessity; including the rise and progress of the church, its growth in numbers and religious work, etc. . . ." Then in 1898 the German Baptist Brethren Historical Association organized, with headquarters at Germantown. Its object was "to collect, preserve and diffuse the history of our church."

Almost immediately a Niagara of scholarly works began to flow from the press. Middle District's Martin G. Brumbaugh was the first to go into print—with his *A History of the German Baptist Brethren in*

Europe and America, published in 1899 while he was president of
Juniata College. A classic, it stamped him the denomination's
pioneer historian and was a feat of prodigious scholarship. Some of
the material for this monumental study had been gathered in the
summer of 1896 while he was in Germany studying at the University
of Jena. Most of his sources, however, were found in the vast private
library of Abraham Cassel.

Brumbaugh's history made the Brethren aware, as never before,
of an important aspect of their past: the vigorous literary and
intellectual activity of colonial ancestors. It revealed that the greatest
cultural force among German-speaking colonists had been the Sauer
press, not Franklin's, as historians thought. Moreover, it brought to
light Brethren involvement in the founding of Germantown
Academy and the fact that even earlier, almost as soon as they had
landed in Pennsylvania, the church fathers had set up a school of
their own, woman-taught.

Brumbaugh lamented that, when researching his volume, "with
one exception, no member [of the denomination] has aided in the
work, although repeated appeals were made."[1] That one exception
was Abraham Cassel, a third of whose holdings Brumbaugh acquired in 1899 for $2,500, paid for out of his own pocket. Its seller, a
native of Harleysville, Montgomery County, was a great-great-
grandson of Christopher Sauer through his mother, who was also a
great-granddaughter of Peter Becker. From its start he was a
stockbroker and booster of Juniata College, to which he sent his
daughter in 1877. At the time, Cassel's library ranked as one of the
largest private collections in the country—some fifty thousand
books, pamphlets, and broadsides—dwarfing many public and college libraries.

The part of this coveted miscellany that Brumbaugh purchased (it
included three boxes of Cassel correspondence) he turned over to
Juniata College, where it resides today in the Archives of the L. A.
Beeghly Library. The young college president hoped to make
Juniata the chief repository of Brethren publications, past and
future. In 1900 he sent out circulars to one thousand ministers in
the Eastern states, asking for old books, magazines, newspapers,
almanacs, and anything else that might have been published by
members of the church. The response was disappointing, and the
project never panned out.

Nevertheless, the German Baptist Brethren Historical Association, whose executive committee Brumbaugh began to chair a decade before his death in 1930, kept alive the zeal for preserving
historical records. Others from Middle District were officers of the

association in its infancy: Frank F. Holsopple, a son-in-law of James Quinter and then a Juniata College professor, and Lawrence Ruble of McVeytown, a farmer-teacher who later became County Superintendent of Mifflin County schools. Another early officer was Harry H. Nye, who did not, however, come to Central Pennsylvania until 1930, when he joined Juniata's faculty as a history instructor.

Men such as these gave a new stature to church history within the denomination by the time the first decade of the 1900s had run its course. By then other histories had appeared, like Juniata graduate George N. Falkenstein's *History of the German Baptist Brethren* (1901), or even *History of the Tunkers and the Brethren Church* (1901) by Henry Holsinger, the man who caused the great split of the 1880s after leaving Middle District. The approach of the church's bicentennial year—1908—prompted several queries calling for some suitable commemoration at Annual Conference at that time.

The program that took place was history-oriented, the twenty-four speakers all looking back at the past, for the most part. Among the impressive list of those who prepared papers were a number of individuals who at one time or another lived in Central Pennsylvania: Tobias T. Myers, Solomon Z. Sharp, Adaline H. Beery, Galen B. Royer, Henry B. Brumbaugh. Their addresses were published in *Two Centuries of the Brethren*, the introduction to which was written by M. G. Brumbaugh, himself one of the speechmakers. Since then books as well as several doctoral dissertations, some of them re-worked and published, have been written by Brethren scholars on various aspects of the denomination—its sociocultural heritage and patterns, its peace testimony, its educational history, its changing attitude toward social involvement, its links to European Pietism and Anabaptism.

Meantime, the Brotherhood's Historical Committee came into existence, the creation of Annual Conference in 1945 and a belated concession to those history buffs who since 1898 had urged that an organization of this kind be incorporated into the general church body. Among other designated functions, this committee was given the charge to "stimulate" research and writing on the Brethren, to "secure" valuable church records and make them available—which the colleges were also asked to do—to "encourage" members to draw up family genealogies, and to develop two historical depositories: a central one in Elgin, Illinois, the location of denominational head-quarters, and another in the historic Germantown Church. The Historical Committee has lacked neither in leadership nor in carrying out its duties ever since.

Historians and other scholars have also found a forum in two periodicals published in recent decades. The late Floyd E. Mallott, while professor of church history at Bethany Theological Seminary, introduced and edited *Schwarzenau,* issued between 1939 and 1942. Then there is today's *Brethren Life and Thought,* established in 1955 as a journal of opinion and scholarship. Although independently owned—by the Brethren Journal Association—it is published in the interests of the denomination.

The Brethren, then, have come a long way in historical awareness since Martin G. Brumbaugh's forerunning volume appeared at the nineteenth century's close. It laid the foundations upon which historians of later generations have built. Fittingly, Brumbaugh's formative influence on Brethren scholarship and historiography did not go ignored by Brotherhood officials. When he died in 1930 the General Education Board of the Church of the Brethren paid tribute to him by saying, "He rendered an immortal service in discovering and preserving for the church her early historical records. He inspired on the part of the church an undying interest in the founders and early traditions of our faith."[2]

The Rise of State and District Histories

Not long after Brumbaugh's book of 1899 came out, district histories began making their appearance. In 1907 a small volume on Southern Illinois was prepared, to be followed by *A History of the Brethren in Virginia* (1908). During World War I others came on the scene—on Pennsylvania's Eastern District, on Northeastern Ohio, on Western Pennsylvania. The list grew with the years, but some of the early histories were not confined merely to districts. *The Church of the Brethren in Lebanon County* had a 1916 publication date, for example, while *A History of the Brethren in Virginia* had preceded it by eight years. Congregations were chronicled too, like the *History of the Coventry Brethren Church in Chester County* (1898). But as for district histories, there was another spurt in literature of this kind after Annual Conference set up the Historical Committee in 1945. District historical committees were appointed to pursue in earnest the preservation of records and other items of antiquarian value. Their work continues, one important aspect of which has been seeing to it that district histories are periodically updated or, in some cases, completely rewritten.

Writing Middle Pennsylvania's Past

The 1925 *History of the Church of the Brethren in the Middle District of Pennsylvania* is strangely silent about an informative little booklet titled *A Brief History of Claar Congregation,* which was printed in 1908 upon the occasion of the Brotherhood's bicentennial celebration.[3] This sixty-page sketch was written by David M. Adams, who pastored the congregation from 1907 to 1909. He later served the denomination in pastorates in Western Pennsylvania and the Midwest before leaving the ministry in 1922 and taking over as editor of the *Cove News.* Adams's account of the Claar Brethren provides valuable historical and biographical data. Nothing like it—on the congregational level—has turned up since.

The most important historical work to follow was the 1925 history, which was fundamentally designed, as its preface indicates, to be a chronicle of the District's "several" congregations and not an overview of the Brethren in Middle Pennsylvania. The idea of such a history apparently originated with James A. Sell of Leamersville, who was a great spiritual and intellectual force in the District during his long life of over one hundred years. The matter of a history got support at District Meeting in 1911, and Sell and George S. Myers from the New Enterprise church and Snake Spring's William S. Ritchey were named to a Historical Committee to gather material from the various churches.

Despite a lack of interest in the District generally, the threesome kept doggedly at their assignment. George Myers, who ran a lumbering business, assumed the arduous chore of researching all church publications. He also made it his task to collect and index all statistical data on ministerial elections. James Sell himself worked at drafting a narrative account of congregational origins and growth from material supplied him. The project dragged out, and then in 1920 Myers died. District Conference that year added two more men to the Historical Committee: Juniata College's Tobias T. Myers and Galen B. Royer. Next year, the appointment of Jacob Kinsel of Altoona, Oscar R. Myers of Juniata College, and Mahlon J. Weaver, then of Roaring Spring, expanded the Committee to seven members. By 1921 the end seemed to be in sight, and District Meeting endorsed the Committee's recommendation that the Mission Board finance the projected history when it was ready to go to press. Receipts from its sale, it was agreed, would go toward repaying the Board.

But the work bogged down, and in 1923 James Sell called for the appointment of an editor to bring the history to its completion. Galen B. Royer, a man of extensive writing and editorial experience, accepted the position and put the finished manuscript in the hands of the printer, who was never identified, by late 1924. The book was ready next April and sold for $4.40 a copy ($3.90 for the 810

advance copies). Fourteen hundred copies of the 561-page history
were printed, but 311 remained in sheet form. It was bound in cloth,
though a few morocco copies were made. M. G. Brumbaugh, then
president of Juniata's College for a second time, wrote the introduction. James Sell's original manuscript was deposited in the College's
library vault (now it is in the Middle District Historical Library in the
Archives).

The Historical Committee disbanded and there matters stood for
the next two decades. Then Annual Conference's action in 1945 to
make the preservation of historical materials a Brotherhood concern
caused some Sunday School leaders in Middle Pennsylvania to raise
the question of bringing the 1925 history up-to-date. But no one
pressed the suggestion until the District Board brought it up
seriously again in 1957. Four years later, District Meeting authorized
the Christian Education Commission to appoint a committee to
investigate the possibility of revising the old history.

The original committee, chaired by Clarence Rosenberger, included Clyde Stayer, Ernest Brumbaugh, Clair Holsinger, and John
Swigart. This new Historical Committee saw its task as threefold: the
collection, preservation, and publication of historical materials related to Middle District. An appeal went out to congregations to elect
historians to assist in this undertaking. As for the third objective, the
committee mulled over several options: (1) reprint the 1925 history;
(2) publish a supplement of the same nature for the period after
1925; (3) publish a new history that would tell the whole District
story in an interpretive and topical fashion; or (4) publish a new
history and reprint the 1925 history.

The Committee finally decided, with the counsel of Dr. Donald F.
Durnbaugh of Bethany Theological Seminary, on option three—a
topical, interpretive history that would stress personalities,
movements, and ideas. It further determined that a professionally
trained historian should be sought out to prepare such a history.
And so in January 1967, Earl C. Kaylor, Jr., a member of the history
and religion departments at Juniata College, was so commissioned.

Out of the Wilderness

1
Origins of the Brethren
in Europe and Colonial America

How many eighteenth-century Brethren pioneers in Central Pennsylvania were of birthright status is hard to know. Some families, like the ancestral Brumbaughs, were converts but a short time prior to colonizing the woods and valleys of the Juniata basin. However, the religious descent of most early Brethren settlers is unknown. Interestingly, the immediate post–Revolutionary War era marked the migration into Middle District of two direct descendants—a grandson and a great-granddaughter—of Alexander Mack. Both are buried in Morrisons Cove.

Genesis of Brethren Ideology

RADICAL PIETISM

The Church of the Brethren got its start in Germany in 1708 as a small sectarian movement at Schwarzenau, a little village on the banks of the stream Eder, in Wittgenstein, a county in Westphalia. This territory was part of the German Palatinate. Alexander Mack, a mill owner and the sect's founder, was a man of some means who had come under Pietistic influences after rebelling against the spiritual lethargy of the Reformed Church in which he had been reared.

Pietism was a movement in reaction to the seeming lifelessness of Lutheran and Reformed orthodoxy. It stressed the devotional life—earnest Christians gathered in small groups to study the Bible, sing hymns, and engage in prayer—rather than theological discussion, which Pietists looked upon as a source of division and strife within the church. Its message also stressed the mystical experience, practical and intense preaching, extensive pastoral work, and devotion to human welfare. The Pietists reemphasized the priesthood of all believers, giving their movement a strong democratizing thrust.

Christianity was a way of life, they insisted, not a creed; hence Pietists downgraded their confessional traditions and affirmed the common experience of Christ as the definition of Christian identity.

Pietism appeared as a reform movement within German Protestantism in the second half of the seventeenth century. At first Pietists, in seeking to renew the church and recover the spirit of the Reformation, posed no institutional threat, and they were far from being heretics. But soon some Pietists became more negative and iconoclastic toward the church structures of their day. They came to view the hierarchical state churches as utterly decadent; their own model of order, discipline, and worship was to be found in the New Testament. Hence the radicals began to advocate a separatist stance toward the state churches. Historians have labeled this development Radical Pietism. To contemporaries, its adherents were known as Separatists.

The Radical Pietists, however, separated not only from the state churches but from organized religion. The late Dr. Floyd Mallott of Bethany Theological Seminary wrote of these Separatists: "They repudiated clergy, sacrament, organization, church buildings, bells—everything that suggested organized religion."[1] In berating and defying the established churches, which at that time were decidedly a political force, the Separatists inevitably clashed with the law. Now stamped as heretics, they were subjected to persecution and punishment by civil authorities: fines, imprisonment, exile, property seizure, and, though rare, martyrdom.

ANABAPTISM

The historical matrix of the Brethren, then, was Radical Pietism. Alexander Mack, himself barely escaping prison, was a Separatist fugitive who eventually found refuge in Schwarzenau in 1700. Schwarzenau was one of a few places in Germany offering asylum to religious dissenters. There in late summer 1708 Mack and seven other Separatists, four men and three women whom he had gathered for Bible study, submitted themselves to rebaptism by threefold immersion rather than by pouring. It was this mode of baptism that eventually gave them their popular name—Dunkers or Tunkers (from the German word *eintuchen,* to dip)—in America. Originally, the Mack group avoided a formal appellation, content to call themselves "brethren." In Europe outsiders called them "New Baptists (Neue Täufer) or Schwarzenau Baptists," writes Dr. Donald Durnbaugh, "to distinguish them from the Mennonites (Alte Täufer) with whom they had so much in common."[2]

Except for the baptismal method, the Schwarzenau Brethren adopted the principal doctrines and practices of the Mennonites, who baptized by affusion. The Mennonites traced their origin to Menno Simons, a contemporary of Martin Luther who late in the Reformation era emerged as the foremost leader of main-line Anabaptism, that peaceful and evangelical left wing of Protestantism which, coming as it did out of the mass of common people, spawned so many sects.* These sectarian Anabaptists or Rebaptizers, while holding to the major religious principles of the reformers, were rejected by society because they sought to reintroduce certain practices and doctrines discarded or neglected by the state churches. Most Anabaptists concerned themselves primarily with an attempt to restore conditions of primitive Christianity as described in the New Testament. Theirs was an experiential faith rather than one based on theological speculation.

Their major break with Protestantism was over the nature and composition of the church. They denied the validity of the folk church, which embraces the whole population of a given territory and into which children are born and baptized. The Anabaptists viewed church membership as both voluntary and exclusive, dependent on adult decision or religious experience. It is a community of saints, composed of the regenerate only. Thus they repudiated infant baptism and practiced adult rebaptism; however, they did not advocate one preferred mode. This emphasis on believer's baptism represented a novel historical position. To be sure, certain medieval sects had renounced infant baptism, but none rebaptized adults.

Anabaptists further conceived of the church as a form of *Gemeinde* or fellowship, committed to mutual aid, rather than an organization. Gradually, however, some of them, like the Mennonites, took on a more churchly character. Generally, the worship of Anabaptists centered in the Lord's Supper, which was preceded by a love feast and the washing of feet. The "holy kiss of charity" and anointment of the sick for healing were also important rites.

Like most sects, the Anapatists were reserved, if not critical, in their relation to the state and in their attitude toward social conventions and culture. They stressed nonconformity with the world— valuing simplicity of life and dress, abhorring personal ambition, scorning oath-taking and legal redress. Their communities laid great stress on literal obedience to the Sermon on the Mount and the other teachings of Jesus. Strict disciplinarians and bound by rigid

---

*I use the term *main-line* Anabaptists to distinguish them from the more fanatical agitators at Münster, Westphalia, in the 1530s, whose short-lived movement was marked by violence and moral laxity.

The love feast is still central to Brethren worship, as this recent picture of the sanctuary at Middle Pennsylvania's Pine Glen Church illustrates.

moral taboos, Anabaptist groups imposed severe censures on members for misconduct and heresy.

Another of the cardinal tenets of the Anabaptists was the complete separation of church and state. This was absolutely essential, they argued, to guarantee religious liberty, a principle no less crucial in their credo. History taught them that the union of state and church invariably promoted the persecution of dissenting groups. The Anabaptists were perfectionists who believed that society—the established church and civil government—was incapable of being transformed. The state, therefore, served no positive function; it was a device solely for restraining sin. By its very nature it must be coercive, not cooperative. Anabaptists admitted, upon New Testament authority, that civil government is of divine appointment with legitimate authority over citizens. But this authority cannot violate individual conscience. Ultimately, Anabaptists taught, Christians must "obey God rather than man." For these reasons, Christians must not hold public office or engage in social action.

This emphasis upon allegiance to the demands of God rather than to the needs of society was rooted in Anabaptism's perfectionistic impulse. Perfectionism is the belief that it is possible to attain near-perfect obedience to the Gospel as a moral response to divine grace. This concept never symbolized to the Anabaptists, however, the actual attainment of moral and spiritual perfection; actions and attitudes always fall short of this vision. Rather, it underscored for them the primacy and transforming character of love. They interpreted the New Testament ethic to be a love ethic.

The doctrine of perfection served as grounds for both their separatism and their pacifism. As Edward L. Long, Jr., has written:

> Concern for complete and perfect obedience in one's own life may not be combined with an ethic acceptable to all the world. The Anabaptists totally and completely rejected the use of armed coercion by members of their own fellowship, yet referred to the sword as "ordained for use outside the perfection of Christ." They did not try to construct a Christian ethic acceptable to, and valid within, a community outside of Christian commitment. Their key ethical concept has been total fidelity within the fold rather than universal responsibility within the world, and they have been willing to live apart from the mainstream of the world's life in order to "obey God rather than man."[3]

As Perfectionists and Separatists, the Anabaptists opposed all war and military service. But their brand of pacifism went beyond religious opposition to killing in warfare. Some scholars refer to the kind of pacifism they exemplified as vocational pacifism. The vocational pacifist is persuaded that the essence of the New Testament love ethic is nonresistance to evil, that is, defenselessness or passive obedience. The hateless life, according to the nonresistant ideal, means, in imitation of Christ, the meek acceptance of personal injustice for the sake of obedience to God. Pacifism of this type does not seek to alter, change, or overthrow the social order, or to abolish war. It can and usually does result in civil disobedience but not as a technique to effect political or societal reconstruction. Its quiet posture is alien to strident public protest and unacceptable to the moral crusader. Thus, though true rebels, Anabaptists pacifists were known as "The Quiet Ones in the Land" *(Die Stillen im Lande)*. Vocational pacifism is simply a way of life, a form of witness to a higher morality, a total commitment to the example of Christ.

By contrast, scholars speak of "modern" or "activistic" pacifism, a peace stand historically represented by a group like the Quakers and great personalities like Mahatma Gandhi and Martin Luther King, Jr. The motif here is "nonviolent resistance to evil." Explains Edward Long, Jr., "Believers in nonviolence regard the duty to oppose evil by every means short of violence to be an important part of Christian obligation. Martin Luther King became a pacifist only after he realized that nonviolence provides a way in which to oppose evil without the use of military techniques."[4]

Activistic pacifists make two un-Anabaptist assumptions about the world and the peace witness. First of all, they believe that society—

and the state—are capable of being changed in life and character,
like individuals. Political and social involvement, which includes
holding public office and engaging in reform action, is seen as a
legitimate way to remodel sinful, coercive society into a more Christian, peaceful order. Second, the activistic pacifist feels morally
compelled to resist evil, to make nonviolence a positive method to
outlaw war and eliminate societal ills, to become a crusader for social
progress. The Church of the Brethren would by stages move into
this second camp, but until the present century Brethren pacifism
belonged to the Anabaptist mold.

Brethren historians agree, then, that Anabaptism and Radical
Pietism were two lines of influence upon Alexander Mack's little
band at the beginning. The political climate in Wittgenstein changed
after 1720, and the Schwarzenau congregation, now faced with
persecution, migrated to Holland, where there was religious tolera-
tion. Gradually, however, they cast aside many beliefs and ways of
the Radical Pietists, like community of goods, antisacramentalism,
and celibacy. The very decision to form a fellowship, highlighted by
rebaptism, in 1708 violated the antiorganizational prejudices of the
Radical Pietists. "The best way to understand the early Brethren,"
Donald Durnbaugh puts it aptly, "is to see them as a Radical Pietist
group which approximated an Anabaptist view of the church." He
concludes, "To be sure, they retained some characteristics of their
Pietist background but they were almost indistinguishable by the
outsider from the Mennonites."[5]

Growth and Persecution

Before any formative contact with the Mennonites, however, the
Schwarzenau Brethren were quite active in gaining converts to their
following. Soon after 1708 they were sending preachers on tours of
the Rhine Valley and to Switzerland to establish new fellowships. In
all, there developed four other Brethren centers, either as a result of
missionary activity or the relocation of an existing, persecuted
group. Two branches, one at Marienborn and one at Epstein, later
merged at Krefeld, a city in the Lower Rhine Valley northwest of
Düsseldorf and then under tolerant Prussian rule, to escape persecution. Krefeld was a commercial city that the Mennonites had made
a prosperous center of German textile industry. There the Brethren, who had begun arriving in 1715, experienced their first close
association with the Mennonites.

About this time the Schwarzenau congregation itself found it
necessary to migrate in a body. According to Durnbaugh, the
reasons are not clear, whether because of an unfavorable change in

the political picture or mounting economic hardship.[6] Martin G. Brumbaugh, however, attributes their flight to bitter persecution.[7] For whatever cause, they went to Holland in 1720. Like the Brethren at Krefeld, the Schwarzenau pilgrims found refuge with the Mennonites—in their marshland colony of Surhuisterveen. This would be home for them until 1729, when the Mack-led Wittgenstein group, who tradition says introduced the first potatoes to Hollanders of that area, departed for the New World. At Surhuisterveen the Brethren apparently took up ice skating, something they had never heard of before and which at first they considered a devilish activity.[8]

Socioeconomic and Cultural Origins

Obviously, life was not easy for the European Brethren, who sacrificed much in terms of security and personal comfort for their religious convictions. It would be interesting to know more fully the social, economic, and educational background of the men and women to whom the denomination owes its genesis. Records are spotty and often fail to reveal pertinent information, but a search of published sources, like Donald Durnbaugh's *European Origins of the Brethren,* is not altogether a fruitless enterprise.[9]

There is, of course, considerable information on Alexander Mack. He was probably the best-born and by far the most well-to-do of the church's progenitors. His father was an influential and respected citizen of Schriesheim, a town near Heidelberg and far south of Schwarzenau, where he twice served as mayor and was a council member of long standing. Mack's wealth—land, mills, and vineyards—was largely inherited in 1706 when he was twenty-seven. His father-in-law, also a town councillor, left him a sizable additional legacy in 1714. This fortune he exhausted for the welfare of his followers by the time he sailed for America.

Floyd Mallott speculates that Mack used up the bulk of his private resources during the seven years the Schwarzenau folk had their goods in common.[10] This is likely true, as is his further observation that, with few exceptions, the Old World Brethren belonged to the "poor laborer and peasant class," their poverty magnified by the fines and jailings meted them.[11] A Swiss Separatist, in a letter written from Krefeld to friends in Switzerland in 1719, speaks of the "Schwarzenau Baptists" as "gathering a great number of poor people."[12] At that time Luke Vetter, one of the original eight, and his wife and four children were on public relief at Krefeld, as was at least one other Brethren family.[13]

Though some Brethren, hailing from rural and grape-growing

areas, were probably counted among the peasantry, there are no direct references to them as farmers in extant sources. This is a curiosity, suggesting that perhaps Mack's followers were less people of the soil than tradition maintains. Their dozen or so years at Schwarzenau hardly encouraged tillage as a livelihood since the forested, mountainous land around that village was described by Mack himself as "poor and rough."[14]

Documents do provide, however, frequent mention of the Brethren as craftsmen. A nineteenth-century Mennonite historian, writing about his people at Surhuisterveen, relates that there were "many artisans" among the thirty families from Schwarzenau that relocated there.[15] Of Alexander Mack's four male comrades at the Eder-stream baptismal scene, we know that Andrew Boni was a linen weaver and George Grebe a gunsmith. Grebe, according to a contemporary account, had been a "rich" court gunsmith at Kassel, who after fleeing to Schwarzenau was reduced to living in a one-room hut there, penniless.[16] The occupations of the other two, Luke Vetter, the charity case at Surhuisterveen, and John Kipping, are unknown. Peter Becker, a leader at Krefeld, was a serge weaver, at least while a resident of that city. Other trades specifically identified with the Brethren were shoemaker, tailor, capmaker, sackmaker, buttonmaker.

While we get some fairly clear clues about the socioeconomic status of primitive Brethren, we must rely on surmise when discussing the extent of their schooling. Only one of their numbers, John Lobach, a buttonmaker by trade and one of the famous Solingen prisoners, refers to his education. He had apparently received a good one, but not at the university level. For a time he taught a private school, while recovering from an illness that kept him from his workbench. His beautiful letters, especially to his mother from prison, and an autobiographical sketch exhibit a sensitive, cultured, literate mind.[17]

Regarding the male members of the founding epoch, particularly the leaders, it is safe to say that theirs was more than a rudimentary education. One Brethren educator points out that "they were a studious people who were willing to meet to study their textbook, the Bible, in depth and that they were sufficiently educated to make their own evaluations of what they studied. . . . Their leader and others who were with them in their early years in Germany did have an awareness of some of the significant scholarship of that area and time."[18] Alexander Mack had a literary knack and authored two tracts as doctrinal guides for his disciples in addition to composing hymns and poetry.

He was not the only one with a poetic bent. John Naas, next to Mack the most influential European leader—a man of commanding figure who, though tortured, heroically refused military service for the King of Prussia—also composed hymns. So did Peter Becker, the Krefeld elder who set in motion the wholesale Brethren exodus to America.

Women, of course, held no status as leaders of the young movement, their nondomestic and intellectual outlets curbed by the mores of that age. Nor were they privileged with a formal education, though probably few if any were illiterate. However, observes Durnbaugh, "It is significant that women played a role in every area of Brethren expansion."[19] They made up a solid segment of the order—about a third of the European membership—and proved to be loyal and supportive spouses in the uncertain lives of their husbands. Moreover, the hardships they patiently endured as empty-handed homemakers, often on the move, all bespoke a religious dedication every whit as daring and steadfast as that of their menfolk.

These men and women of the Schwarzenau generation never attracted a large following. The number that joined the church probably added up to few more than 250 by the time the American hegira got underway. The European phase of Brethren origins ended with the 1730s, the handful that remained relapsing into separatism or joining kindred groups such as the Mennonites.

Colonial Beginnings

The first contingent of Brethren to emigrate to America were Krefelders, led by Peter Becker in 1719. A quarrel over church discipline, which involved an intimate friend of Becker's, split that fellowship and provoked a mass exodus. Durnbaugh thinks economic and outside religious pressures also contributed to the decision to go to Pennsylvania. Several Mennonite families from Krefeld had already settled in William Penn's colony, at what came to be called Germantown, a distance of two hours' walk from Philadelphia. Whether these first Pennsylvanians directly influenced the Krefeld Brethren to make the perilous Atlantic crossing in pursuit of religious freedom and economic independence is not known. But some of their letters, telling of unlimited opportunity, abundant land, and, above all, liberty of conscience, must surely have fallen into Brethren hands. These testimonials would likely have been reinforced by pamphlets and agents advertising Pennsylvania all over Holland. At any rate, forty families (two hundred persons), well-nigh the whole fellowship, chose to accompany Peter Becker on the oceanic journey to Penn's mecca.

Quaker convert William Penn, who obtained his wilderness terri-tory in America in 1681 as settlement of a large debt owed his father by the king, dreamed of founding a religious utopia in the new world. He called what he set out to do "an holy experiment." He looked upon his colony as a trust committed to him by God. In many respects, it was a veritable "melting pot," deliberately and success-fully designed to produce a diversified society, self-governed. The province attracted men and women differing in race and language and religion. This was quite in contrast to the Puritans of New England, who were frightened by the idea of a heterogeneous state and erected civil and ecclesiastical barriers to prevent it.

In his new social order, Penn wanted to prove, in the words of Floyd Mallott, "that religious liberty was practical, that pure Chris-tianity could be maintained without a State Church, that govern-ment could be carried on without war and oaths."[20] Pennsylvania as a testing ground of democratic principles, freedom of worship, and brotherly love forthwith became a beacon of hope to the oppressed overseas. In eighteen years (1682–1700) its population increased forty-fold—from five hundred to twenty thousand. By the time the Brethren had all removed to Pennsylvania—in 1733—the number of inhabitants had grown to about 75,000. Seven years later, the proprietary Province stood as the fourth most populous colony in America.

Among the colony's earliest pioneers, the Brethren benefited much from its benign rule and long-lasting peace with the Indians, but, by the same token, they made a contribution of their own to the vitality and success of Penn's dream. Leavenlike, they, along with the Quakers and other German Pietists, helped to shape that large part of America, where, as one historian has expressed it, "the family, the church and the community are still the foundations of a generous and simple life."[21] The Brethren were also party to the economic progress of Penn's province. As frontier farmers, they added an element of strength to the economy, taking a part in making the wilderness a garden spot, by hard work and thrift, and, along with other "plain people," cultivating the "Dutch country" into the gra-nary of Pennsylvania. They and their Pennsylvania Dutch neighbors became the backbone of the agricultural population in the Keystone State.

Circumstances forced the Brethren to turn to farming, no matter what kind of work the men had done in Europe. Those who accompanied Peter Becker in 1719 found most of the land around Germantown sold, and so only half the families settled there. The rest moved deeper into the interior, where land was more readily available.

This later proved to be the pattern of dispersal for the Surhuisterveen congregation. They also emigrated in a body, in 1729, at the urging of the Becker party. The congregation, led by Alexander Mack, chartered the ship *Allen* and sailed out of Rotterdam. Fifty-nine households (126 persons) made up the passenger list. This was the last migration en masse by the Brethren. Others would come to Pennsylvania during the 1730s, but usually in single family units. The Naases—father, mother, and daughter—came in 1733, followed by son Jacob's family in 1735. They were among the last arrivals.

Like the earlier Brethren seafarers, John Naas took the Rotterdam-to-Philadelphia route, a journey of about fifteen weeks ordinarily. Ocean passage then was a hazardous adventure, compounded by horrendous shipboard conditions. Naas, in a letter to his son written in diary form, described the daily dangers and handships he experienced on his ship, the *Pennsylvania Merchant:* fierce storms, becalming delays, numerous deaths among the young and old, constant fighting, widespread sickness, poor diet and hunger, filthy water and thirst, overcrowding, lack of sanitation, and lice.[22] Andrew Boni, one of the Schwarzenau eight, crossed the Atlantic on the *Allen* with Alexander Mack, and in a subsequent letter to a cousin in Germany warned of kidnappers, lurking in the port city of Rotterdam, who sold their victims into servitude.[23] The high cost of crossing the Atlantic, in terms of blood and tears, not to speak of cash, was not unknown to the Brethren, so their decision to migrate from the land of their origin was not a trivial matter.

How they were able to pay for the trans-Atlantic fare is not clear. It does not appear, however, that they came as "redemptioners," adults who sold themselves into servitude for a limited period to defray the costs of their passage from Europe. This was a common practice among the Germans, beginning about 1722, when the traffic in redemptioners increased sharply, and continuing until 1810. The transportation of this kind of human freight became "big business" with sea captains, and conditions on their ships often rivaled in horror those that prevailed on ships engaged in the African slave trade. Apparently, the *Pennsylvania Merchant,* on which John Naas came across, included indentured servants among its passengers, although the shipboard life did not equal the squalor and privations of the worst vessels of this sort.* Naas himself confessed, while cognizant of the trials of others, "I personally did not have much hardship—very little actually."[24]

The reception he got when his ship moored in Philadelphia's harbor was hardly that of a redemptioner and probably duplicated the welcome given the 1729 incomers by the Becker-led migrants of 1719. Said Naas, "Brethren and sisters came to meet us in small boats with delicious bread, apples, peaches, and other refreshments of the body, for which we praised the great God publicly on the ship, with much singing and resounding prayers."[25] The viand-bearing greeters were all from the congregation at Germantown, among them Alexander Mack.

Naas was much impressed by the general welfare of the Germantown Brethren. He remarked to his son, "Our people are getting along well, one better than the next, but no one has scarcity."[26] Some had acquired considerable land, as many as two hundred acres or more. Others owned between forty and one hundred acres of ground.[27] Already by 1733 the Brethren, who came as poor aliens, were among the chief landholders of the colony. Alexander Mack, however, in his mid-fifties, lived in a little one-story house he had built on a half-acre lot.

When John Naas made his appearance the Germantown church had been in existence a decade. A puzzle to historians is why the members waited four years after they migrated before officially organizing. One explanation attributes the delay to disunity because of differences on church policy and marriage dating back to Krefeld days. Another interpretation points out the difficulties of starting anew as a church group when the families scattered to look for available land. Whatever the reason, the Krefeld exiles held no common religious services until the winter of 1722, when Peter Becker and John Gumre opened their homes for worship. These two men and others had taken it upon themselves that autumn to visit all the scattered Brethren in the "back country." It was these visitations that sparked interest in periodic house-meetings and eventually the decision to unite in a fellowship. The historic event took place on Christmas Day, 1723. Peter Becker was elected elder and baptized six persons, after which the love feast was held in the home of John Gumre, through whose land Wissahickon Creek, the baptismal site, gently flowed. Twenty-three communicants were in

---

*Indentured servants were of two general types: voluntary (redemptioners and apprentices) and involuntary (felons and debtors). Ordinarily, apprentices were children or young men untrained in a trade. The chief class of indentured servants in colonial Pennsylvania were the "redemptioners."

that company and formed the nucleus of the "Mother Church" at Germantown.

In the autumn of 1724 all of the men in the congregation (fourteen) made an evangelistic swing through the hinterland—as far north as present-day Pottstown and westward into Lancaster County, then known as Conestoga. The expedition resulted in two new congregations, Coventry and Conestoga—both, of course, small. Still, the outlook was promising.

But problems and divisions lay ahead. The troubles started with the baptism of Conrad Beissel, the posthumous son of an alcoholic baker. A religious exile, he had come to Pennsylvania in 1720 and spent a year apprenticed to Peter Becker as a weaver. He then left Becker's house and, with some friends, lived as a hermit in the Conestoga wilderness along Mill Creek. There he became the leader of the new congregation, whom he soon introduced to celibacy and sabbatarianism. Unstable, charismatic, and egomaniacal, Beissel has been described by one social historian as "not unlike [what] Adolf Hitler might have become if he had followed a religious vocation."[28]

As might be expected, his ministry to the frontier Brethren at Conestoga proved a stormy one and in no time caused the disaffection of the Mother Church. Not even Alexander Mack, after he reached America in 1729, could reason with Beissel or effect a reconciliation. In the midst of the tumult, Beissel suddenly betook himself some eight miles deeper into the wilderness, taking shelter in a hut along the Cocalico Creek. There in 1732 he founded Ephrata, which by the latter part of the decade had become a full-fledged monastic community.

The cloistered Ephrataites and their "Superintendent" were tireless in seeking proselytes among the Pennsylvania Dutch population, the Brethren included. They even evangelized the Germantown church. This led to a stunning exodus of seventeen adults and several children during 1738 and 1739. Some of these defectors were among the ablest and most active members, two of whom were sons of Alexander Mack (one, the founder's namesake, did return and for fifty-five years was a Brotherhood leader). The schism of the 1730s came at a bad time for the struggling Brethren. An umbilical relationship existed between Germantown and its offshoots in those pre–Annual Conference days; a blow to the Mother Church was a blow to all. Alexander Mack had died in 1735, and at first his guidance was sorely missed. But Peter Becker at Germantown, and elsewhere John Naas, Martin Urner, Michael Pfaultz, and others, would fill the breach, reorganizing the shattered forces and exerting a stabilizing influence until the crisis had passed and men the caliber

of the two juniors, Alexander Mack and Christopher Sauer, came on
the colonial scene.

Colonial Growth and Westward Migration in Pennsylvania

Even before the younger Mack and Sauer rose in prominence, the
revitalized Brethren were planting other congregations in the colonies. These were less the result of a missionary thrust than the side
effect of a surge west and south for more attractive farmland. By
1740 Brethren pioneers were scattered over five Pennsylvania
counties: Chester, Bucks, Berks, Lancaster, York. With the 1740s
they began to move into Maryland, Virginia, North Carolina, and
South Carolina.* Rivalry in the Ohio Valley erupted into the French
and Indian War in 1754, exposing the frontier settlements of
Pennsylvania to havoc and disaster, but neither hostilities nor the
westward mountains deterred some of the hardiest Brethren. A few,
presumably trekking the famous Braddock Road, located in the
colony's far southwest—Washington County—as early as 1759 or
1760, claiming land by squatter title. The western reaches of Bedford County (now Somerset County) attracted yet others about
1762.

But at the end of the French and Indian War in 1763 the valleys
and coves of South-central Pennsylvania were inhabited by only a
few colonizing Brethren. For good reason, as we shall see in later
chapters, most of the church's frontiersmen had chosen to bypass
the territory. This would change, however, within another two
decades, though most of the settlers would hail from Maryland and
not from the eastern counties of Pennsylvania.

In 1770, when the Brethren began homesteading the colony's
interior, the number of individuals belonging to the church in
Pennsylvania was still remarkably low. The Baptist historian Morgan
Edwards compiled a census that year showing 419 Brethren families
and 793 members in the Province. He estimated, on the basis of
family size for that age, that slightly less than three thousand
persons were closely identified with the Brethren. By Edwards's
tally, there were but fifteen congregations and four meetinghouses
and only eight ordained ministers.[29] Overall for the colonial Brethren, he listed forty-two preacher-elders and over fifteen hundred
baptized members.

Edwards's statistical report appeared when the Church of the
Brethren was in its sixth decade of existence. In those sixty years the

---

*There were also a few New Jersey Brethren at this time, in the Amwell area (Hunterdon
County), where John Naas was elder until his death in 1741.

church had been transplanted from its place of birth in the Rhine Valley of Germany to Penn's Colony in America. At Germantown the Brethren formed their first congregation in the New World. It became, because of able leadership, the center of influence for new churches during the colonial period. From Germantown and its environs, the Brethren moved westward to the Susquehanna River, thence pushing on, before the Revolutionary War, across obstructing mountains into Western Pennsylvania. Not until after the American Revolution, however, does the history of the Brethren in Middle District begin.

2
The Scene in Central Pennsylvania: 1750 to 1800

Topography

Originally, the Middle District of Pennsylvania covered all the territory west of the Susquehanna River and east of the Allegheny Front (the mountain wall from Bedford to Altoona), and stretched the whole way from Maryland to New York. Historians employ the term *old west* to designate this part of Penn's Woods during the colonial period. In 1892 the present District boundaries were established, reducing them to the five county South-central area: Bedford, Blair, Centre, Huntingdon, Mifflin. In many respects the topography of this region makes it one of the most scenically beautiful in the state.

The District falls into what geologists call the ridge and valley sector of Pennsylvania. As we shall see in the next chapter, the nature of this landform influenced to some degree the pattern of Brethren migration into this part of the state. Parallel mountain ridges, lying close together with intervening fertile valleys, cut diagonally through the District in a northeast-southwest direction. In some places the ridges, of moderate, uniform elevation, are deeply incised by stream erosion, creating picturesque "water gaps"; at other places, shallower, V-shaped depressions form "wind gaps." Between these mountainous barriers stretch limestone valleys, varying in width, that have been farmed since pioneer days.

Also a prominent and important feature of the District's landscape is the Juniata River, with its three branches and their main tributaries. The Juniata, which rises in the District, traverses it on a west-to-east course and divides it in almost equal halves. The Juniata Watershed makes of South-central Pennsylvania a tracery of ever-filled streamways as mountain ravines pour their rainfall into the valleys below. Brethren and other settlers found this webwork of riverheads a valuable resource for power, transportation, and domestic use. It also provided ready-made baptismal sites by the score.

Of the Juniata's branches, the Little Juniata is the northernmost, rising in a gap west of Altoona in Blair County, then flowing northeast along the Allegheny Front to Tyrone, where it turns abruptly eastward toward its confluence with the Frankstown Branch just east of Alexandria, in Huntingdon County. Its tributaries are Bald Eagle, Spruce, Shaver's, and Standing Stone creeks.

The Frankstown Branch has its source in the northern end of Bedford County, flows northeast to Ganister in Blair County, on by Williamsburg, and continuing in a northeastern direction, to Alexandria. Feeding it along the way are Canoe and Clover creeks.

In the extreme south, the Raystown Branch begins in the eastern slopes of the Allegheny Mountains, wends its way through Bedford County eastward to a point between Everett and Breezewood, where it takes a northeasterly course into Huntingdon County until it unites with the Little Juniata a few miles east of Huntingdon to form the Juniata River proper. Coffee Run, Yellow, James, and Trough creeks are the only feeders of consequence to the Raystown Branch.*

From the Raystown juncture, the Juniata, after looping southward at Mount Union, resumes a northeastern bearing to Lewistown, in Mifflin County, a short distance beyond which it begins angling southeast toward the Susquehanna River. East of Huntingdon, the river itself is fed by Aughwick Creek from the south and Kishacoquillas and Jack's creeks from the north.

Early Roads and River Travel

Before the American Revolution there were few roads of any importance in what is now Middle District. South-central Pennsylvania, since long before the coming of the white man, was criss-crossed by Indian trails that were still heavily used by the natives as late as the 1750s. Early buckskin pioneers and traders began about that time to widen these dim pathways, with room enough only to walk "Indian file," into bridle paths, or pack trails, to permit the passage of a horse and its rider. But developing such routes into roads came very slowly because the cost was prohibitive in this sparsely settled and heavily wooded part of the state.

Forbes Road was the most important artery to cross the District in

---

*The construction of the Raystown Lake in 1973 all but obliterated James Creek and Coffee Run by its backflow.

colonial times. Paralleling the Turnpike of today, it was built in 1758 to expedite the march of General John Forbes against Fort Duquesne during the French and Indian War. It extended the already existing cross-colony wagon road from Philadelphia to Bedford, which passed through Carlisle, to the fork of the Ohio River. For many years after the Revolution it was known as the Pennsylvania Road or Great Road. In 1773 a road was hacked out from the Maryland line to Bedford (Route 220) to link up with this provincial east-west artery.

The first road within Mifflin County, a makeshift affair, opened in 1767, from Sterret's Gap in Juniata County, through Lewistown, to Reedsville in Kishacoquillas Valley. It was frequently blocked by rock slides in Mann's Narrows.

Road building in Huntingdon County began in the 1770s. One early road, laid out in 1774, ran south from Huntingdon through Woodcock Valley to the "great road" at Everett in Bedford County (Route 26).* At McConnellstown the road branched down Hartslog Valley across the Juniata River to Alexandria and on westward to the Water Street narrows. Another road in operation by the mid-1770s originated where the Aughwick enters the Juniata River along Route 103, led south to a point near Shirleysburg and from there through Shade Gap to Burnt Cabins, also on the Great Road (Route 522 south of Shirleysburg). Both roadways of the seventies were thirty-three feet wide, and no attempts were made, even until years later, at either ditching or filling; it was simply a matter of removing obstructions.

During the Revolution highway construction received little attention in the District, but the return of peace brought renewed efforts. The Assembly in 1787 authorized a fifty-foot-wide state road between Hollidaysburg and Blairsville (Route 22), which by 1796 extended all the way to the Ohio line (completing a second transstate thoroughfare). Another major road in 1787 ran from Huntingdon via Three Springs to Fort Littleton (Route 655), another juncture with the Great Road. In 1790 a road linking Lewistown and a ferry point near Mount Union began to bear traffic. The tables for Pennsylvania in the census of 1790 contain a map that shows a road from Huntingdon to Spruce Creek and up the valley between Tussey Mountain and Bald Eagle Ridge (Route 45) to where it merged with one from Lewistown (Routes 322 and 144) near Centre

---

*I have used modern place names rather than colonial designations. In some cases, present towns did not exist in those days. Also, I have identified the various roads by current route numbers, but these are not to be taken literally. Sections of these highways have been relocated over the years.

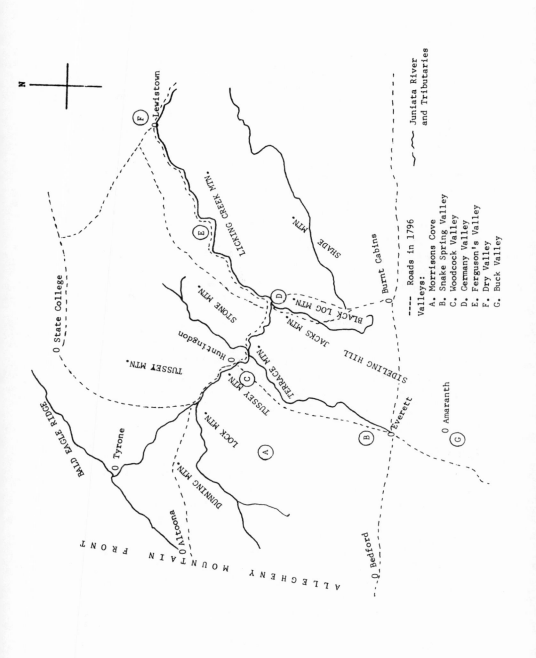

Hall in Centre County.[1] Another is shown from Mill Creek up Big Valley to Reedsville (Route 655), intersecting the Lewistown-Centre Hall axis. A third is shown branching off Route 522 and running the crest of Black Log Mountain to the Juniata River.

Such was the system of interconnecting roads in the District by 1800. There were, of course, a few other roads, mere narrow passageways, built solely for local use. As noted earlier, road building then involved no engineering; it was wholly dependent upon compulsory labor required of all taxables. Little care was taken to avoid steep inclines. There were no bridges; fords and ferries had to suffice. Much of the year wagon traffic was impossible because of weather conditions and poor upkeep. The first decade of the 1800s, however, set abroach an era of turnpike construction that better served the transportation needs of a fast-growing state, not to mention its South-central counties.

Meanwhile, an act of 1771 had designated Pennsylvania's larger streams as public highways. In the District the Juniata, with its three branches, naturally came to be the main water thoroughfare. (Many of its smaller tributaries, as well as other streams of Central Pennsylvania, were later declared open for boats and raft passage.) Arks— flat-bottomed, blunt-nosed boats—were soon familiar sights all along the river valley, carrying lumber, farm produce, and other cargo. The first ark, invented by a German settler (Kryder) at Huntingdon, floated downriver to the Susquehanna in 1796. Boat traffic of this sort on the Juniata shifted to the canal when the main line through Central Pennsylvania opened in the 1830s.

Early Settlements

Prior to the mid-1750s that part of Central Pennsylvania bounded by Middle District was owned by the powerful Iroquois Confederacy of New York. The Penn family, ever eager to deal fairly with the red man, had promised not to invade hunting grounds not legally purchased. But some Scots-Irish, in defiance of this agreement, began squatting on land in what is now Fulton County. In response to repeated Indian protests and to preserve peace, the provincial government in 1750 took steps against the trespassers, drove the whites back east, and burned their homes and crops. That is how the village of Burnt Cabins got its name, eleven homes having been put to the torch. But even as deep in the midlands as Morrisons Cove, three log houses were reduced to ashes by the same punitive measure.

The Albany Treaty of 1754, however, cleared the way for col-

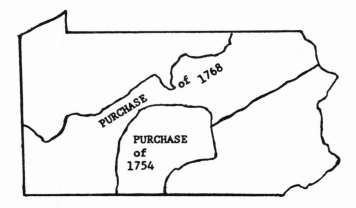

onizing the interior region. This treaty with the Iroquois, who held all the Indians of Pennsylvania in subjection, gave the Penn heirs ownership of a large wilderness area, stretching west of the Susquehanna to the crest of the Alleghenies and from the southern boundary of the Province to a line struck on a northwest-by-west diagonal from the mouth of Penn's Creek. The tract, which encompassed several counties, included all of Bedford, Blair, Huntingdon, Mifflin, and about half of Centre. The Pennsylvania Indians, especially the Delawares and Shawnees, were bitter against both their overlords, the Six Nations, and the people of the Province for a cession in which they had no voice. They repudiated the treaty, and another one was negotiated in 1758. But their resentment kept the heartland frontier in turmoil for two decades.

Indian traders had been operating in the interior of Pennsylvania by the 1740s, but the first white settlement was made by a man named Ray in 1751. He built three cabins along the southern branch of the Juniata River near the present site of Bedford, and for a decade the place was called Raystown. In 1758 Colonel Henry Bouquet built a stockade fort with large store houses there, which soon took the name Fort Bedford. Another stronghold was erected farther east—at Juniata Crossings—where the stream intercepted Forbes Road. Around these defense works a small colony of civilians permanently gathered. The town of Bedford, which boasted about one hundred families in 1763, was laid out in 1766. The population dropped to twenty families in 1773, but by 1800 inhabitants number 789.[2] In 1771 Bedford County was created out of Cumberland County, with its seat at Bedford. All of present-day Huntingdon and Blair counties were included in this division.

The next settlement in the District was Huntingdon, founded in

1767 by Dr. William Smith, an Episcopal minister and first provost of the University of Pennsylvania. Located on the Juniata River, it had by 1792 a population of eighty-five families. In the 1790s neighboring settlements (like Alexandria and Petersburg) grew up along the river and in adjacent valleys. The peopling of the northern half of Bedford County by the 1780s had so increased that in 1787 the Assembly set off the new county of Huntingdon, with its first town designated the seat.

The third in succession was Lewistown, some thirty miles down the Juniata from Huntingdon. When the western part of Cumberland County became Mifflin County in 1789, the organic act seated it at the mouth of Kishacoquillas Creek. That year a town was chartered and given the name Lewistown, which by 1800 had a population of 523.[3]

Elsewhere in the District, the population was more scattered and town-founding was delayed. It is true that in what later became Blair County some towns were on record in the 1790s, for example, Hollidaysburg (1790) and Williamsburg (1795). But in 1814 the former claimed but seven buildings and the latter counted just twenty families.[4] Blair County, formed from Huntingdon and Bedford counties in 1846, was made up largely of isolated farmsteads in the late eighteenth century. Except for the Philadelphia-to-Pittsburgh overland route, which passed through Frankstown and Hollidaysburg, there were no public roads integrating that part of the District.

Centre County, organized in 1800 out of Mifflin and Lycoming counties, need not concern us here, since it has entered the District's history only in recent decades.

The Brethren and Indian Troubles

FRENCH AND INDIAN WAR

Grievances against the white man by the Indians of Pennsylvania had accumulated over a period of several decades by the time the French and Indian War (1754–1763) broke upon the scene and gave rise to war-whoops and bloody massacres all over the back-country. As we saw above, the treaty of 1754, confirmed in 1758, especially outraged the Delawares and Shawnees, who claimed the Juniata Valley as a hunting ground. As a result, they joined forces with the French on the promise that their lands would be restored to them.

The French hoped to use the Indians to terrorize the countryside, drive settlers off their farms, and so ruin Pennsylvania's economy. To meet this threat, the Province erected a chain of some two hundred forts over the mountainous frontier during the course of the war. Garrisons patrolled the wilds between. These defenses did not stop the Delawares, led by their chiefs—Captain Jacobs, Captain Beaver, and "Shingas the Terrible"—who made devastating raids into Central Pennsylvania, attacking farms, killing livestock, burning houses, and murdering the settlers or carrying them off as captives. Dread of the Indian's tomahawk and scalping knife was everywhere felt.

Uriah J. Jones, in his history of the Juniata Valley, which appeared in 1855, claims that the few Brethren of Morrisons Cove, along with others, suffered severe hardships at the hands of the Indians during this period of violence. Critical of their pacifism, he bitterly wrote that "in the predatory incursions of the French and Indians, in 1756–63, and, in fact, during all the savage warfare, they not only refused to take up arms to repel the savage marauders and prevent the inhuman slaughter of women and children, but they refused in the most positive manner to pay a dollar to support those who were willing . . . to defend their homes and their firesides, until wrung from them by the stern mandates of the law."[5]

It was he who first told of John Martin, said to be a pioneer Brethren preacher in the Cove, whose family was led into captivity at that time. In hopes of securing the release of those loved ones still alive, Martin made the following appeal to the provincial government, to whom the Indians promised to deliver all captives:

> August 13, 1762
> The Humble Petition of Your Most Obedient Servant Sheweth, Sir, may it pleas Your Excellancy, Hearing me in Your Clemancy a few Words. I, One of the Bereaved of my Wife and five Children, by Savage War at the Captivity of the Great Cove, after Many & Long Journeys, I Lately went to an Indian Town, viz., Tuskaroways, 150 miles Beyond Fort Pitts, & Entrested in Co'. Bucquits & Co'. Croghan's favor, So as to bear their Letters to King Beaver & Cap'. Shingas, Desiring them to Give up One of my Daughters to me, Whiles I have Yet two Sons & One Other Daughter, if Alive, Among them—and after Seeing my Daughter with Shingas he Refused to Give her up, and after some Expostulating with him, but all in vain, he promised to Deliver her up with the Other Captives to y' Excellency.[6]

History does not say whether the family was reunited. One story states that the wife and four children were killed and only the eldest daughter returned.

It is quite possible that Jones erred in placing Martin in Morrisons Cove, which some historians think he confused with the Great Cove in Fulton County since there is no record of any settlements in the

Blair County Cove until after the French and Indian War. Whatever the case, Martin apparently was not one to turn the other cheek to his enemies. William White, an early settler on the Juniata, writes in a letter dated August 17, 1763, that Martin

> seeing an Indian coming up to a house where he was, fired at him, upon which the Indian raised a yell and took [to] a tree. . . . Martin, imagining there might be more Indians near him, ran to a company at work and told what had happened, [and] when they went to the place, found some blood and excrement, from which they concluded he was shot through the bowels.
>
> They followed his track down to the bottom, where they saw the tracks of six or seven more, but, being a small party pursued no farther.[7]

Elder James Sell obviously knew nothing of this incident when he wrote for the 1925 district history that, in all of the trying experiences of frontier life before the Revolutionary War, no Brethren of Central Pennsylvania had compromised the church's peace principle.[8]*

Another family with a Brethren heritage—Replogle—also met with Indian violence during the war. Rinehart Replogle, Sr., who had settled somewhere in Bedford County as early as 1750, had a fifteen-year-old daughter, Margaret, stolen by Indians in 1766. Margaret was gone twelve years before she was able to make her way back home. It all began on a gala day in her community:

> The neighbors were having a husking party in which the men of the neighborhood spent the day husking corn and the women met at the same place and spent the time quilting. In the evening the young people met and had their husking party or "Husking Bee" as it was called.
>
> Margaret's mother was at the quilting. Her father had for some reason remained at home. During the day the dogs were greatly disturbed and the father went out but he also returned without finding the cause of their barking. When it was time for the mother to return home, Margaret and her brother went to accompany her. On their way the Indians sprang from behind the trees where they were hiding, seized her and carried her away. The brother outran the Indians and on reaching home fell in a swoon at the doorway.
>
> On the same day the Indians also captured a young man who had attended the husking party, his wife and their little babe eight or nine months old, burned their home so the people would think they had been burned and would not seek for them. These captives, including Margaret, were forced to wade along the banks of a stream all night in order to elude the whites who would be searching for them. Margaret tore her silk handkerchief, which was red, and her apron into shreds and let them

---

*There is the possibility that John Martin the Indian fighter and John Martin the Cove preacher were two different men, although Brethren tradition says not.

catch on anything growing along the banks or projecting over the water, hoping they would be seen by those looking for her. But these little shreds never told their story to whom it was intended and Margaret remained with the Indians seven years.

The little babe that had been captured found conditions so much different from its little cradle by the fireplace that it cried and sobbed all night and on into the next morning, while its mother sought in vain to comfort it. The Indians thought its cries might betray them. An old Indian approached him with his tomahawk and told the mother if the babe uttered another cry he would split its head open. The little one seemed to have sensed the situation because it at once ceased its crying, and from then on not one sound was heard.

On their raids the Indians took household articles that they could make use of. The young father was made to carry a very heavy load, one that he was hardly able to bear. The mother carried the babe and Margaret only a long handled pan. The Indians' cruelty was shown in the treatment accorded the father. One day he was forced into a contest in which the Indians were lined up on both sides of a course he was given to run. When he was not able to make the run in the prescribed time, they struck and lashed him into unconsciousness.

At one time when they were roving about, game and other food was scarce. They had not been able to obtain food for the tribe for several days. While they were holding council in the evening Margaret overheard them discussing the killing of her for food. A young brave begged for her life and asked that they wait until the next day. If they were unable to find food until the next evening he would give his consent to the slaying to save his people. The next day they came upon a trader's horse that had died upon the trail. Here they pitched camp and remained until all the meat of the dead horse was consumed. In the evening when she thought they were all asleep she cut herself a piece of the meat and put it over the fire to broil. When it was done, one of the Indians arose, took the meat and ate it. After waiting a long time, feeling sure that all slept, she prepared a second piece. It met the same fate. Then she waited until she felt she could wait no longer and broiled a third piece. She was luckier this time and declared it was the most savory piece of meat she had ever eaten.

At another time when they had been without food they told her to go and make a fire by a log, and that she must not look back. She went as bidden but kept watch as much as possible to ascertain what was going on. Whenever the fire started to burn she would stir it out with a small stick. The Indians thought she was stirring it about to make it burn. Soon she heard the Indian "Joy Shout." Looking, she saw some of the young Indians, who had been hunting, running and shouting and bearing a deer on their shoulders. Her life was spared once more. The deer was roasted on the fire that had been intended for her. She said that never afterward did she feel safe while with the Indians.

Although she was soon separated from her white friends, she was always kindly treated and during her entire sojourn with the Indians she was never asked to share her tent, even with a child.

One of the young braves aspired to her hand. He placed his blanket over the door of her tent. An Indian woman told her that if she was willing to be his mate, she should take his blanket into her tent; but if she did not wish to accept his offer she should allow it to remain there three days. She could not meet such a fate and always hoped for a release from the Indians. Thus the young brave received his answer.

The clothes of the white babies that were stolen were kept. At the birth of an Indian babe it was given to Margaret to be dressed in white man's clothes. The little papoose thus dressed was passed along the tribe. After all had seen and admired the little one it was given back to her. The clothing was then removed and the Indian baby dressed in skins. The white baby's clothes were put away and kept.

The Indians sold her to the French. The French sold her to the English and the English set her free at Detroit, which was then Fort Detroit. A woman with a two year old child was set free at the same time. When freed, they started at once on their journey back to their separate homes in Pennsylvania. They walked the entire distance. They were passed by traders upon the trail but as only women of ill repute were found upon the trails they were not asked to ride. Their food consisted of what they found along the way.

While lying sick in a village on her way home Margaret overheard them speaking of a boy that had been found wandering about, who could speak only the Indian tongue. She asked that they bring him to her. He proved to be the little fellow who had been stolen the day of the corn husking in Pennsylvania.

Her parents hoped that if still living she would communicate with them in some way; but as the days passed into months and months into years their hope died, but not so with her brother. When nearing home, while sitting on a log to rest, a man approached her. She recognized him and asked where he was going. He replied that he was going to a nearby village to see if he could obtain some information in regard to his long lost sister who had been stolen by the Indians. That if he obtained no word of her today, he would be sure she was dead. As he started on his way she called to him by name and told him that she was his long lost sister. Beside himself with joy and so overcome with what he had heard, without a word he turned and ran to carry the glad news to the anxious ones at home.

She told of the great rejoicing that attended her home coming, that her father almost lost control of himself over his joy, and of the great assemblage of neighbors from far and near who wept and rejoiced with great rejoicings over her safe return.

We can only conjecture the harrowing experiences the girl must have had in her search for her home and in her wanderings about, alone in the wild country.[9]

REVOLUTIONARY WAR

Many of the settlers in Central Pennsylvania had fled their homes long before Margaret Replogle was kidnapped, taking refuge in the more thickly populated occupied regions along the Susquehanna. Once peace was restored, they returned to begin anew. There was no further Indian terror on the frontier until the American Revolution (1776–1783).

This time the Indians were the allies of the British, and their forays throughout the Juniata Valley again forced a number of people to flee to safety. For protection, those who stayed behind erected with their own hands twelve new forts, while the ones at Huntingdon and Bedford were enlarged. To these they would resort when danger threatened.

The Indians, based in Detroit, began to terrorize the interior soon after the Americans declared their independence. The British by then were offering handsome bonuses for patriot scalps. In late fall 1777 an alarm was spread among the settlers, and those who chose to stay and face the peril (about half the population) made for the nearest fort with all dispatch—except for the Brethren. They refused to be forted or to pull out. A few, however, did go into hiding when the Indians swept through the area, concentrating their pillage in Morrisons Cove (between Martinsburg and Roaring Spring). Nevertheless, thirty of them were massacred in less than forty-eight hours, according to Uriah J. Jones, though Brethren oral tradition says twenty.[10]

Jones described the Brethren as standing by meekly while their women and children were butchered and scalped. Allegedly, the bereaved men merely said at the sight of this horror, "Gottes wille sei gethan" (God's will be done). Afterward this was remembered as the "Dunkard Massacre," and so impressed were the perpetrators that years later, during the War of 1812, some of them inquired of Huntingdon volunteers fighting in the Niagara campaign whether the "Gotswilthans" still lived in the Cove.[11] How many Brethren were taken prisoners during the Cove raid is not known, although folklore does mention that two members of the Houser family, the father and a son, were killed while working in the fields.[12] One Houser son, Jacob, escaped on horseback, while his mother's hiding place went undiscovered. Another brother and a sister were captured and later released.

After the "Dunkard Massacre" the main body of Indians worked their way toward the Kittanning warpath that followed the Juniata across the District and then struck a northwest course from Hollidaysburg through the Horseshoe Curve gorge. But a few stragglers lagged behind, and they were party to the Jacob Neff episode, the most famous legend of Roaring Spring history.

As Uriah Jones tells it, Neff, a Brethren who operated a mill at the present site of Roaring Spring, discovered two Indians one morning lurking in the woods nearby. He kept a loaded gun in the mill, and, seizing it, took aim out a window and killed the older one. Taking to his heels, he was chased up a hill by the other Indian, who got off a shot at him but missed. Then, face to face forty yards apart, each began frantically to reload—pouring in the powder, jamming home the bullet, yanking out the ramrod, priming the charge. Neff was the quicker and coolly shot his duelist through the head, despite all kinds of acrobatics by the Indian to throw off Neff's fire once he saw the muzzle of the miller's musket leveled at him.[13] Neff then escaped to the nearest settlement, which Jones does not identify, where a force was raised and the mill revisited. They found it burned to the ground and the corpses of the Indians taken away.*

Another version has Neff, after his duel, going to Stonerstown, where some Cove settlers had sought refuge, for help. There several companies of twelve men each organized to return to the Cove to see what damage the Indians had done and drive them out. One of these squads was led by Neff and went to Roaring Spring. A battle took place when the Indians ambushed the scouting party. All of the white men were killed except Neff, who managed to dispose of his second Indian that day with a rifleball in the head.[14]

Jones claims that the Brethren excommunicated Neff and, because he had defended himself, would not patronize his mill after he rebuilt it. This action, Jones said, eventually forced the miller out of business. But James Sell disputes part of the Jones account and adds more details in the 1925 district history. Sell denies that Neff ever owned the mill he worked or rebuilt it. He argues that Daniel Ullery was the original owner, and it was he who put up a second one after the arson of 1777. As for Neff's expulsion, Sell writes:

> He was counseled by the church for his violation of her peace principles. He did not plead justification. He admitted that he was wrong to take human life but said his deed was done under strong temptation and excitement. He was excused, but required not to speak of his act in company in a boasting or justifying way. This restriction he frequently violated and he was expelled from the church.[15]

Another story about Indian atrocities in the Revolutionary era has to do with the Dibert ancestors of Middle District. The exact year is not known—probably 1781—and it was first told by Mrs. Emma Replogle, whose schoolman father is dealt with in chapter 8. In her book, *Indian Eve,* Mrs. Replogle says that Indian marauders in the Bedford vicinity (Dutch Corners) murdered the parents of the first Dibert family and some of the children, and burned their house.

---

*J. Simpson Africa, in his history of Huntingdon and Blair counties, gives a slightly different narrative. He got his information from Jacob Shenefelt, whose father was an early settler and preacher in Morrisons Cove. The Shenefelt story, however, seems to be a conflation of the Jones account and the tale about the postduel ambush that Neff survived.

Two boys and a girl were abducted. One boy, seven years old, was made to walk over the bodies of his parents, the mother still alive. The family had just baked bread and churned butter, and the Indians forced the children to take these things with them and to carry a lot of bedding. The Diberts had a horse with a bell on its collar, which was used to raise an alarm when Indians were around. Wanting the bell, the raiders cut off the horse's head to get it. Then they rang the bell at the homes of other settlers in order to lure them out. Eventually, all three of the children, though scattered, were rescued by soldiers.[16]

The Brethren had not yet penetrated into other parts of Middle District during the years of the Indian scare, hence the widespread bloodshed elsewhere in the Juniata Valley did not involve them. The worst of the tragedies were over by 1782, the last murder occurring in late summer 1781. The surrender of Cornwallis that October at Yorktown practically ended the war, though the Treaty of Paris did not come until September 1783.

With peace, settlers began filtering into Central Pennsylvania by several routes, in steady numbers. Among these postwar pioneers were to be found not a few hardworking, venturesome Brethren. They played a major role in turning the timbered valleys of the then isolated interior into productive farmland.

3

Brethren Pathfinders

Information on the Early Brethren Hard to Find

The 1925 district history says, without documentation, that as early as 1755 a "colony of Brethren" had entered Morrisons Cove through Loysburg Gap and gradually made their way northward to its more spacious parts.[1] Nothing more is mentioned about these pioneers—who they were, whence they came, where they struck roots. If the 1925 history is right, then the first Brethren settlers of Middle District must have been squatters who established "tomahawk claims" on the land they occupied.* The Albany Treaty of 1754, as we saw in the last chapter, opened Central Pennsylvania to settlement, but no land sale in the Cove is recorded until much later—in 1766—and then no Brethren was involved. Actually, there is no positive proof that any Brethren at all were pioneering in the Cove by 1755, and certainly not a "colony" of them, which implies a sizable group. Quite likely, then, this is an unfounded tradition.

Perhaps John Martin and his family, the victims of Indian brutality in 1763, were the first Brethren in Middle District. But anything about Martin's life—his past, where exactly in the Bedford-Blair County area he lived, or what qualified him for election as Clover Creek's earliest preacher—is a mystery. Except for his experiences with the Indians, he is only a name to us.

By the time of the Revolution, there is evidence to suggest the presence of a number of Brethren settlers in Morrisons Cove, and apparently a few others were scattered elsewhere in the Juniata Valley. But the facts are scanty and provide no clear, comprehensive picture of these pioneering families. Probably they constituted a majority of the Cove colonists, but we have no idea what their population amounted to. Nor do we know precisely the scope of their distribution in the Cove, although Neff's mill at Roaring

---

*It was frequently the practice of pioneers, before legal titles were obtained, to blaze or deaden trees in marking out a claim of land they planned to settle.

Spring would lead us to think they were early concentrated in that vicinity.

Meanwhile, a few Brethren, bypassing the interior, had taken up life anew among the rolling hills of Southwestern Pennsylvania. But for their fellow believers the extreme frontier line in the Keystone State, as late as 1800, was marked by the Allegheny Front, where the "old west" ended.

The Brethren and Frontier Life in Central Pennsylvania

Prior to 1779 the Penn family, as proprietors, owned the soil of Pennsylvania, and all purchases of land from them carried the obligation of an annual quitrent in perpetuity. The quitrent could be paid in wheat, flour, beaver skins, or other commodities; or it could be satisfied with a token payment, such as a red rose or Indian arrow. This practice, a carry-over from feudal Europe, met with resistance from the start, and was considered wholly out of place in a colony founded upon democratic ideals. Thus the reluctance of farmers to pay this kind of tribute resulted in a poor collection of quitrents. Feudal land tenure in Pennsylvania was abolished soon after the Revolution, in 1799, by the so-called Divesting Act. All lands not yet sold were turned over to the Commonwealth, and all farmers were granted full and undivided ownership of their property.

The process of acquiring a land title in pioneer days was most cumbersome. The first step was to make application (this was called a warrant) to the land office in Philadelphia. On approval of the warrant, that office authorized a survey that had to be made within six months. The survey was then recorded, giving the applicant legal claim, although the land might not be paid for until much later. According to the Land Act of 1792, title (called a patent) was not to be conveyed unless a settler, within two years, had actually occupied his tract and begun clearing and working it. This law set the price of land, depending upon its location, between thirteen and twenty cents an acre, a drastic reduction from earlier rates.

The typical frontier family was young and poor, and the law of 1792 made it easier for them to buy enough acreage for a backwoods farm. Most young couples had to borrow from parents, since there were no banks to extend credit. The early going for them on the frontier was usually a struggle, for rarely did a new farm support a family until the second year. Their living at first had to come from forest and stream and from the meager supply of food they brought with them. A large proportion of their time initially went into clearing the timber and not into raising crops. Husband and wife worked side by side, a few acres at a time, in subduing the forest.

What method of ground-clearing the Brethren pioneers of Central Pennsylvania used is not known. Probably it was the "Yankee method," named for the practice of New Englanders, whereby trees were felled, saplings and underbrush grubbed up, and all but the largest stumps pulled or dug out. This was the common procedure among Germans, in contrast to the Scots-Irish, who preferred to girdle rather than cut down trees.

Pioneer farmers of the 1780s and 1790s in Central Pennsylvania were as dependent on wildlife as on crops and livestock. Practically every one of them was a hunter and trapper. Game helped to feed and clothe their families, and animal furs were used to barter for supplies. It is highly probable that some kind of firearm could be found in every Brethren farmstead of that time, peace principles notwithstanding. Deer, bear, squirrels, and turkeys were plentiful in the mountains, and the streams abounded with fish and aquatic mammals. In 1784 squirrels were causing so much crop damage in Bedford County that authorities levied a bounty of two pence a scalp on the rodents.

Wolves could also prove troublesome, especially when, desperate from hunger, they would wreak havoc on livestock. Sheep and calves were the most desired prey. Sometimes the wolves attacked people. Mary Brumbaugh, whose family was among the very first to settle in Morrisons Cove, once had a harrowing experience with these beasts. She was married to Samuel Ullery and had settled near New Enterprise sometime in the late 1780s or early 1790s. One evening she went for the cows and got lost in the woods. Wolves appeared and forced her to climb a tree to get out of their reach. She sat in it all night, listening to the family blowing horns and searching for her. In the morning she found the way home, where she had left a nursing baby.[2] John Wineland, who began farming near Rebecca Furnace in 1780, had a similar adventure. He often traveled from house to house in the Cove mending shoes. On one expedition he saved his life by using a stout hickory club to drive off attacking wolves while he was traveling at night.[3]

The home of a Brethren family was a log cabin, of course, the most common abode of pioneers, usually located near a spring or stream. Often, however, before the log house was built, it was necessary to live in crude shelters, even tents, as did Nicholas Fouse when he and his family settled near Williamsburg in the Cove. He was married to Margaret Brumbaugh, kin to Mary Ullery, and eventually, in 1793, they put up a small cabin of four rooms, made of hastily hewn logs, with a crude chimney in the center and a fireplace on both sides for cooking. It had a clapboard roof, the shakes riven from blocks of pine or hemlock, and an earthen floor.[4] For years the Fouse household—in common with all their neighbors—had to make do with bare floors underfoot.

The Fouse children never forgot the hardships they and their parents endured in eking out an existence before the forest around them was turned into a prosperous farm. One daughter remembered how coffee was a special treat, brewed but once a week, always on Sunday morning. All fabrics were homespun and all clothes homemade, the flax and wool coming from the farm itself. Almost every one of the seven Fouse sons learned how to weave, spending his evenings over the loom.[5]

Nicholas Fouse, like all frontier settlers, had to produce nearly everything his family needed. Because of industrious pioneers like him, Morrisons Cove in time gained notability as a great grain-growing region, corn being the favorite crop. But flax, wool, and potatoes were also important staples. Its agricultural reputation, however, came after 1800. Before that, the area was almost totally isolated from mills and markets because it lacked roads and water transportation.

Both before and after 1800 an important mode of transportation in Central Pennsylvania, besides horseback, was the Conestoga wagon. It hauled many pioneers, including the Brumbaugh and Fouse families, and their possession to new inland home sites. A Fouse daughter recalled, "Preparations were made to emigrate [to Morrisons Cove] early in the spring of 1789. It was essential to procure a covered wagon and a yoke of oxen for the undertaking. Into that vehicle were packed the smithing tools, necessary wearing apparel, bedding, food, etc."[6] It also served as a shelter for the whole family en route.

The overland course the Fouses took from Washington County, Maryland, was the same one the Jacob Brumbaugh menage followed the previous year. Indeed, it was the only way they could have gone in the 150-mile trek. Striking the road that looped south from Chambersburg through northern Maryland, the migrants bumped over its rough, ungraded surface as it swung back north along the eastern base of Sideling Hill to intersect the Pennsylvania Road about twenty-five miles from Bedford. They then headed west in the direction of that village, turning north at Everett and passing up Yellow Creek to the Loysburg Gap, where the road ran out, then through the Gap into the Cove.

Meanwhile, to the east, in Germany Valley, Joseph Long, progenitor of a line of Brethren preachers, would soon himself be clearing a forest farm. But he had to find his own way into the Aughwick bottoms since there was no road, not even a footpath. He blazed trees to mark his trail to the spot where he would build a little cabin; later, he made the track a wagon road. But how he got to the Valley from Lancaster was never told. Most likely he took the Pennsylvania Road to Burnt Cabins and headed up the road to Shirleysburg, built in the mid-1770s. From that place he probably blazed the way to his cabin site.

Centers of Brethren Settlements and Earliest Families

As noted in chapter 1, the Brethren formed a very small religious body in Pennsylvania at the time of the Revolutionary War. Their numbers fell far short of one thousand when that conflict ended. Prior to 1783 Middle District could count only a handful of fellow-believers, about whom little or nothing can be learned. Not until the postwar 1780s did the first permanent occupation of Middle District by the Brethren begin, some settlers relocating from eastern counties but most moving in from northern Maryland. They tended to cluster at three principal points: Morrisons Cove, Germany Valley, and the Lewistown area.

MORRISONS COVE

Called the Great Cove until about 1770, this rich farming land, with no public road until the 1800s, is about thirty-nine miles long and twenty miles wide. It is surrounded by mountains, foothills of the Alleghenies: Tussey on the east, broken ranges and spurs on the north, and Cove or Dunning on the west. It begins at Pattonsville, Bedford County, and ends at Williamsburg on the Juniata River. The first large land purchases were made in the Cove in the mid-1760s, but the Indian menace delayed large-scale settlement for another two decades.

It would seem that the John Martin family were the first church members to pioneer in Middle District—about 1760. But aside from Martin's Indian exploits, the only other thing we definitely know about him is that he was one of Clover Creek's first preachers. If he did lose all of his family except a daughter to the Indians, then he must have remarried. The census of 1790 lists two John Martins in Huntingdon County (which then included Blair County), both households reporting females over sixteen years old.

This is all that is known about Brethren pathfinders until the Revolution, when Jacob Neff became infamous as an Indian-slayer.

Though excommunicated, he apparently stayed on in the Cove, to judge from the census of 1790. The mill Neff operated at Roaring Spring when he fought off the Indians in 1777 was owned by Daniel Ullery, himself presumably Brethren.* His mill was the first one in the Cove and in 1795 was sold to his son John. Another son, Samuel, settled near New Enterprise soon after 1780 and became a very influential minister there. It was said that while living in Maryland he served as a packer in the French and Indian War.

Among the original settlers of Roaring Spring was also the Jacob Houser family, which was tragically victimized during the Great Cove massacre. Martin and Jacob, Jr., survivors of the bloodbath, became successful farmers.

Neighbors to the Housers and Daniel Ullery were the Christian Hoovers, whose family head was another of the earliest ministers. Hoover owned a linseed oil mill on Plum Creek, not far from East Sharpsburg.

John Metzger was a Brethren pioneer who came to America from Germany in 1758, indenturing himself to pay for the voyage. After working off his obligation, he betook himself sometime during the Revolution to the Cove, where he married an Ullery daughter and lived about halfway between Fredericksburg and Martinsburg. The Clover Creek Church stands on part of his original tract.

One of the most prolific and prominent pioneering families in the Cove was the Brumbaughs. One bloodline traces back to (John) Jacob Brumbaugh, an orphan refugee from Germany who arrived in 1750.[7] He made his way across the frontiers of Pennsylvania and Maryland to find a home in Washington County, on Conococheague Creek, which winds in great loops through a fertile valley along the Mason-Dixon line a few miles north of Hagerstown. Many German immigrants had situated in that locality. There in 1760 he married Mary Angle, who was said to be the first Brethren convert west of the Blue Ridge Mountains, a convert of famed pioneer missionary George Adam Martin. Brumbaugh, a Lutheran, eventually joined his wife's church.

Some interesting, but unsupported, stories have been written about Brumbaugh's alleged friendship with George Washington. J. Maurice Henry, in his history of the Brethren in Maryland, claims that both General Edward Braddock and Washington put up a night or two in the Brumbaugh home during the French and Indian War.[8] Apparently, though, Jacob did serve in the disastrous Brad-

---

*The 1925 history gives confusing data on this mill. At several places it says that Ullery built it, but gives two different dates for its erection, both after 1777. Obviously, the mill could not have been destroyed at the time of the Brethren massacre, as the book states.

dock campaign of 1755—but as a packman, his religious scruples keeping him from actual combat. During the Revolution two decades after, he was one of Western Maryland's leading contributors—in money and provisions—to the war effort. Henry implies that Washington later rewarded his patriotic but pacifistic packman by arranging the patent for his large land holdings in Central Pennsylvania, but there is no proof of this.

In 1788 Brumbaugh left the Conococheague country and, as we saw earlier in this chapter, traveled by Conestoga wagon to Morrisons Cove, locating near New Enterprise. He seems to have built a saw mill that same year to help clear his original grant of 337 acres. In time he acquired over six thousand acres in Middle Pennsylvania, together with large tracts of land in Maryland. When in his sixties, in 1794, he moved across Tussey Mountain into Woodcock Valley, joining some half dozen or so other German families with similar Pietistic leanings. But that story will be told later. His seven children united with various denominations, only two, Mary and John, becoming Brethren.

Mary was the mother treed by wolves, and her husband was Samuel Ullery. Her younger brother John was twenty years old when father Jacob took up residence in the Cove. He married a Cove girl and bought land near his parents' farm. He became a minister, as did his son, David.

A second Brumbaugh lineage starts with progenitor John Henry, a German emigré in 1754 who also ended up along the Conococheague. All four of his sons—Jacob ("Jockel"), George ("Yerrick"), John, and Conrad—were born abroad and pioneered the Cove. In fact, there is the tradition that Jacob and George, when well into life, were occupying a tract of land near Rebecca Furnace at the time of the Indian outbreaks in the late 1770s. They left, it is said, and did not return until the danger had passed—perhaps in 1780.

Jacob was twice married, fathering fifteen children. Sometime after 1794 he left the Clover Creek site to join his Brumbaugh kin (probably cousins) in Woodcock Valley. The next decades recorded a complex web of marriages among the Brumbaughs, Bowerses, and Garners, the Valley's original families. There is no record of "Jockel's" religious preference, but some of his numerous offspring joined the Brethren, and son George became James Creek's first elder.

George, on the other hand, as one of Clover Creek's primal elders, raised an entire family of Brethren (twelve children). He married a daughter of John Metzger, and they began life together near Fredericksburg. After her death, he took as wife the widow of Christian Hoover, the oil mill operator.

George's and Jacob's brother John emigrated to the Cove in 1785 and settled close to the present site of East Sharpsburg. His wife was a Metzger, perhaps a sister to George's spouse. He took a warrant for fifteen hundred acres, stretching from Roaring Spring to Tussey Mountain, but obtained no patent until 1792. For some reason, he got the nickname "stocking weaver." John and his wife had three daughters but also raised a boy left on the doorstep of their Maryland home by some Scots Highlanders passing by. They named him Brumbaugh, and when he grew up he learned to play the violin and became known as "Fiddler Jack." This pastime would suggest that he was not Brethren, nor probably was his foster father, although there is no evidence one way or another. The mother and one daughter, Margaret, definitely were.

Margaret married Daniel Camerer, a German immigrant, at Conococheague, and they followed her parents to the Cove about 1795. The Camerers had prospered in Maryland and for years were regarded as among the wealthiest of the earliest settlers. Daniel bought seven hundred acres from his father-in-law; included in the tract was almost all of the site where the town of Martinsburg now stands. There were nine children in the family, and two of the sons built the first Brethren church in Martinsburg.

The fourth of progenitor John Henry's boys was Conrad, who, with brothers Jacob and George, was in the Cove by the mid-1770s. Like them, he vacated his land during the Indian troubles, joining a militia company in Cumberland County. Afterward he returned to the Cove, where tax lists show him as owning three hundred acres in 1783. He had been well educated in Germany, and later, when pioneering in the Johnstown area, taught school. He was a Brethren minister.

Only Conrad's oldest son, John, remained in the Cove, marrying a daughter of John Metzger, who spent his last days with the Brumbaughs. He was well established along Clover Creek by 1800. Later he put up a grist mill on the stream. Like his father, he was called to the ministry, though neither man is listed as such in the 1925 history. In 1818 John moved to Miami County, Ohio.

The Brumbaugh clan clearly left its mark on Morrisons Cove, but there were other early Brethren settlers about whom less information exists. One of them was John Wineland, who came to the Cove from Virginia about 1780 and married Hannah Brumbaugh, Jacob's daughter. They did much of their courting in the harvest field, presumably while John was a Brumbaugh hired hand. It was he who sometimes encountered wolves in making his shoe-mending rounds of scattered farms. They lived on a farm on the later site of Rebecca Furnace.

Then there was John Holsinger, a widower of Brethren parentage from Franklin County who sometime around 1780 took possession of land just south of Bakers Summit on the eastern slope of Dunning Mountain. In 1797 he married Elizabeth Mack, a great-granddaughter of the church's founder. Holsinger, a minister, was closely associated with Samuel Ullery in consolidating the Brethren of the Cove after the Revolution. John and Elizabeth were progenitors of a distinguished lineage of church leaders, some of whom were the founders of the Dunnings Creek congregation.[9]

Other longtime Brethren names like Dibert and Replogle crop up in the records of the late eighteenth century, but whether their forefathers were church members is not clear. A "Rhinehart Replogle" appears in the 1790 census, and in 1798 his son Daniel married Nancy Brumbaugh, a daughter of George. They lived near Waterside, as did some of their thirteen children, and were Brethren.

The name of Daniel (Paulus) Paul in the 1925 history is only a cryptic line in Clover Creek's registry of its early ministers. But now we know that he, too, like so many early settlers was an immigrant, in 1763. The name Paul is probably of French Huguenot derivation. Eventually, Daniel came to the Cove with his family, presumably before 1780. His farm was located on Piney Creek, four miles north of Martinsburg. He was known in the community as "that old Frenchman." One of his boys, Henry, became another of George Brumbaugh's sons-in-law.[10] Apparently, he was part of that ministerial triad, including George Brumbaugh and John Martin, responsible for bringing the Clover Creek congregation into existence.

Jacob Shenefelt is also only a name in the 1925 history's enumeration of Clover Creek preachers. Of German origin, he was from near Hagerstown, Maryland, where his parents farmed along Antietam Creek. His father, Henry, bought four hundred acres for him from "stocking weaver" John Brumbaugh, and in 1795 Shenefelt moved his family into the stone house Brumbaugh had originally built for himself at East Sharpsburg. The 1925 history has him elected a minister at his new location in 1793, which must be a mistake.[11]

Other Brethren would follow these pathfinders into the Cove soon after the turn of the century. Their life would only be a little less harsh than that of their predecessors. Here in 1806, for instance, came Alexander Mack's grandson, William, to live out his years with daughter Elizabeth and her husband, John Holsinger, in their Bakers Summit home. Thus for a period of roughly two decades, the Brethren of Morrisons Cove, though relatively isolated, could feel a special bond with their spiritual father and those other intrepid souls of Schwarzenau repute.

The pattern of Brethren settlement in that part of Middle District where William Mack chose to spend his last days is obvious. There were three centers in the Cove: New Enterprise (or what the 1925 history calls the headwaters of Yellow Creek); Roaring Spring-Martinsburg; and Clover Creek. Often pioneer parents were accompanied, or soon after followed, by some of their grown children and families. As might be expected under the circumstances, there was a good deal of intermarrying among the Brethren families. For, remembered Jacob Shenefelt, Jr., who had moved to the Cove as a boy, until the 1800s the Brethren and Lutheran were the only religious bodies there.

GERMANY VALLEY

This part of the Aughwick Valley in Huntingdon County, located between Shirleysburg and the Juniata River, received its name in recognition of the preponderant number of Germans that settled here. Pinched in by low ridges on the east and west, it is five miles in length. Though Shirleysburg was an old Indian trading post and fort, Germany Valley in the early 1790s was still unexplored terrain.

Here in that decade came Christian Long. He was born in Pennsylvania—probably in Lancaster County—about 1769 and lived to be eighty years old. He was the son of Joseph Long, the pioneer who literally tree-blazed his way into Germany Valley in search of a future home. The father, born in 1727, likely became Mennonite while growing up in Lancaster County. Whether he later converted to Brethrenism cannot be determined. But it would appear that son Christian was a devout Brethren by the time he himself put up a cabin in Germany Valley, despite being married by a German Reformed clergyman.

Christian's father, who departed Lancaster County for Maryland in 1787, acquired over nine hundred acres of Morrisons Cove land in the early 1790s. But he soon sold them off and never lived in the Cove. Instead, in 1795 he squatted on virgin soil in Germany Valley, the first white settler there, three years before applying for a warrant on some twelve hundred acres on both sides of the Aughwick Creek.[12]

The following year (1796), Christian and his wife, Elizabeth Baker, joined the parental Longs. Their first child was born in 1797. In 1802, at age thirty-three, Christian was given a ministerial call when the Brethren of the Valley (six of them) decided to organize. Two sons, Christian, Jr., and Peter, walked in his pastoral steps, though both eventually left the homestead area.

Another of Germany Valley's hinterlanders was Jacob Lutz, who had apparently married Christian Sr.'s sister, Catherine, before migrating from his Maryland farm. They made their appearance in 1796, about the same time as Christian. Catherine became the Valley's seventh church member, and her husband its second minister.

Their daughter Catherine married Andrew Spanogle, whose father, John, a Dutch immigrant, had settled temporarily somewhere in the vicinity of Shirleysburg (but apparently not in the Valley itself) perhaps as early as the late 1780s. The Spanogles, father and son, both became ministers, John at Warriors Mark, where he relocated, and Andrew at Germany Valley. Andrew, bilingual, gained some notice as an evangelist in the East and Midwest.

The Secrist brothers, Daniel and Peter, whose wives and themselves were among the half-dozen Brethren to organize the Aughwick congregation, were probably ante-1800 pioneers in the Valley. Daniel was elected the first deacon, but, other than that, the record on the Secrist families is totally blank.

The only language spoken by the original Brethren settlers of the Valley, of course, was German. Not until after 1806, when English-speaking John Hanawalt began preaching, was the sound of another language heard in their services.

LEWISTOWN AREA

Dry Valley

Sometime before the Revolution, John Rothrock came from Northampton County and laid claim to land four miles northeast of Lewistown.[13] His religious connections are not known, but his son Joseph, who farmed the homestead until his death, was one of the earliest ministers of the Kishacoquillas Valley congregation, as the pre-1800 Brethren of Mifflin and adjoining counties called themselves. Joseph was the first-known Brethren to settle in Dry Valley, an area curiously misnamed since its meadows are well watered by Jacks Creek. Scenic Route 522 also runs the length of the valley on its way to Selinsgrove. Joseph had a son called Abraham, who succeeded him in the ministry and eldership.

Ferguson Valley

George Rothrock was an uncle of Joseph, and in 1773 he obtained title to land in Ferguson Valley. Today the Spring Run church stands in this Valley, located a few miles northwest of McVeytown and thirteen miles long. It extends west from Yeagertown, with Jacks Mountain on the north and Oriskany ridges on the south.

George may or may not have been Brethren, but his twin daughters, Susannah and Mary, born in the Valley, were baptized in 1794 at age twenty-one in Spring Run. Cousins of Dry Valley's preacher-to-be Joseph Rothrock, they were the first to receive a Brethren baptism in their home valley.

The sisters married Hanawalt brothers; Susannah married George and Mary, John. The father of the Hanawalts, Henry George, was German-born (about 1724) and immigrated to America as a redemptioner in 1745. The man to whom he was bound out had purchased land in Ferguson Valley at a sheriff's sale, and when Henry married his daughter the 550-acre tract became theirs. They traveled from Carlisle by horseback, following bridle paths. Their log cabin was later replaced with a more commodious house, and the farm was dubbed "Old Mansion."

Henry was not Brethren, nor were his sons until after marrying the Rothrock twins. Their marriages, however, produced churchmen of note in the District. Mary's husband, John, was the Hanawalt who introduced English services to the Aughwick congregation. He and Mary moved from Ferguson Valley and did their farming one mile east of Mount Union.

George and Susannah, who raised their family on the Old Mansion Farm, were parents of Joseph Rothrock Hanawalt, the first minister to preach in English in the Lewistown area. He was a regular attendant at District Conference and not a few times could be found at Annual Conference, where he often was appointed to important committees. He was Spring Run's first bishop.

Joseph R. Hanawalt married a daughter of John Swigart, Sr. Swigart migrated from Germany about 1790, first settling in Berks County, then in Ferguson Valley in 1792. If not a Brethren beforehand, he probably became one after marrying Abraham Miller's daughter, Catherine. This union gave rise to the Swigart lineage, so important in the history of Juniata College and several District churches.

The 1925 history mentions a Jacob Kinsel, another Berks Countian who took up life in Ferguson Valley about the same time as John Swigart, while in his mid-thirties. He soon became "a leading spirit" among the Brethren in Mifflin County, signaled by his call to preach. Apparently, however, only one of his descendants, Michael F. H. Kinsel, took an active interest in the church at Spring Run.

Granville

Also an early settler was John Swigart's father-in-law, Abraham Miller, a migrator from Dauphin County sometime in the last quarter of the eighteenth century. He carved out a farm near

Granville, along the Juniata River, about five miles south of Lewistown. His background is a blank, but tradition holds that he was the first minister in the Kishacoquillas Valley congregation.

This survey of pioneering Brethren families in the Lewistown area, as of the other District enclaves, shows the considerable extent to which they intermarried. Such a practice only served to perpetuate their Germanic speech and ways.

OTHER BRETHREN SETTLEMENTS

Woodcock Valley

Woodcock Valley stretches southwest of Huntingdon for a distance of about ten miles. It lies between Warrior's Ridge and Terrace Mountain, Route 26 running almost exactly down its middle. One of the oldest settled valleys in Huntingdon County, it was a favorite haunt of Indians, whose great East-West warpath went through part of it.

Earlier I mentioned Jacob Brumbaugh's trek over Tussey Mountain from Morrisons Cove in 1794 to begin anew in Woodcock Valley. By then aged sixty, he took nine of his remaining children with him to join six or so other non-Brethren German families already there. This move served to plant the seed of Brethrenism in that Valley, eventually producing the line of Brumbaugh in the District so intimately linked to religious publications, educational reform, and other forms of progressivism—social as well as political.

Probably Jacob located directly on the site where in 1804 he built a stone house, now listed in the Pennsylvania Register of Historic Places. Stone houses were a rarity in the central part of the State at that time, and it was probably the second erected by the Brethren of Middle District. (See Jacob Studebaker below.) Its interior design reflected the typical larger Brethren domicile in older eastern counties: swing-back and movable partitions on the first floor to allow use as a meetinghouse.

Brumbaugh descendants married into other families of pioneering origin, like the Garners, Groveses, Boyers, Norrises, and Peightals, gradually enlarging Brethren influence all over Woodcock Valley. In time, too, later generations of Brumbaughs established themselves along the Raystown Branch, on the east side of Terrace Mountain, creating another pocket of Brethrenism.

Snake Spring Valley

The year 1782 was probably when Jacob Snyder, Jr., a Virginian who lived for a time near Hagerstown, Maryland, first set foot in what later was called Snake Spring Valley. The Valley, located a short distance northwest of Everett, got its name in a curious way, at least according to the *Primitive Christian*. It said in 1877 that

> before the days of canal-boats, railroads and telegraphs, goods were forwarded from Philadelphia to Pittsburgh, and from the westward, on pack horses . . . and as they passed to and fro along this road, they stopped at this spring to water and eat their lunch, and as the place was infested with snakes . . . received the name Snake Spring.[14]

Before long this term was used of the Valley itself, so this tradition says.

Several brothers and sisters of Jacob, Jr., had preceded him into Central Pennsylvania by a couple of years. He himself apparently did not put up a cabin of his own until 1786, after marrying and becoming a father. He moved wife and son into an earthen-floor hut, their home for a decade and a half. The 1925 history lists him as an early minister, but whether he came of Brethren antecedents or was a convert is an elusive question. At any rate, his son John married a daughter of Samuel Ullery, the New Enterprise circuit rider who did so much to keep the Cove Brethren in regular touch. If not beforehand, the Snyders, as a result of this marriage, now entered the ranks of Mack followers.

Mary Snyder, a sister of John, married Jacob Studebaker of the Valley sometime before 1790. The census of that year shows a family head of that name with ten children. According to the 1925 history, Studebaker built a large stone house in 1803, where the first love feast in the Snake Spring vicinity was held. This stone residence was likely the first Brethren-built one in the District, antedating Jacob Brumbaugh's by a year.

Artemas

Deep in the mountains of southern Bedford County, a few miles north of the Maryland line, stands the hamlet of Artemas. To this even yet out-of-the-way place, about the time of the Revolutionary War came Joseph and Rachel Bennett from parts unknown. Joseph is listed in the 1790 census as head of a family of six (four sons). The parents must have been Brethren at the time of their arrival, since their remote location kept them isolated from any contact with even the closest church members—at Snake Spring Valley—for decades. The name Bennett was synonymous with the Artemas congregation for the whole of the nineteenth century.

Warriors Mark

This area lies to the east of Bald Eagle Ridge, not far from Tyrone. The earliest Brethren settlers here, the 1925 history states, were John Spanogle and Henry Nearhoof, both later elevated to the ministry. Neither was Brethren originally—obviously not Spanogle, who was a Revolutionary War veteran. Spanogle, with his parents and two brothers, migrated from Holland to America, soon after which the father died. The family separated, and John, after his military service, took his mother with him to the Shirleysburg neighborhood, where he married. The stay there was brief, and sometime in the late eighties or early nineties he moved on to Warriors Mark. There his mother married a Nearhoof. John and his wife had ten children in all, though the census of 1790 lists only one son at home. Some of the Spanogle offspring married into families with prominent Brethren names later on, such as Buck and Cox. Son Andrew became a minister, the far-traveling evangelist at Germany Valley mentioned earlier.

Nothing much is known about Henry Nearhoof, except that in 1790 he had a family of two sons and a daughter. Apparently, his farm adjoined that of John Spanogle, whose mother married either Henry or one of his sons. *The Christian Family Companion* said in 1869 that he was the first minister in the Warriors Mark congregation, later to be joined by Spanogle. Generations of Nearhoofs have been identified as Brethren ever since.

It would have been helpful to know more about the contribution that women made to planting the church in Middle Pennsylvania. As mother and helpmate, the distaff side certainly played an important role in helping the pioneer family cope with the hardships and hazards involved in opening the frontier. And on her, more than on the "head of the family," fell the responsibility of nurturing the tender sentiments that kept backwoods life from lapsing altogether into the pitfall of barbarism. How many husbands or fathers who became leaders in the church had been brought into the Brethren fold because of feminine suasion makes interesting speculation.

4

Rural Churches

A Rural-Oriented District

Central Pennsylvania, primarily because of its physical geography, has remained essentially agrarian and sylvan in character. In all of Middle District there are only two urban areas, Altoona and State College, but their combined population does not total one hundred thousand. And only four boroughs—Lewistown, Tyrone, Huntingdon, Hollidaysburg—boast a populace of five thousand or more, Lewistown being the largest with about seven thousand. Thus the numerical strength of the District is to be found in its countryside and village congregations. The rural areas account for ninety percent of the church buildings and nearly sixty-two percent of the membership. These congregations in the open country, however, tend to be small, half of them with a membership of less than 150. Some of them, as a result, have resorted to yoked cooperative pastoral programs in order to survive.

In Middle District the agrarian values of the Brethren heritage are still important. But they are eroding under the onslaught of modern society, a condition true for the Brotherhood as a whole. Rural isolation is a thing of the past, thanks to technology, which puts the city only minutes away and brings the blandishments of a consumer economy into virtually every farm home today via radio and television.

Central Pennsylvania Less Isolated after the Mid-1820s

The early circuit-riding preachers of the District faced a formidable task in trying to maintain contact with scattered members and congregations as long as travel was limited to horseback. This mode of transportation—over lonely, poor roads through unimproved country—was dangerous and unpleasant. But with the first decades of the nineteenth century came the heyday of road making and canal construction that helped open up the interior. This was the era of turnpike building, when scores of toll roads, some of them macadamized (paved by layers of compacted small stones) or planked, not only linked nearby communities but ran the length and breadth of the District. The pikes promoted stagecoach service and long-distance freight hauling by Conestoga wagon.

Meanwhile, in January 1825 an editorial appeared in the *Huntingdon Gazette* noting that, while the turnpike craze was still raging (and would continue for another quarter century), "now we are all agog in this and many parts of the country on the subject of canaling." The famous Erie Canal would be completed later that year, and its threat of capturing the trade of the great West roused the people of Pennsylvania. A number of canals were constructed, but the most important was a main line—four hundred miles long—from Philadelphia to Pittsburgh that also included railroad mileage. The portage system of ten inclined planes over the Allegheny Mountains, connecting Hollidaysburg and Johnstown, was a railroad sensation. Through Middle District, the canal, which carried boat traffic between Hollidaysburg and Lewistown before the whole main line was opened in 1834, followed the course of the Juniata River and its Frankstown Branch by way of Williamsburg.

Then in 1850 came the Pennsylvania Railroad, when a single track was completed from Philadelphia to Huntingdon. In two years' time, trains were running the length of the Commonwealth. Branches began to radiate through Central Pennsylvania. In 1872 Morrisons Cove got one of these branches, tracks being laid from Altoona to Newry, Roaring Spring, Martinsburg, Henrietta, and Williamsburg.

By that time the Huntingdon and Broad Top Railroad had been opened—in 1856—to Mount Dallas, a distance of forty-five miles, bringing rail travel to Woodcock Valley and points south. At Mount Dallas connection was made with the Bedford and Bridgeport Railroad so that trains ran daily between Huntingdon and Cumberland, Maryland.

In 1874 the East Broad Top Railroad, a narrow-gauge line (three feet), was operating its entire length—between Orbisonia and Robertsdale.

Soon after the century's turn, the invention of the automobile put Henry Ford's "Model T" on farms everywhere and compelled the rapid development of a highway system. The Lincoln Highway (Route 30) and Route 22 became the two most important cross-state arteries, passing through the southern and northern sectors of Middle District, respectively. But in the beginning these advances disturbed many Brethren, who were slow to accept the motorcar because they felt that it violated the principles of the simple life. Not until 1919, for example, did the New Enterprise congregation remove the stables that stood next to the church, and only in 1922 were the hitching posts finally taken out.

Other amenities enjoyed by townspeople as the 1900s commenced were things of the distant future for country folk. Electrification, the telephone, indoor plumbing, central heating—these did not become available to rustic living in many areas until the 1930s or later.

The town had a strong attraction for Americans after the Civil War, and the Brethren were no exception. Rural areas of the District suffered somewhat from this drain on its members. Also, as available land shrank, the 1880s witnessed a considerable exodus of church members to the West or, in several instances, to Maryland's Eastern Shore.

Individual Congregations

The first comprehensive numeration of the Brethren took place in the early 1880s. Howard Miller, who joined the church when introduced to the Brethren as a teacher at Lewis Kimmel's Plum Creek school in Indiana County, began working privately on a census of the Brotherhood in 1877, a task opposed by not a few Brethren. Then in 1880 the federal government, in connection with the census of that year, appointed him enumerator of all noncombatant and nonlitigant secular and religious organizations in the United States.

This led to the publication of his informative compilation, *Record of the Faithful: For the Use of the Brethren. Being a Statistical Record and a Complete Directory of the Brethren Church for the Years 1881–1882.*[1] Brotherhoodwide, he reported, there were almost fifty-eight thousand members, Pennsylvania accounting for 14,557 of them. In Middle District, he listed twelve congregations, all rural except Huntingdon. The eleven country churches had a total membership of 2,492. Nearly half of this constituency hailed from Morrisons Cove.

Today, forty-one congregations in Middle District fall into the category of rural. Historically, they were organized in the following chronological order.

CLOVER CREEK (1790)
MEMBERSHIP: 205

The Clover Creek congregation, according to the 1925 history, had its genesis in 1790 with twenty members. But these figures are based upon tradition and cannot be taken as facts.

Few records of this early company have been preserved. For about

half a century, as was the Brethren custom, the members met in their homes for public worship. Clover Creek was the first church of the District to entertain Annual Conference, in 1823, although minutes for that year and the next, for some reason, were never published. This event took place on a farm halfway between Fredericksburg and Martinsburg.

Clover Creek's first church building was erected in 1841 where the present one now stands. A low, one-story structure with a basement, it stood on the mountain slope and was known as the "Brumbaugh House," since most of the surrounding farms were owned by descendants of the pioneer Brumbaughs who settled in the Cove. Later, the village of Fredericksburg sprang up just below the church, along Clover Creek.

Four years later John and James Camerer put up a dual-purpose building—a dwelling and a meetinghouse—in Martinsburg, as a convenience for the members in that part of the Cove. It still stands, opposite the present church structure.

Next in Clover Creek's growth came the Diehl's Crossroads church, in 1855. Prior to this, services in the Henrietta environs, by mid-century important for iron-ore mining, were held in the farm home of Isaac Burget.

Clover Creek again played host to Annual Conference, this time in 1863 on the John Brumbaugh farm. The church was converted into a dining hall, while Conference business took place in a nearby grove. Neighboring barns served as preaching sites. Soon-to-be-marytred John Kline presided over the wartime Conference, which was addressed by Daniel P. Saylor in an eloquent plea for money to help those Brethren who had suffered property loss in the recent battle of Antietam.

The 1870s saw a new church built at Martinsburg, the Crossroads church remodeled, and two new meetinghouses go up—one at Williamsburg (Fairview), in the northern end of the parish, and one in the western part, near Roaring Spring (Albright).

As for the mother church, Henry Brumbaugh thought in 1873 that something should be done to improve its own facilities. He wrote in his *Pilgrim:*

> This thing of women, especially those having children to care for, sitting on seats without backs during two or three hour services, is an act of penance done with exceeding bad grace.[2]

A typhoid-fever epidemic swept Fredericksburg the summer of 1881. There were twenty-seven cases, of whom eight died. It had been nearly twenty years since the community, which in the early eighties had a population slightly over one hundred, had been struck by a disease of this nature and severity.

On the brighter side, 1881 was the year the congregation decided to take Henry Brumbaugh's advice and rebuild the home church. The original one was torn down and in its place rose a larger one (43' x 63'), with basement, costing $1,496.98. The following November it was decided to have preaching every other Sunday night.

In all, nine churches over the years, either directly or indirectly, were nurtured into independent existence by Clover Creek: Martinsburg, Crossroads, James Creek, Huntingdon, Fairview, Williamsburg, Smithfield, Albright, and Roaring Spring.

From 1925 to 1936, the Clover Creek congregation included three churches: Martinsburg, the home church, and Diehl's Crossroads, the last having been rebuilt in 1906 (40' x 55'), debt-free, at a cost of $2,300. By 1930 Clover Creek, with more than seven hundred members, was the third largest congregation in the Brotherhood. But in 1936 Martinsburg became autonomous, and then in 1972 Diehl's Crossroads struck out on its own under a part-time ministry.

The years have seen several remodeling projects. A rededication service on April 24, 1938, marked the completion of a major refurbishing program ($3,696.84) in the middle of the Great Depression. The most recent reconstruction work was in 1961, when an educational wing was added and the sanctuary refurnished. The one-story annex (42' x 32') on the south side contains six classrooms on the ground floor and six in the basement, a nursery, a heating system, and rest rooms.

As in most Brethren churches, the early leadership at Clover Creek was furnished by the free ministry. Even as recently as the 1930s, the congregation had as many as eight resident ministers. From 1936 to 1953 the church moved away from the free ministry to part-time pastorates. Then in 1953, purchasing the former Brumbaugh property for a parsonage, the church obtained a full-time pastor in Lloyd B. Stauffer, who served till 1957. Since his time there have been Elmer E. Ebersole (1957–1960), Harold L. Bowser (1960–1965), vacant (1965–66), Richard C. Wenger (1966–1973), and Charles H. Heltzel (1973–   ).

NEW ENTERPRISE (1796)
MEMBERSHIP: 356

As we have seen in the two previous chapters, New Enterprise was a center of Brethren activity by the last quarter of the eighteenth century. Earliest records put Cove-pioneering Brethren on the Three Springs branch of Yellow Creek in the northwestern corner of Bedford County. Though they would organize as the Yellow Creek congregation, it is not to be confused with the church of that name today. In 1785 a deed signed by Benjamin Franklin conveyed a tract of land consisting of 269 acres to Samuel Ullery and Jacob Brumbaugh, and it is on a part of this land that the first New Enterprise church stood. In 1796, then, the Brethren in the south-

ern end of Morrisons Cove organized as the Yellow Creek congregation, its territory embracing all of Bedford and much of Fulton counties. Fourteen congregations today occupy this original area.

As far as is known, the Samuel Ullery mentioned above was the first minister of Yellow Creek. Ordained in 1810, he had oversight of the congregation until his death in 1822. He was buried in the cemetery close to where the New Enterprise church was later built.

In 1820 the Snake Spring Valley congregation, which included the southern portion of Bedford County and a small section of the Cove (now the Koontz parish), formed out of Yellow Creek. Work began at Hopewell (the present Yellow Creek congregation) about 1830, leading to an organized church there two decades later, and a meetinghouse.

Meanwhile, in 1840 a meetinghouse had been built at New Enterprise. It was Yellow Creek's first. Before that time the members met for worship in their homes. Then the Holsinger church near Bakers Summit was erected in 1850. Twenty-two years after this, two identical churches (each 32' x 45' and frame) went up at Waterside and Snyder.

It soon became apparent that Yellow Creek's congregational bounds were far too large to manage efficiently. And so in 1876, on the strength of a fifty-six to thirty-five vote, the members allowed the creation of what came to be called the Woodbury charge. For the time being, the New Enterprise-centered congregation retained the name Yellow Creek.

The next year, Yellow Creek entertained Annual Conference, which held its sessions in the Ober barn on the outskirts of New Enterprise. The church itself was used for a dining hall.

But its days were numbered. Thirty-eight years old, it was demolished in 1878 and replaced by a new structure (80' x 50'), which was frame and had a basement. Its sanctuary was then the largest in the District, with a seating capacity of eight hundred. At the front of the sanctuary was a platform, a kind of chancel two-steps high, marking a departure from the one-level floor traditional with the Brethren—a departure more and more common in church construction by the late 1800s.

In December 1880 Yellow Creek completed and dedicated a small church building (34' x 40' x 12') at Dutch Corners (Imlertown). The work there never really got going, and in 1908 the building was sold. About this time, the one at Snyder was also disposed of, ending involvement there.

Meanwhile, as recounted in chapter 7, the Progressive Brethren split did not bypass the group at New Enterprise. At a special assemblage on August 16, 1883, presided over by outsiders James Quinter, James Sell, and Solomon Buckelew, twelve names were stricken from the roll because of their secessionist sympathies— among them a minister and two church officers.

In April 1895 the congregation legally changed its name to New Enterprise. Explains the 1925 history, this action was taken because "in the Hopewell congregation not far away was a post office named Yellow Creek and many confused this name and the one of the congregation." (The next year Hopewell, with District approval, chose to call itself the Yellow Creek church.)

New Enterprise became the legatee of a church at Salemville in 1908, upon the death of Leah Burger. She and her husband, John, who died around 1883, had built the church in 1882, intending that it be interdenominational but allowing it to be christened the Dunker Baptist Church. Of substantial size (60' x 40'), it had a bell and an expensive Brussels carpet on the floor, and was enclosed by a white picket fence. At Leah's death, she left the church to the New Enterprise congregation because she felt that there were not enough people in Salemville to support the church on their own. According to an article in the *Morrisons Cove Herald* (January 27, 1966), the deceased widow's prized Brussels carpet was taken up sometime later and auctioned off at eleven cents a yard. Pieces of the floor covering were seen in many homes throughout the Cove for years after. Services were held in the Salemville church until recently (it was sold and relocated in 1980).

The large church house erected in 1878, a one-big-room type, was not suited for Sunday School use. Therefore, at a cost of $2,650, this

Salemville Church, sold to Mennonites and moved in 1980.

was remedied in 1915 by dividing part of the sanctuary into class-rooms, arranged so that they could be opened into the main auditorium. Some twelve hundred worshipers heard Dr. Charles C. Ellis of Juniata College speak at the rededication service on October 31.

The year 1918 marked a change in ministerial policy. At that time the congregation forsook the free ministry and adopted the pastoral system. H. Stover Kulp, later destined to Brotherhood fame on the African mission field, became the first full-time pastor. But he served just one year, 1918–19. He was followed by George E. Yoder, coming from the Norristown church, who continued until 1927. Daniel O. Cottrell came next, 1928–1935, to be succeeded by Wilfred N. Stauffer, 1935–1945.

During the Stauffer pastorate, the original Waterside church was sold and the present building purchased in 1936. Twenty-three years later, Waterside began a pastoral program of their own and in 1963 became a separate congregation.

After Wilfred Stauffer there followed Cletus S. Myers, who served from 1945 to 1951. He was pastor when the present New Enterprise church was built, still the only place of worship in the village. The decision to build was made on Sunday morning, February 2, 1947, at a council specially called by the Official Board. But still to be resolved was the question of location: in town or on the old church site. This was finally determined in January 1948. At a special council on the 4th, the members voted for a town site and authorized selling the 1878 building and the parsonage. The congregation then purchased the Ebersole property, including ten acres of land from Henry R. Snowberger. This property included a house next to the building site, which became the parsonage. The parsonage was rebuilt and modernized in 1966.

The new edifice, constructed of native limestone and Gothic in architectural design, was dedicated by President Rufus D. Bowman of Bethany Theological Seminary on January 14, 1951. The auditorium has a seating capacity of three hundred, with additional seating capacity for 150 and two hundred in the balcony and narthex, respectively. The sanctuary is 43' x 72' and the Sunday School end of the building measures 30' x 72'. A large social room is in the basement. In 1970–71 extensive improvements were made in the sanctuary ($17,000).

Pastors since Myers's time have been Wayne H. Dick (1951–1958), William F. Smith (1959–1968), vacant (1968–69), Ira W. Gibbel (1969–1975), J. Ronald Mummert (1975–1978), and Lee G. Bowman (1979–   ).

SPRING MOUNT (1800)
MEMBERSHIP: 64

Although, according to the latest figures available, the Spring
Mount membership is one of the smallest in Middle District, much
of the early Brethren activity in the northern reaches of Huntingdon and Blair counties was instigated by this rural congregation.
At least three churches—Tyrone, Bellwood, Juniata Park—sprang
up out of its territory. According to the *Record of the Faithful,* Spring
Mount was organized in 1800 with twelve members. Today this
small settlement of twenty homes, also known as Cross Roads, lies
one mile north of Warriors Mark at the foot of Bald Eagle Ridge.
The village took its name from a nearby spring, although originally
the congregation was called Warriors Mark. The membership was
scattered, located in Warriors Mark, Tuckahoe, Bald Eagle, and
Sinking Valley.

Andrew Spanogle told Henry Holsinger in 1869 that his father,
John, a Revolutionary War veteran of Dutch antecedents, and
Henry Nearhoof were the congregation's first ministers. The red
brick house built by Nearhoof, still standing just west of Spring
Mount, has movable partitions in the west room on the second floor,
indicating the early Brethren of this area typically met in private
homes for worship. Other family names among the early Brethren
settlers here included Beck, Auteberger, Grazier, Buck, and Grain.
It was in 1856 that Jacob Beck, a native of Warriors Mark
Township who was called into the ministry in 1833, deeded to the
congregation a three-quarter-acre plot of ground on the corner of

his farm adjacent to the village. On it the members in 1857 put up a 40′ x 40′ frame structure still in use today. By this time Graybill Myers, in one of his frequent moves, had taken up residency in Tuckahoe at the extreme northern bounds of the congregation, just a few miles from Altoona. He and Samuel Cox, whose knowledge of the Bible was legendary, tried to minister to the widely scattered Brethren, but their work languished.

After the Civil War, the life of the church was revived by Henry R. Holsinger. In 1865 he began publishing the *Christian Family Companion* in Tyrone, which fell within the Spring Mount's congregational limits. The people made him a minister in 1866, and the young publisher, with the help of James A. Sell, then a twenty-year-old licensee working in Holsinger's office, soon started a Sunday School and did much to add new members to the church rolls. Both men moved away a few years later, and much of the gain was lost. There were troubles, the nature of which was never revealed. An item in the *Primitive Christian* in Janaury 1877 observed that the church had "never been unified" and that it had "personal problems." At this time services were usually held in the afternoon, to accommodate preachers from Altoona, most notably Graybill Myers, who after 1873 was paid one dollar a round trip.

Joseph W. Wilt, the man who would for the years ahead be instrumental in starting five missions in the District (all to become self-standing congregations), conducted the first revival in 1877 when thirty-six came into the church. Two years later, Wilt became pastor and moved to Spring Mount, operating a carriage and buggy shop. Over the next half decade he raised the membership from fifty to 126. Sometimes in this period Spring Mount Brethren also worshiped in the Mount Vernon schoolhouse.

After Wilt's pastorate Spring Mount went into decline again. As a last resort, the congregation asked the District Mission Board to take over in 1898. Between 1904 and 1920 the pastors of the Altoona and Tyrone churches, William Howe, Walter S. Long, and Charles O. Beery, filled the pulpit as they were able. In nice weather, Beery bicycled his way to Spring Mount. During these years there were no regular church services. The Sunday School, however, met unfailingly.

Regular pastoral care resumed in 1920 when William N. Hoover purchased a farm and began his work there. Until the 1920s the entrance to the church building was at the back, away from the main road. In 1923 council voted to put in a front entrance, which meant reversing the sanctuary and making other major changes. The pastor and a deacon, Walter Cox, did the carpenter work. Electric lights were installed at the same time. More recently, beginning in May 1956, an extensive improvement program was undertaken on a pay-as-you-go basis, which continued for a decade or so at a cost in excess of ten thousand dollars.

Earlier, on November 15, 1950, incorporation papers brought about changing the old congregational name of Warriors Mark to Spring Mount.

Ten years before this, in 1940, William L. Gould replaced William Hoover as pastor, serving until 1944. Since then there have been: Sheldon Snyder (1945–1949), Harold L. Bowser (1950–1954), Homer F. Hoover (1954–55), substitutes from Juniata College (1955–1957), R. Eugene Miller (1957–1959), substitutes from Juniata College (1959–1965), Paul R. Yoder, retired Juniata College physics professor (1965–1975), and Ralph Z. Ebersole, who in 1976 accepted the call to serve as yoked pastor for both Spring Mount and Tyrone congregations.

AUGHWICK (1802)

MEMBERSHIP: 278

The Aughwick congregation perhaps holds more historical interest for the Brethren of the District than any other parish. As Dr. Donald Durnbaugh has pointed out, "Its Germany Valley meetinghouse is the oldest building in the district (1836), it was the scene of two early annual meetings (1839 and 1855), it has preserved the oldest congregational record (1847), and it was the site of the first meeting of the Middle District (1861)."[3]

It was near Aughwick, we saw in chapter 3, that the first white settlers in Huntingdon County established themselves. Pioneering the way was Joseph Long of Lancaster County, who put up a crude cabin in Germany Valley sometime in the late 1790s. Other families of German origin followed in later decades—the Spanogles, the Ebys, the Lutzes, the Wakefields, the Garvers, the Swanes—some of them occupying land owned by Long. It was from among these early residents of Shirley Township that the Aughwick congregation developed.

The church organized about 1802, Christian Long, Daniel Secrist, and Peter Secrist and their wives making up the six founding members. Christian Long, son of Joseph, was chosen minister and Daniel Secrist, deacon. Two years later, Jacob Lutz received a ministerial call, apparently soon after his baptism. His wife, Catherine, had earlier joined the congregation as its seventh member.

Long and Lutz preached in German, a liability in reaching out to the surrounding English community. Accessions came slowly until 1806, when John Hanawalt, who spoke English, was elected to the ministry. After that, states a historical sketch of Aughwick in the *Brethren's Almanac* for 1878, "things seemed to move a little faster" and "the church began to spread out its borders considerably."

Germany Valley, oldest church building in the District (1836).

In the pattern of the earlier Brethren, the Aughwick members at first worshiped in private homes. Later, in keeping with another Brethren custom of the nineteenth century, a schoolhouse was used when the membership grew too large. This was probably in the early 1830s and lasted for only a short period.

Then in 1836 the congregation erected a "low stone church" (40' x 65') for eight hundred dollars. The oldest meetinghouse in the District, it still serves the Brethren of Germany Valley, nearly a century and a half later. Says the 1925 history, "It is a splendid monument to the devotion, courage and sacrifice of those earlier days." Significantly, this remained the only stone church in the District until the Huntingdon Brethren built theirs in 1910.

Soon after 1836 the Aughwick Brethren hosted the first of two Annual Conferences to be held within its bounds, both before the

Civil War. The invitation for the first one, held in 1839, was probably extended through Christian Long, several times a member of Standing Committee, as he was in 1838 when that body selected the place for the next year's assembly. On whose farm the 1839 session took place is not known.

The business was relatively routine, only a half dozen queries being dealt with. But James Quinter remembered that there followed an awakening of "considerable religious interest" in Germany Valley.[4] Schoolmaster Quinter, his journalistic career still a thing of the distant future, was in a position to know, for he was partly behind the area revival. Following Annual Conference, he and John H. Umstad of Philadelphia stayed over to do some preaching in the Valley.

By the 1840s Aughwick had turned out an unusually large number of ministers in its short history. "Preacher factory" was the way some began to refer to the congregation at this time, according to Christian Long. Fourteen ministers had answered the call in the forty-eight years to 1850. Some of these men moved away from the congregation and gave strong leadership elsewhere in the Brotherhood. Among them were Christian Long, Jr., who became an evangelist of some note in Illinois and Iowa, and Enoch Eby.

Eby "went West" in 1855, farming in Illinois and Kansas. Between 1873 and 1899, he was, except for two years, regularly a member of Standing Committee. Eleven times he presided over Annual Conference, and in 1877 he went to Denmark to help Christian Hope establish a mission church.

Another of the Aughwick "factory" products was John G. Glock, born in a German village on the banks of the Neckar River. Licensed in 1842, he began to keep a congregational account book of communion expenses. The earliest entry dates back to 1847, antedating by a couple of decades record-keeping by any other church of the District.

In 1855 Aughwick entertained its second Annual Conference, John B. Garver's farm serving as the scene of the event. The *Shirleysburg Herald,* the local paper, estimated there were four thousand Conference-goers, while the noncommittal *Huntingdon Journal* put the figure at "several thousand."[5] Upon the sponsoring congregation fell the burden, custom then dictated, of providing meals, lodging, and horse feed for all who came from any distance.

In contrast to the 1839 Brotherhood congress, the one for 1855 debated many weighty issues—from marital problems to membership in the Know-Nothing Party to the use of weapons in self-defense to patenting inventions to erecting tombstones to questions of divorce and adultery. Christian Long was again a member of Standing Committee. The Shirleysburg reporter thought that all went smoothly, commenting that "good order and respectful conduct prevailed throughout the entire meeting and nothing occurred in anywise to mar the comfort, nor interrupt the proceedings and religious exercises of that most *peculiar* people."[6]

The expenses incurred hosting Annual Conference as well as cash amounts received were dutifully entered in the congregation's financial record book. Nine years later, in October 1864, Aughwick began to minute its council meetings, another District first. The initial scribe, who wrote in a clear, neat hand, never identified himself. John B. Garver, who later joined the ministerial ranks, became clerk in 1867, his job until 1874.

The 1860s also brought further historical luster to the Aughwick church. In 1861 the newly formed Middle District of Pennsylvania held its maiden meeting here. The man who had initiated the call was Graybill Myers of the Warriors Mark congregation, himself an 1839 Aughwick ministerial offspring.

With the decade of the seventies came many advances, both in the area and in the Aughwick congregation. A railroad now ran from Mount Union to Shirleysburg. In 1872 the Germany Valley meeting-house was refurbished. Pews got backs and, in a daring innovation, carpeting went down on the aisles. Henry Brumbaugh liked the covered aisles and wondered why, though a novelty, "a thing of such real benefit is not generally adopted."[7] By the early seventies Aughwick's membership exceeded two hundred. However, the greater part of the congregation no longer lived in Germany Valley but in the Hill Valley area.

Thus the matter of putting up a church in Hill Valley was discussed in council as early as August 1872. The go-ahead decision came the next spring when a two-thousand-dollar limit was placed on costs. John Spanogle, James R. Lane, Henry Rhodes, George Garver, and Michael Myers made up the building committee. They oversaw the erection of a brick structure (40' x 50') that was dedicated on Saturday, September 19, 1874. It was built on the farm of Elder James R. Lane, two and a half miles south of Shirleysburg, surrounded, said the *Pilgrim,* by a "beautiful grove," an "excellent spring," and a "stream of water." At a New Year's Day council meeting three months later, the new meetinghouse was given the name Sugar Run.

The previous year, while work progressed on the Sugar Run

church, the Aughwick congregation voted that "all those members residing in Mifflin County be stricken off to Spring Run."[8] How many this lopped off the membership roll is not known.

Sugar Run Church.

Despite the realignment of congregational lines with Spring Run, Aughwick churchgoers were still widely scattered. Many had sought homes in the promising valleys that laced southern Huntingdon County. Hares Valley, to the west, became the habitation of several Brethren families. They began meeting in the Lincoln schoolhouse and soon their numbers grew. William Spanogle, newly licensed in 1877, took a special interest in the Hares Valley group. His work prospered, and on January 1, 1879, the Aughwick congregation authorized building a church "at or near Lincoln School house." This was done, much labor being donated, within the next year. The frame building (32' x 36'), located about three miles from Mapleton Depot, became the Beech Run Church.

In October 1884 the Aughwick people erected a fourth meeting-house, this one in Black Log Valley, about ten miles from McVeytown. Dedicated by James Quinter, who had recently merged his publishing business with that of the Brumbaugh brothers in Hunting-don, it was then accessible only by a steep, rough, mountain road. John Shope, a third-degree minister since 1879 who farmed in

Black Log Valley, did most of the preaching for the half-hundred or
so Brethren living between the Black Log and Shade mountains.

After a few years, however, Shope defected to the Progressive
Brethren. He took with him many of the Black Log people as well as
the bulk of members at Beech Run, where he had been a prime
mover in starting a Sunday School. In fact, the Beech Run ranks
were reduced to as few as two before the Progressive schism had run
its course in the District.

Despite this exodus the congregation numbered as many as 250 in
1887 and boasted seven resident ministers. That year, it was divided
on a trial basis into three subdistricts, two ministers assigned to each.
This system of ministerial placement worked so well that it was
continued for several years.

With the new century, a Sunday School was organized in the
Enyeart schoolhouse, located between Orbisonia and Rockhill, a
small community to the south. This was in April 1904, and before
long local preachers—James Lane, Robert M. Wakefield, John
Garver, Seth and Christian Myers, and Samuel A. Norris—took
their turns holding worship services at the same place. A revival
conducted in late summer by William F. Spidle, a school teacher,
home minister, and ex-Methodist, won thirty persons, mostly adults,
into the church.

A church house was the next step in accommodating this latest
sector of growth in the Aughwick congregation. Named to the
building committee were George Renecker, Thomas O. Cloyd, and
Howard Norris, who was also the contractor. The church (35' x
40'), built for fourteen hundred dollars, was dedicated on March 11,
1906.

Forty-nine years later, the Aughwick congregation voluntarily
underwent a three-way division. With the 1955 District Meeting's
blessing, Germany Valley and Sugar Run remained as part of the
original Aughwick congregation, while Beech Run was given its
autonomy and Rockhill and Valley Point united as a separate
charge.

The year 1961 was another important one for the Aughwick
congregation. It was an anniversary year, marking the centennial of
the first District Meeting and a century and a quarter since the
building of the Germany Valley meetinghouse. Donald Durnbaugh,
then teaching at Juniata College and later to become one of the
denomination's foremost historians at Bethany Theological Seminary, prepared a pamphlet for the occasion, "Brethren Beginnings
in Middle Pennsylvania." He was also one of the featured speakers at
the District-sponsored anniversary service on Sunday afternoon,
May 14, held at the Germany Valley church. With him on the

program was Morley Mays, then Juniata's academic dean. The District moderator, Berkey E. Knavel of Roaring Spring, presided over the celebration.

No extensive structural changes have been made in either the Germany Valley or Sugar Run churches since they were built, although the latter did undergo a general renovation in 1974. Since 1957 Aughwick's parsonage has been a large, frame house on Garber Street in Mount Union.

The 1920s ended an era of home ministry for the congregation. Its pastors since then have been: DeWitt H. Miller (1921–1923), Alexander M. Stout (1923–1926), H. Will Hanawalt (1927–1937), Jacob T. Dick (1937–38), Martin and Marian Scholten, an early team (1938–1947), E. Myrl Weyant (1947–1953), David C. Emerson (1953–1957), Albert M. Haught (1957–1967), Raymond Risden (1967–1969), Victor S. Norris (1969), Howard L. Ogburn (1969–70), John D. Keiper (1970–1975), Roy C. Myers (1975–1977), and Harold M. Kenepp (1977–   ).

Oil painting of early Snake Spring Brethren by Barnard Taylor. Note the once-distinctive simple clothes, typically bearded men, and bonneted women.

SNAKE SPRING VALLEY (1820)
MEMBERSHIP: 220

This church is located five miles north of Everett on Route 36. Into this Valley, whose unusual name is explained in the preceding chapter, came Jacob Snyder from northern Maryland in 1782. Here he built a shack in which he lived and for a while taught school. As noted in chapter 3, it is not clear whether he was Brethren upon his arrival or even the first of that faith to settle near the Valley's once popular spring. The 1925 history, at any rate, has Brethren here in the 1790s who were ministered to by Samuel Ullery, the pioneering preacher from New Enterprise. Elected a deacon, Snyder built a brick house in 1811 that doubled as a place of worship.

Around 1820 the Brethren of the Valley formally organized, a designated line dividing it from Yellow Creek (New Enterprise) on the north but leaving it boundless on all other sides. Hence its territory reached south to the Maryland line, eastward into Fulton and westward into Somerset counties.

Isaac Ritchey, reared in the Reformed Church, became the first minister and first bishop of the congregation. At his death in 1845, Jacob Snyder acceded to these offices, which he held until 1848, the year he died. Meanwhile, Jacob Steele, another ex-Reformed communicant who became a widely traveled farmer-evangelist, had been called to the ministry and began to do the first preaching in English. But German so prevailed among the Brethren of the Valley that he was not advanced to the eldership until 1872. His ministry of nearly sixty years, however, was largely devoted to the Yellow Creek congregation.

The Snyder upstairs-sanctuary served the Snake Spring people for half a century, until 1860 when they put up a frame building on the lowlands of the Daniel Hershberger farm. The contractor was Martin Hoover, who afterwards built several churches in this congregation.

Soon other meetinghouses began going up under Snake Spring's aegis. In 1862 the Yellow Creek house was erected on land owned by Jacob Steele on the Hopewell-Loysburg road. The Koontz house came next, in 1865. Then in 1872 the Brethren in the Clearville neighborhood got the Cherry Lane church, while those at Artemas were churched in 1879. The Bush Creek meetingplace near Rays Hill, long since abandoned, was an 1883 project.

By 1890 there was a growing demand for a new home church, the old location not to everyone's liking. Thus in 1890 another one—the same size as its predecessor (40' x 60') but with an eight-foot high basement—was built on the present church site at a cost of $1,763. Originally, this site was part of the John S. Baker farm.

Still more churches would be erected within the Snake Spring territory. The townspeople of Everett built theirs in 1893 and in 1895 the residents of Buck Valley, in Fulton County, theirs. As the 1925 history rightly observes, "Perhaps there is not another congregation in the brotherhood that has such a record of building meeting-houses as Snake Spring Valley." Eventually, of course, this vast parish was subdivided into independent congregations centered around these various churches.

When the Sunday School movement took hold in the District, Snake Spring was one example where a meetinghouse was enlarged to accommodate modern needs in religious education. Thus in 1913 the members spent twelve hundred dollars to add on more Sunday School space.

The next development came in March 1943 when the church council established a building fund of one thousand dollars and designated the offering on the first Sunday of each month for that purpose. Then, ten years later, in accordance with the plans prepared by Church Architect Forrest U. Groff, work began on a major remodeling program that cost approximately $32,000. In 1958 the congregation bought for a parsonage the property adjacent to the church for ten thousand dollars. Since then both the parsonage (1976 and 1979) and the sanctuary (1978) have undergone renovations and improvements.

The Snake Spring church operated on a free ministry plan until January 1950, when council took action to pay ministers on a by-the-sermon basis. Ministers who have served since 1925 include: Isaac Wareham (1932–1958) and Marshall Van Horn (1938–1958), who alternated every other Sunday during those years; Don Leiter (1958–59), H. James Pearson (1959–60), and D. Luke Bowser (1962–1964) on a full-time schedule; Robert W. Detwiler (1964–1972) and Richard C. Wenger (January–August 1973) on a part-time arrangement, the latter while the pastor of Clover Creek; Galen E. Hoover (1973–1975), who inaugurated a yoked parish with the Cherry Lane church; and Victor S. Norris (1976–1980), under a continuing yoked pastorate.

DUNNINGS CREEK (1840)
MEMBERSHIP: 248

Dunnings Creek was originally part of the Yellow Creek congregation, whose bounds westward extended to the leeward side of the Allegheny Mountains. In that foothill country, comprising two Bedford County townships, St. Clair and Napier, the Dunnings Creek Brethren in the 1840s assigned themselves a territory running twelve miles east and west and twenty-five miles north and south.

A nucleus of Brethren had settled near present-day Pleasantville by 1843. In that year George M. Holsinger, whose mother was

Elizabeth Mack, a great-granddaughter of Alexander Mack, and Moses Rogers were called to the ministry. Holsinger, in 1841, had moved across the Cove Mountain from Bakers Summit to a farm three miles west of Alum Bank. In the fall of 1843 the small colony of Brethren at Dunnings Creek began the erection of a log meetinghouse, finished the next year, on three-quarters of an acre donated by Christian Mock, whose wife was a member. This log building, located two miles from Pleasantville, became known as the Mock Church.

Holsinger and Rogers were inexperienced pulpiteers, and much of the early preaching was done by outsiders—like Aughwick's Christian Long and Yellow Creek's Martin Miller. But these men preached in German, creating a communications problem for the local valley dwellers, who found it more to their advantage to call upon ministers from the Conemaugh congregation, near Johnstown, for English preaching. Levi Roberts, nearly seventy years old, and Peter Lutz, much younger, would walk twenty miles over the mountain to preach for them. There was also John Mineely, a cripple, who came by horseback about once a month to hold services.

The Mock Church still stands, although very much dilapidated and unfit for regular services. The *Gospel Messenger* reported in 1892 that June 17th of that year had been set aside to clean up the church and the graveyard, which had fallen into neglect. Forty workers turned out, including a number of children, who gathered moss and placed it around the weed-choked graves their elders had cleared off. According to the denomination's paper, the last regular service at the Mock Church was held in mid-September 1893.[9]

Today the original wooden peg benches without backs, the pulpit standing flat on the floor, and the Spartan decor give one a good idea of what the atmosphere in the historic log-walled relic must have been like a century and a quarter ago. In September 1954 a

Historic Mock Church, built in 1843 and still standing.

special service was held there to discuss the possibilities of restoring the church. Nothing definite, however, came out of these proceedings. Meanwhile, a great turn had come in the life of the Dunnings Creek Brethren in the year 1870. Because of their isolation and the cramped quarters of the Mock Church, the little group had been holding its love feasts in barns. But in 1870 they built a "love feast house," meaning one with a kitchen and big enough to accommodate communion-goers. Located in Dunker Hollow, which is about a mile and a half northwest of the small town of Ryot and not far from the old Mock place, it went by the name Holsinger House. The 40' x 50' frame building, with two front entrances, cost the congregation about five hundred dollars. (The Holsinger church is not to be confused with the Holsinger congregation.)

Then numbering fifty, the members, motivated by the enthusiasm generated by a new place of worship, decided to organize and did so on January 15, 1871. They officially named themselves the Dunnings Creek congregation and elected John S. Holsinger their elder.

In 1874 Dunnings Creek transferred to Western District. Though on the eastern slope of the Alleghenies, roads and transportation conditions made the new congregation more readily a part of that district than the one that spawned it. Thirty-eight years later, however, in 1916, the situation had changed, and Dunnings Creek came back into Middle District's fold.

Meanwhile, the congregation, grown somewhat scattered in the nearly four decades of Western District affiliation, had built two more churches. One was at Point, four miles northwest of the Napier Station, and was built in 1893. (In 1958, by request of the Point members, this group became an independent fellowship.)

Then, in 1905, a frame church (36' x 50'), costing $3,600, was built in New Paris, a town north of Shellsburg and about fifteen miles northwest of Bedford, the County Seat. From 1927 to 1930 the New Paris church, its numbers in decline, was closed for regular worship. Mr. and Mrs. Ross Callihan were the members largely responsible for putting the New Paris church back into full-time service.

Between 1925 and 1940 the following ministers served the congregation at intervals: George Rogers, Madolin Boorse Taylor, D. Howard Keiper, Glen E. Norris, Eli S. Keeney, and Thomas B. Mickle.

John E. Rowland became the first full-time salaried pastor in 1940, remaining eight years. After him came Elmer E. Ebersole (1947–1957), followed by Fred A. Driver (1957–1959), during whose first year the Point people, as noted above, withdrew to form an independent Brethren group. Next was Thomas E. Shoemaker (1960–1966) and then Charles W. Palmer (1966–1973).

The Palmer pastorate saw in 1971 the construction of a new $190,000 brick church near the village of Ryot, on Route 96. Two years later, however, the congregation suffered a severe wrench when eighty-one members followed Charles Palmer in establishing the Faith Brethren Bible Church.

The minister from 1973 to 1980 was John M. Foster, and in 1979 the congregation burned the mortgage on its parsonage. With Foster's leaving, Mary Lou Hall was called on an interim basis, to be followed a few months later by Herbert E. Schimpf, full time.

SPRING RUN (1848)
MEMBERSHIP: 252

This congregation, whose church stands two miles north of McVeytown, originally fell within the territorial bounds of the old Kishacoquillas Valley parish, which embraced a scattered Brethren population in parts of Huntingdon, Centre, and Mifflin counties. In September 1865 the Kishacoquillas members opted to divide into two autonomous parts, the western branch called Spring Run and the eastern, Dry Valley. Earlier, in 1858, identical church houses had been built at each end of the parish.

Who the Brethren were who first preached in the Spring Run territory is not fully known. Tradition holds that two of the early preachers were Henry Nearhoof of Warriors Mark and Peter Shellenberger of Lost Creek, but it is believed that John Swigart, who came from Berks County about 1792 and settled on a farm in Ferguson Valley, was the first resident minister. About the same

time, Jacob Kinsel, also a Berks County ex-resident, became a Ferguson Valley farmer. Another early settler with some claim to honors as the Valley's initial preacher was Abraham Miller, an emigrant from Dauphin County. Of the three, only Jacob Kinsel is said to have been a bishop.

Other ministers of the last century up to the Civil War were Joseph Rothrock, Abram Rothrock, John Hanawalt, Henry Snyder, John Spanogle, Adam Young, Reuben Myers, Peter S. Myers, Archibald Van Dyke, and Daniel Eshelman. John Hanawalt may have been the first English speaker in the congregation. About 1845, the members decided to conduct half their public services in English. Gradually, German was abandoned, during which time the church grew rapidly, attracting many prominent families familiar only with English.

This sudden membership gain, beginning about 1850, created the need for a suitable meetinghouse. For many years the Brethren met in private dwellings. Some twenty homes were used, the worship services arranged in rotation, thus making an appointment at each place about every twenty weeks. Later, meetings were held in schoolhouses. Barns usually housed love feasts. The promising gains made in the area around McVeytown, a village that in 1850 was made a station on the newly constructed Pennsylvania Railroad, led to formal organization in 1857 with a membership of 157. Then, as noted earlier, a church was built at Spring Run in 1858, and seven years later came the separation from Dry Valley.

Soon after the Civil War broke out, Stone Valley, an area twelve miles northeast of Huntingdon, became mission territory for the Spring Run congregation. In 1862 Samuel Musser, a Methodist from near McAlevys Fort, attended a love feast at Spring Run and was so deeply impressed that he prevailed upon the members to preach in his community. When this happened, he was baptized a Brethren and eventually elected to the ministry. Joseph Hanawalt and Solomon Z. Sharp, the ex-Mennonite who was a pioneering educator in the Brotherhood, answered the call first, Sharp providing a regular ministry every three weeks during the years he headed Kishacoquillas Seminary.

But the thirty-or-so-mile trek worked a hardship on him, and from 1865 to 1867 Archibald Van Dyke, the future father-in-law of John B. Brumbaugh, the publisher and educator, resided in the area and provided the ministry. He was followed by James Sell, who resigned as associate editor of the *Christian Family Companion,* to give two years as a carpenter at McAlevys Fort. Meetings were held there, at Brush Ridge and at Bear Meadow, and in various schoolhouses.

For a time in the 1870s the Presbyterian Church in Manor Hill, an architectural treasure today, was a frequent preaching site. Van Dyke put in a second pastoral stint in the Valley, living on a farm in Chilcote Hollow, midway between Huntingdon and Manor Hill, from 1873 to 1878. In all, about two dozen members were cultivated in Stone Valley, whose population was largely of Quaker descent. The work there was finally abandoned about 1890.

In 1892 Spring Run built a second church, in Bratton Township near Mattawana, where Brethren had been meeting in the local schoolhouse since the 1860s. The *Pilgrim* and *Christian Family Companion* indicate that two unsuccessful attempts were made to house members living south of the Juniata River in 1874 and 1875. At the June council meeting in 1893, the members named the new church building Pine Glen.

The Spring Run church was remodeled in 1909, when the original raised seats were removed. In 1923 there were more improvements, highlighted by the addition of eight Sunday School rooms. Further remodeling occurred in 1947, 1951, 1953, and 1970.

In 1941 the congregation went on a full-time pastoral program. Prior to then, however, post–Civil War ministers have been Abram Myers, Samuel J. Swigart, George H. Swigart, Reuben Myers, John C. Swigart, and Lawrence Ruble. It was Perry Huffaker, a song leader well-known in the Brotherhood, who got the nod in 1941 and moved into a new parsonage. During his ministry Pine Glen and Spring Run, in 1946, became separate congregations.

Since he left in 1949, there have been Henry W. Esbensen (1949–1951), D. Luke Bowser (1954–1959), Frederick A. Driver (1959–1965), Wilfred N. Stauffer (1965–1967), J. Philip Shankster (1968–1974), and Earl D. Rowland (1975–   ).

HOLSINGER (1850)
MEMBERSHIP: 177

The Holsinger congregation traces its history back to 1850. In that year the Yellow Creek members erected a frame meetinghouse (for $620) on a corner of John M. Holsinger's farm, near Bakers Summit. Quite a settlement of Brethren had located in that southern Cove region during the early 1800s, and John Holsinger, whose wife Elizabeth's ancestry traced back to Alexander Mack through her paternal line, became the prime mover in putting up a place of worship for the Brethren of Bakers Summit. At the time, he was Yellow Creek's bishop.

Years later an interesting legend sprang up and persisted about this shuttered church in the woods off the road to Lafayettesville. Tradition maintained that the church shutters would fly ajar, even when there was no breeze, each time an event of serious importance occurred in the community. Thus, according to the old tale, ghosts were thought to warn the good people on the Summit of impending trouble.

In August 1876 the Yellow Creek congregation, in a council meeting held at the Holsinger church, voted to subdivide and create from within its boundaries another parish that included Woodbury, Claar, Lower Claar, and a part of Clover Creek. On November 11 the members of this new territory met in the Holsinger house and adopted the name Woodbury. In 1890 the Holsinger church, as a wing of the Woodbury congregation, was assessed in value at five hundred dollars, with a reported seating capacity of four hundred.

In another dozen years, however, the aging building, one of the oldest church structures in the Cove, was outgrown. The Bakers Summit people decided to raze the church of legend and build larger. A farewell service took place on September 9, 1912, featuring such speakers as John B. Fluck, only days away from his eighty-third birthday, the irrepressible James A. Sell, and George S. Myers, later one of the three original committee members appointed to prepare the 1925 history.

The second and present building (40' x 60'), brick, and costing $3,200, was dedicated on April 6, 1913, debt-free. Sell and Fluck again collaborated in conducting special services on that day.

Major improvements on the church did not occur until the mid-1950s. The sanctuary was completely renovated and refurnished, new classrooms were added, the vestibule was enlarged, and the men dug out the basement. President Calvert N. Ellis of Juniata College was the guest speaker on March 24, 1957, dedication day.

The next important event in the history of the Holsinger congregation occurred in 1960 when, along with Curryville, it severed its ties with Woodbury. However, the Holsinger and Claysburg churches, being only a few miles apart and both small in numbers, decided in 1961 to join together and share the work of one pastor. This lasted until 1963, when the joint pastoral arrangement ended.

In the spring of that year the Holsinger members broke ground for a parsonage on a wooded plot donated by Jacob S. Snyder. The total construction cost of fifteen thousand dollars was kept down by volunteer help.

Twelve years later, in April 1975, the congregation celebrated its 125th anniversary. This was also an occasion to dedicate $16,000's worth of improvements.

Before 1960, of course, the Holsinger members were under the pastoral care of Woodbury. From 1960 to 1963, during the Holsinger-Claysburg union, A. Lester Bucher was the minister. Then in 1963 Ivan B. Walker, for fifteen years a pastor in Eastern Pennsylvania, moved into the church's tree-shaded parsonage on a full-time basis. He remained at Holsinger until 1968, when his replacement was Blair C. Harshbarger, who served to 1976. Since 1977 E. Myrl Weyant has been the pastor.

MAITLAND (1856)
MEMBERSHIP: 143

Maitland's congregational roots go far back into the last century. Originally, it was called the Lewistown or Dry Valley charge, for which a place of worship was built in 1858 four miles northeast of

Lewistown (now on Route 522). The 40' x 60' frame structure, a crossroads church, cost its builders two thousand dollars. In 1916 the congregation officially took the name Dry Valley when a subgroup in Lewistown split off.

This left Dry Valley with a membership of 139. Its resident ministers were Samuel J. Swigart, Edward M. Howe, Samuel J. Steinberger, Jacob H. Richard, and John B. Shellenberger. Samuel Swigart did double duty as bishop. There was further membership attrition in 1921 with the formation of the Burnham church, which took ninety persons. Only Bannerville remained within the fold.

This is the way things stood until 1955, when Bannerville chose to become a separate congregation. With this move, Dry Valley got District Conference's approval the same year to take the name Maitland, the rural community where its church building stands.

In time the Maitland church needed care, and according to the *District Echo,* the congregation in 1937 was "striving toward the accumulation of sufficient funds to remodel and beautify our church building, which vision we hope will become a reality in the near future." More recently, in 1963, Maitland built an educational wing (48' x 72') that included, among other things, fourteen classrooms. The project was completed for about $50,000, volunteer labor cutting costs by almost half. Further modernizing of the physical plant came in 1968–69 when the sanctuary was redone and carpeted. At the same time, the members improved the exterior of the parsonage, a frame, four-bedroom dwelling about one mile from the church, at a cost of $5,500. Most recently, in 1979, the congregation began construction on an entirely new structure, including a fellowship hall, next to the one now in use, the cost of which is projected to exceed $130,000 (this does not include the cost of furniture and other appointments for the sanctuary). When it is ready for occupancy, the plans are to raze the present one.

Like several other congregations in the District, Maitland had to endure the stormy waters of a fundamentalist split. George B. Reedy, interim pastor from 1961 to 1963, brought the issue to a head. In 1965 he started the Independent Lewistown Area Bible Church, a splinter group made up from various congregations of the area.

Maitland's supported ministry goes back to the 1930s and Alvin S. Cox, who served until the pastorate of H. Quinter Rhodes, which began in 1955. Rhodes was followed by George Reedy, after whom came Stephen G. Margush (1964–1969), Raymond Risden (1969–1972) who died in office, and Wilbur E. Fether (1973–   ).

JAMES CREEK (1858)
MEMBERSHIP: 45

A *Gospel Messenger* article in 1887 states that the James Creek congregation, named for the stream that ran close by, was formed in 1858.[10] There had been Brumbaughs in Woodcock Valley since before 1800. From this prolific family sprang a long list of distinguished church leaders in the nineteenth century, some of them among the Brotherhood's most progressive thinkers.

Woodcock Valley, which eventually attracted other Brethren, was originally part of the Clover Creek congregation. George Brumbaugh, who lived on "Timothy Meadows," the family homestead in Woodcock Valley and was called to the ministry by Clover Creek in

1820, received ordination rites in the late 1830s, serving both mother and daughter groups as bishop. His son, Isaac, elected a minister in 1832 and an elder a few years later, became the overseer of James Creek upon its formation, a position he held to his death in 1871.

Henry B. Brumbaugh, the *Pilgrim* publisher who grew up along the Raystown Branch of the Juniata River, noted in his diary that James Creek, in council session, decided to build on Saturday, May 9, 1859. An entry soon after refers to services held in a Valley schoolhouse, which was probably one of several used by the James Creek people for years. Worship also took place, so tradition holds, in the stone house on the old Brumbaugh homestead.

The 1925 history gives 1860 as the year the James Creek church was built, but Henry Brumbaugh's diary dates its dedication as August 25, 1861. Brick cased and a short distance from Marklesburg, it stood for over a hundred years before being razed to make way for the recently constructed Raystown Lake.

In early 1872 the congregation, which then had ninety-nine on its roll, decided to build a meetingplace along the Raystown Branch for a sizable group of members living there. Henry Brumbaugh, made the congregation's secretary at that time, wrote in his diary for Saturday, May 4, 1872: "Went down to the river to make arrangements about building a M. House." The first service at the Bethel house, or the "Corner" as it was commonly referred to, was on Saturday, February 1, 1873, according to the Brumbaugh diary. The frame structure was small, its dimensions 30' x 36'. The members themselves cut and planed the timber for it.

Meanwhile, a cluster of Brethren had sprung up farther down the Valley, near Entriken. There in 1873 the Coffee Run church (30' x 36') was built at a cost of $492.50. Services were rotated among the three churches, although there was preaching every Sunday evening at James Creek. Beginning in 1899, services were held at James Creek every Sunday and at Bethel and Coffee Run every two weeks.

By the mid-1880s Brethren in the upper end of the Valley—at Grafton (now Hesston)—were holding regular services in the village's Lutheran church and schoolhouse. There was talk of building at Grafton, but nothing ever came of the idea.

In 1878 a group of members withdrew for the purpose of organizing a congregation at Huntingdon. Among them were the founders of Juniata College.

During the 1880s many Brethren families moved out of Woodcock Valley, one large contingent relocating on Maryland's Eastern

Shore. The situation became so bad, because of deaths and re-movals, that even the *Gospel Messenger* commented on it. One writer lamented in 1899, "Only a few members live in this place." The *Gospel Messenger* carried ads about the fertile farms then available in the James Creek vicinity.

The Coffee Run group was hardest hit, and in 1914 their church was disposed of. The Bethel church was sold in May 1948, torn down and removed, its furnishings auctioned off. Some minor improvements were made in the James Creek building over the years, but nothing major.

In the early 1970s the Army Corps of Engineers condemned the one-hundred-year old church, since the backwaters of the proposed Raystown Lake would encroach that far up Woodcock Valley. The James Creek members held their last love feast in the doomed structure on September 30, 1973, and soon after it was razed. Fortunately, the congregation, compensated handsomely by the government, was able to move immediately into the vacated United Methodist church, a frame structure and in fair repair, in nearby Marklesburg. At first leasing the facility, they purchased it for $26,000 in 1974.

Ministers since 1925 have been Irvin B. Brumbaugh, Galen B. Royer, John E. Rowland, John Endres (1934–1936), John Grimley (1936–37) Galen B. Royer (1937–1942), D. Luke Bowser (1943–1945), George Gardner (1945–46), Eugene E. Ankeny (1946–47), D. Luke Bowser (1947–48), George H. Tinsman (1948–49), Harold L. Bowser (1949–50), G. Wayne Glick (1950–1953), O. Clyde Bush (1953–1964), and C. Roscoe Wareham (1964–   ).

YELLOW CREEK (1872)
MEMBERSHIP: 301

Originally, the Yellow Creek congregation, centered at New Enterprise, embraced all of Bedford County and much of Blair and Fulton. For the formative years of this territory, from which fourteen congregations were ultimately carved, see the New Enterprise sketch.

What is now the Yellow Creek parish had its beginning about 1830 in the farmhouse of Samuel and Esther Stayer, a few miles south of Hopewell. It was the product of a series of meetings, probably conducted by preachers from Snake Spring or New Enterprise, which led to seven conversions, one of whom was Jacob Steele. Soon after, the twenty-nine-year-old Steele, a cooper-turned-farmer, was elected to the ministry, an office he filled for nearly six decades.

According to the *Christian Family Companion,* he was an inveterate
tobacco user who was never able to shake the habit.[11] By 1860 services
were being held in an old log schoolhouse near Tatesville and the
present Bethel church.

The number of members in Hopewell Township increased
rapidly, and in 1862, with the aid of Snake Spring Valley, they were
able to put up a frame structure (40' x 70') on a plot of ground

along Yellow Creek and across the road from the present church site
(on Route 26, nine miles north of Everett). The lot was sold to them
by Jacob Steele, who along with Henry Clapper had been providing
pastoral care. By then the congregation had for some time been
going by the name of Hopewell, a village five miles to the north.

As mentioned earlier, a log schoolhouse along John's Branch,
near Tatesville, was a frequent meeting place for Brethren of that
area. On January 9, 1872, the Bethel group, as they were called, and
the Hopewell group combined, a union that obtains to this day. The
Bethel Brethren erected a small church in 1885 on a parcel of land
four miles northeast of Everett, off Route 26, purchased from
Jeremiah E. Gates for one dollar.

By the late 1880s the Hopewell church had been outgrown, and
the members decided to tear it down and build anew. In 1899 they
erected a frame building (40' x 60') across the road at a cost of
$22,000. At that time, according to the *Gospel Messenger,* the congre-
gation encompassed 150 square miles.[12]

Meanwhile, the members had petitioned the 1896 District Conference at Aughwick to change their church name from Hopewell to
Yellow Creek. This request was granted, since the previous year the

New Enterprise congregation had dropped the appellation of Yellow Creek for its present one.

With the coming of the new century, the Bethel people saw themselves in need of better quarters. And so in 1903 they put up a larger facility (35' x 50') at a cost of two thousand dollars.

The first major renovation of the 1899 church house came years later, in 1955, and included, among other things, the addition of six Sunday School rooms. Bethel followed suit a year later with the addition of more instructional space. Then in 1957 the two churches

Bethel Church.

purchased land midway between them, in the open country seven miles north of Everett along the main highway, for a parsonage. Built for $22,000, it was occupied for the first time in the spring of 1959.

Elders and free ministers since the Steele-Clapper era have included George W. Brumbaugh, John S. Rush, David A. Stayer, Dorsey I. Pepple, Joseph H. Clapper, Sr., and Emmert Frederick. Those numbered in the full-time pastoral ranks have been Charles H. Heltzel (1957–1962), Richard A. Grumbling (1963–1969), David K. Hanawalt (1969–70), Ivan B. Walker (1970–1973), Ralph F. Thomas (1973–1977), and Joseph A. Lewis (1977–1980).

LEAMERSVILLE (1873)
MEMBERSHIP: 253

Leamersville was originally part of the old Frankstown—later called Duncansville—territory. The Brethren in that small community, a few miles south of Duncansville on present-day Route 220, were by the early 1870s quite eager to have a house of their own.

Since 1865 they had been worshiping in a rented Methodist Episcopal church. On November 9, 1872, it was decided at a Carson Valley council meeting to build a church on Andrew Snowberger's place near the town of Freedom. But Daniel Sell, farmer-brother of James, David and Brice, changed that decision by donating a lot at Leamersville for building purposes. His revered brother, James, was made, says the 1925 history, "solicitor, treasurer, architect, and head carpenter." On Christmas 1873, a Thursday, Leamersville dedicated its house (30' x 40'), which cost $640.

Over a quarter century of steady growth led to the decision in 1904 to divide the Duncansville charge into two independent congregations: Leamersville and Carson Valley. Leamersville organized on June 24 of that year, and David D. Sell was chosen bishop. His brother, James, after thirty-two years in the position, voluntarily resigned to make way for younger blood. The lay members numbered forty.

Soon the old building was outgrown, and the congregation met in it for the last time on April 3, 1910. The thirty-eight-year-old building was sold and a new church built on a plot of ground donated by John Sell and Martin Greenleaf, directly across the road. It, too, was a frame structure (38' x 60'), without basement and costing three thousand dollars. Again, James Sell was solicitor and contractor, doing much of the work himself—at age sixty-five. Dr. Charles C. Ellis, Juniata College's future president, spoke at the building's dedication on September 18, 1910, for which James Sell had written a special hymn.

In 1921 Leamersville's Jeremiah Snowberger began a Sunday School in Claysburg for the nearly one hundred Brethren in that vicinity. The mission work there is told under the Claysburg account.

About this time there was agitation to remodel the Leamersville church to provide better Sunday School facilities for the home group. As a result, in 1922 the building was raised five feet in order to make classrooms and install a steam heating plant. Two years later the congregation wired the interior for electric lights.

On October 17, 1940, the church suffered a great loss when fire swept through the frame structure, causing extensive damage. It took eleven thousand dollars to restore the building, which was completed the following year.

Sunday, September 2, 1945, was a big day in the life of the congregation. On that date the members joined in public acknowledgment of James A. Sell's one-hundredth birthday. His remarkable career receives in-depth treatment in the sketch on Carson Valley, where he presided as elder for over three decades.

In 1965 extensive improvements were made in the physical plant. At a cost of $25,181 the congregation added a new educational wing. Mortgage-burning day came not long after—in July 1973. There has been other remodeling work in the last decade.

As for Leamersville's spiritual leadership, it was, of course, at first provided by the free ministry. Those who served in this capacity were David D. Sell, James A. Sell, Brice Sell, Michael Claar, and Jacob Zimmerman. In 1921 George W. Rogers of Dunnings Creek became the congregation's first supported pastor. Then in 1924 John B. Miller, for twenty-one consecutive years a member of the District Mission Board, succeeded him for the next few years.

Other ministers, on a supply basis, were: from 1924 to 1935, Samuel Weyant and Leonard R. Holsinger; from 1935 to 1940, George Rogers, Jacob Kinsel, Horace Clapper, and J. L. Bowman; from 1940 to 1944, Dean Walters, Joseph J. Shaffer, Quinter Showalter, A. Emmert Frederick, and Merle Heinz.

In 1944 William L. Gould accepted a full-time pastoral call with the understanding that a parsonage would be provided. This was arranged through the purchase of a house in East Freedom for $2,500. (In 1950 a parsonage was built beside the church for $17,500.) Gould served three years, and since then there have been J. Stanley Earhart (1947–1953), Ordo M. Pletcher (1954–1962), Kenneth R. Blough (1962–1968), Earl D. Dietz (1968–1972), and Christian R. Arndt, Jr. (1972–   ).

CARSON VALLEY (1874)
MEMBERSHIP: 315

According to the 1925 history, Carson Valley's past is rooted in a body of Brethren settlers who, soon after 1760, concentrated near

Frankstown, once a famous Indian trading post, a few miles east of present-day Hollidaysburg. There is serious question, however, whether the Frankstown Brethren date back that far. More likely, they did not appear in those parts until around 1800. Nevertheless, when they did, the 1925 history is probably right in saying that they so completely occupied "the good lands along the Juniata River that it took the name of 'Dunker Bottom,' a name appearing in legal papers to designate the location of properties."

Eventually, these Brethren pioneers began to hold services, calling themselves the Frankstown church, although probably there was no formal organization. This was around 1800 and involved some

twenty persons with a Brethren background. Tradition had it, according to church historian James Sell, that Yellow Creek provided some of the earliest preachers. James Quinter wrote in 1877 that Frankstown's first known resident minister was one John Cripe, about whom nothing is known.[13]

The first resident bishop of the "Frankstowners" was David Albaugh, a Marylander who located near Duncansville. He came into possession of a large tract of land and built himself a house with removable partitions, making his home adaptable for worship. Albaugh, somewhat irregularly, began preaching without the usual formal call to the ministry. In time, however, this call came, and he was soon advanced to the bishopric. His son, David, Jr., eventually followed in his steps.

In the early 1800s, the date unknown, Frankstown Brethren

joined with the Mennonites and Lutherans in building a church, probably the first in that part of the valley. Constructed of logs, it stood on the hill above the Geeseytown cemetery (along Route 22).

But the future of Frankstown, incorporated as a borough sometime in 1831 or 1832, was doomed. In 1841 it had a population of 350, but the borough went into rapid decline after it lost out to Hollidaysburg as a canal and railroad terminus in the Pennsylvania System. Meanwhile, the Brethren had gradually vacated the "Bottoms" and the surrounding fertile farms, selling out to the Scots-Irish, who had not been the best of neighbors. Some of the members headed West, while others settled in the Duncansville area. Here lived all the preachers by then, and so in 1866 the congregation's name was changed from Frankstown to Duncansville.

For nearly half a century the Duncansville Brethren had been worshiping in a meetinghouse, put up by the community, that stood on the present site of the Carson Valley church. It had been built soon after David Albaugh, Sr., made his own home available for worship. It was a crude structure, known as the "Old School House" since it served both church and school purposes.

The "Old School House" came down soon after 1850 to make way for the Carson Valley cemetery. This left the church without a place of worship and private homes and schoolhouses had to be used. Then in 1853, on an acre of ground sold by David Albaugh, Jr., from his farm near Duncansville, the Brethren of the Upper Juniata Valley for the first time got a church building exclusively their own. It stood about a mile from the main line of the Pennsylvania Railroad.

The Duncansville work prospered under the pastoral activity of Albaugh the younger, Jacob Burkhart, Graybill Myers, and Daniel M. Holsinger. By the early 1870s the Albaugh church was outgrown. Moreover, according to the *Christian Family Companion,* the "regular meetinghouse was too much an out-of-the-way place."[14] Plans were thus made to build a new church—at Carson Valley, about a mile and a half north of Duncansville and six miles south of Altoona (on Route 764). The congregation disposed of the old church for $334 and in 1874, at a cost of $1,350, rebuilt at the new location—putting up a 34' x 43' structure equipped with a basement.

For a period of ten years, between 1870 and 1880, the church doubled in size. By the 1880s about half the congregation lived in the vicinity of Carson Valley, while the other half lived in and around Leamersville, four miles south of Duncansville. As early as 1873 the congregation had seen fit to erect a small church house at Leamersville to better serve the needs there. The 1870s, too, were the decade when the Altoona mission became an "arm" of the Duncansville parish.

Duncansville's membership numbered 140 in 1877, but the spurt of growth it enjoyed during the seventies came to an abrupt halt with the Progressive schism of 1882. As pointed out in chapter 7, it looked for awhile as if this liberal-minded congregation might join the Holsinger schismatics en masse. But, of course, this did not happen, although there were numerous individual defections. For years to come, the work of the congregation suffered from the shock of the Progressive incident.

For thirty-two years, from 1872 to 1904, Duncansville's bishop was James A. Sell, a remarkable man who lived to the age of 102. Untrained but brainy, he was widely known throughout Central Pennsylvania as a preacher, author, poet, orchardist, and journalist. With the exception of a brief period in his early life when he lived at McAlveys Fort (midway between Huntingdon and State College), his entire life was spent in Blair County—fifty-two years of it at Leamersville, with shorter residencies in Hollidaysburg, Altoona, and Martinsburg.

James Sell was born on November 23, 1845, the son of Daniel and Rachel (Detwiler) Sell. He was the sixth of nine children born to his parents. His ancestors on the paternal side came to America from Alsace-Lorraine in 1729 and settled in Adams County. His maternal forebears came from Switzerland.

The Blair Countian grew up on a farm in Freedom Township, obtaining a minimal common school education. But his constant companion in later life was a pocket dictionary, and he acquired a fine command of language that was evident in all his sermons, addresses, and writings.

On October 24, 1865, when he was not quite twenty-one years old, the then Frankstown church called him to be their minister. Seven years later he was ordained to the eldership, making him the youngest bishop in the Brotherhood at that time. In his early years in the ministry, he was known as the "boy preacher" and his services were in wide demand.

In 1866, after a brief try at schoolteaching, Sell accepted a position as Henry Holsinger's assistant in the offices of the *Christian Family Companion,* published at Tyrone. He there learned the printing trade and helped launch a secular paper, the *Tyrone Herald.* He did not long follow the journalistic profession, leaving Holsinger to work as a carpenter in Altoona and elsewhere for several years. Then in 1885 he acquired a farm in Freedom Township, which, in a pioneering venture, he converted into a commercial peach orchard.

He continued in the business for a score of years, a horticulturalist par excellence in the eyes of later successful fruit growers of the County.

A civic-minded man who held various public offices, James Sell was always interested in the cause of education. He played a lively role in the starting of Juniata College and for twenty years was chairman of its Advisory Board.

Elder Sell, a man of high literary attainments, wrote much throughout his life. He was the first person of his denomination to publish a book of poems. His writings included the *Lost Children of the Alleghenies,* a true story of the lost brothers George and Joseph Cox, and still regarded by oldtimers as a classic. James Sell was also blessed with the instincts of a historian. He collected the data that made possible the publication of the 1925 history, and he assisted his son, Jesse, in preparing a history of Blair County that appeared in 1910.

Freedom Township's most distinguished citizen of those days was married to Esther B. Stiffler of Canoe Creek in 1867, a union that bore four sons. Their seventy-three years of wedlock set a Blair County record.

In the early part of 1904, Duncansville, under Elder Sell, divided into two congregations, Carson Valley and Leamersville. The Duncansville congregation as such now became nonexistent. With this reorganization, Brice Sell, brother of James, became Carson Valley's resident bishop, while Levi B. Benner and William N. Hoover took over ministering to the eighty-four members.

Carson Valley, upon the 1904 division, at once became involved in building missions within its territory. A mission was started at Lakemont the same year the church was organized, but for unknown reasons it was abandoned. A mission began at Hollidaysburg in 1908, ministered to by William Hoover. In another year it gained independent congregational status. After work at Bennington, begun in 1912, proved unsuccessful, another attempt at a Lakemont project had to be given up because of ministerial shortage.

Meanwhile, the work at home was prospering. The 1874 church building was remodeled and dedicated on August 13, 1917. The ministers at that time were Levi B. Benner, Frank E. Brubaker, and Jacob W. Hoover.

The church continued to call young men into the ministry over the years, some going forth to serve elsewhere, others, like Homer F. Hoover and Joseph J. Shaffer, staying on home ground. In 1947, however, the free ministry was discontinued, and the church sought the services of a part-time pastor. This position was filled in March

1948 by C. Russell Snyder of Altoona's Twenty-Eighth Street congregation, who pastored at Carson Valley until December 1955.

Under Elder Snyder's leadership, the church continued to grow and found it necessary to make provisions for larger facilities. The decision to build, after Forrest Groff, the Brotherhood architect, was consulted, came in 1951. The groundbreaking date was November 1, 1953. Much of the construction was done by volunteer labor. This fact, along with some setbacks like the collapse of one wall, delayed completion until 1964 of the brick-cased church, the cost of which approached $116,000. Its occupancy, however, had taken place earlier—in 1959, and over the next five years worship and work went on together until dedication day.

By that time the pastoral picture had changed. In 1955 Snyder moved on, and C. Roscoe Wareham of Martinsburg, a teacher at Altoona High School, gave ministerial leadership for the next four years. There was no regular minister after that until 1962, when Perry B. Liskey began his duties as Carson Valley's first full-time pastor. To house the Liskey family, the congregation built a twenty-four-thousand-dollar brick parsonage on a plot of ground adjacent to the church.

The Liskeys left in 1970, to be followed by Herman B. Turner (1971–72). Then came a pastorless interim of a year, after which R. Eugene Miller of Saxton, whose previous occupation had been that of carpenter, became Carson Valley's present minister.

WOODBURY (1876)
MEMBERSHIP: 324

Woodbury is a quiet hamlet of less than three hundred residents on the southern fringe of Morrisons Cove, just south of where Routes 36 and 866 intersect. Originally, the Brethren of that area belonged to the Yellow Creek congregation, which in late summer 1876 subdivided into two parishes. One became New Enterprise, the other part—embracing Woodbury, Claar, Lower Claar, Queen, and a portion of Clover Creek—remained with the mother group. But a few months later, in November, members from the Woodbury area voted to become a separate congregation. Included within the ambit of the new parish were the Brethren of the Holsinger and Curryville territories.

The membership, some 243 strong, quickly acted to build a church, a frame structure 77' x 45' with a large basement and central heating. Daringly, the Woodbury people also decided upon seats "with backs." The worship facility cost $3,090 and was dedi-

cated on October 14, 1877, by James Quinter. It was located on a plot of ground belonging to Rhinehart L. Replogle, about a half mile north of the village on Route 36. The large, well-kept lawn surrounding the spacious home of Rhinehart Replogle adjoining the church provided a beautiful setting for the services of baptism. On this property was a never-failing spring, walled in with huge sandstones. Water flowed from the spring to a specially constructed baptismal pool. Not until 1944 did the church have an indoor baptistry.

The change from a free ministry to a full-time pastoral program, as at most congregations of the District, was a gradual and much-discussed question. Woodbury took the latter step in 1924, engaging John E. Rowland from Pennsylvania's Southern District. The next year he and his family moved into a parsonage erected in Woodbury.

By this time the taxation system adopted in 1882 was on its way out as a source of congregational income. But Dr. Raymond R. Stayer, a dentist from Denver, Pennsylvania, who grew up in the Woodbury church, vividly recalls the "church tax" method. The "collection basket," he remembers, was passed only on special occasions such as revival meetings, when the evangelist received the total amount collected as a "love offering." The rest of the time church income derived from individual assessments. His grandfather, Rhinehart R. Stayer, was the tax collector for many years. Writes Dr. Stayer:

In a little brown notebook was the list of the members with an amount of tax listed following each name. Grandpa was a natural for the job. He was jovial, well-liked, and fearless when it came to buttonholding a delinquent. He was a retired farmer . . . and spent much time driving from farm to farm visiting and collecting tax.

In the family circle, there were frequent comments such as "G. C. goes on pretty big for one who hasn't paid his church tax."

At a Sunday service, Elder "John," their last names were all Stayers, would announce, "Brother Rhinehart will sit at Burkets Store next Tuesday for the convenience of the Curryville people to pay their church tax," or another time it would be Potes Store in Bakers Summit for the members of the Holsinger Church.

Down through the years since, the Woodbury house has undergone periodic improvement—in 1928, 1944, 1953, 1959 (when a $50,000 education wing was added), and most recently, 1974.

In 1960 the membership voted to subdivide into three congregations, with Woodbury and Curryville having full-time pastoral service each and Holsinger sharing, part-time, the ministry at Claysburg. The parsonage, located in Woodbury and owned jointly by the three churches, was purchased by Woodbury.

Up to 1960 the pastors since the Rowland years (1924–1931) were: Joseph H. Clapper (1931–1943), Joseph E. Whitacre (1943–1947), Harper M. Snavely (1947–1951), Rufus McDannel (1951–1954), and Earl K. Ziegler (1954–1960). After the division, Delbert E. Hanlin served to 1963, followed by Homer J. Miller (1963–1971) and Raymond R. Boose (1971–   ).

BEECH RUN (1879)
MEMBERSHIP: 104

The Beech Run, or Hares Valley, church, as we saw in the sketch of Aughwick, was built in 1879. As further noted, the Progressive split of the eighties ravaged the congregation so badly that by 1900 its membership had dropped off to one family. Services were abandoned for a period of time.

Then in May 1922 Huntingdon called Alexander M. Stout, a seminary student at Juniata College, to the ministry. Soon after being licensed, Stout, a Hoosier State native, looked up the lone Beech Run family, started a Sunday School, and gave weekend pastoral care. In 1923 Stout accepted the Aughwick pastorate, and the District Board placed Galen Blough, a student at Juniata College's Academy, in charge of the Hares Valley work. By the fall of 1924 the *Gospel Messenger* could report a membership of twenty-two there.[15] Despite this upward turn, preaching services, so the District Minutes indicate, were still held only every other week as late as 1930.

Until 1928 the church continued to be served by Juniata students. But in that year John M. Pittenger, a Juniatian and returned missionary from India, began his twelve-year stint at Beech Run at the request of the District Mission Board. The Pittengers lived in the Mission House in Huntingdon, which had largely been financed by the Brethren Sunday Schools of Central Pennsylvania.

Over the next decade there was talk from time to time about effecting an organization at Beech Run, but nothing was done until 1938. That summer the pastor, in company with Elder George Detweiler, Huntingdon's minister, and Charles Brechbiel, carried a petition to the Aughwick council meeting, held in the Sugar Run house. Permission was granted the Beech Run group to elect trustees, deacons, and such other officers as needed. This was done on the evening of October 11, 1938. By then the membership had grown to fifty-four.

Growth was steady enough that over the next decade and a half there developed strong sentiment for congregational autonomy. This matter came up formally at an Aughwick council meeting on October 18, 1954. Council concurred, and in 1955 action by District Conference released Beech Run from Aughwick's control and seated its delegates.

In the last forty years the Beech Run church, which stands three miles south of Mapleton Depot on Route 655, has undergone much renovation. In 1939 the large posts were removed from the center of the sanctuary, new seats were installed, and the old pot-bellied stoves were replaced with central heating. Also, at this time kerosene lamps gave way to incandescent bulbs. Carpeting went down on once-bare floors the next year. Alterations to the outside entranceway followed in 1945. Then came the addition of a vestibule and bell tower in 1952. More classrooms were added two years later, two in the basement, three on the main floor, and one on the second floor. In September 1959 the congregation purchased the Lincoln schoolhouse next to the church, which was put to use as a fellowship hall. Beautification of the sanctuary and two classrooms, and the installation of new stained-glass windows constituted a project completed in the spring of 1966. The cost was over eight thousand dollars. The most recent remodeling involved adding a kitchen to the schoolhouse, a $13,000 effort.

The pastors since the time of John Pittenger have been: Martin Scholten (1940–1947), Warren F. Groff (1947–1949), Glenn C. Zug (1949–50), Robert Jones (1950–1953), Raymond R. Smith (1953–1966), O. Clyde Bush (1966–67), Tobias F. Henry (1967–1974), vacant (1974–75), John B. Johnson (1975–1978), and Raymond E. Hill (1978–   ).

UPPER CLAAR (1886)
MEMBERSHIP: 317

The history of the Upper Claar congregation goes back to the early nineteenth century, when a few Brethren families began to push westward across Cove Mountain into the northeastern salient of Bedford County. This was rugged, hilly country of dense forests.[16] One of the earliest pioneers was Frederick Claar, the son of a German immigrant, who in the fall of 1800 hacked out a farm on which the Upper Claar church now stands (four and a half miles northeast of Claysburg). The twenty-year-old settler and his wife, both non-Brethren, were led to unite with the church through the preaching of Yellow Creek ministers living in the western part of Morrisons Cove and holding services in the home of the young couple.

The Claars, husband and wife, were baptized in 1816. Others were baptized later, worship taking place in their barns in summer, their homes in winter. Soon these accommodations proved inadequate, and the little band of worshipers decided to build a church. Frederick Claar donated a plot of land on his farm, and in the summer of 1851 a little frame structure (36' x 26') was erected and dedicated. It stood across the road from the present Upper Claar church. Weekend services every four weeks continued under Yellow Creek's ministry.

In 1876, as we saw elsewhere, two new congregations formed out

of Yellow Creek: New Enterprise and Woodbury. With this subdivision, the Claar farm Brethren fell under Woodbury's jurisdiction. A decade later, the group across Cove Mountain felt strong enough to organize as a separate body. They called themselves the Claar congregation, in honor of the family so prominent in their religious life. Called to be their presiding elder was the recently ordained John L. Holsinger of Dunnings Creek.

With steady growth, more space was needed. Thus the congregation put up a new church, completed in 1891, which came to be called the Lower Claar house. Located a mile and a half east of the old church, it cost about $3,100 and was built by Jacob Fries. This place now became the spiritual center of the congregation (see the historical sketch of Lower Claar).

But nostalgic attachment to the original church site prompted a number of members—whose parents and kin were buried in the adjacent graveyard—to begin construction of another meetinghouse near the old one in 1892. In 1908 an addition (34' x 32') to the church was built, costing $1,500.

In the new century's first decade, the Claar congregation also came into possession of a Union Chapel (1906) located about four miles west of Claysburg. It provided ministerial care there for five decades. Then in 1913–14 a church was built at Queen, which, for a few years, gave Claar members four places of worship. This all changed in May 1916 when an amicable division created three unallied congregations: Upper Claar, Lower Claar, and Queen.

At the time of this subdivision, James Sell, the dean of District bishops, was given oversight of Upper Claar. The next year Taylor

L. Dively replaced Sell as elder and would remain uninterruptedly in that office until the late 1960s.

Taylor Dively was also one of three resident ministers at the time of the 1916 division, along with Frederick C. Dively and Samuel C. Weyant. These men and others, like Archie Hoskin, gave Upper Claar pastoral service as home ministers until the 1950s, when the congregation opted for a full-time cleric.

Periodically, the Upper Claar church since 1908 has undergone improvements. A basement was excavated in 1927 to provide both a small kitchen for preparing love feasts and a central heating plant, and in 1933 came the ultimate modern convenience, electric lights. Other improvements included drilling a well in 1939 (before this, water had to be carried) and indoor rest rooms in 1946. The next major renovation project was putting up an educational wing, which was dedicated by President Calvert N. Ellis of Juniata College on September 27, 1959. The annex added eight Sunday School rooms. Ten years earlier, in 1948, the members had erected a marker on the site of the original Claar church built in 1851. It memorialized Frederick and Christian Claar, the congregation's organizers. In 1967 the church again completed a structural addition and the remodeling of the sanctuary.

Meanwhile, the people of the parish had for some time felt the need for a full-time pastor. But there was the problem of a parsonage. This was remedied when the members decided to put the money from a several-year-old building fund into constructing a manse. John Musselman donated a lot directly below the church, and work on the parsonage started in 1954.

Into the house moved E. Myrl Weyant, who had become Upper Claar's pastor in October 1953. After he left in 1956 the two Claar churches agreed on a yoked ministry, beginning with Ralph Z. Ebersole's pastorate in January 1957. Post-Ebersole pastors have been Glenn O. Hassinger (1961–1965), A. Harrison Smith (1965–1968), Taylor L. Dively (1968–1972), and George H. Snyder (1972–   ).

A decade before George Snyder's call, Upper Claar discontinued its relationship with the aforementioned Union Chapel. At first services were interdenominational, but because the Brethren far outnumbered those of other faiths, the Poplar Run facility was placed under Upper Claar's custody. Ownership, however, still resided with the several denominations. Beginning during the Depression, the District for years provided funds for its support. Finally, as the work declined in the post–World War II period, the trustees of the chapel deeded the ground and building to the Emmanuel Baptist church in October 1962.

Meanwhile, during the war the work at Queen, which had long been languishing, came to an end.

FAIRVIEW (1891)
MEMBERSHIP: 87

The Fairview church, located two miles south of Williamsburg at the northern end of Morrisons Cove, was built in 1874. Previously, beginning about 1864, services for Brethren in that part of the Cove were held in schoolhouses. Preachers came from the Duncansville

and Clover Creek congregations. They included familiar names like Graybill Myers and James Sell from the former and George Brumbaugh and Daniel Holsinger from the latter.

A petition from Fairview members led to Clover Creek's approval for a church house in the upper valley. The building (38' x 42') was dedicated by Henry R. Holsinger, the future Progressive dissident, on October 25. Its cost totaled over $1,300, and, like most Brethren churches then, had no elevated pulpit. According to the *Primitive Christian*, Fairview had seventy or eighty members by 1881. Sunday School growth and the need for love feast conveniences resulted in an annex (20' x 35') in 1890.

The next year, mother church Clover Creek granted Fairview its independence. The congregation formally organized on September 26, making John W. Brumbaugh, a descendant of the original Brumbaugh settlers, its presiding elder. Joseph S. Snowberger was the only resident minister within Fairview's territory, and he succeeded Brumbaugh as bishop in 1894.

The congregation prospered, and eventually built, with Clover Creek's help, another meetingplace at Smithfield, four miles north of Martinsburg, in 1893. Then in 1912 Fairview authorized a church structure in Williamsburg, where the flour, paper, and silk mills had attracted Brethren. Both places were granted congregational autonomy in 1917. Until 1922 the three groups received joint pastoral care from William H. Holsinger (1918–1920) and Grover L. Wine (1920–1922).

From that year to 1957 the following men gave part-time ministry to Fairview itself: Galen B. Royer (1922–1925), Isaac B. Kensinger and Ernest A. Brumbaugh cooperatively (1925–1947), Ernest A. Brumbaugh (1947–1949), Prof. Harry H. Nye of Juniata College (1949–1954), and Dr. Tobias F. Henry, also from the College (1954–1957).

In 1957, at District urging, the congregation inaugurated a full-time pastoral program. Gerald Walizer of Pennsylvania's Southern District came to Fairview that fall and was its minister for five years. During that time the congregation—in 1963—went off District support.

The Fairview Brethren have made some major improvements in their facilities in the last two decades. A parsonage was built near the church in 1960. Then five years later the congregation, having amortized the parsonage loan of $9,500 in the autumn of 1964, dedicated a five-room educational annex to the church, which also was given a new entrance.

Since the pastorate of Gerald Walizer, there have been Raymond P. Gordon (1962–1978), Mrs. Mary Lou Hall of Curryville on an interim basis (1978–1980), and Guy S. Fern (1980–   ).

LOWER CLAAR 1891)

MEMBERSHIP: 97

The early history of Lower Claar is included in the sketch of the Upper Claar congregation. That account refers to the erection of a second church building for those people in 1891, on a plot of ground donated by Miss Catherine Duncan, a mile and a half east of the first one and more centrally located. Then in 1916 came the congregational decision to subdivide.

At the time of this three-way split, Lower Claar, debt free, had fifty members. David M. Adams, a former pastor at Claar who later left the ministry for newspaper work, stepped in to fill the dual position of bishop-preacher. In 1908 he had published a sixty-page history of the Claar congregation.[17] His departure after five years and the use of supply ministers, the 1925 history indicates, worked "greatly against the growth of the congregation."

But Lower Claar was far from moribund, and until 1957 managed reasonably well with visiting preachers, among them Dorsey I. Pepple, the District record-holder in years of pastoral service, some Juniata College professors—like Harry H. Nye, Tobias F. Henry, and Morley J. Mays—and Kenneth I. Morse, who preached regularly till leaving the District to become editor of the *Gospel Messenger*.

For some time prior to 1957, however, the Lower Claar people had felt the need for a full-time pastor. At the urging of G. Quinter

Showalter, their moderator, they approached Upper Claar, already pastored full-time, about a yoked ministry. The proposal met with favor, and in January 1957 Ralph Z. Ebersole began serving the two churches (see the Upper Claar sketch for the list of pastors since then).

Two years later over $32,000 went into extensive remodeling of the basement (which provided a fellowship hall), equipment, redecorating the sanctuary, and landscaping. In 1971–72 further improvements were made in Christian education facilities and in the church interior.

BANNERVILLE (1892)
MEMBERSHIP: 135

Bannerville is a small village seventeen miles northeast of Lewistown, a short distance off Route 522 from McClure. In it is located the only Church of the Brethren in Snyder County. (Actually, it is practically on the Mifflin County line.) Originally, it was an outlying post of the Dry Valley congregation, which was headquartered at Maitland.

The credit for starting a Brethren mission point there properly belongs to Mrs. Maggie Shellenberger, a Lutheran who converted to the Brethren after her marriage. She and her large family had in 1876 moved to Bannerville, where husband Enoch opened a store. Her adopted community was churchless, and so in 1879 she began a Sunday School in the local schoolhouse. Two years later preaching was introduced, ministers from Maitland filling the pulpit every eight weeks.

In time, interest seemed to justify erecting a meetinghouse. A building committee was formed, made up of Enoch Shellenberger, Daniel Zuck, and Andrew Spanogle (Spanogle was later a chief

instigator of a home for the aging in Middle District). The frame church (35' x 50') cost $1,500 and was dedicated on January 3, 1892.

The membership soon built up to forty or so, but the lack of a resident minister deprived the congregation of proper care. At the time the 1925 history was published, the number had dwindled to twenty-five or less.

But the picture brightened soon after that. About 1930 Melvin Fleming, Bannerville's minister, held a revival in a schoolhouse at Three Rivers, in the course of which he baptized forty persons. All of them subsequently carried their membership to the Bannerville church.

Slow but steady growth necessitated enlarging the church building. In 1945 the congregation excavated a basement and in 1949 enlarged the church's main entrance. Further revamping in 1954 provided an annex of three Sunday School rooms.

The next year, in October 1955, District Conference endorsed a petition from Bannerville asking for independent status as a congregation. Maintaining full-time pastoral services became a problem, however, for the Bannerville charge under its newly gained independence. Thus in 1964 the congregation entered into joint pastoral relations with the Lewistown church.

Ministers since the 1920s have been: Joseph H. Fleming (1923–1943), Merrill R. Peters (1943–1963), vacant (1963–64), Kenneth Martin (1964–1966), vacant (1966–67), Ira F. Lydic (1967–1974), and Walter E. Coldren (1974–   ).

RAVEN RUN (1893)
MEMBERSHIP: 238

The Raven Run church group near Saxton, in the northeast corner of Bedford County, was once a part of the Hopewell congregation, now known as Yellow Creek. Probably the first members of the Church of the Brethren to locate in Raven Run Valley were Samuel I. Brumbaugh, Martin Hoover, and John B. Dilling, but exactly when that was is not known. In 1878 they erected a brick church (28' x 40'), which, beginning in 1885, also housed a Sunday School.

By the early nineties there were nearly a hundred Brethren living in the Valley and around Saxton. On November 25, 1893, at a council meeting in the Hopewell church, it was decided to form a new congregation on the northern fringes of the parish, to be

known as the Raven Run congregation. Hopewell's ministers were to supply Raven Run until other arrangements were made. The two deacons, John Dilling and Jonathan Hoover, were authorized to call a council meeting for organizational purposes. This took place on December 16, and receiving the call as elder was George W. Brumbaugh, the bilingual preacher and much-respected churchman from Clover Creek. The next year Samuel Brumbaugh began his half century as Raven Run's pastor.

Out of this fast-growing parish two other congregations soon formed: Stonerstown and Riddlesburg. This did not hurt Raven Run's own growth, however, and by 1910 the need for a new church was obvious. Thus on March 26 of that year came the decision to build. The first church was torn down, and a building committee composed of Frederick Hoover, David P. Hoover, John P. Ritchey, Samuel Brumbaugh, and Philip Richard supervised the construction of a brick building (35' x 50') with a basement under part of it. The cost was $2,500 besides donated labor. The ever-popular pulpiteer, Charles C. Ellis of Juniata College, dedicated the new church on December 18. On that day eight hundred dollars was raised toward the $1,200 indebtedness.

On December 31, 1917 two adjoining tracts of land were purchased. On this ground stood a log house, which was torn down in 1933 and in its place went up a new frame house for the custodian and his family. This house later became the parsonage, which in 1955 underwent extensive remodeling.

On January 30, 1949, the church was partially destroyed by fire. Reconstruction began in March, resulting in a larger building (35' x 66'). During the time of rebuilding, the Raystown Brethren opened their doors to Raven Run members who worshiped with them until the rededication service on September 25, 1949.

The latest remodeling of the church occurred in the early seventies. On January 4, 1969, the congregation voted to enlarge the restored building of 1949. The brick and concrete addition, volunteer labor keeping its cost to just under $45,000, includes the Ned Miller Memorial Library, pastor's study, nursery, nine Sunday School rooms, and a 20' x 80' basement. Dedication day was April 29, 1973.

Up to that time Raven Run had had but three pastors. Samuel I. Brumbaugh terminated his fifty years of pastoral service in 1944. Percy R. Kegarise succeeded him, giving the congregation twenty years. There were interim ministers from October 1964 to September 1965. Then David C. Emerson took over the pastoral reins and served until 1976, followed by incumbent Roy C. Myers.

AMARANTH (1895)
MEMBERSHIP 51

Once a postal station and originally known as Fairview, Amaranth lies tucked among the hills of Fulton County near the Maryland line (a mile and a half from the Amaranth exit on Interstate 70). It is one of three congregations outside the five counties making up Middle District. By the early 1880s a handful of Brethren had taken up residence in Buck Valley and Whip's Cove, an area about twelve miles northeast of Artemas, where a colony of Brethren had existed since Revolutionary times. A church had already been built at Artemas in 1879, and its minister, John Bennett, whose grandfather had been a Brethren pioneer in the area, joined with men from Snake Spring Valley to preach to neighboring Brethren. Their labors centered around the McKibben schoolhouse. Services were held once a month, on Saturday or Sunday evenings.

In 1895 the baptism of twelve persons brought the number of Brethren living in Buck Valley close to a score. That same year the Snake Spring Valley congregation, which had sired the Artemas mission, helped them build a frame church out of lumber cut from the surrounding mountain slopes. Title to the land and property is still held today in trust by Snake Spring. But the Buck Valley Brethren became a part of the Artemas fold beginning in 1897. When the name-change, from Fairview to Amaranth, took place is not known.

Buck Valley, though the 1920s saw a steady influx of Mormons into the area, was never a mecca for Brethren. The congregation barely held its own. Nevertheless, District Conference at New Enterprise in 1929 gave the green light to dividing Artemas into three separate charges, the other two being Amaranth and Glendale. John Bennett, the patriarch of Artemas who lived into his eighties, served as elder at Amaranth until his death in the late 1930s.

Unfortunately, the Artemas congregation was itself already in decline by the time of Bennett's death. During the Depression the Brethren at Artemas began sharing their building with the Christian Church. The end for them came in 1959, when a commission from the District arranged with the last two members to turn the church over to private owners for the sum of one hundred dollars.

But in Buck Valley the story was different. Their church building has been revamped twice in recent years. In 1960, at a cost of $3,981, a basement was poured, a furnace put in, and a vestibule added on. Then in 1966 other improvements, inside and outside, amounted to $3,704. That same year, the congregation went off

District support. Since then there have been other renovations, including the addition of a Sunday School room in 1976 and the paneling of the basement—at a cost of over nine thousand dollars.

Ministers who have supplied the pulpit or pastored at Amaranth since the days of John Bennett have been G. Landis Baker, E. A. Edwards, Howard Whitacre, Daniel M. Vickers, Mrs. Evelyn Eppley, A. Lester Bucher, Harry L. Brubaker, Harry L. Knisely, a Juniata student (1960–1962), David B. Clapper (1963–1970), Raymond R. Smith (1970–1973), and Fred D. Hendrickson (1973–   ).

ARDENHEIM (1896)

MEMBERSHIP: 82

A *Gospel Messenger* article in 1898 identified the territory that later came to comprise the Ardenheim congregation as "one of the old preaching points" in Huntingdon County.[18] It stated that services were first held in the Sugar Grove schoolhouse, about three miles northeast of Mill Creek (along Route 22), sometime during the 1840s. However, an item in the *Pilgrim* in September 1875 mentions only five or six members among the "Ridge" dwellers.

The earliest Brethren to settle in the Lick Ridge area were from Path Valley, Franklin County—the Goodmans, the Ruperts, the Numers, the Bollingers—many of whom later went West. Their location put them within Aughwick's purview. Elders from that congregation would ride horseback some twenty-five miles to preach to those Brethren clustered along Sugar Grove Run. Among these preachers were Abram Funk, John Glock, John Spanogle, and James R. Lane. Michael Bollinger, a Sugar Run resident, also did some preaching before going West, where his pulpitry fame spread far and wide.

At first the Sugar Grove Brethren met every sixteen weeks, then every eight weeks. By the late 1870s they were meeting twice a month and conducting a summer Sunday School. About 1880 a second summer Sunday School began in the Woodville schoolhouse at Ardenheim, then a railroad station. Baptisms over the years were held at various places—some in Sugar Grove Run, others at Germany Valley, a few at James Creek, and later all at Huntingdon.

When the Brumbaugh brothers, Henry and John, moved the *Pilgrim* office to Huntingdon, they frequently preached at Sugar Grove, since it was nearer than Germany Valley or their home church, James Creek.

In 1878 the Ridge members became identified with the Huntingdon congregation after it separated from James Creek.

Beginning with the 1890s, the stretch between Ardenheim and

Mill Creek began to build up. In 1894 William J. Swigart, a teacher-trustee at Juniata College, and John B. Brumbaugh, one of Juniata's founders, led a revival in the Woodville school, each preaching alternate evenings. The response was so encouraging that the Huntingdon Brethren immediately took steps to build a house of worship in the vicinity. On Wednesday, October 17, 1894, Henry Brumbaugh, according to his diary, drove his buggy from a bank meeting to Ardenheim to help stake ground for a new church. There, in 1895, contractor Otis Brumbaugh erected a brick-veneered building (38' × 50') two miles east of Huntingdon on Route 22, costing $1,700.

The next year, on April 26, Ardenheim organized as a congregation in its own right. Its elder and principal preacher until 1935 was W. J. Swigart, who lived to be eighty-nine years old. He made Ardenheim a kind of training school for budding student ministers from Juniata College, who often preached for him at his invitation. Usually, in accompanying their mentor, young college clerics had to make the ten-mile round trip to Ardenheim and back on foot—the way "W.J." did it for years.

Beginning in 1928 Elder and Mrs. Swigart went to Florida each year for the winter months. The congregation elected two young men, Charles Cisney and John W. Endres, to the ministry to fill the pulpit during the pastor's winter absence. Both had taken their preelection training—in Bible, English, and public speaking—over a six-year period under Professor Swigart. During the 1940s two Juniata students, Earl Kaylor (1946) and Harold Kenepp (1949–50) preached at Ardenheim, along with Lewis Knepper (1946–1949) from Huntingdon and Roy Myers, a young licensed farmer from Black Log Valley. In May 1952 Myers was made full-time pastor. He served until September 1956, when he accepted a call to the Juniata Park Church. Daniel Vickers of near Altoona put in the next year as pastor, to be succeeded by Wilbur Fether, another Altoonan, from 1957 to 1959. Raymond Smith of Orbisonia became pastor then, combining his Beech Run ministry with that of Ardenheim until 1964. Merle L. Hoover was the minister from November 1965 to February 1970. Orbisonia also produced the next pastor, Victor S. Norris—for the next half dozen years. The minister from 1976 to 1980 was Chester A. McCloskey of Altoona.

Wired for electricity in 1928, the Ardenheim church has undergone periodic repairs and refurbishing in subsequent decades. Since 1968 the members have put nearly $14,000 into improvements, including an addition for Sunday School rooms, a nursery, and a library.

ALBRIGHT (1898)
MEMBERSHIP: 258

The late 1700s found more than one Brethren family in the vicinity of the curious water flow called Roaring Spring because of its peculiar noise. Early records reveal such common names as Neff, Ullery, Hoover, Martin, and Brumbaugh. Near the spring Daniel Ullery, who had come into possession of the "Mill Seat Land" tract about the time of the Revolutionary War, built the first grist mill in that part of Central Pennsylvania. Several years later he sold all his property, part of which fell within the bounds of what became the borough of Roaring Spring, to his son John. The latter, who added considerable acreage to his father's holdings, in 1821 himself sold out to a non-Brethren and moved away.

Other church members about this time also departed the area, leaving the ranks badly depleted. The few who remained held services regularly in their homes or in schoolhouses close by. But the fifty years that followed saw the membership build back up.

In February 1878, therefore, Clover Creek, the parent congregation, decided that there were enough members living in the vicinity of Roaring Spring to justify building a church house there. John W. Brumbaugh, whose grandfather had been a pioneer in Morrisons Cove, and Jacob L. Wineland were appointed a "committee on location." They accepted Samuel B. Albright's offer of ground on his farm, which was located about a mile south of the borough line.

The Roaring Spring Brethren drew up plans for a 40' x 32' frame building. The seven-hundred-dollar construction cost was met by levying a per capita tax on members: fifty percent on men, twenty-five percent on women.

Though now themselves housed, the folk in and around Roaring Spring did not constitute an independent congregation. For many years after 1878, they joined with the mother church in a once-a-month Sunday service at Clover Creek.

By this time the paper mills had located in Roaring Spring, bringing an influx of new residents. The little Brethren church on the outskirts of town attracted its share of these newcomers. In the spring of 1894 it experienced what the *Gospel Messenger* termed a "Great Awakening." Through a series of meetings conducted by two young Cove-area ministers, John R. Stayer and Brice Sell, thirty-eight baptisms were recorded.

The membership on the westernmost fringe of the Clover Creek territory was clearly ready for congregational status. This came in May 1898, and the church took the name Roaring Spring. The first minister to the 135-member group was John R. Stayer. British-born Thomas B. Maddocks served as elder.

Before long, however, the feeling grew that there should be a church in town. Many Brethren youth were attending services of other denominations there, frequently renouncing their childhood faith. In February 1910, therefore, council voted to allow those residing inside the borough to go ahead and build. A year later the town group retained the old name Roaring Spring while the country division called itself Albright. It was agreed that, since a boundary line between the two congregations would be hard to establish, individuals could make their own choices about where they wanted to hold their membership. Some sixty-odd persons stayed with the Albright church.

In 1923 the congregation completed an extensive remodeling program, debt free, thanks to the vigorous leadership of Jacob Kinsel of Altoona, their pastor at the time. The church was practically rebuilt at a cost of $3,700. Brick-cased outside and redecorated inside, it got electric lighting, central heating, and a basement for Sunday School work. Since then, the church house has undergone the usual periodic renovations.

Jacob Kinsel, a one-time printer, journalist, and medical student, stayed on as pastor until 1927. He was followed by Dorsey I. Pepple, who combined banking with preaching all the years of his ministry. "D.I." (he preferred to be called by his initials) gave thirty-three years to the Albright congregation. A resident of Woodbury, where he became president of the local bank in 1942, Pastor Pepple retired from the ministry in 1970 at age eighty-five. He lived into his ninth decade, passing away in April 1980. Over the years he held many District offices and served seven times on the Standing Committee of Annual Conference.

Albright's pastor from 1970 to 1980 was Joseph G. Moyer, who came from the Indian Creek church in Montgomery County. The Moyer family was the first to occupy an Albright-owned parsonage, including a brand new one in 1975. Since 1980 the pastor has been George D. Ebersole.

STONERSTOWN (1901)

MEMBERSHIP: 99

The village of Stonerstown is adjacent to Saxton borough and only a few miles from the Raven Run church. The first Brethren to move into the community—a short time before 1880—were two women: Mrs. Mary Elisa Fockler, a stepdaughter of Jacob Steele, the earliest English preacher in the Snake Spring congregation, and Mrs. Susan Keely. Mrs. Fockler was a member at Woodbury and Mrs. Keely at Yellow Creek.

By 1883 more Brethren sisters had taken residence in Stonerstown: Mrs. Catherine Ritchey, Mrs. Mary Smith, Mrs. Rebecca Smouse, and Mrs. Hannah White. At first some of these ladies walked the approximately three miles to Raven Run to attend services. Then, to minister to them and their families from time to time, there came to Stonerstown such preachers as George W. Brumbaugh and Samuel Ritchey from Yellow Creek, and from

Snake Spring, John B. Fluck and David Clapper, father of Grace, the early China missionary.

In 1893 this little band rented an old Lutheran church and engaged Silas Hoover for a revival meeting. Two years later, Mr. and Mrs. George H. Dilling moved from the Raven Run congregation to Stonerstown. They are credited with being the leaders in the plan to have the parent congregation purchase the abandoned Lutheran church, a weatherboarded log structure. It took a lot of persuasion to bring Raven Run to this decision, but the purchase was made in 1895—for three hundred dollars.

One of the early preachers at this mission point was William I. Book, principal of the Stonerstown High School. He later became a professor of physics at the University of Pennsylvania. Dr. Book also was for many years a trustee of Juniata College, where a chair of physics is named for him. Another of the early preachers was the College's Bible professor, John B. Brumbaugh, a longtime member of the District Mission Board, who in 1902 became the mission's elder. In 1901 he had reported at District Conference that Stonerstown then had sixteen members, ministered to every other Sunday. He emphasized the necessity for a regular pastor for the mission.

This was not possible, however, until 1907, when William A. Gaunt accepted a call, moving from Huntingdon to Stonerstown. But the congregation was unable to meet his ten-dollar-a-month salary, and so his pastorate was terminated in 1909. The membership then numbered nearly one hundred, but a strike by trainmen of the Huntingdon and Broad Top Railroad brought on a local depression, the impact of which was felt by the treasury of the Stonerstown church. In fact, recalls Miss Dessa Ritchey in her booklet, "Stonerstown Church of the Brethren: Its Beginning," written as a Christmas gift for her family in 1962: "The next year some of the most active members moved from the community to secure better employment."

Herman B. Heisey (1911–1913) and Charles O. Beery (1913–1915) gave pastoral leadership during those hard times. Then a great boost to the work came in 1914 during a revival conducted by Harvey S. Replogle of the Scalp Level church in Western Pennsylvania. The 1925 history says there were forty-three accessions as a result of this revival, but the Stonerstown Minute Book reports twenty-six—twenty-one by baptism and five by reclaiming.

Nevertheless, the need for a new building, which had been talked about since 1908, became more urgent. In August the members met with the Mission Board, and it was decided to erect a brick-cased structure (43' x 64') with a basement, steam heat, electricity, and an indoor baptistry behind the pulpit. The site chosen was almost opposite the old church. The towered building, which cost $8,495, was dedicated on August 27, 1916. Five thousand dollars was raised toward the debt during the course of the day.

John P. Harris, a Virginian born near Staunton, was the pastor then, and John Brumbaugh, the congregation's elder until 1920, wrote for the *Gospel Messenger* that "Brother Harris . . . carefully managed every detail and worked hard" while the church was going up.[19] His pastorate, during which the congregation "grew rapidly," came to a close in 1925.

The building debt was cleared the next year, on the tenth anniversary Sunday, August 29. The pastor then was Leonard R. Holsinger, who continued to live in Martinsburg. He resigned in 1935 to accept a pastorate in Ohio. Frederick C. Hollingshead and Professors Harry H. Nye and Paul R. Yoder provided part-time ministerial services over the next two years. Then O. Clyde Bush (1937–1939) and Chester N. Baird (1939–1942) served as full-time pastors, to be followed by E. Paul Dilling (1947–1961) on a part-time basis. Glenn P. Davis was next, from 1961 to 1962, and since then Daniel M. Brumbaugh, a public school teacher now retired, has been Stonerstown's pastor, also on limited time.

During Brumbaugh's leadership, the congregation has incorporated, in 1963, and made extensive repairs to the church plant. In November 1965 action was taken to tear down the parsonage across the street from the church and build a new one. Today an income-producing rental for the congregation, it was completed in 1967.

ROCKHILL (1907)
MEMBERSHIP: 137

In the Aughwick sketch we saw how the Brethren at Rockhill Furnace, today a small community of 480 residents south of Orbisonia, organized a Sunday School in 1901 that grew into a worshiping body needing a church building. Rockhill at century's turn was a company town that belonged to the Rockhill Iron and Coal Company. Here were located the depot of the East Broad Top Railroad, its yard, and other buildings (the railroad was owned by the RICC).

The Brethren got their place of meeting after the RICC donated two lots on a prominent corner of one of the best streets. By dedication day in 1906, the congregation had raised all but $150 of the $1,400 needed to put up the 35' x 40' frame church built solely

by donated labor. Somehow Mary S. Geiger, the wealthy Philadelphia widow who gave liberally to Juniata College, became interested in the Rockhill project and made a substantial donation. Weekly worship services, however, were still a thing of the future.

The next major step in the development of the congregation came in 1955, when the Aughwick charge underwent a threefold partition, at which time Rockhill and Valley Point combined pastoral services under David C. Emerson, the minister at Aughwick. He resigned there in 1957 and served the yoked parish until succeeded in.1966 by Homer F. Hoover, who was followed by Tobias F. Henry (1966–67). on April 11, 1967, the members voted to secure a full-time resident minister, ending the yoked ministry, and proceeded to purchase and remodel a two-story brick parsonage in Orbisonia along Route 522. Ronald A. Beverlin became pastor in 1967, and two years later effected a reyoking with Valley Point. At this time, the Rockhill-Valley Point charge entered into an interesting experiment in ecumenical cooperation with Baptist congregations in Saltillo and Three Springs. This experiment was the brainchild of Ronald A. Beverlin and was called Christ Parish. Eventually, the Baptist Church in Three Springs withdrew from the federation. David K. Webster was Christ Parish's minister from 1976 to 1981.

Meanwhile, in 1969, sometime after Ronald Beverlin had assumed the Rockhill pastorate, the congregation built an educational unit on the church. Then in 1976 a baptistry was placed in the sanctuary in memory of Mrs. Bertha Chilcoat, a highly respected member of the church and the community. Other renovations have also recently been carried out.

RIDDLESBURG (1908)
MEMBERSHIP: 54

Riddlesburg, south of Saxton four miles on Route 26, was originally part of the Raven Run congregation. The *Gospel Messenger* gives John B. Brumbaugh of Juniata College, for many years a dominant member of the District Mission Board, much credit for beginning the work at Riddlesburg, although the account of that church in the 1925 history, written by John's brother, Henry, makes no mention of his contributions. Instead, the 1925 history speaks of Thomas C. Lear's efforts to engage Charles O. Beery, then Tyrone's pastor, to hold a two-week meeting, during April 1906, in the Knights of the Golden Eagle Hall. This resulted in seven baptisms, upping the Raven Run membership in Riddlesburg and Defiance to an even dozen, representing six families.

At once these members began holding weekly prayer meetings in their homes and soon requested the parent church to provide a preaching ministry. But Raven Run's ministerial staff was small, and so on May 27, 1906, the congregation decided to put the work at Riddlesburg in the hands of the District Mission Board. For the next four years the preaching was done in homes—in those of Thomas Lear, Christian Oaks, and Melvin Reed. One of the regular preachers at this time was William A. Gaunt, a transplanted West Virginian then living in Huntingdon. In the spring of 1907 the Riddlesburg group got the District Mission Board's go-ahead nod to build.

In July they organized with fourteen charter members and elected John Brumbaugh as elder. Prior to this, however, back in April, the Riddlesburg people had convened in Christian Oak's home and appointed a building committee comprised of William Gaunt, Henry H. Brumbaugh, and Thomas Lear. Gaunt, their pastor, gave untiringly of his time soliciting funds for the new church, a brick-veneered building (35' x 50') with a towered entrance that cost $3,860.75. It was dedicated on September 13, 1908.

The following spring Riddlesburg was recognized as an independent body, giving Middle Pennsylvania twenty-six congregations at that time. In the seven decades since, the church building, though well maintained, has undergone no major renovations.

Ministerial duties prior to 1949 were carried out by the following men: William A. Gaunt, Herman E. Heisey, John B. Miller, John P. Harris, Charles O. Beery, Leonard R. Holsinger (1921–1931), O. Clyde Bush (1934–1940), Charles H. Heltzel (1942–1948), and since 1949, in one of the District's longest pastoral tenures, Horace G. Clapper.

SMITHFIELD (1917)
MEMBERSHIP: 146

The Smithfield church stands in the fertile Piney Creek Valley four miles north of Martinsburg. The early settlers of that vicinity, of course, fell within bounds of the Clover Creek congregation, which in 1891, as we saw elsewhere, gave the Fairview people—on the other side of Piney Ridge—their independence. The Smithfield-Beavertown road was fixed as the dividing line between the two groups, the Smithfield residents north of this road remaining with the mother church.

About this time, ministers from Fairview and Clover Creek began preaching once every two months at the Smithfield schoolhouse. Among these early preachers were George W. Brumbaugh, Joseph Snowberger, Andrew Detweiler, and William H. Holsinger. They also conducted Sunday School during the summer months.

In 1892 John R. Bashore moved to Barbara and became the resident gadfly for a church at Smithfield. A farmer-laypreacher, he had a great passion for missions. It was his custom every spring to offer twenty-five cents to any boy or girl who would invest it for a year and then give its earnings to some missionary cause. He was the prime mover in organizing an "evergreen" Sunday School at Smithfield in the late 1890s.

Earlier, in 1893, Jacob D. Smith donated land for a church site on which Fairview and Clover Creek helped erect a 35' x 45' place of worship. The plain, frame building cost $2,300. At this time the preaching interval was changed from the eighth to the fourth Sunday. Clover Creek and Fairview continued to take turns supplying preachers.

In another fourteen years the work at Smithfield, which made steady headway, led to a petition requesting permission to form a separate congregation. Both Clover Creek and Fairview had to take action on this appeal, which they did in February 1917. Then on May 4 the petitioning group organized and officially took the name of Smithfield. The sixty charter members elected William Holsinger their elder and pastor, who until 1922 was also joint pastor at Fairview and Williamsburg.

Smithfield's church house was heated by two coal stoves until 1929, when a furnace was installed and other renovations were made. Further improvements followed in 1939, with electric lights replacing kerosene lamps. Electricity came to that area largely through the efforts of Heaster L. Smith, church janitor for forty-six years, who began to despair of finding replacement parts for kerosene lamps, which were fast becoming obsolete. This problem, plus the recognized advantages of incandescent lighting, prompted him to lead the fight to get an electric line extended through that community. After initial disappointments, his efforts ultimately led to the beginning of the Valley Rural Electric Cooperative in the Cove—all because of Heaster Smith's desire to see the Smithfield church adequately lighted.

Church enlargement came in 1949, when the basement was excavated for Christian education purposes. The cost of over five thousand dollars was paid before dedication on November 20. General redecoration and the installation of new sanctuary furniture constituted an early 1960s project. In 1979 over $100,000 was expended to add eight Sunday School rooms and extensively remodel the entire church building. This included putting a baptistry in the basement.

The 1960s were also a time when the Smithfield congregation began to express "conscientious objection" to Brethren membership in ecumenical movements. They initiated a query in 1963 urging Annual Conference and District Conference to withdraw from the National and World Council of Churches. This query produced a study by the District, dealt with in greater detail elsewhere, lasting several years.

Men who pastored the church after William Holsinger were Isaac B. Kensinger (1924–1928), Dorsey I. Pepple (1928–29), George S. Batzel (1929–1933), Ira C. Holsopple and Homer F. Hoover (1933–1939), A. Emmert Frederick (1939–1962), and Walter Snyder (1962–   ).

KOONTZ (1922)

MEMBERSHIP: 185

This congregation, located in the southernmost section of Morrisons Cove, two miles below Loysburg, began as a part of the Snake Spring Valley charge. Very little is known about its origins. John Koontz, Sr., came into Morrisons Cove in the spring of 1837 and bought a farm from David Loy. About this time other Brethren families moved into the community. Among them were Peter Baker, John N. Teeter, Jacob Guyer, Sr., David Stayer, John H. Miller, and Henry Miller. No record exists indicating when these Brethren began to hold public worship, although it must have been around 1840.

The Koontz home was the scene of many of these meetings. The preachers—Isaac Ritchey and Andrew Snowberger—came from Snake Spring Valley, across the mountain. Then in 1865 Jacob

Koontz became the first resident minister. That year a church was erected on a part of his farm, the cost unknown. The call of John B. Fluck in 1879 made that progressive-minded educationist the Koontz church's second home preacher.

By the turn of the century the Koontz members felt the need for a larger church. In 1903 they put up a frame building (40′ x 60′) costing $1,800.

The Koontz church remained leagued with Snake Spring until April 29, 1922, when it organized as a separate congregation. David T. Detwiler and Yellow Creek's elder, David A. Stayer, guided the proceedings. A New Enterprise farmer, Herman Guyer, got the nod as presiding elder. He was at the time one of five resident ministers, the others being Henry Koontz, Elmer Butts, Tobias F. Henry, and Howard Hershberger. There were ninety-nine lay members.

The first major remodeling project came in 1963, when five thousand dollars went into reconstruction of the basement, providing a social room, classrooms, modern kitchen facilities, and a new heating system. Three years later the church completed a wholesale revamping of the sanctuary. During the 1970s the members spent over $17,000 on further improvements, including the addition of a foyer in 1978.

In 1967 Koontz and nearby Waterside combined their pastoral programs, thus ending for the former a history of nonsalaried, part-time ministers. For a parsonage, the two congregations, beginning the next year, rented a one-story brick residence in Loysburg.

Koontz's ministerial force since the 1920s has included Isaac

Wareham, O. Clyde Bush, R. Eugene Miller, Clifford Fluke, Edgar M. Detwiler, Merle Detwiler, Howard W. Bernard, who served full time (1968–1976), Timothy L. Monn (1977–1979), and Louis D. Bloom (1980–   ).

GLENDALE (1922)

MEMBERSHIP: 87

About 1910 some of the Brethren in West Virginia began to move into Alleghany County, Maryland, just across the Pennsylvania line directly south of Bedford. By 1915 the Bibles, Dollys, Teeters, Mallows, Millers, Morrals, Aults, and other families were there without a Church of the Brethren to attend, the closest one being in Artemas, some thirteen miles northwest.

With the help of Elder John Bennett of Artemas, for more than three decades that village's postmaster, James W. Bible, Benjamin Y. S. Deeter, and several others, it was decided to build a church along Flintstone Creek, to be an arm of the Artemas congregation. In a quite isolated location, the church was constructed in 1921 by Lewis Strawser at a cost of four thousand dollars. The congregation would later take the name Glendale. Today the church stands along Route 40 at Flintstone, Maryland, one of three outside the bounds of Middle District proper.

Because the Flintstone Brethren had no financial resources, merchant-farmer-postmaster-preacher John Bennett carried a note on the debt, backed by the pledges of the members. As it turned out, not a few pledges were ten years or more in being repaid; some never were. The building was dedicated on June 18, 1922. A week before, twenty-four people were received into the church and eighteen were baptized at the Gilpentown Bridge by John H. Cassady of Juniata College.

Late in 1930 it was brought to the attention of the church by members of the John Bennett family that he was in ill health and did not have the money to pay on the church note. The congregation was asked to take over the payments, and it was decided to take pledges for the year 1931, due monthly. Of this amount, the pastor, G. Landis Baker, was to get ten dollars a month and John Bennett the remainder. Because of hard times, however, Baker was never paid all that was owed him.

At the end of the first ten years, there were thirty-three members at Glendale. The roads were being improved, and Sunday School was now held year-round instead of only during the dry months.

In 1939 the congregation, with Pastor Howard Whitacre's help, voted to build a parsonage in Flintstone. The deed was put in the pastor's name since he was personally financing part of the cost—with the understanding that if he left, the church was to have first chance to buy it. When the Whitacre pastorate ended in 1945, Glendale's budget could not stand the strain of a mortgage, and so the parsonage passed into other hands.

In 1949 the church building was extensively renovated and the basement excavated. With the 1950s and the inevitable demise of the mother congregation Artemas, Amaranth and Glendale went their separate pastoral ways. John H. Buffenmyer took over Glendale's pulpit in 1951 where he remained until his death in 1973. During his ministry there was some discussion whether Glendale should affiliate with the West Marva District or remain with Pennsylvania's Middle District. In July 1967 the congregation opted to stay with its original district home.

After John Buffenmyer's death, Glendale was served by supply preachers. Then, beginning in November 1977, Paul K. Wharton of Altoona accepted a full-time call. In 1979 Earl Harper took over the pulpit. Meanwhile, in 1975 the members had begun to use new Christian education facilities (five classrooms), a self-help project that started in 1970 and cost slightly more than seven thousand dollars.

CHERRY LANE (1924)
MEMBERSHIP: 93

The 1925 history reports that, sometime before the Civil War, a few Brethren families had located in the vicinity of Clearville, a village five-and-a-half miles due south of Everett. These families, territorially within the charge of Snake Spring Valley, first met in the home of Daniel Snyder. Later they used the several neighborhood schoolhouses.

Except for Graybill Myers, the ministers that served this group—Henry Hershberger, Jacob Steele, Andrew Snowberger, Jr., William S. Ritchey, and Jacob Koontz—were, of course, products of the mother congregation. Besides Daniel Snyder, other prominent household heads making up the Clearville-area contingent were Thomas Dibert, John B. Smith, Isaac Ritchey, and John Dibert. Daniel Snyder and Thomas Dibert later were on the building committee that erected the Artemas church in 1879.

Earlier, in 1872, Clearville Brethren had gleaned a church of their own (38' x 48'). In time, by 1913, this meetinghouse was outgrown and a new one built. It was put up on land donated by Daniel

Snyder, where the building still stands. The frame structure (40' x 60'), with a large kitchen attached to the rear, provided the Clear-ville group with a "love feast house," thus laying, says the 1925 history "the foundation for future growth."

On May 10, 1924, the eighty-four members there organized into a separate congregation, taking the name Cherry Lane. Their first presiding elder was Ira C. Holsopple, pastor at Everett. Ralph Cox, a Warriors Mark native who pastored in Illinois and Wisconsin before settling within the Cherry Lane parish, was the church's first salaried minister, from 1924 to 1930.

On Cherry Lane's fortieth anniversary, May 10, 1964, the members celebrated the completion of a major remodeling project. The dedication speaker was Guy Fern, a former pastor.

Then, beginning in fall 1975, Cherry Lane and Snake Spring officially initiated a yoked parish relationship, having been since 1973 sharing the pastoral services of Galen Hoover. The two churches are ten miles apart, in open country.

Pastors since the Cox years, have been: A. Jay Replogle (1930–1935), Emmanuel Edwards (1936–1938), Charles O. Beery (1938–1946), Guy S. Fern (1946–1954), Lawrence E. Thomas (1954–1956), Perry B. Liskey (1956–1962), John D. Keiper (1962–1965), Harold M. Kenepp (1965–1968), Joseph E. Whitacre (1968–1971), Galen E. Hoover (1971–1975), and Victor S. Norris (1976–1980).

CLAYSBURG (1927)
MEMBERSHIP: 192

Claysburg is a Blair County town that lies along old Route 220, just about midway between Altoona and Bedford. The church there

had its inception in the early part of 1921, when Burdine Claar of the Leamersville congregation urged that a Sunday School be started to serve its nearly one hundred Brethren residents.

The Claar congregation, within whose bailiwick Claysburg fell, gave permission to begin work. Burdine Claar secured the use of a large second-story room in the old Bank Building that summer. From the Leamersville church, however, came the Sunday School's organizer and first superintendent, Jeremiah Snowberger. The school was held on Sunday afternoons all summer, closing down for the winter and then resuming the next spring with an average attendance of approximately forty.

In the summer of 1922 some of the District leaders recognized the opportunity of opening a mission church in Claysburg. A roofed-over tabernacle was erected on the site of the present church, and John R. Snyder, a leading evangelist in union tabernacle work who located in Huntingdon in 1922, preached the first sermon on August 16. A series of revival meetings followed into late fall, producing no less than thirty-three baptismal candidates. When cold weather set in, the meetings were held in the I.O.O.F. Hall across the street.

John B. Miller of Curryville, Leamersville's sixty-six-year-old pastor, carried on the work in the hall and tabernacle. In 1926 the District Mission Board completed construction of the present church and parsonage—a duplex facility, as was then a common architectural arrangement among many denominations. Daniel B. Maddocks of Altoona, a car shop foreman, was the architect of the brick structure with a towered entrance, erected by considerable volunteer labor.

The year 1926 was also when the Claysburg fellowship officially organized, in September. Charles L. Cox received the pastoral call, and Maddocks was elected elder. During Cox's twenty-six-year pastorate there were 332 accessions, either by baptism or by letter.

Years later, when Woodbury subdivided, the Claysburg and Holsinger congregations, following a study of their pastoral programs, decided to try a yoked ministry. This arrangement continued for two years, from 1961 to 1963.

In 1974–75 a remodeling and beautification program put the interior of the Claysburg church in excellent physical condition. The men did the work, supervised by Jack Freeman. Earlier, in 1971, chimes had been donated to the congregation in honor of Charles Cox.

Successors to Pastor Cox have been D. Paul Green (1952–53), Paul E. Ritchey (1953–1955), Otho Hassinger (1955–1959), A. Lester Bucher (1959–1963), Charles W. Palmer (1963–1966), Albert M. Haught (1966–1976), Joseph A. Miller (1976–1978) and Marvin G. Reeves of Oklahoma, who at age fifty-two decided to change vocational directions and become a pastor (1978–   ).

PINE GLEN (1946)
MEMBERSHIP: 460

In post–Civil War years Pine Glen schoolhouse, south of the Juniata River near McVeytown, Mifflin County, was a regular preaching point in the Spring Run congregation. Services were held on a twice-a-month schedule. After some agitation, two unsuccessful attempts were made—in 1874 and 1877—to give the Brethren of the Pine Glen vicinity a meetinghouse. Then in 1892, when Reuben T. Myers, John Yoder, Abraham Myers, Jacob Miller, and Michael F. H. Kinsel constituted a building committee, things began to happen.

That year the congregation acquired land from Abraham and Mary Grassmire and put up a church (40' x 60'), patterned after the Maitland and Spring Run houses and, like them, costing two thousand dollars. Much of the material was donated, the largest cost being the slate roof. Volunteer labor further kept expenditures down. William J. Swigart of Juniata College, who had grown up in the Spring Run congregation, was the dedication speaker on January 23, 1893. Nearly four hundred worshipers crowded into the new facility to hear "W.J." preach. His relative, George H. Swigart, an early believer in education and for forty-three years a schoolteacher, served as the first elder.

At their June business session, the Spring Run members the next year voted to name the Bratton Township church Pine Glen.

A long time passed before any major work was done on the 1893 structure, although the need for Sunday School rooms prompted minor renovations at different times. It was cramped classroom space that led to digging out the basement in 1935 for additional Sunday School space and for a central heating plant.

By the time of World War II Pine Glen had grown to be almost as large as the mother church, and so in 1946 its members petitioned District Conference to be organized as a separate congregation. This was granted, and on October 4 two members of the District Ministerial-Mission Board, Tobias F. Henry and Paul R. Yoder, both of Juniata College, took charge of the organizational meeting. Lawrence D. Ruble was elected moderator.

Next year the front of the church was remodeled, making five classrooms available and adding a baptismal pool. In 1951 the sanctuary got new carpeting and new pews, installed at a cost of four thousand dollars.

Prior to 1949 Pine Glen shared pastoral services with Spring Run. But with the former's independent status, there was increasing pressure for a pastor of their own. Thus in 1949 J. Richard Gottshall moved to the community in this capacity, serving to 1958.

His ministry coincided with the seventy-two-thousand-dollar remodeling project of the mid-fifties. This project had its origin in April 1953, when the trustees brought an item of business to council asking that a fifteen-member planning committee be established to study the needs of the congregation for more classrooms and auditorium space. Such a committee was created in July and began its work at once. A year later it got approval to engage Forrest Groff of Elgin, Illinois, to work up preliminary drawings. These drawings were received a couple of months later and given thorough study by the planning committee. In August 1955, upon the committee's recommendation, the Groff-drawn plans received the membership's approval.

In October 1955 the congregation purchased additional ground from the Cemetery Association for expansion purposes. The plans called for moving the old building to a new foundation and putting on a 34' × 81' addition. The project was completed in the fall of 1958. Almost half of the $72,000 construction cost was already paid off.

In 1960 the congregation built a one-and-a-half story frame parsonage across the road from the church. Then eight years later, on October 13, the members, after a decade of faithful stewardship, were able to burn the 1958 church mortgage.

Pastors since J. Richard Gottshall's resignation in 1958 have been David H. Markey (1958–1961), Guy S. Fern (1962–1970), Lee A. Weaver (1970–1978), and, in a return engagement, J. Richard Gottshall since 1979.

PARKVIEW (1949)

MEMBERSHIP: 70

For a number of years, a mission existed in the Kline school, just outside the limits of Burnham. A congregation officially took rise there in 1949 upon District approval. With three thousand dollars borrowed from the then Mission-Ministerial Board, the local Brethren had earlier erected a one-story concrete-block church at Parkview Terrace and Parcheytown Road, opposite Kishacoquillas Park. It was dedicated on March 13, a few months before the District gave the Parkview congregation its autonomy.

One of the most active members in establishing the congregation was the former Hazel Yetter (she later married Earle Strauser), who became Parkview's longtime treasurer. Another prominent member was Alvin S. Cox, who provided pastoral services when the fellowship organized and saw it through its formative years. He was followed for two years by Carl Lauer. From 1952 to 1957 J. Donald Plank, Burnham's minister, carried on pastoral duties at both places. Henry H. Moyer then filled the position at Parkview until 1960, and the following year Earle Strauser began the first of his two pastoral stints there, resigning in 1968. During this period, in 1964, the church building was extensively remodeled. Harvey Wilson continued in the part-time ministerial tradition there from 1968 to 1971.

In 1971 Parkview purchased a parsonage and called Earle Strauser for a return limited pastorate. Upon his approaching retirement in 1977, the congregation hoped to go on a full-time pastoral program. But this did not materialize and M. Leslie Campbell, who had been ordained by the Bible Fellowship Church of Allentown, Pennsylvania, came as a part-time pastor. He terminated his service in March 1980. During his last year the Parkview sanctuary underwent a ten-thousand-dollar renovation, debt free.

VALLEY POINT (1955)

MEMBERSHIP: 48

Black Log Valley lies athwart the Huntingdon-Juniata County line, northeast of Orbisonia seven miles. The soil there, said the *Gospel Messenger* in 1884, was not so "productive" as some of the

neighboring valleys, but the Brethren and others had long brought it under cultivation. That region, we learned earlier, was part of the far-flung Aughwick congregation.

According to the *Gospel Messenger*, Brethren living in the Valley numbered about sixty in the early 1880s. Ministering to them at the time was John Shope, a farmer from Black Log who had been licensed by the Aughwick congregation in October 1879. Because of the concentration of members in the Valley's upper end, a church was built there and dedicated on October 19, 1884, its site in Lack Township, Juniata County. The new meetinghouse, only four hundred dollars owing on it when James Quinter preached the dedication sermon, boasted a usable basement, a rather unusual convenience for Brethren churches of that era, especially those rurally located. In the Aughwick Minute Book, this building was always referred to at first as the "Bryan Run Chapel." The donors of the land, George Smith and his wife, wrote into the deed that the property was to revert back to the owners or their heirs if the church fell into disuse.

Following dedicatory services, John Shope, who became an elder three years later, held a six-week revival during which he baptized some ninety persons. The building debt, in the course of the prolonged preaching mission, was further reduced by two hundred dollars.

The Minute Book for Aughwick council meetings shows that on May 30, 1895, the new church was permitted to organize "separately" but remain "under the supervision of Elders at Germany Valley." Besides Shope, other early preachers at Black Log were James R. Lane, Seth W. Myers, Robert M. Wakefield, and Thomas Chilcote.

However, as mentioned in the Aughwick sketch, John Shope united with the Progressive Brethren Church in 1890. Fourteen other Black Loggers followed suit, although several of them, but not Shope, eventually returned to the fold.

Records are practically nonexistent, but apparently by the mid-1930s the Bryan Run Chapel or Upper Black Log Church, as it came to be called, was standing idle most of the time. The summer of 1934, a union Sunday School was conducted there, a Methodist superintendent in charge. And in 1935 H. William Hanawalt, Aughwick's pastor, wrote, "The outlook for the future of the Brethren Church [in Black Log Valley] is not good."

By this time Black Log Brethren were worshiping at the Valley Point church, located in Huntingdon County closer to Shirleysburg. This church, about which the 1925 history is strangely silent, was built around 1888 on land bought from a family named Mateer. It was used only in the summertime, on Sunday afternoons. Collection was taken every other week and often amounted to only seven cents or a little more.

Later the Brethren sold the building for $125, and it became known as the Union House. Any denomination, except Catholics and Jews, could worship there. By 1921 it had become the church of the United Brethren in Christ. Two years later it had come back into the hands of the Aughwick congregation, but under what terms is not known.

The situation in Black Log Valley, however, as Pastor Hanawalt correctly assessed, showed little promise until after World War II. In fact, in the early 1940s the District Mission-Ministerial Board was almost ready to advise Aughwick to abandon the Valley, leaving it to the Christian Missionary Alliance Church.

In 1955, as noted previously, Aughwick subdivided into three distinct congregations, one of which was the Rockhill-Black Log alliance. David Emerson, up to this time Aughwick's pastor, now took over this new charge. Valley Point became Black Log's principal place of worship, services at Upper Black Log to this day being only a rare event.

However, in 1959 Valley Point withdrew from its union with Rockhill. Fern D. Dunmire, a home minister from McVeytown, was named pastor. His pastorate ended in 1969 when Rockhill and Valley Point were reyoked under Ronald A. Beverlin. It was at this time that these two Brethren churches and the Baptists at Saltillo and Three Springs federated to form Christ Parish, mentioned in the Rockhill vignette.

As it remains today, Valley Point is still a part of Christ Parish. In August 1979 a ground-breaking ceremony marked the start of construction of a Christian education wing (two rooms) and a new basement at Valley Point, the work to be done by volunteer labor from the congregation. David K. Webster, who succeeded Beverlin in 1976, ministered to the Valley Point members till 1981.

POINT (1958)
MEMBERSHIP: 88

As we saw in the historical sketch of Dunnings Creek, Point church was originally part of that congregation. The church building itself (30' × 40') was erected in 1893 and stood four miles northwest of the Napier Station, not too far from New Paris and three miles northeast of Schellsburg.

Dunnings Creek provided the preaching ministry until 1956,

when the Point church decided to go its separate way pastorally. Raymond P. Gordon of New Paris accepted Point's pastoral call, serving until May 1962. During his pastorate, in 1958, the congregation got the District's blessing to organize as an autonomous group, retaining as elder Edgar M. Detwiler, who was also the elder of Dunnings Creek. After Gordon's six-year ministry, Point elected Michael Olivieri of Roaring Spring to be the pastor. He continues in that capacity at the present time. From time to time, of course, the Point church building has undergone renovative improvements down through the years.

CURRYVILLE (1960)
MEMBERSHIP: 266

The beginning of the Curryville charge dates back to March 1906, when the Woodbury congregation acceded to the wishes of Brethren living in or near Curryville and decided to give them their own place of worship. A basementless brick structure (40' × 60'), costing $2,958.02, was erected and dedicated that December. Samuel S. Rhodes, active in the Sunday School, donated the ground.

Curryville, six miles south of Martinsburg, was in bygone years located on the Morrisons Cove Branch of the Pennsylvania Railroad. In 1928 the Brethren there remodeled their church, adding a tower, balcony, Sunday School rooms, and an aid society room at a cost of $4,600. Beginning in 1938 and continuing several years, the men dug out and finished the basement.

On April 12, 1950 this building was destroyed by fire—at the very time members were planning a service to dedicate recently completed improvements. The loss was set at fifty thousand dollars, with only three thousand dollars' fire insurance carried by the congregation.

At the quarterly council meeting held at Woodbury two days after the destructive blaze, it was decided to proceed at once in replacing the Curryville church. The new edifice (41' × 81'), set off by a large tower, had a price tag of $58,000. It was dedicated on August 26, 1951, with Rufus P. Bucher and Juniata College President Calvert N. Ellis the speakers for the occasion. The membership at that time was 175.

On April 1, 1960, Curryville became a separate congregation. The members erected a parsonage in 1961 ($26,800) a short distance from the church, and in 1962 acquired a school property for religious and social use across the highway. In 1976 the church sanctuary was completely remodeled at a cost of $40,000.

Curryville's first moderator was Chester P. Guyer. Robert Blair, a Juniata graduate and a Wooster College professor today, was interim pastor until he entered Bethany Theological Seminary. The next pastor was Lee A. Weaver (1961–1970), who was followed by Ronald F. Madeira (1970), James O. McAvoy (1970–1972), John J. Cassel (1972–1975), and Claude B. Hall (1975–   ), whose wife Mary Lou has recently served interim pastorates for three District churches: Fairview, Dunnings Creek, and Everett.

WATERSIDE (1963)
MEMBERSHIP: 202

The Brethren at Waterside, today a small community midway between Woodbury and Loysburg on Route 36 in the heartland of Morrisons Cove, belonged to Yellow Creek before that congregation, in 1895, changed its name to New Enterprise. As mentioned earlier in the New Enterprise account, the Brethren put up a church (32' × 45') on a hill at Waterside in 1872. Four years later a Sunday School was started there, reporting in 1878 an average attendance of forty-three.

By the time another generation had passed, however, the future of the Waterside church was somewhat in doubt. The New Enterprise Minute Book reveals that on January 9, 1924, the congregation decided to discontinue services at the "Hill" house until "further action" in the spring. In April the church was locked up and its library moved to New Enterprise. But the next month services were resumed, and on Sunday afternoons the ministers were instructed to

work out the preaching schedule. Prospects brightened and on July 14, 1926, New Enterprise voted to make repairs on the aging Waterside building.

For want of a better place to worship and because of quarry operations close to the church, some Watersiders in the mid-1930s began talking of disposing of the 1872 building. Then in 1936 the Church of God sanctuary, about three-quarters of a mile north, became available. A committee—Oscar Beach, Frank Huntsman, Abe Replogle, Levi Guyer, A. B. Replogle, and William Over— looked into the matter that summer and reported that the neighboring church could be purchased for $610. The New Enterprise congregation, however, moved slowly and not till September, by a vote of 27 to 17, was the deal finally approved. The 1872 building then became the property of the New Enterprise Stone and Lime Company, which paid four hundred dollars for it and used it for storage purposes.

This relocation seemed to give the Waterside church a shot in the arm, and the work there made significant growth. There was soon need for more Sunday School space, and in 1948–49 the interior was remodeled to provide a balcony with rooms under it. This was done at a cost of $3,200 dollars.

Ten years later Waterside petitioned New Enterprise to begin their own pastoral program on a trial basis. Permission was granted, and Isaac Wareham gave eight months in 1960 on a part-time schedule. His successor, R. Eugene Miller of Saxton (1960–1967), introduced a full-time pastorate.

In July 1962 the growing congregation launched a program to add more educational rooms. The annex (20′ × 45′) was completed the next spring and cost fifteen thousand dollars, two thousand of which was in donated labor. The dedication day speaker on Sunday, April 21, was Dr. Nevin H. Zuck, pastor at Elizabethtown and moderator of Annual Conference the previous year. Upon Miller's resignation in 1967, the Koontz-Waterside churches entered into a full-time yoked ministry under Howard W. Bernhard (1968–1976). See the Koontz sketch for the ministers who have served since 1976. During the decade of the seventies there were periodic programs to improve worship facilities at Waterside.

DIEHL'S CROSSROADS (1972)
MEMBERSHIP: 63

The early history of Diehl's Crossroads, home church of the late Ella M. Snowberger, the historian who wrote eleven volumes of *Recollections of Bygone Days in the Cove,* is traced in the Clover Creek portrayal.

As we saw, Diehl's Crossroads, located a mile east of Curryville at Henrietta, assumed its congregational independence in 1972, after 117 years under Clover Creek's wing. A supply ministry sufficed until 1974, when Harry L. Brubaker, formerly of Western Pennsylvania and a farmer near Roaring Spring, became part-time pastor. His first year the congregation completed a $1,200 remodeling program that included erecting a front-entrance portico topped by a twenty-two-foot steeple.

Brubaker was pastor until summer 1978. Charles O. Guyer, then a licensee from New Enterprise, replaced him in a part-time capacity. Guyer, who has since been ordained, was replaced by Calvin Shoenberger, Jr., of Altoona in 1980.

BLACK VALLEY (1975)
MEMBERSHIP: 81

For some forty years or more, the Cherry Lane congregation provided ministerial assistance to scattered Brethren in the wild, mountainous area of southeastern Bedford County. Sideling Hill slices through those parts, five miles south of Everett, on a diagonal axis. There at two places, Black Valley and Pleasant Union, services were conducted in union churches by denominational representatives of both the Brethren and the Christian Church.

In the fall of 1973, however, Cherry Lane took action to dissolve this arrangement. The reason given was that the members desired "to yoke with one parish, a Church of the Brethren, therefore strengthen their Brethren heritage, as well as local strength based on

worship services every Sunday." As a result, both Black Valley and Pleasant Union petitioned the District to be admitted to congregational status in the Church of the Brethren. Such recognition was given only to Black Valley at the 1975 District Conference. But the District's newest congregation became the second one—like State College—to profess dual denominational loyalties. It is yoked with the Bedford-Fulton Christian Conference and goes under the name Black Valley Federated Church of the Brethren and Christian. Ministers of the two groups share each other's pulpits on a regular basis.

Black Valley adopted a constitution on September 22, 1975. O. Clyde Bush of Curryville has been their pastor from the start, while Everett's Bryce Means has been the only moderator.

5
Town Churches

Town Missions

Because of their rural heritage, the Brethren were slow to develop interest in towns, to say nothing about cities. Not until 1895, for instance, did Annual Conference officially approve city mission work. But after the Civil War, when the nation experienced a great urban growth and agriculture was beset by periodic recessions, Brethren youth began the trek to urban areas. This trend prompted one man to write the *Christian Family Companion* as early as 1873 wondering why the Brethren always erected their churches in the countryside. He advised, ". . . in this age of the world, our meeting-houses should be built in towns. The time has come when we must build our meeting-houses where the people are."[1] Middle District's own Graybill Myers the year before had publicly commented that he "feared the brethren are too timid about letting their light shine in cities and towns."

James Sell, at age twenty-nine on the threshold of his long ministry in the District, had some thoughts on the matter too. He wrote the *Christian Family Companion* in 1874 to put forth one reason for the absence of Brethren town churches:

> The question has been often asked, why do the brethren not preach more in the towns and cities? The plain truth of the matter is just simply because we have but few preachers who are able, Paul-like, to defend themselves when they are encountered "by certain philosophers of the Epicureans and of the Stoics" who generally inhabit such places.[2]

Nine years later, Henry Brumbaugh spoke to the same point. He observed in the *Gospel Messenger,* when reporting on Altoona's new church building:

> That city churches will require more care and pastoral labor must become an established fact before we can expect success in city work. The

minister in charge must have a master mind. He must be not only a good preacher, but in addition, must possess good executive ability.[3]

He went on to urge the Brotherhood to adopt some kind of program or create some board to give city congregations financial help and guidance.

Already, since the District Conference of 1873, it had been proposed that Brethren of Central Pennsylvania build a church in "some city or town every year."[4] There was a particular interest at that time in starting a mission point in Altoona, a goal soon realized. Later the creation of the District Mission Board in 1886 provided a formal organization for fostering town missionary projects, though progress was slow. As late as 1906 the Board was still pledged, said Juniata College's John B. Brumbaugh in a *Gospel Messenger* editorial, to establishing churches in the "principal towns of the district." Brumbaugh, who gave over a quarter century to the Board, went on to say, "We are not in sympathy with the idea that the Brethren church is not adapted to the cities and towns."[5] And so for many reasons, among them concern over the bad influences of an urban setting and its threat to the simple life and to nonconformity, the Brethren were still debating the advisability of city churches well into the first decade of the twentieth century.

But an interesting fact has gone ignored, as far as Middle Pennsylvania is concerned. Not only were its post–Civil War leaders outspoken apologists of town/city churches, but in Altoona and Huntingdon the District can claim two of the half dozen earliest such congregations in Brethren history. No other district did as well.

The last third of the 1800s was, of course—in Pennsylvania as well as in the nation at large—a time of unprecedented urban expansion. When the Civil War broke out, the urban population of the state amounted to about one-third of the total. In 1880 nearly forty percent of the people were living in cities, and by century's turn nearly fifty-five percent of Pennsylvanians lived in towns of twenty-five hundred or more inhabitants.

Actually, few states suffered such a major internal relocation of its population as Pennsylvania in the last quarter of the nineteenth century. In 1870 the state had only fifteen cities with a population over ten thousand. But in 1900 there were forty-three of them at widely distributed points within its boundary. This urban population explosion almost took on the scope of geometric progression. Scranton, for example, tripled in size in thirty years, Pittsburgh quadrupled its populace, while Johnstown residents increased six hundred percent.

Lure of District Towns

Pennsylvania's phenomenal demographic shifts in the late 1800s, however, were not generally reflected in its center-state counties. That section, as the last chapter demonstrated, remained primarily rural and mountainous timberland. Altoona, to be sure, was one city in Middle District to match the unparalleled urban expansion of the post–Civil War decades. It grew from 3,500 in 1870 to nearly 39,000 in 1900, a growth rate of better than one thousand percent. Tyrone's population was well-nigh as dramatic, the number of its residents increasing from 1,800 in 1870 to about eight thousand by 1896. Huntingdon, meanwhile, also made a notable jump—from 1,890 in 1860 to six thousand in 1900. But other than these three places, the population picture was quite ordinary.

Elsewhere in the District, the citizenry of Lewistown was slightly over three thousand in 1890, that of Hollidaysburg a little under three thousand, that of Bedford 2,200 (about the same size as Bellwood), while Roaring Spring, with 920 people was almost twice as big as Martinsburg. Up north in the District, the whole of State College Township numbered only 1,666.

By 1902 there were churches, if not autonomous congregations, in almost all the towns along the main line of the Pennsylvania Railroad within the limits of the District. Mount Union was one exception, but hopes were expressed at the time that a church would presently exist there too. But that, of course, did not happen. The railroad was an important factor in luring District Brethren to the towns along its tracks. A natural terminal point because of its geographical location, Altoona was in large measure a creation of the Pennsylvania Railroad and has remained essentially a railroad town. The locomotive repair shops and yards there and in adjacent towns—Hollidaysburg, Tyrone, Bellwood—provided many jobs. And, even farther down the line, Huntingdon in the 1870s became the site of a freight car works.

Other industries provided opportunities for employment. The paper mills at Tyrone, Williamsburg, and Roaring Spring had large payrolls. The iron and steel factories in Burnham employed a sizable force of laborers. Industrial concerns such as these and smaller businesses of all kinds made the town seem an occupational mecca to job-seeking country youth.

At first the Brethren gravitated toward blue-collar labor. But as more of them finished high school or earned diplomas at Juniata's Business College (established in 1891 and some years graduating more students than either the College itself or the Academy) they entered the white-collar ranks, as office workers or secretaries. With the twentieth century, increasing numbers of church youth preferred teaching positions in town schools over rural ones, many quickly moving into principalships. Other professions, though, like law or medicine, were largely ignored by the Brethren. Nor had many as yet gone into business for themselves in the towns.

Brethren town-dwellers by the early 1890s began to enjoy conveniences unknown by their country kin. The telephone became available, Juniata College, for example, installing one in 1881. Indoor plumbing brought the creature comfort of hot and cold running water, symbolized by the bathroom. Streets were paved, the streetcar appeared, and after 1900, indoor electrification was common.

The move to town led to significant changes in the life-style of a congregation. As James Sell and the Brumbaughs argued, the town church required a new strain of minister: trained, full-time, and salaried. It meant a break with "the-little-white-frame-church-in-the-country" concept of architecture. The red-brick structure, with an elevated chancel and Sunday School classrooms, became the new model. Its indoors baptistry spelled doom, even for the country congregations, to the traditional creek-side baptismal rite.

For present purposes, the term *town* has arbitrarily been defined as a place with a population of two thousand or more. Such a definition, in actuality, pretty much coincides with the measurement used by the United States Census Bureau to designate *urban* (at least 650 families). Today Altoona is the District's largest urban area (62,900), followed by State College (33,778). Of the other eleven towns with Brethren churches, Tyrone is the most populous with 7,072.

Everett (684) and Roaring Spring (669) boast the largest membership rolls in the District, while Martinsburg (492) ranks third. In all, town churches represent about thirty-eight percent of all those on congregational rolls.

In the Church of the Brethren at large, the number of urban members has increased rapidly since World War II. The report of the General Brotherhood Board to the 1968 Annual Conference, entitled "An Urban Ministry for Today's People," listed 336 non-rural congregations in the denomination. Yet, at that time this figure represented only one-third of the total number of congregations.

MARTINSBURG (1871)
MEMBERSHIP: 490

From the Clover Creek congregation, as its historical sketch in chapter 4 shows, sprang several church groups, of which Mar-

tinsburg is one. The town of Martinsburg, in the heart of Morrisons Cove, was built on land once owned by the early Brethren colonist John Brumbaugh. He owned fifteen hundred acres reaching from Roaring Spring to Tussey Mountain, obtained in 1792. Part of this land later became the possession of Brumbaugh's son-in-law, Daniel Camerer, whose two sons, John and James in 1845 put up the first meetinghouse for the Brethren in Martinsburg. This building filled the dual capacity of church and dwelling, and it still stands across the street from the present building. In 1866 a Sunday School was started, and by 1870 the house-church had become too small. Clover Creek decided to sell it that year and made preparations to build a new corner-lot edifice. This one, brick and 48' × 38', was ready in 1871, according to the *Pilgrim,* which claimed that people were turned away at its dedication, so great was the attendance. Preaching at Martinsburg, of course, in a multi-church congregation like Clover Creek, was at first a once-a-month event.

The Martinsburg group made steady growth, and in 1917, twenty years before it was carried out, they pushed to become a separate congregation. For reasons unknown, it was considered best to wait. But the pressure to build larger in town was not ignored, and in 1920 came the decision to tear down the old church and erect a new one on the same site. The building committee of Moses R. Brumbaugh, Ira Brumbaugh, Henry Brumbaugh, George B. Wineland, and James Wineland oversaw the construction of a modern church plant (75' × 74'), brick-cased and flanked by two towers. The cost was $36,496.26. The speaker on February 26, 1922, dedication day, was District-born Milton C. Swigart of Germantown, where his pastorate witnessed the growth of that historic congregation from less than fifty to over four hundred. More than seven hundred heard his dedicatory sermon.

As yet the church was served by local ministers, among whom were Jacob K. Brown, Moses R. Brumbaugh, Frederick R. Zook, Charles B. Smith, Isaac B. Kensinger, and Leonard R. Holsinger. It was in recognition of these men and others, who one time or another had preached at Clover Creek and Crossroads, that the new building was named the Martinsburg Memorial Church of the Brethren.

In October 1925 Charles O. Beery came from Juniata Park to become the first full-time pastor. He stayed for five years. By 1930 Martinsburg, with its nearly five hundred members, was Clover Creek's largest subcharge.

Aubrey R. Coffman, one of only a few Brethren ministers then with an earned doctorate, followed in the pastorate after a three-year hiatus, from 1933 to 1945. The present parsonage adjoining the church property was purchased in 1933. It was during Coffman's tenure that Martinsburg finally separated from Clover Creek—in 1936, taking 513 members off the mother church's roll.

Millard G. Wilson succeeded Coffman, putting in a half-dozen years. During his ministry Memorial Church saw the need for providing more adequate educational facilities. And so plans, blue-printed by C. H. Deardorff, the retired Brotherhood architect, that called for removing the east wall of the church and reversing the sanctuary, met with council acceptance in July 1950. Soon the Building Fund was increasing by two thousand dollars a month.

In November 1951, the new wing now open for Sunday School use, worship services were moved to the basement to make way for remodeling the sanctuary. This part of the renovation program was completed several months later, and the first service in the reversed sanctuary was held on March 30, 1952. A week-long series of evangelistic meetings, April 13–20, preceded dedication day, the speaker for which was Dr. Paul M. Robinson, president of Bethany Theological Seminary. The cost of the improvements totaled $136,585. Later more than ten thousand additional dollars was spent on a parking lot.

Despite a debt of $64,500, Memorial Church burned its mortgage within seven years—at a ceremony on Sunday, September 21, 1958. Since 1958 was the 250th Anniversary of the founding of the Church of the Brethren, commemoration of this event got equal billing with the mortgage-burning service. In the past decade some major maintenance work has been necessary, and a twenty-thousand-dollar Mohler organ was installed.

Pastors since Wilson left in 1951 have been Roy S. Forney (1951–

1960), Floyd H. Mitchell (1961–1971), Gale D. Crumrine (1971–1978), Ronald F. Madeira, interim (1978–79), and Kenneth O. Holderread (1979–   ).

ALTOONA, FIRST CHURCH (1874)
MEMBERSHIP: 301

The nucleus of a Brethren group in Altoona first appeared sometime in 1870 or 1871 through the preaching activity of Graybill Myers, who belonged to what was then called the Duncansville congregation. At first services were held in some of the homes. Later a hall on Sixth Avenue was rented for a brief period, after which came use of a Methodist Chapel closer to center-city on the same street. Once a month the worshipers met, and by 1872 their membership numbered a dozen or so.

Then in early December 1872 Elder Myers, in a letter to the *Pilgrim*, proposed that the District help finance a church in Altoona as part of its home missionary thrust. He wrote, "I think there is more prospect of success in town . . . if we had a house of worship."[6] Foresightedly, he went on to observe, "It is evident Altoona will be . . . the main place for manufacturing stock for the [rail] roads, so it will require thousands of hands." His suggested that every member of the District be assessed fifty cents for the project.

District Meeting at Clover Creek the following spring endorsed the idea, thus paving the way for one of the first city congregations to be formed in the Brotherhood since that of Philadelphia First Church in 1813. A local building committee, composed of Samuel

Cox, Conrad Imler, and Robert McFarlin, looked at several possible sites. The trio finally recommended purchase of the Methodist Chapel itself, which had since been put up for sale for fifteen hundred dollars.

The Chapel, actually an unremodeled dwelling place about three-fourths of a mile from the train station, disappointed *Pilgrim* publisher Henry Brumbaugh. He thought the batten-sided meeting-house (16' x 46') to be "cheaply built" and "not the kind to be in Altoona, especially when backed by the district."

Extensively renovated, the Chapel became a permanent church home on June 21, 1874, dedication day. Two weeks later the first Sunday School organized (twelve males and twenty-nine females). Soon bimonthly services gave way to weekly ones. Not till Saturday evening, September 27, 1877, however, did Altoona Brethren cele-brate love feast in their own place.

And not until 1879 did they liquidate the mortgage on their sanctuary. A few congregations reneged on their assessments, the depression of the mid-seventies working a hardship on the people. But the officers of District Conference and a number of congrega-tions honored the debt and pressed for its payment. Few area Brethren, however, matched the sacrificial gift of Woodbury's Jacob Miller. A furniture-maker and church elder, he personally contrib-uted $310, every cent of it borrowed, to the Altoona mission.

For eight years after the Chapel was bought, oversight of the Altoona Brethren, by common consent, rested in the hands of the Duncansville congregation. James A. Sell, Duncansville's bishop, handled the preaching duties, assisted by his brothers, David and Brice, and Graybill Myers.

Beginning June 1, 1881, quarterly council meetings were estab-lished. This was the first step toward the goal of autonomous status openly advocated by some of the members. Finally, on July 4, 1882, Altoona became a separate congregation, its bounds marked by the city limits. There were thirty-six charter members, and James Sell was elected bishop.

By this time the little corner church had become too small for the steadily growing membership. Moreover, serious structural defects, as Henry Brumbaugh feared, had developed. Most members recog-nized the need for larger quarters but, remembering recent finan-cial struggles to pay off the old Chapel, were reluctant to push ahead. Nevertheless, on January 7, 1882, a special council meeting was called to consider building. Only nine members attended; seven voted to go ahead with plans, two voted against such a move. This was hardly a mandate, but during the summer of 1883 work began on a projected $3,300 building at the original old-Chapel location, Sixth Avenue and Fifth Street.

On February 14, 1884, James Quinter, president of the then Brethren's Normal College in Huntingdon and an editor of the *Gospel Messenger,* led in the dedication of the uncompleted structure. The day was wet and unpleasant, but attendance was good. The new building, frame and two-stories high, with the "audience room" on the second floor, was more to Henry Brumbaugh's liking. He noted in his diary that it was a "good and well arranged house."

But once again lack of funds plagued the Brethren of Altoona, then a city of twenty-five thousand. To meet the emergency, Elder Sell canvassed the District and raised about a thousand dollars. While the new church was still under construction, Joseph W. Wilt moved from Warriors Mark and became an Altoonan. He became active at once in the affairs of the congregation and worked tirelessly to help lift the debt. No less idle were the women of the church. The Sisters' Sewing Society, organized on July 21, 1885 (probably the first of its kind in the Brotherhood), volunteered to be responsible for part of the indebtedness. At last, with spring 1889, the ledger was wiped clean.

That summer, council meeting authorized constructing a baptistry in the back yard of the church. Seven years later permission was given to install an inside one. Already—since April 1892—there was an organ in the Sunday School room. District Conference took a dim view of this innovation, advising that "the object of so much trouble be removed from the School." But the congregation sided with the Sunday School officials, who assumed full responsibility for setting in the organ.

Through the years leading up to the transition to a regular pastor, the pulpit was filled by Joseph Wilt, Daniel Brallier, Benjamin Ranck, and others. By century's turn the membership had grown from a handful to upwards of two hundred. As a result, beginning in the mid-1890s, there was persistent talk of the need for a salaried ministry. The *Gospel Messenger* was currently urging this system upon the Brotherhood, especially in the case of city churches. There, argued its editors, untrained lay preachers were at a grave disadvantage. The issue at Altoona was not finally resolved until July 3, 1904, when a special council gave a call to Walter S. Long, a former District pastor then at Germantown.

The spiritual leadership of the new pastor widened the influence of the congregation in the city. Growth continued. Before long the need for additional space became all too evident. In January 1906 council created the "Church Extension Fund," to be cared for by a three-person committee: the pastor, Mrs. Harriet Kipple, and Ardie Wilt, son of Joseph, and a future trustee of Juniata College. They were "to make plans and carry on the purpose of the fund."

There was no concerted solicitation campaign and thus progress was slow. By June 1915 the amount in the fund was less than nine hundred dollars. By this time, however, the desire for a new church was greatly increased among the members. The recent erection of a forty-one-hundred-dollar mission at Twenty-Eighth Street had awakened enthusiasm for better facilities at First Church. On October 1, 1915, in council session, the members called for a committee to secure plans and get an estimate on costs. The committee reported back on January 7, its recommendation to proceed at once to build carrying by an almost unanimous vote. The new church building was to go up at the old Chapel location.

It was further decided to purchase an additional twenty-five feet on Sixth Avenue for four thousand dollars, thus increasing the building lot to 72' x 120'. The old church would, of course, have to be razed, the salvaging of which was contracted out for a return of one thousand dollars. The last service in it was held on May 14, 1916.

During the construction period the congregation had use of the nearby German Evangelical Church. The World War delayed progress somewhat, but on November 17, 1917, the completed structure was dedicated. First Church Brethren now had a fine brick and stone edifice, housing an auditorium seating five hundred, seventeen individual classrooms, and a large up-to-date parsonage. The total cost—for lot, parsonage, and church—came to $56,309.65.

This time the Altoona Brethren avoided financial embarrassment. The willingness on the part of the three hundred members to meet the challenge head-on was manifested by the fact that, although no large gifts were received, almost the entire membership faithfully made monthly contributions. Less than seven years after occupancy, on First Church's Golden Jubilee Anniversary (July 6, 1924), the congregation took part in an impressive mortgage-burning ceremony.

Meanwhile, First Church, largely through the efforts of Joseph Wilt, had mothered four mission points in the Altoona area. All four eventually became independent congregations. First came Bellwood (1894), then Juniata Park (1905), Twenty-Eighth Street (1910), and Riggles Gap (1914).

Walter Long, as First Church's earliest full-time salaried pastor, gave forty years to the Altoona flock, retiring in November 1944. Few ministers in the Brotherhood have given more years to one congregation. During Long's pastorate the membership tripled. The church offerings had almost trebled, from five thousand dollars a year to fourteen thousand. Long bequeathed all his real estate and personal property to First Church, his home at 308 Wordsworth Avenue being still its parsonage.

Succeeding pastors have been Herman B. Heisey (1944–1948), Stephen G. Margush (1949–1962), vacant (1962–1964), Donald H. Fornwalt (1964–1967), James T. Costanzo (1967–68), Vincent Porte (1968–1970), and Guy S. Fern (1970–1980).

First Church has undergone no major remodeling programs in the years since its erection, but, of course, it has been diligently maintained.

HUNTINGDON (1878)
MEMBERSHIP: 346

As Dr. Donald F. Durnbaugh once wrote, "an unusual convergence of religious, educational, and publishing enterprises marks the beginning of the Church of the Brethren in Huntingdon. Thus the first Brethren place of worship was located in a publishing plant, whence it moved four years later to a college chapel, remaining there over thirty years until a separate church edifice, the Stone Church, was erected."[7]

The first Brethren to put down roots in Huntingdon was Dr. Andrew B. Brumbaugh, who began practicing medicine there in April 1866. In June he was joined by his wife and two children—from their home in nearby Marklesburg. Some months later, David and Jane Deniser from Germany Valley became fellow-residents. The doctor then importuned his cousins, Henry and John Brumbaugh, to move their young church paper, *The Pilgrim,* from Marklesburg to Huntingdon in 1873. With them came Emma A. Miller and Wealthy A. Clark, two publishing assistants. In the spring of 1874 there entered the *Pilgrim* office Eleanor J. VanDyke, later to become the wife of John Brumbaugh. Now Huntingdon, a county seat on the main line of the Pennsylvania Railroad with a population in the early 1870s of some three thousand souls, had nine members of the church.

This little band held prayer meetings in each other's homes but attended worship at James Creek, home church for the Brumbaughs, some eleven miles south of Huntingdon. This was a great inconvenience, of course, and soon the Huntingdonians began talking of a place of worship in the borough. Said Henry Brumbaugh, "We felt that there was work for the Master right here for us to do, and that we must make a way for it."[8]

Promised one hundred dollars from the District, they began fixing up a first-floor room in the *Pilgrim* building at the corner of Washington and Fourteenth streets. It took almost two years, and then all was ready for the dedication service on Sunday, June 20, 1875. Peter S. Myers, a self-taught, well-educated man who later was in the vanguard of those establishing the Church of the Brethren in California, and Archibald VanDyke, father of Eleanor, preached that day from a pulpit donated by Dr. Brumbaugh. The 1925 history notes that this use of a pulpit was a "radical" innovation, since the long table, behind which sat all the ministers in attendance, was the accepted rostrum. From the start, therefore, the Huntingdon church had within Brethren circles the reputation of being dangerously progressive.

The next year, 1876, marked a milestone in the life of the Huntingdon Brethren. First, the Huntingdon Normal College, later renamed Juniata College, opened that April under Jacob Zuck's tutelage. Then in October James Quinter, publisher and revered Brotherhood leader, moved to Huntingdon after the Brumbaughs and he merged their papers. He at once became the recognized spiritual leader of the infant group.

The Normal made steady growth, and the membership of the Huntingdon group increased correspondingly. Many Normal students were baptized into the congregation, sometimes at the old canal, sometimes at the Juniata River. Before long the James Creek congregation decided that the Huntingdon fellowship should stand on its own feet, a step that was taken by the daughter church on September 28, 1878. James Quinter became their elder, joined in the ministerial ranks by Henry Brumbaugh and William J. Swigart, a Normal School teacher and trustee. The membership then stood at thirty-six. Huntingdon thus became, like Altoona, one of the very earliest town churches in the Brotherhood.

Soon after organizing, the Huntingdon Brethren followed the Normal when it relocated in the spring of 1879 on the present campus. Founders Hall was occupied by the school in April, and its spacious chapel, which could accommodate five hundred persons, became the new home of the congregation. The ample space of the church-chapel was in sharp contrast to the relatively cramped quarters of the 16' x 65' room in the *Pilgrim* building.

For thirty-one years the College chapel was home for the Huntingdon Brethren. In that time over 750 persons received baptism, not a few of them students, now immersed in the outdoor baptismal pool on campus instead of at riverside. Thirty or so were called to the ministry by the church, many of whom went out as foreign missionaries.

But by 1905, said the *Gospel Messenger,* a number of people wanted a "real church building," not a college chapel. In the words of H. B. Brumbaugh, although "the chapel had proved to be a Bethel of consecration and . . . a place of sacredness because of the sweet memories that clustered in and around the place, yet it was a house of mixed services. . . . Therefore, a large number of our people had an anxious yearning and a longing desire to have erected a house or temple that could be wholly set apart and dedicated to the Lord's service."[9]

A building committee was formed, with I. Harvey Brumbaugh, then acting president of the College, as chairman. The architectural idea for Stone Church would come from his wife, Amelia, née Johnson. It was patterned after a countryside chapel she had once seen in England. The architect for Stone Church (45' x 93') was Edward Tilton, the man who designed many of Andrew Carnegie's public libraries and who had drawn the plans for Juniata's Carnegie Library and Huntingdon's J. C. Blair Hospital. Built on a lower-campus lot leased to the congregation for ninety-nine years, Stone Church was erected at a cost of $19,312.75 and dedicated on December 11, 1910. The main dedication day speaker was Dr. Martin G. Brumbaugh, then superintendent of Philadelphia schools and president of Juniata College. Offerings and pledges on that Sunday amounted to more than $7,900 dollars, which together with monies already in hand, virtually cleared the indebtedness on the building.

Since 1910 other noteworthy events in the history of Stone Church have been entertaining Annual Conference in 1944, the erection of a Christian education wing in 1956, which culminated years of planning, and a series of major renovations between 1970 and 1980 amounting to over $90,000.

Down through the early decades, the Huntingdon church enjoyed the services of a distinguished lot of free ministers, many of whom were administrators and professors at the College. In May 1905 John B. Brumbaugh, one of the College's founders, was appointed pastor, part-time at first, then full time. He retired in 1914, and since then the pastoral ministry has been filled by J. Harry Cassady (1914–1918), Galen K. Walker (1920–1926), Foster B. Statler (1926–1937), George L. Detweiler (1937–1941), Tobias F. Henry (1941–1947), John C. Middlekauff (1947–1959), Stewart B. Kauffman (1960–1970), and Richard L. Landrum (1971–1980).

EVERETT (1891)
MEMBERSHIP: 684

Everett, located at the intersection of Routes 30 and 26, originally fell within an undivided area cared for jointly by the Yellow Creek and the Snake Spring Valley congregations. In 1887 a church was built at Fairview, five miles east of Everett, but until the early 1890s that was the closest meetinghouse to the town itself.

Then on April 1, 1891, Elder David S. Clapper and his family moved to a farm near the north borough line. There were almost a score of Brethren already living in the immediate vicinity when the Clappers made their appearance. Very soon these people expressed a desire for worship services. Elder Clapper, then in his mid-forties, placed seats on his barn floor and in May began to hold preaching services every two weeks. He also spent much time in pastoral work. In the fall, at harvest time, the barn was vacated and the seats moved across the road to a grove. When cold weather set in, the worshipers made use of an unoccupied church close by.

By then thirty-two members had been added to the Everett group. The next summer a dwelling was purchased, moved to a place near the Clapper farm, repaired (making a room 16' x 24'), and furnished—all for ninety dollars. Here a Sunday School organized and here, in late October, the first love feast was held, Conrad G. Lint of Meyersdale officiating.

Everett became an official congregation on December 16, 1893, electing George W. Brumbaugh of Clover Creek, a farmer and blacksmith who preached in both German and English, as elder. By 1895 forty-two members were added to the original membership. Upon the accidental death of Alfred T. Simmons, called to the ministry at Everett in 1894, and David Clapper's removal to Kansas, the burden of leadership after 1895 rested largely upon John S. Hershberger, a local businessman and later a Bedford County judge. By this time Everett had a population of two thousand and was building up rapidly.

There was need for a more commodious place of worship, and in 1895 a building committee recommended the corner of Second and Water streets as the site for a new church. The location was accepted, and on it was reared a brick-veneered building (35′ x 35′ x 14′) with a projecting vestibule (7′ x 10′) at a cost of $2,244. The brick for the casing was made by John S. Hershberger and his brother James, a business partner. The church, seating 350 people, was dedicated on October 6, 1895. By then sixteen hundred dollars had already been raised.

According to the *Gospel Messenger,* the new church had "ample hitching room and large shade trees."[10] It was the first Brethren church to be built in a Bedford County town, the paper emphasized.

From the beginning to 1912 the free ministry provided pastoral care. During these years the growth of the church continued, so that by 1913 it was necessary to enlarge the 1895 building. In that year it gained a rear addition (35′ x 18′), a north-side annex (43′ x 13′), and a 10′ x 10′ entrance tower on the north front corner.

These additions provided ten class rooms for Sunday School, the rooms on the north side able to be opened into the sanctuary when needed, which became a common architectural device for the Brethren in those years. The seating capacity did not change, although the new building included an inside baptistry, replacing the backyard pool.

The remodeled church sufficed until 1945, when the need for additional Sunday School space and a larger sanctuary became so urgent that the church authorized a building committee to study the situation. In the fall of 1949, Forrest U. Groff, the General Board architect, began to draw preliminary plans. Final plans were not approved until August 1950. They provided for wholesale overhauling of the existing structure and the addition of a large educational wing on the back. The cost came to $95,316.14.

Dedication of the enlarged church was preceded by a week-long series of meetings, the preaching done by guest ministers. The dedicatory message itself came from Rufus D. Bowman, president of Bethany Theological Seminary, on Sunday afternoon, February 3, 1952.

Then on Friday morning, August 9, 1968, catastrophe struck the church's administration building, which was located several hundred feet to the rear of the main church structure. The annex, which housed the church office, the pastor's study, and some Sunday School rooms, was destroyed by fire. A $115,000 education wing was built in 1970 to absorb these facilities.

Everett's full-time pastors have been Mahlon J. Weaver (1912–1918), Ira C. Holsopple (1918–1926), Edgar M. Detwiler (1926–1948), Stewart B. Kauffman (1948–1953), Robert G. Mock (1953–1958), Fred M. Bowman (1958–1962), J. Earl Hostetter (1962–1973), Philip K. Bradley (1974–1977), and David S. Young (1978–1980). Mrs. Mary Lou Hall followed in a pastoral role on an interim arrangement.

TYRONE (1894)
MEMBERSHIP: 199

Tyrone the town had its beginning in 1850 when its first building went up. It grew to 125 by 1864 (the year Henry R. Holsinger moved there), a by-product of the Pennsylvania Railroad. Located about seventeen miles northeast of Altoona on Route 220, the town originally fell within the bounds of the Warriors Mark (Spring Mount) congregation.

Tyrone was the birthplace of the Brotherhood's first weekly paper, the *Christian Family Companion*. The publication began in May 1864, with the future firebrand, Henry R. Holsinger, as editor and

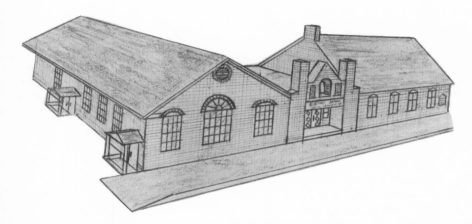

publisher. Two years later Clover Creek called him to the ministry. Joining him as associate editor in April 1866 came James A. Sell, licensed the previous October in his nineteenth year. The Warriors Mark congregation, widely scattered, was in decline, and the presence of these young ministerial recruits, says the 1925 history, "gave a new lease to the life of the church." James Sell left the editorial staff in 1868 and was replaced by Joseph W. Beer, himself licensed, who a dozen years later followed his employer into the Progressive Brethren fold. Holsinger once praised Beer as being "one of the most logical and forcible public speakers of my acquaintance."

According to the *Christian Family Companion,* Holsinger rented and fitted up a hall in Tyrone for public meetings in 1869. The first service took place on June 6, James Sell and Isaac Myers of Union County doing the preaching. A Sunday School, organized the year before, also met in the hall. The Tyrone mission and Sunday School, however, were discontinued in 1871 when Holsinger moved his publishing business to Meyersdale.

Tyrone was without preaching services until the mid-1880s, when Samuel S. Gray, an ex-Methodist from Centre County, who married a Brethren and was licensed at Warriors Mark in 1877, began to preach on occasional Sundays in the home of Harvey N. Stewart. Then in 1890 the little band moved to a second-floor room in Goheen's Hall, corner of Columbia Avenue and Twenty-First Street. Samuel Gray found it difficult to keep after the work and in 1892 turned it over to John B. Brumbaugh of Huntingdon. The College founder and Bible professor looked after the mission, unpaid, for the next two years. Then at his suggestion the District Mission Board stepped in and assumed charge in February 1894. Three months later the Tyrone members, numbering nineteen, organized as a congregation. They chose no bishop since they remained under the care of the Mission Board.

Through the Board's guidance and financial aid, the Tyrone group had already purchased, for three hundred dollars, a corner lot at Adams Avenue and Eighteenth Street. There they erected a brick church (32' x 47') without a basement, which cost $1,632.89. It was dedicated May 5, 1895, with a debt of only $547.21. The speaker was Juniata College's up-and-coming president, Martin G. Brumbaugh, on his way to the governor's chair.

Ministers from Huntingdon supplied the pulpit until April 1897 when Walter S. Long, who had been the first head of the Brethren home for the aging at Shirleysburg, took pastoral charge, as the District's earliest salaried clergyman ($300 a year). He served till 1900 and was succeeded by Theodore R. Coffman for the next five years. Then followed Charles O. Beery (1905–1913) (during whose pastorate the congregation obtained a parsonage adjacent to the church), David P. Hoover (1913–1917), and William M. Ulrich (1918–1921).

There was no resident pastor for the next two years, at which time James W. Fyock took up the work. During his four-year pastorate the church was enlarged in 1925, providing more classroom space. Then came John N. Snyder's ministry (1927–1943), during which the basement was dug out to give more Sunday School room. The church made great gains in those sixteen years, more than two hundred being added to the membership. The work progressed so well that in 1928 the congregation at last became self-supporting. For a time during the Depression Tyrone sponsored a Sunday School at the Mountain Orchard schoolhouse in Decker Hollow.

John Snyder died in December 1943, and the church was without a resident pastor until Bryon Reihart's coming in October of the next year. His was a three-year pastorate, after which D. Luke Bowser, a Bethany Seminary student, filled the pulpit on an interim basis for several months. At this time—in January—the recently remodeled basement was dedicated.

In September 1948 Mahlon J. Weaver, approaching retirement age, resigned his pastorate at Bellwood to accept Tyrone's call. He pastored there three years before retiring.

The pastorate of Wilmer R. Kensinger (1952–1958), Weaver's successor, saw the erection of a new church building. It went up directly back of the old one, and on August 18, 1957, the 250-

member congregation heard their moderator, Dr. Tobias F. Henry of Juniata College, preach the dedication sermon. Kensinger's unexpected death in early summer 1958 left the church pastorless for several months, supply ministers from Juniata College filling the pulpit void. During this interval the parsonage was renovated and put in order for the next pastor.

That was Herman L. Baliles (1958–1965), under whom the mortgage note on the church was burned in a special ceremony held August 15, 1965. That September, Baliles moved on, to be succeeded by Ralph Z. Ebersole, a student at Juniata College, who served till early 1969. (Until 1968 he also was half-time manager of Camp Blue Diamond.) In May 1966 the Ebersoles, Ralph and Betty, moved into a new brick parsonage on Hamilton Street, near the hospital. The large lot for the $24,000 home was donated by Mr. and Mrs. Ivan Ray and Mrs. Mary Albright.

When Ralph Ebersole took over as executive director of Camp Blue Diamond in 1969, he was followed by Stephen G. Margush, who had pastored several Middle District churches. Margush stayed till 1975, and after a year's lapse, Ralph Ebersole returned to his former charge, which in 1976 became a yoked parish with Spring Mount.

BELLWOOD (1897)
MEMBERSHIP: 154

Bellwood, located five miles north of Altoona off Route 220 on the way to Tyrone, originally, like Tyrone, came under the ministerial mantle of the Warriors Mark congregation. Occasional services were held in the community's schoolhouse beginning sometime in the 1880s. Bellwood, Antis Township's largest community, had a population at that time of slightly over two thousand. Among the visiting preachers from the Warriors Mark church were two ex-Methodists, Samuel Gray and Samuel Cox, and Conrad Imler, a local resident. Two well-known ministers outside the congregation, Graybill Myers and James Sell, also brought the Word.

Not until 1894, however, was a real effort made to establish a mission. At that time five members lived in the vicinity. The person who took the initiative was Joseph W. Wilt, recently ordained elder of Altoona's First Church, who rented the first floor of a one-time store and began preaching in March. A month later a Sunday School, the attendance of which averaged eighty-one for 1894, came into existence. This Sunday afternoon school grew rapidly, crowding the small downstairs quarters. An adjoining storage room was

taken over and the partition removed. But this space was soon outgrown, necessitating a move upstairs.

Within a year the membership numbered twenty-two, and the thought of building a church was much on people's minds. The decision to do so came at a special meeting on June 10, 1895, at which time Joseph Wilt, Charles L. Douglas, and Harry Laird became a Building Committee to see the project through. Pastor Wilt carried the matter to his home church and through it petitioned the upcoming District Conference in May for approval and financial help. District sanction came without a hitch, and in December Bellwood had a church. The brick building (40′ × 56′), which cost two thousand dollars, was dedicated by Juniata College's William J. Swigart.

On April 11, 1897, the sixty-three members officially organized as a congregation. Joseph Wilt remained as elder-pastor. Within another few years the building debt was entirely erased.

In 1899 Wilt, a fifty-three-year-old businessman who had built up the membership from five to seventy-three, resigned and the District took over. It appointed Josiah B. Brumbaugh, a former schoolteacher who had just moved to Bellwood from near Henrietta, to oversee the church and do the preaching for two hundred dollars a year. He was pastor eleven years and was followed by John B. Miller (1910–1912), who commuted each week from a farm near New Paris. After him came Charles O. Beery, also pastor at Tyrone, for one year. From 1913 to 1920 Daniel B. Maddocks, a foreman in the Altoona car shops, provided pastoral care.

Two revivals held by David P. Hoover, the minister at Tyrone, during 1914 and 1915 resulted in eighteen accessions, raising the membership to ninety-five. At the same time there were 105 on the Sunday School rolls. Space was at a premium, and so the congregation promptly assented to an extensive remodeling project. Plans were finalized in June 1915, and on October 3, rededication Sunday, the congregation met in a remodeled house with three added classrooms, a new concrete baptistry, a choir platform, recarpeted floors, a kitchen, a new heater, electric lights, redecorated walls, and a new roof—all done at a cost of $1,600. Pledges and cash raised at the rededication service covered the entire debt.

By 1920 Bellwood was strong enough to support a resident pastor. That year it purchased a parsonage for $2,500, and issued a call to Virgil C. Holsinger, a former high school principal whose home was near Williamsburg. The Holsingers took the Bellwood pastorate on partial support, with Virgil given the privilege of teaching or continuing his education at Juniata.

Holsinger resigned in June 1924 to teach in the Williamsburg schools. The pulpit was supplied until October 1, when Galen Blough, a student at Juniata, became the second resident pastor. Three years later, Blough's charge had become totally self-supporting, no longer in need of partial District support.

In subsequent years major building projects have been accomplished in the church plant. A basement went under the sanctuary in 1925 and the church entrance was altered. New classrooms became available in 1933, bringing an end to curtained-off areas in the basement. In 1950 three lots were purchased at the rear of the church for possible future expansion and parking facilities. Elgin's Arthur L. Dean provided architectural plans for the addition of an educational unit in 1958. This work was completed in 1960. Then in January 1962 the members voted to go ahead and completely overhaul the sanctuary, which had been a part of the original Dean drawings.

More recently, in December 1965, the congregation acted to purchase the Carlin property, adjacent to the church lot, made available when the John Carlin family, heretofore a bulwark at the Bellwood church, moved to Whittier, California. This property, acquired for $3,800, was then razed, part of the grounds landscaped, and the rest converted into parking space. In 1968 the church bought a parsonage, an older house completely renovated inside, at the corner of Eighth and Tuckahoe streets.

Since Galen Blough's time, the ministers at Bellwood have been: H. Paul Cox (1930–1940), the first local member to be ordained, O. Clyde Bush (1940–1945), D. Luke Bowser (1945–1947), Mahlon J. Weaver (1947–1950), Eugene E. Ankeny (1950–1953), Arthur L.

Croyle (1953–1955), Homer F. Hoover (1955–56), Richard A. Grumbling (1956–1964), Oscar R. Fike (1964–1969), John M. Foster (1969–1973), Donald F. Hoover, Jr. (1973–1976), and Robert D. Hoover (1976–   ).

ALTOONA, JUNIATA (1907)
MEMBERSHIP: 50

As we have seen in the case of several present-day churches, Joseph W. Wilt of Altoona was an active home missionary in Middle District in the late 1800s and early 1900s. He is credited with starting

five missions, all of which became self-supporting congregations. One of them was Juniata Park.

When First Church, Altoona decided to call a full-time pastor in 1904, Joseph Wilt, their spiritual leader at the time, was freed to give his attention to starting a mission at Juniata, an industrial suburban section of the city. Fourteen members lived in the city's outskirts, and in 1905 they built a church at the corner of Ninth Avenue and Third Street. It was brick (48' × 49'), with a crenelated six-sided tower entrance, and cost $4,766. It took less than nine years to amortize the heavy mortgage, with District help.

Formal organization came on April 26, 1907, outsiders Henry B. Brumbaugh and James A. Sell overseeing the proceedings. The fifty-nine members adopted the name "Juniata Park" and made Pastor Wilt their bishop. (Since the late 1960s the congregation goes by the shortened name of Juniata.)

In 1914 Elder Wilt began preaching every two weeks at Riggles

Gap, a village about seven miles northeast of Juniata. This led to the erection of a church there in 1917. From that date to 1949 Riggles Gap and Juniata Park constituted a joint congregation.

On July 1, 1919, Charles O. Beery became the twin congregation's first supported pastor. He continued in this capacity until 1925 when the Martinsburg church called him to the pastorate there. Others that ministered to the Juniata Park-Riggles Gap group until 1949 were Ira Holsopple, Earl C. Bowser, Roy K. Miller, Joseph J. Shaffer, Purcel R. Bratton, Martin C. Banks, Wayne Carr, and Lowell Martin.

After the 1949 division, Howard L. Alley, a returned missionary, served for a few years and was followed by Roy C. Myers (1956–1967). During Myers's ministry, after the death of George Ross at Riggles Gap in 1960, there was another pastoral jointure between the two congregations until 1964. The Myers years also witnessed a major construction effort—a $60,000 education wing, completed in the spring of 1966. The congregation had to struggle to pay back a $30,000 loan from the General Brotherhood Board, but it persevered and in 1972 celebrated with a mortgage-burning service.

A minor schism occurred in 1975 when several members withdrew from the congregation to follow Richard Brown, a lay non-Brethren fundamentalist from Claysburg who worshiped at Juniata and was interested in starting an independent church. But the loyal members gracefully survived the crisis.

Post-Myers pastors have included Charles H. Heltzel (1967–68), Ivan B. Walker (1968–1970), Merle H. Hoover (1970–1972), Harold F. Horst (1972–1974), and G. Robert Wharton (1975–   ).

BURNHAM (1908)
MEMBERSHIP: 147

A woman was behind the first Brethren activity in Burnham, the same woman who had earlier started things up in Bannerville—Maggie Shellenberger. The pattern was the same, first a Sunday School, then preaching. In the fall of 1907, while visiting her daughter, Mrs. Ida Wilson, the sixty-five-year-old widow saw in Burnham borough, adjacent to Lewistown, "the need for religious instruction among the lowly of the place." Burnham was then part of the Lewistown branch of the Dry Valley congregation (Maitland). It was also Mifflin County's industrial center, boasting two large iron and steel companies.

Burnham's Brethren Sunday School began in the home of David Goss, with six people present. Next Sunday, fifteen showed up. About two months later the school moved to a private two-room

house on Pine Top. Soon there was a demand for preaching, which
was provided by John B. Shellenberger, a merchant-preacher and
son of Maggie. In January and February 1908 John Shellenberger
conducted special services over a six-week period, meeting once in
the Pine Top house, and then, because the attendance was so large,
in the home of John A. Filson, Sunday School superintendent, the
rest of the time.

The need for a church house now became apparent. The matter
was taken up by the Dry Run church, which gave its okay, stipulating
only that costs not exceed two thousand dollars. To a building
committee were named John Filson, John Breininger, and John
Shellenberger. The new church (35' x 50'), located at 640 Freedom
Avenue, was frame, its basement and main floor fitted out with
classrooms. Dedication day was December 20, 1908.

There was steady growth in the years that followed, and it soon
seemed wise for the mother church to grant Burnham its independence, which in 1916 had been done for Lewistown. And so on
March 26, 1921, Burnham gained its freedom. At the time, it had
seventy members, while Dry Run was left with a membership of
eighty. John Shellenberger continued on as pastor of the newly-
organized congregation.

The 1950s were a decade of physical expansion. In 1951 the
congregation purchased a parsonage at 803 Freedom Avenue.
Three years later a building committee was formed to study the
feasibility of adding a wing to the church. But the committee found
this to be inadvisable, and so plans were formulated for greater
things.

On September 11, 1954, church council voted to purchase a

property several blocks away, on Freedom Avenue, which included a house and a building site. The purchase price was $8,300. It was decided at this time to sell the old parsonage and make the pastor's home the house next to the site of the projected new church. At the same meeting the congregation further acted to hire the Wells Company, a professional fund-raising organization. Forrest Groff, then the Brotherhood's architect, prepared preliminary drawings, which were presented to council on March 17, 1956, and tentatively approved. In 1957 Burnham incorporated, a move made necessary in order to borrow the money for building.

In the fall of 1958 Pastor Clarence Quay sent out a church letter stating: "There is $28,479.40 in the Building Fund. The Building Committee will request council for permission to build when the fund reaches $30,000. December 20th will be the 50th anniversary of the dedication of our present building. With a little extra effort we can reach the $30,000.00 goal by December 20th. This would put special significance in our anniversary letter."

A second pastoral letter on January 8, 1959, informed Burnham members and friends that the $30,000 goal had indeed been reached by the target date. An important council meeting, therefore, was called for January 25, 1959. At this gathering came permission to build.

Ground-breaking ceremonies at 541 Freedom Avenue took place on April 12, 1959. The cornerstone was laid on July 26, at which time Calvert N. Ellis, president of Juniata College, spoke. The preacher for the dedication service on December 27 was William M. Beahm, dean of Bethany Theological Seminary. The total cost of construction and furnishings came to $115,102.50.

In 1967 the Burnham church acquired a two-acre recreational site from the Standard Steel Company. The members erected on it a picnic pavilion that seats one hundred.

The pastoral roster at Burnham over the years reads as follows: John B. Shellenberger (1908–1926), H. William Hanawalt (1927), Wilbur C. Swigart (1928–1942), Carl N. Lauer (1943–1945), Eli S. Keeny (1946–1950), Wilbur C. Swigart (1951), J. Donald Plank (1952–1957), Clarence E. Quay (1958–1962), Carmon E. Sollenberger (1962–1968), J. Donald Plank (1968–1977), and Norman R. Cain (1978–   ).

HOLLIDAYSBURG (1908)
MEMBERSHIP: 259

Before 1872, according to the *Pilgrim,* no Brethren had ever preached a sermon in Hollidaysburg, which in 1846 had become the

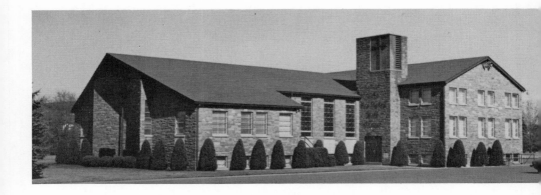

seat of justice for Blair County. Henry R. Holsinger was doing some preaching in a schoolhouse there that fall. But very few Brethren lived in the town, which had grown prosperous with the advent of the Pennsylvania canal and railroad system, until after the turn of the century. Nothing permanent, however, grew out of the 1872 school services.

That would not happen until April 26, 1908, when a half dozen town residents began a Brethren Sunday School in Stultz Hall, corner of Mulberry and Wayne streets. Interest was strong, the attendance soon averaging over twenty-five. From this beginning came regular preaching, starting with the service conducted by James Sell on September 13. By next spring average attendance for the sermon was close to one hundred.

The Carson Valley congregation quickly moved, with District sanction, to establish a separate mission point at Hollidaysburg. This was done on August 29, 1909, with thirteen charter members. Among them was William N. Hoover, a schoolteacher-turned-railroader, who became the group's first elder and pastor. That fall the place of meeting was moved to the Wolf Building, corner of Allegheny and Front streets, and the time of services was switched from afternoon to morning.

Reported the *Gospel Messenger* about post-1909 progress, "new quarters had to be secured several times, so steady was the mission's growth." A building fund came into existence at once, prompted by James Sell, who would raise $1,200 on his own outside the congregation. The 1925 history tells how he turned over four pennies as seed money for the fund. This was to honor a gift from a certain woman, Emily R. Stiffler, donated by her years before toward a building in town. Though poor, she had written for many of the church papers, and her gift consisted of two postage stamps.

On April 14, 1911, the congregation, which was self-supporting from the onset, paid $650 dollars for a lot on Pine Street. Some three years later came the church building (36' x 50'), brick-cased, with an inside baptistry, an annex (12' x 25'), and a roomy basement, said the *Gospel Messenger,* that could be converted into Sunday School rooms. The total cost, including the lot and furnishings, amounted to $5,250. J. Harry Cassady of Huntingdon, a pastor-evangelist of rising reputation, gave the dedicatory sermon on November 29, 1914. For the occasion James Sell composed a special hymn, which was printed as part of a souvenir booklet. In another three years the congregation was out of debt.

William Hoover continued his free ministry until 1918, when Joseph J. Shaffer, an educator who later became an Altoona principal, was given the pastoral call. He was Hollidaysburg's first full-time pastor and served until 1923, to be followed by Walter C. Sell (1924–1927). During the Sell ministry a lot for a parsonage was purchased in 1924 next to the church. But it was another fourteen years before a dwelling went up on the site.

The immediate post–World War II years were momentous ones for the Hollidaysburg Brethren. In 1948 an expensive Moller pipe organ was installed in the sanctuary. Then at their July business meeting in 1953, the members voted to relocate the church on the outskirts of town, north along Logan Boulevard. Ground-breaking for the new facility took place three years later, and on Sunday, October 26, 1957, worship was held in the old church for the last time. Dedication for the new stone structure, costing about $148,000, occurred on September 14 of the following year. By that time the congregation had, in 1938, built a brick parsonage four blocks from the present church. A decade had not passed before, in 1967, the Hollidaysburg people celebrated with a mortgage-burning ceremony.

After Walter Sell there have been the following pastors: Wilfred N. Stauffer (Juniata student, 1931); Joseph J. Shaffer (six months, 1931); Franklin J. Byer (1933–1935) who was also serving at Williamsburg and then from 1935–1945 was full time at Hollidaysburg; Ralph G. Rarick (1946–1949); Daniel C. Haldeman (1950–1954); Raymond E. Martin (1955–1958); Ivan C. Fetterman (1958–1968); Ronald F. Madeira (1968–1978); and the Spaeths, Harry and Ada, a husband-and-wife team (1978–   ).

ROARING SPRING (1910)
MEMBERSHIP: 669

The Albright sketch in the last chapter mentions how the townspeople of Roaring Spring got a church in 1910. As pointed

out, for some time prior to that year the need for a town church was evident. The paper mills had attracted to the borough a number of Brethren, whose children began attending elsewhere rather than at Albright. A Sisters' Sewing Society, says the *Gospel Messenger,* took the initiative on the matter and with proceeds from their sales of "bonnets, quilts, aprons, comforts, etc.," purchased a plot of ground in 1907 for five hundred dollars. There in 1910 a brick church was built at a cost of nine thousand dollars, its crenelated tower reflecting the trend of that time in Brethren architectural taste. Juniata College's C. C. Ellis delivered the dedicatory sermon on October 30 to the sixty-member congregation. In 1918 the members purchased a parsonage directly behind the church.

By 1927 the Sunday School, its attendance sometimes exceeding four hundred, had outgrown available space. And so the 1910 structure was given a major overhauling that year, at a cost of about $40,000. The rebuilt facility preserved the basic pattern of the original church, but the sanctuary was enlarged by the addition of balconies and choir space, the baptistry was relocated, and a basement fellowship hall was provided.

The pastors who led the congregation in its early period were Orville V. Long, Ross Murphy, Albert G. White, Mahlon J. Weaver, Leonard L. Holsinger, and Arthur C. Miller. James Sell and Orville Long were the earliest elders.

Roaring Spring's membership grew steadily and by the mid-fifties had surpassed the seven hundred mark. In that decade the church was twice substantially remodeled to accommodate the growing number of worshipers—in 1954 and 1958—at a total cost of more than $168,000. In each case, sufficient funds had been pledged beforehand to cover the projected costs. The 1958 overhaul involved erection of a Christian education annex. In 1970 the congregation dedicated a newly acquired and refurbished parsonage across the street from the old one, purchased from George B. Replogle.

The pastorate between the late twenties and the early sixties was filled by Joseph H. Clapper, Simon P. Early, Tobias F. Henry, Wilmer R. Kensinger, Haddon Q. Rhodes, Carl E. Myers (1951–1957), and Berkey E. Knavel (1957–1965). Floyd E. Bantz became pastor in 1965 and served to 1979; in 1980 he was succeeded by William K. Roop.

LEWISTOWN (1916)
MEMBERSHIP: 146

As we learned in chapter 3, a few Brethren families had settled in Mifflin County shortly before the Revolutionary War. In time—about 1800—a congregation was formed, called the Kishacoquillas Valley church, composed of members scattered in parts of Huntingdon, Centre, and Mifflin counties. Sometime later, the date unknown, the congregation changed its name to Lewistown. The Lewistown church embraced all of Mifflin County until September 23, 1865, when it was amicably decided to subdivide the parish into two charges. The western section took the name Spring Run and the eastern retained the name Lewistown, although it was just as often called Dry Valley. Each section already had a meetinghouse, one at Spring Run and one in Dry Valley, both built in 1858.

The 1925 history states: "With the church house around which the religious interest of the Lewistown (country and city) congregation centered for a whole generation only four miles from the city [at what is now Maitland], and with a big field that taxed the ministry to work, the ministers made no effort to preach at any point in Lewistown city until about forty members resided within its limits." However, the *Christian Family Companion* mentions preaching at Town Hall as early as 1868. Nevertheless, nothing substantial was done until about 1890 when a small group began using the Toll Gate schoolhouse for once-a-month services. Dry Valley ministers took turns preaching: William Howe, Samuel J. Swigart, George S. Myers, Andrew Spanogle, John M. Mohler, Albert C. Steinberger, Jacob H. Richard, and Harry A. Spanogle. Then in 1892 a Sunday School got started, conducted every two weeks. Soon the schoolhouse no longer answered the town Brethren's needs.

The prospects in the county seat, with its population over the five thousand mark, looked so promising that the Dry Valley congregation decided in January 1896 to build a church there. The brick building (40' × 60') at 134 Shaw Avenue was available for worship on January 3, 1897, dedicated that day by James A. Sell. Dry Valley had limited the building committee of Andrew Spanogle, Jacob U. Howe, and Samuel Swigart to an expenditure of $2,500. At the time of dedication, the membership had increased to about seventy.

It soon became apparent, says the 1925 history, that city problems and interests were quite different from those of the country. As a result, it was thought best to turn the Lewistown group loose, which was done in March of 1916. By then it was a flourishing congregation of 217 members. Samuel Swigart became their presiding elder. Already, since May 1, 1915, they had a supported pastor in William Kinsey, a Juniata College graduate and son-in-law of William Howe, long a District leader from Dry Valley.

One of the first things the newly organized congregation did was to push a remodeling program. This resulted in six thousand dollars worth of alterations, the general plans for which were worked out by the pastor. His design called for an entrance tower with crenels and eleven classrooms that could be thrown open to the main auditorium. When J. Harry Cassady, Huntingdon's pastor, preached the dedication sermon on December 3, 1916, the congregation raised $1,424.50 that day, leaving a debt of only a thousand dollars.

In 1920, for the price of six thousand dollars, Lewistown purchased a nine-room parsonage at 37 Shaw Avenue, one block from the church.

Its first occupants were the Herman B. Heisey family. The previous year, Heisey had become pastor, succeeding William Kinsey, and over the next six years the membership at Lewistown skyrocketed from two hundred to five hundred.

Despite this phenomenonal growth, nothing was done to the physical plant until the 1940s. In 1943 the church carried out improvements costing more than five thousand dollars. Two years later the congregation decided to enlarge its outgrown facilities. This was done in 1948 at a cost of $20,000. A two-story addition went up on the rear of the existing church. This annex permitted enlargement of the sanctuary and provided two new chapels, one on the main floor and one in the basement, as well as thirteen new classrooms and other conveniences.

The late 1940s and early 1950s witnessed the unfortunate split in the church over the fundamentalist-modernist issue. Harold Snider, the pastor, tried to turn his Shaw Avenue parish into an independent congregation named Calvary Brethren Church. This led to litigation with Middle District, a story told in full detail in chapter 11.

In 1951 the Lewistown dispute was finally settled when the Pennsylvania Supreme Court ruled against the Snider faction and conveyed all real and church property to the original congregation. Soon after this Supreme Court order, the church reorganized, retaining Earle W. Strauser as elder. That fall Niels Esbensen came as pastor to help put the pieces back together.

In 1961 the church was redecorated and recarpeted at a cost of five thousand dollars. Three years later, Lewistown became yoked in pastoral service with Bannerville, an arrangement that still remains. Recently, parts of the church building were again redecorated and extensive repairs made.

Pastors since Heisey's last year (1925) have been Tobias F. Henry (1925–26), Arthur B. Miller (1926–1928), M. Clyde Horst (1928–1935), Herman B. Heisey again (1935–1940), Harold Snider (1940–1951), Niels Esbensen (1951–1953), Clayton H. Gehman (1953–1957), Lee A. Weaver (1958–1961), Kenneth Martin (1961–1966), Ira F. Lydic (1966–1973), and Walter E. Coldren (1974–   ).

WILLIAMSBURG (1917)
MEMBERSHIP: 237

Williamsburg, like Smithfield, is a child of the Fairview congregation. The paper mill town, located on the Frankstown Branch of the Juniata River, was incorporated as a borough in 1898, about the time the Brethren first began to move into its limits.

Soon after the century's turn it became more and more evident that the Brethren there ought to be churched. The idea gained more force when Samuel S. Bottomfield, a friend of the denomination, donated a lot on West Third Street. This generous act brought the issue of building to a head, and in response the Fairview congregation appointed Joseph S. Bechtel, Joseph S. Sollenberger, Emory Brumbaugh, Frank P. Detwiler, and Jacob B. Snowberger as a Building Committee. They supervised the construction of a brick building (44' x 58'), properly towered, that was completed in 1912 for six thousand dollars. Dedication day, February 18, left the congregation nearly debt free, since $1,935 was raised on that occasion, much of it from among members of the parent congregation.

The Williamsburg mission prospered to the extent that in another five years it was ready to strike out on its own. At services on March 9, 1917, its independence was established with William H. Holsinger elected as elder and pastor, the same offices the sometimes farmer-teacher also held at Fairview. His new charge then numbered eighty members. In 1922 M. Clyde Horst became pastor and served two years. His successor was Levi K. Ziegler, for whom the congregation purchased a parsonage on West Third Street at a cost of six thousand dollars, in September 1924.

Ten years later Williamsburg began construction on a Sunday School annex, the plans for which were drawn by Dr. Paul Holsinger. This addition, costing about $9,400, was dedicated in January 1935. Then in the 1960s the congregation outgrew its Sunday School facilities a second time. Six more classrooms were added and the whole sanctuary extensively revamped in 1969, the cost approximating $35,000.

Pastors at Williamsburg since Levi Ziegler have been: Franklin J. Byer (1930–1935), Charles O. Beery (1936–1938), Wilbur H. Neff (1938–1940), Elmer Q. Gleim (1940–1942), Harry H. Nye (1942–1944), Norman Ford (1944–1946), D. Alfred Replogle (1946–1950), Lloyd B. Stauffer (1951–1953), Paul R. Yoder (1953–54), John Ebersole (1954–1958), Paul R. Yoder (1958–59), Glen E. Norris (1959–

60), D. Howard Keiper (1960–1964), E. LeRoy Dick (1964–1972), Ira F. Lydic (1973–1976), vacant (1976–1978), and Lee A. Weaver (1978–   ).

ALTOONA, TWENTY-EIGHTH STREET (1920)
MEMBERSHIP: 177

A trio of First Church ministers—Joseph Wilt, Daniel S. Brallier, Seth Myers—were the most insistent in that congregation, as the 1900s began, about the need for mission work on the south side of Altoona, a fast-growing section. In April 1909 a committee began to look for a suitable location. A year later it recommended the rental of a hall at Eighth Avenue and Twenty-Third Street. The following July a Sunday School organized, meeting every Lord's Day afternoon on the second floor of this building.

The project grew, and in July 1911 First Church instructed the trustees to purchase a lot (50′ x 120′) at the corner of Sixth Avenue and Twenty-Eighth Street. There a brick church rose up at a cost of $4,488, counting the lot. Walter Long preached the dedicatory sermon on June 28, 1914. For the next two years, however, preaching services took place only on Sunday evenings.

Steady growth soon led to a petition for independence. This was granted on April 4, 1919. There were ninety-three charter members, and Daniel B. Maddocks, a car shop foreman, became the first presiding elder. Benjamin F. Waltz came from a charge in Western Pennsylvania as pastor in May 1920. His beginning salary was eighty-five dollars a month. A parsonage next to the church was purchased for $6,500 and paid off in less than four years.

By 1924 there were over two hundred persons enrolled in church and Sunday School. As a result of this growth more room had to be found. Thus in January 1925 a Building Committee assumed the task of planning an educational wing. This annex was completed and dedicated the same year.

The year 1927 brought 122 accessions to the Twenty-Eighth Street church, most by baptism. The congregation now began to think of a new and larger church in the distant future and accordingly set up a building fund.

After a fourteen-year pastorate, Waltz resigned in September 1934. He was followed the following March by Glen E. Norris, a young minister and returned missionary from Sweden. He served until June 1945, to be succeeded by Henry F. Kulp, pastor at Brooklyn, New York, in January 1946. Kulp's stormy ministry, which in 1949 ended with the breakaway of a large part of the congregation, is treated at great length in chapter 11.

After the Kulp schism, Levi K. Ziegler, Regional Secretary, acted as interim pastor to help rally the Twenty-Eighth Street remnant. This arrangement lasted three years, terminating when C. H. Cameron began his full-time labors in the fall of 1952. At that time the church reorganized with sixty-four members.

Within a half-dozen years the Sunday School, especially the Primary department, had outgrown its facilities. A careful inspection of the forty-seven-year-old structure, however, ruled against the advisability of any extensive remodeling program. And so in October 1959 the decision was made to build and make use of the architectural services of Arthur Dean, the Brotherhood's Building Counselor. Cameron had resigned by this time, and the building program was carried through by his replacement, Donald H. Fogelsanger, a recent Bethany graduate. The motto of the building program was a familiar one: "For the Glory of God and Our Neighbor's Good."

The new site was two lots at Union Avenue and Twenty-Eighth Street. The first services in the L-shaped, stone-fronted church were held on Sunday, October 15, 1961, two weeks before dedication day. The brick structure cost $175,000.

Pastors since 1964, when Fogelsanger resigned, have been Jay E. Gibble (1964–1970), Russell Burris (1970–1975), and Richard G. Bright (1975–   ).

BEDFORD (1957)
MEMBERSHIP: 182

As early as 1928 the Home Mission Board raised the possibility at District Conference of opening work in the historic town of Bedford. Not for another quarter century, however, was any action taken to church that county seat.

After World War II the question of churching Bedford came up again from time to time, but nothing of a deliberate nature was done to bring it about. Then in 1955 District leaders learned that the Bedford Ministerium was planning a religious census of the community. The Middle District, working through the Eastern Regional Office, offered to assist in the survey, which was carried out the latter part of 1955. The Ministry and Missions Commission was furnished cards after the canvass giving the names of those who claimed membership in or preference for the Church of the Brethren.

In early 1956 the District Ministry and Missions Commission appointed a committee of three—Elmer E. Ebersole of Martinsburg, Robert G. Mock of Everett, C. H. Cameron of Altoona—to work out a plan for locating and contacting Brethren residing in Bedford and its vicinity. Letters were sent to pastors of all Middle District congregations, and to many in other districts, asking for the names and addresses of their members in that area. Then a questionnaire was mailed to all those whose names were supplied. The ones that replied to the questionnaire received personal calls by the committee.

After this, the Ebersole-Mock-Cameron trio called a meeting of interested persons to explore the idea of carrying the survey further. From among those attending this meeting, teams of visitors assumed the responsibility of calling on Brethren who had not responded to the poll. The two surveys turned up the information that sixty-five families, totaling 181 persons, indicated deep interest in becoming part of a Brethren church in Bedford. Of these, fifty-six families were of Brethren background, while twenty-eight families claimed no church affiliation.

So promising was this data that the District Board recommended to the 1956 District Conference that the Ministry and Missions Commission continue its study. Action at the meeting designated the Commission "to serve as the agent of the District Board to effect an organization as the need arose." The Commission's three-man committee was enlarged to five with the addition of G. Quinter Showalter of Duncansville and Roy S. Forney of Martinsburg. Meanwhile, with a Bedford church now almost a certainty, the District Board was directed to proceed to secure comity from the Pennsylvania Council of Churches and to clear everything with Brotherhood authorities.

Prospective members met in a mass meeting on January 6, 1957, to elect temporary officers. Five persons from the District were delegated to work with the Bedford Mission Committee in planning worship and fellowship meetings. They were Benjamin Baker, Clarence Knepper, Carlton Livingood, Dr. Mary Mentzer, and their chairman, Ray Replogle.

Nearly one hundred members and friends of the Church of the Brethren in the Bedford area assembled for the first worship service on Sunday, March 17. It was held in the American Legion Hall on East Pitt Street, where the worshipers continued to gather every Sunday afternoon until they had a sanctuary of their own. Nearby pastors did the preaching through the spring. Edward Kerchensteiner, a seminarian from Bethany, served as summer pastor. Then in September Daniel M. Brumbaugh of Saxton, then a teacher at Northern Bedford High School, became part-time pastor for the next four years.

His pastorate helped to lay a solid foundation for future growth at Bedford. In October, upon petition, the Bedford Fellowship was given congregational status by Middle District. That same month Brotherhood architect Arthur L. Dean visited the congregation, viewed the prospective church site, and was engaged to draw plans for a new building. An every-member-canvass in November, as part of the denomination's 250th Anniversary Call, led to the adoption of a ten-thousand-dollar budget. Organizational matters were finally settled in January 1958 when the congregation adopted a constitution and by-laws and elected permanent officers. Articles of incorporation cleared the Commonwealth courts in late March.

The early months of 1958 also evidenced rapid progress in the building program. A ten-acre plot, east of Bedford along Route 30 on a slope overlooking the town, had been purchased the previous fall for $15,525. In a June council meeting the congregation voted to begin construction of the Fellowship Hall, to be the first step in a three-phase building schedule.

A year later, on July 13, a contract for the first unit was awarded to Karns Brothers of Bedford for $48,000. Ground-breaking ceremonies took place two weeks later, Roy Forney officiating. Services were first held in the still-unfinished Fellowship Hall on December 20, 1959. Dedication of the first unit came the following March, with Dr. Tobias F. Henry of Juniata College the speaker.

In September 1961 Joseph M. Mason, a Virginian, assumed full-time pastoral responsibilities. He and his family moved into a newly purchased parsonage at 618 South Juliana Street.

In another four years the Bedford people were ready to move ahead on the rest of the building program, skipping the second phase to complete it all in one fell swoop. On December 9, 1965, council voted to engage Arthur Dean to prepare plans for the sanctuary and classrooms. Architect Dean's final blueprints got congregational approval two years later, on January 1, 1967. On March 28 council acted to secure D.S.A. Inc. of Cleburne, Texas, to supervise the construction, which began following ground-breaking on April 30.

That fall Joseph Mason resigned to become District Secretary, and J. William Stoneback took over pastoral duties. The young minister helped plan the dedication service held on Sunday afternoon, May 5, 1968. The featured speaker was Dr. Morley Mays of Huntingdon, who had been Juniata College's academic dean for twenty years before becoming president elect of Elizabethtown College.

The building program, counting the parsonage, totaled $97,700 in 1968—which did not include volunteer labor. As the dedication brochure pointed out, the District and its churches had responded generously to the Bedford undertaking. In loans and grants, Central Pennsylvania Brethren up to that time had come through with $47,000. No less charitable was the General Brotherhood Board, which provided $53,000 toward the building debt.

On January 1, 1976, just eighteen years after forming, the Bedford congregation became self-supporting. Its indebtedness then had decreased to $21,000, allowing the local people to take the entire burden upon their own shoulders.

Pastors since Stoneback left in 1971 have been: vacant (1971–72), Connell T. Chaney (1972–1976), and John D. Keiper, formerly of Aughwick, who officially took up Middle District residence again on February 1, 1977, after a brief pastorate elsewhere in Pennsylvania. He served until 1981.

STATE COLLEGE (1968)
MEMBERSHIP: 423

The fall of 1968 marked a unique ecumenical event within the District, to say nothing of the Brotherhood. At that time the University Baptist Church in State College became a member congregation of Middle District. The membership there would now maintain a dual affiliation—both with the Church of the Brethren and with the American Baptist Convention. A service celebrating this novel union took place in University Baptist Church on November 24. President Morley Mays of Elizabethtown College, a former District leader and that year's national moderator for the Brethren, was the speaker. Other dignitaries representing the Brethren were District Secretary Joseph Mason, and Dr. Luther Harshbarger, chairman of the department of religious studies at Penn State. For the Baptists there was the Reverend Lee Jeffords, Associate Executive Secretary of the Pennsylvania Baptist convention. Present in a special capacity also was Wayne E. Eberly, one of the influential Brethren in State College, then working on his doctorate at the University.

Churching the university town of State College, set athwart the broad, fertile Nittany Valley, was an idea first broached soon after World War II. But Alvin Cox's report to Elders' Meeting in 1948 on behalf of the Ministerial-Mission Board stated that "upon a thorough investigation . . ., there did not appear sufficient interest upon the residents to start a Mission at this time." This picture changed, however, within another decade and a half. More and more Brethren, on the University staff or as students, were finding their way to State College. Beginning in the early 1960s they formed a Brethren fellowship, involving in time about thirty-seven families. Meetings were held in the lounge of the Penn State Eisenhower Chapel. Among the most active were the Wayne Eberlys, the Lee Byerses, and the George Etzweilers. The fellowship arrangement sufficed for a while, but there arose within the group a deep-felt need for the kind of spiritual nurture that comes with a more stable, pastored relationship. With District backing, they began to explore various alternatives, among them linking up with a local body whose denominational heritage and view of the ministry were similar to that of the Brethren.

The eventual decision to seek affiliation with the University Baptist Church must be seen in a broader context. At that time the Brethren and the American Baptist Convention were engaged in dialogue about closer denominational ties. Both held to similar doctrines and practices and subscribed to a congregational church polity. In State College the Baptists had a solid congregation with a thriving Student Center. Affiliation of the two local groups promised to strengthen their various ministries, especially to University students, in obvious ways. University Baptist Church people were receptive to such a proposition, and so in 1967 a representative committee was formed to give it careful study. The results of this study, of course, are now history.

There has been no attempt to maintain separate denominational groupings in the congregation. Both national bodies are budgeted in outreach giving. At first the members vetoed a name change that would add Brethren or drop any denominational label. But by 1978 sentiment on this matter had changed, and at their business meeting that spring they voted to be known as the University Baptist and Brethren Church.

The congregation originally got its start back in April of 1922, when some thirty Baptists began meeting in what is now the Weaver Building on the Penn State campus. That fall forty charter members organized as a congregation with the Centre Baptist Association. The next June the Baptists bought several lots on the southeast corner of West Nittany and Burrowes streets. An impressive stone structure was erected on this site and dedicated in January 1928. The building was enlarged in 1952–53 and again ten years later with a Christian education wing. The sanctuary was further expanded in 1972 ($80,000).

University Church has had five full-time pastors: Robert A. Selby (1931–1943), Robert H. Eads (1944–1954), Earl F. Spencer (1955–1965), Robert B. Wallace (1965–1973) and Michael Scrogin (1973–   ).

6

The Press and Publishing Ventures

The printing trade as such has never enjoyed much of a vogue among the Brethren. There were two periods in our history, however, when Brethren printers made the press a special agency in the life of the church. Both periods were times of crises for the Brotherhood.

The first period, the mid-eighteenth century, spanned the formative years of the church in the American colonies. It also coincided with the fortunes of the Sauer family press. The Sauer era began when the recent Brethren immigrants, scattered and few in number, were beset by discord and schism. Through their famous press, the Sauers of Germantown made the "Mother Church" a center of influence among the colonial Germans. In the process this family of printers brought the Brethren unwonted status and kept them in public focus on religious and political issues. The Revolutionary War, however, put an end to this.

In the second period the impact of printing was more parochial and less public. This period, which popularized the English press, began just prior to the Civil War and culminated in the post-Appomattox decade. It witnessed a new lot of tradesmen, self-employed job printers, who sought to cultivate an exclusive Brethren readership. They ordinarily functioned as editor-printers, giving as much time to editing and writing as to typesetting. From their shops came a crop of papers vying for acceptance as organs of the Brotherhood.

A few of these latter-day Sauers, more progressive than the others, called for certain reforms. Their image of the church had a modern cast. This outlook, not shared by older members, provoked sharp debate and strife, even rupture. In the end, the reform press prevailed. By the 1880s it had given the Brotherhood a whole new thrust—away from sectarianism.

Much of this story had its setting in Middle Pennsylvania. Here, in a dynamic age of social, cultural, and economic change, a select galaxy of men operated their presses. Of the reformist printers, they stood among the most influential, capable, innovative, and far-sighted. Because of them, in large part, religious journalism found a permanent place in Brethren life and thought.

The Sauer Era

The nineteenth-century printers had one notable quality in common with Christopher Sauer I, renowned colonial printer: all began their trade as greenhorns. Indeed, Sauer's friends had good cause to wonder in 1738, when he opened up his Germantown shop.[1] He was a jack-of-all trades in his mid-forties, whose wife had left him and an only son for the Ephrata Society eight years before. His search for a used press, both in the colonies and Europe, turned up nothing, forcing him, some historians think, to build his own. Moreover, he faced in Benjamin Franklin a formidable competitor, who not only was printing a German newspaper but also monopolized the paper stock in Pennsylvania.

But Sauer, undaunted and resourceful, overcame these early obstacles. The product of his press, the first in America to use German type, took many forms: Bibles, almanacs, newspapers, pamphlets, books, broadsides. The motto on his shop wall, now cherished by the Brethren—"For the glory of God and my neighbor's good"—declared his business code of ethics. When he died in 1758, after a twenty-year career, he was famed as the premier printer for the Pennsylvania Germans. All scholars recognize his central place in the history of colonial printing.

Oil painting of the Sauer print shop by Barnard Taylor.

Scholars also acknowledge that Sauer's press never properly functioned as the official Brethren organ. Actually, his supposed Brethren baptism is a moot subject among historians. Nevertheless, he felt a close spiritual kinship to the Schwarzenau legatees. As long as he lived, his home was open to the Germantown Brethren for a regular meetingplace. Even so, he wrote and printed out of strong personal convictions, not as their designated spokesman. His press was at the service of any German Pietistic group whose views did not conflict with his.

The same independent spirit was shown by his namesake son, Christopher Sauer II, sole heir of the business after his father's death. The younger Sauer, who became one of the richest men in the colonies, was a devout and respected Brethren leader. One writer rates him as "the greatest man the Church produced in the eighteenth century."[2] Burly of build in his prime, weighing 250 pounds, he served as elder of the Germantown congregation, and was a prominent and popular figure at Annual Conference and on the important committees to which he was perennially appointed. But the son, like the father, stoutly sustained the independence of the Sauer press from church control. This policy did not go unchallenged. Sometimes his fellow Brethren exerted firm pressure on him because of what he chose to print.

It was his Brethren beliefs, especially on war, that caused Sauer, at fifty-four, to lose everything. Even though a bitter critic of British colonial policies, he opposed the Revolutionary War on New Testament grounds. His press took a strong pacifistic stand. This brought upon him the enmity alike of both the British and the patriots. The former, when their troops took Philadelphia in 1777, destroyed or confiscated most of the equipment and stock at the Germantown plant, while the latter, after his arrest as an alleged traitor in 1778, disposed of his personal possessions and property at public sale. Sauer, left homeless and penniless, suffered added sorrow in the defection of two sons, business partners with him, as British Loyalists. With this debacle, the Sauer press, after forty illustrious years, came to an ignominious end.

After the war the printing trade was not wholly abandoned by the Brethren. At least one member, Peter Leibert, a little-known but apparently well-regarded Germantown elder, owned and operated a press for thirteen years. A one-time Sauer apprentice and an intimate of the family, he had outfitted himself in 1784 with some of his former employer's equipment that had been seized and sold by the British. He set up a printing office in Germantown in partnership with his son-in-law, a Lutheran. Three years later the partnership was dissolved, and he moved to a new location in town. For a short time his son, probably a Brethren too, worked with him in the office. Leibert revived the Sauer newspaper and almanac, and in time developed into a writer of some merit. In 1791 he printed the first English hymnbook for the Brethren, among whom the German tongue was already in decline. Leibert's press seems to have been very productive, but it never brought him the prestige of the Sauers. Like them, however, he published for an ecumenical audience and not as a Brethren mouthpiece. He gave up his business in 1797.

With that year printing as an influential Brethren trade went into a fifty-year eclipse. In the early 1800s available and cheap land in the South and Midwest produced a generation of Brethren pioneers, lured away from Eastern center of culture to frontier farms and relative isolation. But new members on the fringe areas came into the fold only sporadically. The sectarian Brethren lacked the evangelical zeal of the Baptists and Methodists, two church-bodies whose ranks were crowded with borderland converts. As a result, a half century of benign neglect set in. A big problem for the dispersed constituency was the lack of communication. Apart from annual and district meetings and the local preaching services, most members were kept virtually incommunicado on the state of the Brotherhood. This situation took a turn for the better after a curious little ex-Lutheran pastor, noticeably humpbacked, donned a straight coat. Thanks to him, the printing trade made a comeback in the church.

The Kurtz Era and the First Church Paper

Henry Kurtz, born in 1796, emigrated from Germany at the age of twenty-one.[3] He taught school for two years in Eastern Pennsylvania, and then, in 1819, entered the Lutheran ministry.

Kurtz's pastoral career in the Lutheran denomination proved short-lived, lasting less than eight years. It ended in Pittsburgh during his second charge, when he was deposed by his synod. The trouble began soon after the young pastor took over the parish in 1823 and tried to reform church discipline. He arbitrarily imposed stricter standards, creating open conflict and division in the congregation. Then, before this issue was settled, he used the pulpit to advocate the abandonment of conventional society for life in a Christian communistic colony. His model was the Harmony Society headed by George Rapp in nearby Economy.

Invited to join Economy as a teacher, Kurtz preferred, instead, to move ahead on plans to found his own community, to be called

Concordia. A great deal of his pastoral time was spent publicizing the projected colony, raising funds for it, and recruiting families to settle it. To this end he started a German magazine named *Paradise Regained,* a twenty-four-page monthly.[4] The first issue appeared in September 1825. He continued to publish the periodical on a regular basis until December 1827, although he changed its name to *The Peace Messenger of Concordia.* The editor and chief writer, he did not do the printing work, but jobbed it out locally.

Sometime in 1827 Kurtz, now expelled, had moved his family to a farm in Stark County, Ohio, near the proposed site of Concordia. But support for the colony lagged, and before long the defrocked pastor found himself in a deep quandary about the whole idea. At the same time he became more and more intrigued by his Brethren neighbors. Their life-style seemed to exemplify his own ideals. He gave up his communitarian dreams, and in 1828 was baptized by Elder George Hoke of Canton. Two years later he was elected to the ministry.

Soon after his baptism the new convert decided to combine farming and printing for a livelihood. He purchased a secondhand press from a Canton printer and began to do some job work. Then his editorial instincts took over. He made a try at two German periodicals between 1833 and 1836, a weekly and then a monthly. Probably these were meant for a wider audience than just the Brethren, but both failed for lack of patronage. Among the Brethren he had more success at that time with an English version of a German hymnal. It was adopted by a number of Midwestern congregations.

His reputation spread, enhanced by such publications and by his powerful preaching. Gradually, doors were opened, granting him admission into the church hierarchy. In 1837 he was chosen writing clerk of Annual Conference, a post he filled for twenty years. With this appointment he began printing Conference minutes, both in English and German, on a somewhat official basis. In 1844 he was made a member of Standing Committee, the inner circle of Conference leaders, even before he was advanced to elder, a rare action in those days. Shortly after Conference that year, he received his ordination in the Mill Creek congregation, where he had oversight until his death in 1874.

Kurtz, a lifelong pipe smoker, now began to think seriously about starting a Brethren paper. He was living on a farm near Poland, in northeastern Ohio, having moved there in 1842. His print shop was installed in a springhouse loft, measuring 20' x 24'. Two of his four sons helped out in the shop; the other two took care of the farm.

Already a two-time journalistic loser, Kurtz knew that the odds against the success of a church-related paper were certainly high. Statistically, his reading public would be severely limited, since the current Brethren membership hardly exceeded fifteen thousand.

Nevertheless, the persistent elder was convinced of the need for such a publication. It would serve two purposes: first, restore the unity of a scattered Brotherhood; and second, provide a vehicle through which doctrinal problems could be shared and answered.[5] Then, too, he probably sensed that the Brethren now had more time for thoughtful reading. The popularity of Peter Nead's works seemed to confirm this. Nead, the first Brethren to write a book, had been circulating his theological treatises since 1833.

Still, to avoid a third failure, Kurtz decided to test the sentiment of the denomination on his prospective paper. In 1849 he conducted a canvass of local congregations by mail. The general reaction, he discovered, was quite positive, with most respondents favoring an English edition over a German one. Even so, the more conservative elders voiced staunch opposition. They viewed his brainchild as a worldly innovation, a merchandizing of the Gospel.

Kurtz thought it prudent, therefore, to seek the blessing of Annual Conference. He intended to submit specimen copies to the 1850 sessions for examination. But illness in the family kept him away that year. A query, however, did get on the agenda, asking "whether there is any danger to be apprehended from publishing a paper among us." Conference's response was to table the subject for one year. As a result, Kurtz concluded that he could publish his paper on a trial basis until a final ruling was handed down. Thus in April 1851 the fifty-five-year-old Ohioan issued the first number of the *Gospel Visitor*.

Not for another three years, however, was Conference ready to take a definite stand on the *Visitor's* fate. In 1851 it acted to give the pilot paper tentative sanction for another year, so "that the Brethren or churches will impartially examine [it] . . . and if found wrong or injurious, let them send in their objections at the next annual meeting." The 1852 Conference, after weighing the pro and con reactions to the *Visitor*, determined that "it could not be forbidden" and should be allowed to "stand or fall on its own merits." A final but somewhat anticlimactic seal of approval was given in 1853. The delegates unanimously recommended that since the *Visitor* was a "private undertaking of its editor . . . this meeting should not any further interfere with it."

So came into existence the first periodical officially approved by the Church of the Brethren. One of the oldest denominational journals in America, it underwent a series of mergers and was published at different places, eventually evolving into today's *Messenger*. Beginning in 1852 Kurtz also published a companion paper in German, *Der Evangelische Besuch*. This was an effort to preserve something of the church's Germanic past. But the supplemental edition lost money for him and was discontinued in 1861. The *Visitor*, though, was well received, and its subscription list mounted steadily. After a few years Kurtz expanded the monthly from eight to twenty-four pages. His business outgrew the springhouse loft, and in 1857 he moved his outfit to Columbiana, a neighboring town.

The year before, the *Visitor*'s prospering state had compelled the short-handed editor to hire more help. German born, he felt deficient in his adopted tongue. Thus for some time he had been looking for an English-trained aide, whose chief duties would be editing and writing suitable articles in English. He found such a colleague in James Quinter, a forty-year-old schoolteacher from Fayette County, Pennsylvania. There also came to live with Kurtz that year a sharp-witted apprentice from Morrisons Cove—Henry R. Holsinger. Both recruits were brilliant individuals, but with opposite personalities. Both would leave their marks on the Brotherhood, one for better and the other for worse. And both, as consummate editors, would help to put Middle Pennsylvania, for a period of time, at the center of Brethren publishing activity.

Henry Holsinger and Religious Journalism in Middle District

Henry Holsinger was the District's pioneer printer.[6] On his paternal side, he laid claim to the ancestry of Alexander Mack. He grew up on a farm near Clover Creek, a descendant of a line of Brethren preachers, and in 1854 married Susannah Shoop, a Lutheran from Martinsburg.

Since before his marriage, young Henry had been an avid reader of the *Visitor*. He developed a hankering to become a part of it and learn the printing trade. Thus in the fall of 1856 Kurtz took on the twenty-three-year-old youth as a printer's devil. Bilingual, he learned to set type in both German and English.

But the eager apprentice had grander goals for himself; he had visions of occupying an editor's chair himself. He proposed that Kurtz, about to retire, sell him part interest in the business and name him a coeditor. Holsinger made this bid, no doubt, in the belief that he was as qualified as Quinter, also a novice in the trade. He further importuned his employer to convert the *Visitor* into a weekly. Some Brethren were asking for this, and such a move, he probably hoped, would necessitate his promotion. But Kurtz was banking on Quinter to succeed him, and refused to be swayed by the appeals of his aggressive hireling. So Holsinger, frustrated after a six-month stay, returned to his home area in 1857.

The enterprising farm boy was barely back before he announced plans for a newspaper in Martinsburg. It was to be called the *Morrisons Cove Journal* and would be the first paper printed in the Cove. He had rounded up five hundred pledged subscribers by summer when the Panic of 1857 struck, scaring off wary patrons. The project was then dropped before the would-be newspaperman could go to press. Thwarted in his printing dreams, he spent the next seven years or so teaching school in the winters and working on farms in the summer. But he did not give up and hounded his friends to back him in equipping a shop in Martinsburg.

In the spring of 1863 the thirty-year-old schoolman got his shop, but not in Martinsburg. He bought the office of the defunct *Tyrone Star*, located in the small railroad town some thirty miles north. The office was a cramped second-floor room that contained among its inventory a hard-used Washington handpress and trays of worn-out type.[7] Thus outfitted, Holsinger began his printing career in Tyrone, then a community of about fifteen hundred where five newspapers had failed in the six years since its incorporation. Sometime in May, after the school year had ended, he published the first issue of the *Tyrone Herald*, a weekly carrying the name of an earlier sheet.

By his own admission, the initial months were difficult ones. The nation was in the throes of the Civil War. "Everything seemed gloomy then," he later wrote. "Everybody seemed depressed, and business was dull." Overworked, he was editor, proprietor, printer, and proofreader—all in one person. When school resumed in the fall, he went back into the classroom (presumably in or near Tyrone), which now competed with the pressroom for his time and energy. He had to hire an apprentice boy and rely on the occasional help of a mute printer. How he managed his domestic life during this stage—with his business and school at one place and his family at Clover Creek—remains problematical.

Nevertheless, they were all united in poverty the following May, when he moved his wife and two daughters to Tyrone. They rented a house that had a back lot with a garden already planted. Holsinger later confessed that if it had not been for the vegetables from this garden, his family would have gone hungry many times. He also told the poignant story of how his daughters' pet dog was exploited to stave off hunger in those dark days. One Saturday, after the help had been paid, there was no money left to buy food. So desperate was Holsinger that he sold their dog for a dollar in order to pay the grocery bill.[8]

In the summer of 1864 the *Herald* took a profitable turn for its struggling owner. Probably there was some correlation between this and his increasing political activism. Editorially, he had at first taken an independent position on politics. But in the heat of the 1864 campaign he became an ardent champion of the Republican party. He supported Lincoln and Governor Andrew Curtin, and plugged for giving the ballot to soldiers. While politics put his paper in the black, political infighting soured him. Therefore, in November, as soon as the election results were released, he got rid of the *Herald*. That same month he resigned his school charge.[9]

A new design, one more suited to his religious nature, had taken shape in his mind. He was persuaded that the Brethren would support a weekly paper. He had felt this way, we saw earlier, ever since his apprentice days with Kurtz. The office mail then, open to his perusal, included frequent letters expressing a desire that the *Gospel Visitor* be published on a semi-monthly or weekly basis. Therefore, when the *Herald* editor developed a distaste for secular journalism and began casting about for something more self-fulfilling in his field, he kept coming back to the notion of a weekly church paper.

His mind made up, he got his promotional campaign underway in March 1864. He went to the Spring Run District Conference to seek its sanction for his project. The delegates encouraged him to go ahead "at his own discretion." In May he prepared a specimen copy of his proposed paper, which he named the *Christian Family Companion*. He took it to Annual Conference at Hagerstown, Indiana, and distributed it there (for five cents a copy) among the Conference-goers. He also sent copies through the mail to potential subscribers and advertised in the *Gospel Visitor*.

In that prototypic copy Holsinger lauded his denomination by declaring that

> the Church of the Brethren is now the only religious organization, in the Western World, which teaches the truth, the whole truth, and nothing but the truth, as it is revealed in the New Testament; and which has for its sole object the glory of God and the salvation of the soul.

This was an interesting affirmation, in light of the course of action he would take a decade and a half later. The *Companion*, he stated, would benefit the Brethren in four ways: first, furnish them "with a

weekly journal . . . free from all variety, fiction, [and] falsehood";
second, "afford a medium for free discussions"; third, "give wholesome instruction and kindly admonition"; fourth, supply "interesting church news."

Originally, the Tyrone publisher had intended to begin the *Companion* on a regular schedule in October. But advance subscriptions
lagged. Moreover, by fall he was deeply engaged in a political
contest and back at teaching school. He decided, therefore, to
postpone regular publication until the first of the year. Meanwhile,
to spark patronage, he issued a second sample number in October.
Even so, by late December he had built up a list of only 384
subscribers.[10]

Some Brethren, including a few Holsinger patrons, were fearful
that the *Companion* was coming out in competition with the *Visitor*.
Perhaps, they worried, this would lead to the financial ruin of both.
Holsinger, envisioning a paper of broader scope and purpose,
insisted not. He saw a place and need for each. In the October
specimen he wrote:

> My paper is a weekly Christian Family *Companion,* one that will give
> advice, instruction and information, on all subjects which concern the
> Christian in his pilgrimage through this world and is not designed to take
> the place of any religious journal. The *Visitor* is a monthly *Gospel Visitor,*
> and is dedicated to the vindication and advancement of true Gospel
> knowledge. If both parties stick to their texts, there will be no danger of
> stealing each other's sermons.

It is true, however, that the *Visitor* did suffer by comparison on
several counts once the *Companion* made its debut on January 3,
1865. By modern standards, the virgin weekly—in format, editorial
style, selection of material, reader interest, and quality of paper and
printing—was clearly superior to its older monthly counterpart. The
format of the *Companion* (8" x 10½"), which featured a three-column
page, gave it more of a resemblance to a present-day magazine than
that of the smaller two-column *Visitor* (5½" × 9"). For just a few cents
more per year, a *Companion* reader got twice as much in contents as a
Visitor subscriber. Holsinger did not hesitate to cite this fact on
occasion, belying his claims that the two papers were not rivals.

The *Companion,* to a greater degree than the *Visitor,* set out to
accommodate amateur writers. While a *Visitor* apprentice, Holsinger
had seen badly written articles submitted by aspiring *hommes de lettres*
thrown into the wastebasket. Many of these discarded essays, the
young typesetter deemed, should have been consigned to a better
end. For his own paper, therefore, the thirty-two-year-old editor

adopted the policy that any literary contribution, "no matter how scrawling the handwriting, or how stammering the words," would be put in good shape and honored in print. The *Companion*, he wrote, "will reflect, more, the number and character of its patrons, than the ability of its editor." Years later, he observed that this "feature was very encouraging to young authors, and old men who had experience in public speaking but none at all in writing."[11] From the very first, the young and old of both sexes in Middle District filled the pages of the *Companion* with familiar names—Furry, Brumbaugh, Garner, Hanawalt, Sell, Sharp, Replogle, Wineland, Myers, Snowberger, to mention but a few.

This editorial policy contrasted sharply with that of his editorial peers, Kurtz and Quinter. The *Visitor*, except for published letters, withheld the identity of its essayists, printing only initials. Quinter himself, in fact, wrote under the pseudonym "Clement." Holsinger was counseled to follow the *Visitor's* practice; otherwise, it was charged, contributors would grow vain by seeing their names in print. The *Companion's* editor took a different view. Ignoring the question of vanity, he retorted that a by-line would make a writer more responsible. "In this way authors [would be] brought face to face with each other, and required to meet the issue of their individual productions."

Another principle basic to Holsinger's editorial policy was the "open forum." He invited free and uncensored debate. Many Brethren found this practice objectionable—and threatening. Only a few months after the *Companion* first appeared, Conference received two queries that expressed concern about the troublesome trends in Brethren journalism. They raised the question of how to deal with writers and editors who opposed the "ancient order and customs of the church." Conference ruled that heretical articles were outlawed, and offenders were to be dealt with in accordance with Matthew 18, the traditional disciplinary procedure for Brethren.

Holsinger readily agreed that he could make the *Companion* less contentious and thus more popular by editing out polemic material. "But popularity is not our only aim," he wrote. "We want to do some good to those who do patronize us." Moreover, he was determined to silence a skeptical Methodist friend. This acquaintance taunted him, saying that the Brethren were "not intelligent enough to support a paper."

Despite the open forum, that support came and in good measure, causing growth pains. The less than four hundred subscriptions in 1865 multiplied to over 3,600 in five years. Between 1865 and 1867 Holsinger had to relocate his shop three different places in Tyrone. In the latter year his financial state allowed him to put up a three-story, brick-faced office building. Sometime in 1866 (the year Clover Creek called him to the ministry) he disposed of the old Washington handpress. It was replaced by one having three times its capacity (six hundred copies an hour) and driven by a horse on a treadmill. Then in June 1868 he installed a $1,500 Potter press, powered by a small steam engine. His work force was now made up of an assistant editor, an apprentice boy, a teenage girl (sometimes his older daughter, Ann, stayed home from school to lend a hand too), and another printer besides himself.

As more Brethren homes welcomed the *Companion,* its editor showed signs of becoming a denominational maverick. He grew truculent and played the role of agitator. This became apparent at the first Annual Conference in which he took an active part. In 1867 Conference met at Pipe Creek, Maryland, in a dense grove. Holsinger spoke on one query with such vehemence that he became the storm center of a shouting debate. So intense was the excitement that men and women wept aloud. His father, a revered Middle District elder, was shocked and remonstrated with him in public. He warned, on obvious pragmatic grounds, that such a spectacle could have dire consequences for his business. This ploy only enraged the son. He jumped up, threw his hands in the air, and exclaimed, "Thank God, I am not bound to truckle to the prejudice of any man or set of men, for the sake of my business, so long as I have the use of these two hands wherewith to labor for the support of myself and family."[12]

Holsinger was induced to make amends for his rudeness, but the die was cast. The friction between Holsinger and the ruling elders would never cease. The feeling at Pipe Creek would crop out again and again in following Conferences. It became increasingly clear that the combative editor would not be intimidated; he would compromise on nothing.

Two years later Holsinger set off more pyrotechnics at Conference. He had engaged a shorthand specialist, a reporter from a paper in Washington, D.C., to transcribe a complete record of business proceedings. But Standing Committee intervened before the sessions got underway and passed a resolution against such an innovation. Holsinger was summoned into the inner sanctum and called to account. In defense, he argued for an informed membership. He contended that his readers were entitled to more information than a mere listing of queries and the action taken on each, which was all the official minutes contained. The general Brotherhood, he made plain, deserved to know the substance of the debates that went into the decision-making process.

Holsinger's self-image was more that of educator than of editor, and it was this stance that bothered the reactionary elders. When told that the "sentiment" of the Brethren was against reporting the full text of speeches, he snapped back, "I [regard] it as my privilege, as editor of a paper, to mould public sentiment." Henry Davy, who went Old Order in 1881 and whom Holsinger disliked but respected, had the last word. He said, "You may find it a pretty hard matter to lead the sentiment of annual meeting. The Brethren generally do their own thinking." With that, the ostracized stenographer was sent packing to the nation's capital.

The reporter question remained a *cause célèbre* for several years, and did as much to widen the breach between Holsinger and the elders at that time as his stand on any other issues. In 1871 he took an Associated Press recorder to Conference, but had no more success with Standing Committee than in 1869. *Visitor* editorials were critical of Holsinger's defiant conduct. But the *Pilgrim,* a new weekly published by the Brumbaugh brothers of Middle District, sided with him. A few years later, after Holsinger had given up his paper, the Brumbaughs led the reporter fight. Eventually, Quinter of the *Visitor* was also won over. By 1876 the matter was all but forgotten, and a reporter was no longer *persona non grata* at Conference.

Holsinger's rancorous behavior began to damage his relations in Middle District, where the churches had rallied behind him during the *Companion*'s infancy. By 1869 some of his support there was beginning to erode. That year, District Conference at James Creek entertained a query obviously directed at him. The query was: "Cannot this Council Meeting devise some plan to prevent the prevailing contention of the brethren through the press?" The answer was: "We advise the Elders of the different arms of the church to admonish all brethren and sisters who write for the press, not to send any articles of a controversial nature, on doctrinal points."

The following year, the *Companion*'s editor-*provocateur* added two publications of historical significance to his press's output. One was the *Pious Youth,* the first Brethren magazine for young people. It came out in January 1870. The format of the sixteen-page monthly (later thirty-six pages) was patterned after that of the *Companion.* It included stories and homilies suitable for use in Sunday School work. There were graded Bible games and puzzles, like the ones its parent paper carried at first for adult amusement and instruction. Most of the material, though, was geared for general juvenile reading interest and education. It employed learning devices such as the listing of memorable dates in history. One of its regular features reflected its editor's nostalgia for the German language. The first number of the *Pious Youth* contained a lesson in the pronunciation of the German alphabet. Subsequent numbers added vocabulary drills, and finally entire columns in that tongue. The magazine, however, never became self-supporting, and it was suspended in January 1872.

A more popular publishing innovation in 1870 was Holsinger's *Brethren's Almanac,* forerunner of today's yearbook. The first edition, for 1871, appeared in October and met with instant success. The supply of over three thousand copies, at twelve cents each, was sold out in less than two months. Besides calendrical, astronomical, meteorological, and other miscellaneous data normally found in an almanac, Holsinger included history, statistics, doctrines, and biographical sketches of special interest to the Brethren. Abraham Cassel, celebrated antiquarian and great-grandson of Christopher Sauer, wrote an article for the 1872 edition. (The 1871 issue was printed in Philadelphia, but the one for 1872 by Holsinger himself.) The *Brethren's Almanac* inaugurated the practice of publishing an annual listing of Brethren ministers. The early rosters, of course, were incomplete. But Holsinger thought that such statistics were informative, and he appealed through the *Companion* for cooperation in developing a full and accurate compilation. For many Brethren families, the study of almanacs, next to the Bible, constituted their most important and regular literary activity. Thus within the next decade other church printers followed suit and published almanacs of their own.

By the time his almanac for 1872 was on the market, Holsinger was no longer located at Tyrone. He became unhappy there, isolated from a strong Brethren fellowship. In 1869 he had fitted up a schoolroom for services, but the work languished. And so in 1871 he started to look elsewhere for a new business site. Martinsburg was given consideration, but it lacked a building with adequate office space. The Warriors Mark congregation, hopeful that he would be its pastor, invited his paper there. But Holsinger replied, "We want to do our preaching through the Press."[13] The best prospect was Meyersdale, in Western Pennsylvania. He finally decided upon that Brethren community, despite the urgent pleas of his Middle District friends to stay in the area. The last number of the *Companion* printed in *Tyrone* was October 17, 1871.

As a publisher, Holsinger spent nearly eight years in Middle Pennsylvania. His impact on the Brotherhood during that time was both troubling and formative. Those years, we now see in retrospect, clearly presaged the schismatic stand he would take after 1878. But as John Moore has written, "He was a born editor, and our people probably never had in their ranks a man of finer editorial ability."[14]

Small wonder, then, that he was such a keen judge of journalistic talent. All three of his associate editors, while he published in Middle District, went on to distinguished literary careers. The first one was the later revered elder James A. Sell—poet, essayist, local historican, and genitor of the 1925 history. The "boy preacher" entered the *Companion* office in April 1866, at age twenty and just a few months after his call to the ministry. He stayed a little over two years and helped to guide the *Companion* through its formative stage. John B. Brumbaugh was next, but he remained only four months. Twenty years old, he left to start a paper with his two brothers, and after that a school.

He was succeeded by Joseph W. Beer, a teacher-preacher in his early thirties from Armstrong County. Beer, as gifted in the pulpit as with the pen, became a prolific writer on doctrinal subjects. He went with Holsinger to Meyersdale, and over the next five years continued in editorial work through a series of business mergers that brought him back to Middle District temporarily. In 1878 he and Holsinger founded the *Progressive Christian* at Berlin, Pennsylvania. Later he followed his one-time employer into the Progressive Brethren Church.

The term *Progressive Brethren* was popularized, if not coined, by Holsinger, but, as the *Companion's* editor, he did a like service for his native denomination. If he did not think up the name *Church of the Brethren,* at least he was the first to use it in print. In the *Companion's* first specimen issue he wrote, "I am a member of the 'Church of the Brethren,' generally known by the name of 'German Baptist,' and vulgarly and maliciously called 'Dunkards.' " Beginning with 1867, the title page of each volume carried the clause: "Published by the Editor, by Permission of the Church of the Brethren." Not until 1908, however, was this name formally adopted by the denomination.

Without doubt, Holsinger was a complex person. He had charisma and made many fast friends. But he made twice as many enemies. His mind was sharp, and he worked at improving it. He always carried a small, cheap dictionary in his vest pocket. He once wrote, "A Christian family without a dictionary is like a heathen family without a Bible."[15] He loved to debate. But he could be arrogantly dogmatic, cutting his opponents down by sarcastic remarks. Instead of convincing them, he made them foes. For this reason, James Sell once observed, Holsinger was not appreciated in his day. But, he went on to say, he "did more for the Church of the Brethren than he ever received credit for."[16]

In Sell's opinion Holsinger should have stayed in his home District—among the people who knew him best and accepted him for what he was. Then the feisty publisher, he believed, would not have broken with the church. Sometimes the old elder must have wondered if all would have been different had he remained in the *Companion* office. There were those who thought so:

> During my stay with Bro. Holsinger as associate editor, I had my home with him. We ate at the same table, commenced each day at the same family altar, and walked into the sanctuary together on the Sabbath Day. I stood side by side with him in the work of the ministry, parted with him in love, and [heard] his beloved wife say, "Had you and Henry continued together, this distressing trouble never would have taken place."[17]

An in-depth look at Holsinger's personality and impact on the Church of the Brethren appears in the next chapter.

The Brumbaugh Brothers and the Pilgrim

For most of two years before Holsinger's departure, Middle District was the seat of a pair of adult weeklies. The second paper was the product of three Brumbaugh brothers from the James Creek church—Henry, John, and George. All three spent their boyhood days on a farm along the Raystown Branch of the Juniata River. The ascendant member of this fraternal trio was the faithful diarist Henry, then thirty-four. He farmed and taught school for several years before eloping, at twenty-four, with Susan Peightal, a teenage Lutheran. Afterwards he took up full-time farming at the Branch homestead, making and selling brooms on the side. He was elected to the ministry at James Creek in 1864.

His brother John, youngest of the three, also combined teaching and farming for a living, while George, the oldest, ran a wagon shop. George, himself thirty-six, was given a ministerial call at Clover Creek in 1857, the year before the James Creek congregation was organized. He married a Brethren girl, Fannie Myers, from McVeytown. John did not marry until 1874, when he met Eleanor VanDyke, a company employee.

This triad of brothers found themselves drawn to the printing trade both as a creative outlet and as a way to serve the church. Sometime late in 1869 they formed the J. B. Brumbaugh Publishing Company. John, just out of his teens, was employed by Holsinger at the time, gaining valuable experience. Pedagogues at heart, they originally intended to introduce a juvenile paper. But Holsinger, quite innocently, stole their thunder and announced plans for his *Pious Youth*. Stymied, they offered to buy out the Tyrone publisher.

Henry B. Brumbaugh and John B. Brumbaugh.

Inclined at first to sell, he then reneged, and the bargaining fell through. It was agreed, however, that the Brumbaughs could publish a rival adult paper. Without seeking outright District warrant, they went about preparing a prospectus to be released the first of the year.

The Brumbaughs called their paper the *Pilgrim*. It was designed, according to the prospectus, "for the encouragement of the pilgrim on his way to Zion" and bore the motto: "Remove not the Ancient Landmarks which our Fathers have set." This motto, Henry explained one time, did not imply a reactionary outlook or sectarian bias on the part of the editors. Instead, it meant the landmarks set by Jesus and the apostles. The *Pilgrim*, the brothers hoped, would also attract non-Brethren readers. Moreover, they had no intention of subjecting their patrons to the polemics that characterized the *Companion*. The oblique reprimand given Holsinger by a District query in 1869 was ample warning for them. Their editorial policies would be more temperate; the paper would be aggressive and liberal, but not antagonistic and fractious.

The initial number of the *Pilgrim* was dated January 1, 1870. Printed by Theodore Cremer of the Huntingdon *Republican*, it was sent via the Broad Top Railroad to the Brumbaugh Station. There it was picked up and taken five miles to Henry's home on the Branch farm. Then the brothers, assisted by Henry's wife, folded and addressed each copy, and carted them to the post office for mailing. This inefficient, roundabout process continued until spring, when they set up their own shop. The *Pilgrim* was published semi-monthly until May; after that it came out weekly.

In April Henry sold his place at the Branch and moved to nearby Marklesburg, a quiet hamlet of some one hundred residents. He converted part of his house into an office and press room. The brothers then acquired a used Washington handpress and hired a typesetter. On May 3 they ran off the first Brumbaugh-printed issue of the *Pilgrim*. They also did some job printing on the side. Henry and John bore the brunt of the work load, George being tied down by his wagon and carriage shop in Hesston. The routine consisted of setting type during the day and preparing editorials or writing business letters at night. Many times in those first months, John wrote later, "the villagers could have heard the click of the old frisket in the midnight hours."[18]

The financial picture at the end of 1870 was not bright. With barely three hundred subscribers, the Brumbaughs had lost money. But, as Henry admitted, it had cost them too much to quit. "It was sink or swim." Their plight, he had to confess, was not so desperate as that of Holsinger in his maiden year of publishing. Nor were they plagued by counterfeit money as he was, innocently sent in by unsuspecting subscribers. (Holsinger ran frequent editorials, after starting the *Companion*, to divulge ways his readers could detect bogus currency.)

Undaunted by insolvency, the J. B. Brumbaugh Company plunged into 1871 with high expectations. They set an improbable circulation goal of 3,500. The *Pilgrim* was expanded from eight to sixteen pages, and they raised the subscription rate to $1.25 per year.

The Brumbaugh enterprise, fortified by job work, gained a firmer financial footing during the next two years. In 1871 the *Pilgrim* was going to four hundred post offices. And by the end of 1872 it claimed a clientele in twenty-five states, from Maine to South Carolina and from Pennsylvania to California. There was even one subscriber in Derbyshire, England.

The capacity of the iron handpress was now no longer equal to printing demands. So in January 1872 the Brumbaughs invested close to one thousand dollars in a modern mechanical press. This was a Fairhaven model, adaptable to either steam or water power. But they could not afford to install power equipment, and so the Fairhaven was operated manually. A friend of theirs once quipped that he "would rather make rails than turn the Brumbaugh press."

The purchase of the Fairhaven allowed the brothers, for a brief time, to indulge in a sideline project. The Washington press idled, Henry proposed putting it to use in publishing a local newspaper somewhere. Martinsburg, with a population of about five hundred, struck them as a likely place, since it was less than twenty miles distant and stood at the hub of the Cove area. Nothing had been done about a newspaper there since Holsinger's abortive effort a decade and a half ago. They created the H. B. Brumbaugh Company with John and B. F. Lehman, a shop employee, as editors, The inaugural number of the *Cove Echo,* a weekly, was pressed February 29, 1872, in Marklesburg. The Cove's first paper promised to be: "Independent on all subjects, neutral on none." Early in March the Washington press was transported by wagon over Tussey Mountain to Martinsburg.* After that the *Echo* was then printed there. An office was set up on Market Street above Bollinger's Hardware Store, under Lehman's supervision. The *Echo* was making good progress by September, when Henry and John suddenly withdrew from all personal involvement. Lehman became its outright owner sometime before March 1873. Financial matters, however, were not settled until August of 1874, apparently after some litigation.

This sudden loss of interest in the *Echo* resulted from an unexpected turn of events for the Brumbaughs. In May 1872 Henry had sold his shop-home, and ever since had been scouting around for a place to relocate. Tentative plans had been made in August to move to Martinsburg. But their minds were changed by Dr. Andrew B. Brumbaugh and other relatives, who did not want the brothers to go beyond the bounds of the James Creek congregation. Consequently, the *Pilgrim* publishers opted for Huntingdon, where their cousin practiced medicine. Huntingdon, at that time a bustling borough of three thousand situated along the Pennsylvania Railroad, seemed to them to hold out more promise for business growth than Martinsburg. So in the spring of 1873 Henry bought a lot in the west end from another cousin, Henry Brumbaugh, a brother of the doctor.

Here he built a large three-story brick duplex (still standing), half of it designed for a dwelling, the other half for business purposes. Two days before Christmas 1873, Henry, his wife, and their three-year-old son, Harvey, moved in. Eight wagons, donated by relatives and friends, hauled the household goods and shop equipment the ten miles to Huntingdon. John, still single, took a room nearby. George, however, dropped out of the partnership. He was then the presiding elder at James Creek.

After the shift to Huntingdon, the J. B. Brumbaugh Company prospered, benefiting from a greater market for job printing. The *Pilgrim,* though, failed to gain the large reader clientage claimed by either the *Visitor* or the *Companion* before their consolidation in 1873. The denomination's membership at that time approximated 55,000. From within the Brotherhood the *Pilgrim* probably never

---

*This press is now preserved in Juniata College's L. A. Beeghly Library, still operational.

attracted more than a thousand subscribers, a figure far below that of its two competitors.

Increasingly, the *Pilgrim* editors made themselves heard in church circles, especially Henry, who became a frequent participant in Annual Conference debates. Joined by Quinter, who now owned both the *Visitor* and the *Companion,* they contended doggedly for an old Holsinger cause—a full report of Conference business. The Brumbaughs disagreed with the reactionary elders who warned that the identification of speakers and the printing of their remarks would engender pride. Their bitterest opponents, though, were those elders who disliked having Conference decisions questioned by postmortem editorials and articles. In their view this reflected upon the character of Annual Conference. Printing the full text of debates, they maintained, would only promote widespread skepticism about Conference actions. Brethren schools, dress, an educated and paid ministry, Sunday School work, and kindred progressive ideas aroused high feelings that did not subside when Conference adjourned. Therefore these elders took the hard line: "We don't want a report; other people have no business to know what is going on here."[19]

Quietly but resolutely, the Brumbaughs chose to ignore this kind of mentality. Henry took a stenographer to Conference with him in 1873, and somehow got away with it. He was, however, made to give a public apology, as was Quinter, for publishing articles unsympathetic to past Conference actions. On the reporting impasse, Conference that year made one concession. It permitted a synopsis of speeches to be published in pamphlet form, omitting the names of speakers. But in 1874 the Brumbaughs and Quinter collaborated on a booklet that circumvented this ruling. As a subterfuge, they devised a system whereby speeches were numerically keyed. A copy of the key, which identified each speaker, could be obtained separately upon request.

For the Brumbaughs, as it had been for Holsinger, the principle at stake here was the free press. They used the pages of the *Pilgrim* to applaud this principle, and to plead for the right of an informed Brotherhood. Middle District stood solidly behind them. In 1876 fifteen out of its eighteen churches went on record in favor of an unexpunged Conference report. The matter was resolved at Conference that year by a compromising measure, which had originated in Middle District the spring before. A plenary record could be published, it was decided, but not in any of the Brethren periodicals. It had to be done independently, with the publisher bearing full responsibility for the harm that might result.

At the peak of the "free press" fight, the brothers, who had just launched a school, took on yet another challenge. It seemed to them an opportune time to reintroduce a young people's paper. Holsinger's *Pious Youth* had been suspended in 1872 and the field was now wide open. Therefore in January 1876 they began to publish a paper called the *Young Disciple*. It was the first Brethren paper edited by a female, Wealthy A. Clark (she later married Daniel C. Burkholder).[20] A member of the Aughwick congregation, she had been with the Brumbaughs since 1870. (She relinquished the editorship in 1879.) Under her guidance the *Young Disciple,* which also included selected readings of general interest, became a widely accepted Sunday School tool. The sixteen-page monthly was printed in four parts, one for each Sunday. For thirty-three years it remained the most popular Brethren youth publication, eventually being absorbed by *Our Boys and Girls* in 1905.

The year 1876 turned out to be a bittersweet one for Henry and John. For them it meant not only the initiation of the *Young Disciple* and a normal school, but also the demise of the *Pilgrim.* The termination of the *Pilgrim* came about as the result of a merger. A trend toward the coalescence of Brethren papers had begun in 1873. At that time James Quinter bought out H. J. Kurtz and Holsinger, and combined the *Visitor* and the *Companion.* He moved to Meyersdale, and there published a paper that for two years carried both names of the merged periodicals. In 1876 he shortened its title to *Primitive Christian.* By then the paper boasted a subscription list of six thousand and a reading public of from fifteen to twenty thousand.

As for the Brumbaughs, they had been approached by Quinter and Holsinger about some kind of general consolidation as early as October 1870. It was a hurried conference in the Huntingdon depot. But Henry and John, only in their first year of publishing, apparently were not very receptive to the idea. Little more was said to them about such a possibility for several years. Beginning in August 1874 Quinter, now the proprietor of two merged papers, began to press the brothers on the matter. He made a series of extended visits to Huntingdon over the succeeding months. Finally, in July 1876 the *Pilgrim* owners came to terms.

In October the two printing plants were incorporated into the firm of Quinter and Brumbaugh Brothers, with a capital stock of $20,000. Quinter, the senior partner, took over as editor-in-chief, and the *Pilgrim* Building was made the firm's headquarters. The sheet of this merger kept the name *Primitive Christian,* since Quinter's paper commanded a much wider circulation. The first number of the consolidated *Primitive Christian* went out October 25,

1876. It had nearly ten thousand subscribers. The title page read: "Published by permission of the Church of the Brethren," an unofficial denominational tag borrowed from Henry Holsinger.

James Quinter Comes to Middle Pennsylvania

This latest merger brought to the area, in the person of James Quinter, a man of rare caliber. He had fully vindicated the trust Kurtz placed in him back in 1856. Aged sixty, he had a dozen more good years in him to give to the church in a variety of ways. Quinter was a "God sent man," John Moore wrote of him. Among the Brethren, Henry Brumbaugh declared, "he was known and loved by all." "In the prime of his life," James Sell said, "he bore the laurels of the whole Brotherhood." On a more mundane level, his rise to modest wealth as a publisher had a Horatio Alger touch, coming as he did from a poor family.

James Quinter.

His father died when Quinter was thirteen, obliging the boy to become the family breadwinner. Nevertheless, he finished public school in Phoenixville, in Eastern Pennsylvania, and briefly attended a boarding school in West Bradford. He began teaching school at eighteen, and stayed in the classroom for twenty-two years. Then in 1856 Kurtz invited him to the editorial staff of the *Visitor*. The future president of Juniata College was twice married, his first wife, Mary Ann Moser, falling victim to tuberculosis. His second marriage was to Fannie Studebaker, in 1861.

Quinter devoted nearly fifty years of his life to the church. At twenty-two he was called to the ministry by the Coventry congregation in Eastern Pennsylvania. The George's Creek church, in Western Pennsylvania's Fayette County, ordained him an elder in 1856. The year before, he was named assistant writing clerk at Annual Conference. This appointment brought him into personal contact with Kurtz, then the writing clerk. Kurtz was so impressed with him that he would not rest until Quinter agreed to become his co-editor. In 1859 he succeeded Kurtz as writing clerk, an office he filled with but two interruptions for twenty-six years. And between 1859 and 1887 he was twenty-seven times elected to the prestigious Standing Committee.

The years of Quinter's rise to prominence in the Brotherhood were an age of religious debate. Such able men as Alexander Campbell, founder of the Disciples of Christ Church, and scores of others made debating immensely popular. Every denomination and sect stood ready to defend its doctrinal claims. Quinter entered the polemical arena in 1856, and soon the Brethren looked to him as the champion of their faith and practice. Most of his debates dealt with the more novel Brethren ordinances, such as mode of baptism, feetwashing, and the Lord's Supper. His book *Trine Immersion,* published years later, became a standard Brethren work.

Quinter, the heralded debater, became sole editor and part owner of the *Visitor* in 1864. This was after a three-year stint as principal of the New Vienna Academy in Clinton County, Ohio. While head of the academy, which he started, he still helped to edit the *Visitor.* After his return he and his partner, Henry J. Kurtz, the founder's son, moved the paper's office twice. In 1866 they located it at Covington, and in 1869 at Dayton.

During this time Quinter became something of an authority on hymnology. In 1867 he compiled and published the *Brethren's Hymn Book.* This was probably the best selection of hymns then known in the Brotherhood. It was the income from the sale of this popular hymnal that made him all but financially independent for the rest of his life. (It is interesting to note how the nineteenth-century printers, especially the first ones, promoted hymnbooks among the Brethren—Kurtz, Quinter and Holsinger. Holsinger, while at Tyrone, began work on the first Brethren hymnal with musical notation. He completed it at Meyersdale. Later, after his sale of the *Companion,* the Brumbaughs published a revised edition for him.)

The economic security enjoyed by Quinter did not turn him into a man of leisure. He was a true exemplar of the Puritan work ethic. He was out of bed and at his desk every morning by four o'clock. It is said that he never took a vacation, or allowed himself the luxury of a pleasure trip. Almost every Sunday, for fifty years, he could be heard somewhere from the pulpit.

A kind and gentle person, always well-groomed, he was devoid of humor. He never joked or quipped, and had no time for small talk. He smiled readily, but seldom laughed. John Moore said that he only once ever heard him laugh. That was when Quinter told of how his parishioners at George's Creek put him on a run-down farm. In due time, the publisher chuckled, they learned that their pastor was not "cut out" for a farmer.[21]

This, then, was the man whom James Sell credited with doing more than anyone else "to lift the church to a higher plane in the realm of letters." His place in the Brotherhood as a respected literary figure was secure by the time he came to Middle District. And like many in his new church home, he was uneasy about the proliferation of religious papers. By the late 1870s they were furiously fanning the flames of contention. They pitted not only progressives against conservatives, but both extremes against the moderates. Middle District in 1879 was among the first to voice concern about "the superfluous number of periodicals now published in the brotherhood" and to call for a reduction.

Birth of the Gospel Messenger

By 1880 eight adult papers (not counting the *Pilgrim* and the *Primitive Christian*) had been spawned, all in the 1870s. The earliest was the *Vindicator,* a monthly published at Dayton, Ohio. It became the organ of the Old Order Brethren after the 1881 split. Next came *Der Breuderbote,* in 1875, published at Lancaster. Beginning in 1876, this monthly was co-published with an English edition, the *Brethren Messenger,* at Germantown. It ceased soon after (but was revived in 1884 at Grundy Center, Iowa), and the name of the *Messenger* was changed to *Brethren at Work.* The latter's headquarters was subsequently moved to Mount Morris, Illinois.

The years 1878 and 1879 produced a spate of papers. Holsinger and Beer published the *Progressive Christian,* a weekly, at Berlin. It later became the paper for the Brethren Church, and its name was changed to the *Brethren's Evangelist.* Two other periodicals, short-lived and controversial, were the *Brethren's Advocate* at Waynesboro and a radical monthly, the *Deacon,* at Lewisburg. Solomon Z. Sharp, the well-known educator and founder of Kishacoquillas Seminary in Middle District, started two papers in 1879—the *Gospel Preacher* (it combined with the *Progressive Christian* in 1882) and the *Brethren's Quarterly.*

During the schismatic years 1880–1882, the push for a wholesale merger of all adult papers gained momentum. In 1880 the editors of three papers—the *Primitive Christian, Brethren at Work,* and *Gospel*

Preacher—held a round of merger talks. They met in Huntingdon and at Ashland, Ohio, but negotiations bogged down. Conference then in 1881 appointed a committee to study the matter and bring back a report the next year. Henry Brumbaugh was named one of the six committee members. Their report in 1882 presented two alternative plans. The one accepted included the following proposal:

> We the owners and publishers of the *Primitive Christian* and *Brethren at Work* have this day agreed upon a basis for consolidation on the following conditions:
> Two papers shall be published, one East and one West, or one paper with a branch office, as Annual Meeting and the consolidated form may think to be for the best interests of the church.
> The Annual Meeting shall recognize this paper, or papers, as the case may be, as the official church paper.
> We agree to make ourselves directly amenable to Annual Meeting for the contents and character of the paper or papers.
> We also further agree to purchase at a reasonable price any other papers now published in the Brotherhood, and to merge them into the consolidated paper or papers:
> If the above is not acceptable to Annual Meeting, we hereby agree to sell our respective papers to any company that this Annual Meeting may designate at the price agreed upon between ourselves as the bearer for our proposed consolidation.
>
> Quinter & Brumbaugh Bros.
Miller & Amich[22]

The consolidation was finalized the next year, with the formation of the Brethren's Publishing Company. It was decided to publish one paper but operate with two branch offices, at Huntingdon and Mount Morris. Quinter, now Juniata's president (since 1879) as well as a publisher, was made editor-in-chief. He continued in this position until his death in 1888. The post of Eastern editor went to Henry Brumbaugh. His brother, John, left editorial work temporarily and ran a haberdashery downtown. For a few months in 1884 he substituted as office editor at Mount Morris. This was all that it took to get him back in the harness again, and after returning home was placed on the paper's staff as an associate editor.

The paper born of this merger was given the once-familiar name, *Gospel Messenger,* its title till the mid-1960s. By Conference action it was the official organ of the Church of the Brethren. Its first number was July 3, 1883. The troubled days of 1880–1882 were now over, and the paper's biggest task was to help restore Brethren unity. For a time the *Pilgrim* Building housed the *Gospel Messenger*'s Eastern office. Then in 1885 it was moved downtown across from the Opera House on Washington Street. Finally, in the spring of 1890 the two

branch offices were centralized at Mount Morris. Closing the Eastern department brought to an end a vital chapter in the history of
Middle Pennsylvania. After a quarter of a century, it would no
longer be a part of the Brethren publishing scene.

But prior to the reorganizing of the business, Henry Brumbaugh
gambled on a different kind of journal. This was the *Golden Dawn*, a
thirty-two page religious and educational monthly coedited by
another female, Adaline Hohf (she married William Beery, the
beloved centenarian musician and longtime Juniata professor). The
main purpose of this magazine, introduced in May 1885, was to
promote one of Henry's controlling interests—Brethren schools (it
also contained Sunday School material for those too mature to
appreciate the *Young Disciple*). He hoped that it would help recruit
students for the nascent institutions springing up in the Brotherhood. There was special space allotted in each issue for news from
each of the four schools—Juniata, Spring Creek, Mount Morris, and
McPherson. To his disappointment the *Dawn* was a journalistic dud
and was dropped in August 1887.

The year the *Dawn* expired there developed agitation to give the
church outright ownership of the press. Conference was besieged by
a host of queries asking for a change in the management and
ownership of the *Gospel Messenger*. This mood was precipitated by
the growing sentiment that Conference ought to become a legal
corporation (which it did in 1889). Since 1884, Conference had been
considering the possibility of the church's holding property. Then
the Brethren's Book and Tract Committee, set up in 1885, brought
the matter to a head. It proposed establishing a permanent endowment fund, the interest on which was to be used for book and tract
work. Some Brethren saw wisdom in uniting this activity with a
church paper under direct Conference supervision.

Therefore the 1887 Conference delegated a Committee on Publications to look into the advisability of a church-owned press. The
committee's report the next year recommended that "the Brotherhood . . . purchase the entire outfit and interest of the Brethren's
Publishing Company, and merge this and the Brethren's Book and
Tract Work into one corporation." Middle Pennsylvania, apparently, did not take kindly to this counsel, to judge from District
minutes, though the *Gospel Messenger* editors did. Another nine years
passed before this suggested plan was implemented. Finally, on
April 1, 1897, the Brethren's Publishing Company was dissolved and
its assets transferred to the church. At that time its stockholders
were earning an astonishing twelve percent dividend. When turned
over to the church, the *Gospel Messenger* had a circulation of 15,600
and the *Young Disciple* 18,000.

Under liquidation terms Henry Brumbaugh was to receive, besides a cash settlement, a handsome annuity based on a certain number of shares he had held in Publishing Company stock. Now sixty-one, he had the vigor of a man half his age. In 1888 he had been ordained an elder at Huntingdon, and soon after took over the presidency of Juniata, succeeding Quinter. He held that position until 1893. The next year he helped to found the Union Bank of Huntingdon, being elected vice president in 1895. Up to his death in 1919, however, he maintained close ties with the *Gospel Messenger*. Co-editor until 1908, he retired from full-time duties that year, contributing regularly thereafter as one of its corresponding editors.

John Brumbaugh fell under the same liquidation terms as his brother, but he chose to leave the printing business now once and for all. Called to the ministry in 1888, he was ordained in 1897—a month after the Brethren's Publishing Company went out of business. He taught Bible courses at Juniata, and then later served as pastor of the Huntingdon congregation. Occasionally, he found time to prepare guest *Gospel Messenger* editorials.

Thus the year 1897 ended an era in Brethren journalism. It was an era that saw the church move from a hands-off policy toward Brethren papers to one of censorship and then ultimate ownership and control. Undeniably, the 1880–1882 schism was in large measure a tragic consequence of the printed page. It was this breach that hardened the resolve in the Brotherhood for a noncontroversial press.

But there was a positive side too. It was also an era that made intentional use of papers as an educational medium. To an extent not appreciated today, the press became a force to mold sentiment and shape a new denominational identity. It was an era that produced men and women who challenged the church's "wilderness" mentality—an outlook that emerged with the frontier diaspora after the 1770s and that was marked by withdrawal and antiintellectual stagnation.

Moreover, it was an era of great change and shifting values, both inside and outside the Brotherhood. The emergence of urban America posed serious dilemmas for all rural people—but especially for the Brethren. Middle Pennsylvania, as we have seen, was not a silent bystander in those dynamic years. It could claim its share of those protagonists who enlisted the press to set new bounds of relationship between faith and life.

7
The Progressive Schism

The integrity of Middle District has been tested twice by splinter movements. The first one, Holsinger-led progressivism, was the fallout from a churchwide disturbance. It took its toll in Central Pennsylvania, but did not result in wholesale defection. Holsinger's ideology had always enjoyed general support in the District, but only a few chose to follow in his schismatic path. Proportionately, though, the loss in District membership as a result of the 1882 rift was about the same as that of Brotherhood at large. That schism cost the Brethren, in the course of a few years, five thousand members or one-tenth of their rolls.

The second movement was a Middle District phenomenon that, for the most part, bypassed the rest of the denomination. It was an outgrowth of a long-standing twentieth-century controversy in religious thought: fundamentalism vs. modernism. The impact of this dispute on District churches is traced out in later chapters.

Henry Holsinger Breaks with the Brotherhood

In chapter 6 Henry R. Holsinger's publishing career was described in some detail and his temperamental traits were briefly noted. We saw how he used his papers, the *Christian Family Companion* and the *Progressive Christian,* to promote reform sentiment among the Brethren. In the process, to borrow Elder John H. Moore's words, he most certainly succeeded in "rocking the old ship."[1] The sad thing is that, basically, Holsinger was in accord with the fundamental doctrines of the church. His quarrel with the Brotherhood's ruling elders was mostly over policy and methods. There were those who thought he only reluctantly became a defector. His biggest problem was his abrasive personality.

At any rate, in chapter 6 it was shown that his editorial practices and a series of abusive showdowns at Conference combined to produce a phalanx of opposition to him in nearly every district. By 1873 it was being bruited that Standing Committee was on the verge of expelling him from the church. Thus, to avoid a division, as he later claimed, he went to James Quinter and persuaded him to buy his paper that year.

Constantly moving about for three years, Holsinger eventually landed in Chicago, "anchored at last," he said in one of his letters.[2] He hired on as foreman in a job printing office, the *Christian Cynosure*. On the side he ran a produce commission business. Isolated and lonely, he was pleased to hear occasionally from church leaders. "Had a letter from Enoch Eby today, with one from Isaac Price yesterday. I am still remembered," he gratefully wrote his father in 1876.[3] The heartaches he had caused his father must have been on his mind when he closed with the words, "Truly your unworthy son." His wife, Susannah, loyal to the end, was also grieved by the course of events. To John Moore, who was visiting in their home at that time, she said, "Brother Moore, I never thought it would come to this."[4]

But Holsinger was *not* "anchored" in Chicago, for in the fall of 1878 we find him in Berlin, Pennsylvania. There, with Joseph Beer, who had spent a few years working for Quinter and the Brumbaughs at Huntingdon, he started another paper, the *Progressive Christian*. He was even more outspoken in this paper than he had been in the *Companion*. Others, like Peter Beaver at Lewisburg, Pennsylvania, who published the *Deacon*, a small, radically progressive monthly, soon lined up with him. In 1879 Holsinger provoked a storm of protest as the result of an article that panned Standing Committee, satirizing it as a "secret society."

The ruling body took great alarm the next year when Holsinger himself was ordained to the office of elder. He was given charge of three congregations in Western District: Berlin, Stony Creek, and Somerset. This elevation in the Brethren hierarchy meant that now, as an elder, he was eligible for election to Standing Committee. To some elders, jealous of their quasi-episcopate status, Holsinger posed a subversive threat to existing church polity. He and his cohorts repudiated the sovereignty of Annual Conference and deprecated the power invested in a select coterie of elders—Standing Committee. They declared that all authority resided in the local congregation.

There were, in the main, three points on which Holsinger held different views from the practices of the Brotherhood. As just observed, he denied the authority of Annual Conference to discipline individuals or local churches. He had little use for the prayer veil, and third, he thought the Brethren were fussing too much over the dress question.

An immediate consequence of Holsinger's stepped-up progressive crusade was the Old Order secession during 1881–82. These ultraconservatives had been Holsinger's bitterest foes. Their strength was in the Miami Valley region of Southern Ohio, with enclaves of allies in the states of Pennsylvania, Indiana, Maryland, Missouri, and Illinois. The *Vindicator,* published at Dayton, was their organ. Its articles and editorials were highly critical of Conference for being tolerant of Holsinger's advanced views. The Old Order Brethren held several rump conferences in 1880 and 1881. Finally, in the fall of the latter year most of their leaders and hundreds of laymen were expelled, and their church property was confiscated. These actions were ratified by the 1882 Conference. Ultimately, about three thousand Old Order adherents separated from the mother church.

Meanwhile, some conservatives of the main body grew fearful that strong progressionist sympathy in Middle District would induce others to secede. Accordingly, Moses Miller of Mechanicsburg (the District then included Cumberland County) wrote to Jacob Miller, the elder at New Enterprise and Woodbury, in December 1881:

What I had thought to write to you and others about is this: I fear the Huntingdon [people] and some others are rather helping to drive off some to the Miami faction. You know a few years ago annual meeting decided that brethren should not have Sunday-school conventions. Soon after that Quinter and the Brumbaughs had a program published about [a] Sunday-school convention. Last annual meeting it was decided that the brethren should not call their colleges or schools the Brethren's School. As soon as the report came it had a picture on the cover of a school building, and at the top, "The Brethren's Normal." What does my Brother Jack think of this? The very brother that wrote and printed the decision of annual meeting, to violate and transgress it first.

That is not all. In August attended a Sunday-school convention and giving their proceedings in the paper, calling H. R. Holsinger brother, who, I hold, is legally expelled [this will be explained below]; and mixing in with him and a ring of dandy members. How can you old brethren, who are so near to James Quinter, let it pass? . . . There must be something done in this matter by our next district meeting.[5]

Miller asked that his letter be shared with John W. Brumbaugh at Martinsburg and John Replogle and Daniel M. Holsinger (father of Henry) at Clover Creek.

The 1882 District Conference was held at Snake Spring Valley, the moderator being Moses Miller. Five queries were introduced relating to the current unrest in the Brotherhood. One of them, originating in the Upper Cumberland congregation and obviously framed by Miller, elicited an interesting reaction. The query read:

Inasmuch as the fast element or Progressives, so called, caused a portion of the churches of the Miami Valley, Ohio, and elsewhere, to withdraw from the brotherhood, therefore, we ask District Meeting to ask A M to draw up resolutions agreeable with the Gospel and the general order of the brotherhood.

This was a transparent indictment of the progressive movement, but the session rebuffed the query's proponents and voted to "drop" it. Instead, it supported a petition from Clover Creek requesting District Conference "to instruct delegates to A M to use every legitimate or evangelical means to bring about a compromise that the different (so called) elements may be united." This was a much more conciliatory posture, devoid of any faultfinding.

Meanwhile, the Ashland, Ohio, Conference in 1881 had taken steps that brought the trouble to a focus. It designated a committee to go to Berlin to deal with Holsinger "according to his transgressions." The Berlin committee met with him on August 9, but he refused to be tried in his home congregation without the presence of a stenographer.[6] He also insisted upon a hearing open to members and nonmembers alike. The committee, however, declined to proceed under this arrangement on the grounds that it was contrary to general church usage. As a result, the next day it accused Holsinger of "insubordination to the traditions of the elders," and voted to disfellowship him. This decision, of course, was subject to the approval of the next Conference. Such was his status in the church, then, when Moses Miller penned the letter cited above.

The Berlin committee submitted its report on ostracizing Holsinger in 1882 to the now-famous Arnold's Grove Conference, held near Milford, Indiana. The best part of a day was spent debating it before the delegates ratified the committee's action. When the vote was taken, some seven thousand persons stood en masse. Only about one hundred opposed the motion.

Holsinger, his defenders have insisted, abhorred the idea of being considered a schismatic. He made two unsuccessful attempts to avoid a division in the church. First, at the time of debate on the Berlin committee's recommendation, he presented, through Elder Daniel Moomaw, a compromise paper termed an "olive-branch of peace." It began with an abject apology for past offenses. There followed a short list of promises guaranteeing that his future conduct would be unimpeachably orthodox.

I, H. R. Holsinger, herein set forth the following declaration of purpose and conduct which shall be my guide and standard in my future relation with the church. First, I humbly ask the pardon of the brethren for all my offenses, general and particular, committed in the past either through the *Progressive Christian* or otherwise. Second, I promise hereafter to administer the discipline of the church in harmony with the practices of the church, and will cease to practice or teach any system of church government, not in harmony with that prevailing in the church as set forth by A. M. Third, I promise to cease to speak or write in antagonism to general order and union of its practices now prevailing in the church. Fourth, I promise to cease the publishing of the *Progressive Christian* or any other paper or anything in fact in opposition to A. M. Fifth, I promise to publish these declarations in the *Progressive Christian,* and to harmonize action with the church. I ask that these be placed upon the minutes of this meeting.

But Conference turned a deaf ear to this overture. Then, after the expulsion vote, he and a contingent of supporters drafted a memorial, petitioning Standing Committee to approve a select body representing both church factions, to work out a solution for reconciliation. This request was rejected because it did not come through normal district channels. Twice spurned, the Holsinger wing met a few weeks later at Ashland, Ohio, to organize the Brethren (Progressive) Church.

Progressivism in Middle District

In Middle Pennsylvania the most fruitful proselytizing territory for the Progressives was Morrisons Cove. The pioneer worker for their cause there was William L. Spanogle, one of the most vocal dissenters to the Berlin committee report. Born at Germany Valley (his father was its presiding elder), he was living in Marklesburg at the time of the agitation, a member of the James Creek congregation. In November 1882 James Creek debarred him from fellowship for conducting a preaching mission for the Progressives at Meyersdale. The succeeding month he delivered the first Progressive sermon in the District at the Fairview church. Ironically, Henry Holsinger had been the dedication speaker when it was built in 1874. During December and January if 1882 Spanogle held protracted meetings at the Henrietta Crossroads church. This led to the organization of a like-minded congregation in that area with forty-five charter members, most of them from the Clover Creek fold. He was elected pastor, preaching alternately at Crossroads, Duncansville, and Fredericksburg. Eventually, the Progressive Brethren purchased a union church building at Fredericksburg.

Another eminent early Progressive leader was Rinehart Z. Replogle of New Enterprise, son of one of the first Brethren settlers in the Cove. Articulate and in his mid-thirties, he had been called to the

ministry in 1880. He attended the Arnold's Grove conference to
fight against Holsinger's excommunication. With prescience, he
argued that such severe action "will rend the church from the
Atlantic to the Pacific." He was a prime mover behind the memorial
petition for a compromise, and was named to the committee that
drafted it. He was present at the founding conventions of the
Brethren Church, at Ashland and Dayton. He and his large family
lived in Johnstown at the time of the famous 1889 flood and
survived a harrowing experience, their house destroyed by rampaging waters.

Three Cove churches—Clover Creek, Woodbury, and New
Enterprise—were the hardest hit by Progressive unrest. All three,
with a combined membership of nearly one thousand, held separate
council meetings about the same time, in August 1882, to settle the
trouble. Invited to assist at each church were George Brumbaugh of
James Creek, John L. Holsinger of Dunnings Creek, and James
Quinter. Apparently, Clover Creek successfully resolved its problems, but a prolonged crisis developed at Woodbury and its parent
congregation, New Enterprise. These churches called a special joint
council for December 2, at which time Rinehart Replogle was
disfellowshiped. Another combined council was held February 17,
1883, to hear an appeal from Replogle, who still had not openly
broken with the church. But he and a band of sympathizers walked
out on the council during deliberations. He returned before ad-
journment and announced a meeting the next night in a local
schoolhouse to choose a delegate to the upcoming Dayton convention (he was elected that delegate). By a vote of 39 to 3 (3 absentions)
the council then lifted the membership of thirteen others and passed
the following resolution, according to the 1925 history:

> Inasmuch as the hereinafter named members of our church district have
> identified themselves with the Progressive brethren and have so declared
> to the brethren who visited them, we therefore accept their declaration
> as a withdrawal of their membership from us, and we exclude them from
> the privilege of communion, church council and the salutation of the
> kiss.

Among the thirteen were the church clerk and the church treasurer.
This action was confirmed at the next regular quarterly council,
August 16. At that time 150 voted for expulsion. In all, some thirty
eventually became Progressive communicants.

Carson Valley also felt some tremors from the Progressive disturbance. The congregation had just gone through a decade of steady
growth when the Holsinger issue halted the trend temporarily.

Attrition on a small scale had set in by August 1882. The members in council session that month passed a resolution stating: "In view of the conflicting elements of the Church Progression, etc., the church decides . . . to go on in the even tenor of the way, or stand where she has always stood."[7] This position was reaffirmed a year and a half later, in the face of a minor defection, inspired by the preaching of William Spanogle.

Many District leaders, including Henry Brumbaugh, suspected that one of Carson Valley's most distinguished members, Graybill Myers, would go Progressive. The instigator of District polity in the Brotherhood and architect of Middle District, he was one of the best-known evangelists in the State of Pennsylvania. He was active in the pulpit for fifty years, and allegedly preached in every Brethren church in the Commonwealth. He also made several tours through the Far West. Myers, the brother of five other Brethren preachers, had been Holsinger's elder at Warriors Mark and a warm personal friend. A few weeks after the Arnold's Grove decision, the seventy-two-year-old Eldorado elder wrote Holsinger:

> For my part I will call you my brother until it is proved that you have violated some law. And any member that contends for the whole law, and makes an effort to live it out, is my brother and my sister in the Lord. . . . You know I always was a little more progressive than most of the brethren of my age. . . .
> . . . My life is rapidly drawing to a close, and I do not want to die with animosity in my heart against any person. I take the Saviour's language for my guide, "For whoever shall do the will of my Father, which is in heaven, the same is my brother, and sister, and mother," exclusive of names. In this way I expect to meet the approbation of Him who has power to save.[8]

Myers, however, did not bolt the church, in spite of his liberal views. He told Henry Brumbaugh that "while he always preached that, if he ever found a church that came nearer the truth than the Brethren, he would feel it his duty to go with that church, [though] he has not yet found that church, and therefore knows of no other place to go."[9]

Germany Valley did not escape Progressive pangs either, but their crisis developed much later—about 1891. Nevertheless, trouble did crop up in 1880, revolving around William Spanogle and a few other dissidents.[10] Spanogle resigned as a minister in the congregation and moved to Marklesburg, placing his membership at James Creek. As we saw, he then broke with the Brethren and became a Progressive leader. Another Germany Valley minister, Thomas Chilcote, left the church in 1883 because of a Progressive penchant.

The biggest loss came several years later, in 1891, when fifteen members, involving four families, severed their church relations. John Shope, Jr., who was instrumental in starting the Black Log congregation, led the way, defecting the previous year.

All in all, the Progressive split made only minimal inroads on District congregations. Probably not more than one hundred members shifted allegiance, most of them from the Cove churches. This amounted to about one-tenth of the District membership. The attrition rate was not higher because, on most issues, local and District leaders stood in the vanguard of those working for liberal changes. Therefore, there did not develop in Middle Pennsylvania the sense of desperate frustration felt by many elsewhere in the Brotherhood.

Holsinger in Retrospect

The action of Annual Conference in 1882 shocked Holsinger, and he went into a period of depression. He was disappointed at how few from the Brotherhood had stood behind him or joined his new church group. It was said, however, that "he left more friends in the church than he took out, and some of them remained lifelong friends."[11] In the aftermath of his expulsion, as noted at the onset of this chapter, perhaps five thousand went with him.

Many Brethren were privately critical of Annual Conference for snubbing the "olive branch of peace" declaration. They believed that Holsinger was an honest man and would have abided by his promises. They felt that the Brotherhood incurred blame for driving away a person of great ability who generally accepted the New Testament fundamentals. They admired him for taking a stand for what he believed, in the course of which he set the people to "most vigorous thinking and wakened them up all along the line," as one prominent churchman later put it.[12]

Years later, Howard Miller, Brethren census-taker of the 1880s and editor of *Inglenook* who had been a personal friend of Holsinger, wrote upon learning of Holsinger's death:

> It would be hard to find another person, or to name one, who has so marked the Brethren Church at large. He was about forty years ahead of his surroundings. He was not a scholarly man in the sense of schools. He was a fighter. If he thought a thing ought to be done his plan was to do it, and like all such people, he generally got the worst of it. He was nearly always in hot water in the church.[13]

Continued Miller, in genuine admiration, "if he had his dues, as the world construes such things, he would have a monument for what he did." Unfortunately, the memorial article concluded, Holsinger was not a "good waiter." "He was too impulsive a Peter for that."

As this chapter and the one before clearly indicate, Holsinger was not without his share of postschism well-wishers in Central Pennsylvania, despite the fact that they chose not to shift church loyalties. His home District understood him better than those outside it.

After the Progressive breach Holsinger had health problems, and in 1887 he went to California. There he wrote his *History of the Tunkers and the Brethren Church,* a well-illustrated book of over eight hundred pages. He had hoped the Brethren Publishing House would print it, but that was not to be. His death occurred in 1905, while he was back East visiting in Johnstown, Pennsylvania.

8
The Brethren School Movement: 1856–1876

Early Brethren Resistance to Education

The half century after 1850 not only saw the Brethren rediscover the press; it also was the period that gave the church its six existing colleges. Printing and higher education, of course, were two closely related movements. Both drew their strength from the same cadre of progressives, who felt that the church could not survive in the absence of either. It was the religious press that forced the church to change its position on education. As a result, the Brethren recovered a patrimony almost lost for good during the so-called Wilderness Period, 1778–1850.

Central to the educational reawakening was the progressives' clamor for Brethren schools. Their insistent appeals took on all the qualities of a compelling crusade. This crusade progressed roughly in three stages. Prior to 1875, most efforts were directed at founding secondary schools. Then, from 1875 to 1890, followed the normal school idea. After 1890 came the liberal arts college, the capstone of educational reconstruction in the church. At every stage of this evolution, as the present chapter and the next one will show, Middle Pennsylvania made a major contribution.

Actually, the cultural depression that preceded the mid-century renaissance was something of an aberration in Brethren intellectual history. One need only recall that in the colonial church there was an impressive circle of educated men. Members of this first-generation intelligentsia, to name the more familiar ones, included John Naas, Peter Becker, the Sauers and the Macks, George Adam Martin, Michael Frantz, the two Martin Urners, John Priesz, and Michael Eckerlin. Formal education was important to the founding fathers. The Germantown Church operated a school in its parsonage (taught by a woman), and Christopher Sauer, Jr., was a founder and longtime trustee of the famous Germantown Academy.

But the decades after the Revolutionary War took their toll in learning. For almost a century the church neglected education. Its members, scattered in remote and undeveloped frontier country, sacrificed things of the mind to hew out homes and farms. In some places the Brethren very nearly became an illiterate people. Writes one social historian, at first "the boys learned to read and write and cipher. The girls sometimes attained the same accomplishments; more often they did not." But by 1850, he notes, many children "could barely read, some not at all."[1]

Educational recovery in the church began, it has been said, with the Pennsylvania public school law of 1834. This epochal statute was the first of its kind to be passed in a state with a strong Brethren concentration. Though it was not adopted statewide until some years later, it contributed to recovery in two ways. Bright children from Brethren homes who could not afford "select" or "subscription" schools (privately taught) were now able to get at least a basic education. Furthermore, because of this law, teaching as a career took on new status and security, luring the more ambitious away from the farm.

Among the Pennsylvania Brethren who taught before 1850 were a trio of preachers who, at one time or another, lived in the District— Jacob Miller, Enoch Eby, and James Quinter. In fact, Quinter could very well have been the first of the new breed to take up teaching as a profession—soon after 1830.

Surprisingly, despite the provincialism of the "Wilderness" era, the church never went on record in opposition to public school education. Annual Conference, though often disturbed by "worldly practices" in the schools, refused to challenge the system. Brethren offspring, then, could and did attend the grades with their church's blessing.

The hitch came when these children began to demand more than grammar school training, particularly those aiming to teach. This worried the church hierarchy. To them, any form of education beyond the elementary level seemed superfluous and posed a threat. There was the danger, they thought, that advanced learning would destroy the ideal of the simple life. Hence in 1852 and 1853 Annual Conference labeled colleges and high schools "unsafe" places.

Before 1875 high schools were not included as part of the public school system. Practically all secondary education up to that time was provided by academies. These were basically private schools, supported by tuition and by gifts and endowments; usually they had denominational ties. Beginning with the 1850s, a number of Brethren youngsters found their way to these academies, especially the church-related ones. The result was that some of the most promising of them drifted away into other faiths, or lost their religion altogether.

Beginning of the School Movement

In large part the Brethren school movement originated to stop this drain of talent. It was two ex-teachers, Henry Kurtz and James Quinter, the *Gospel Visitor* publishers, who first proposed a church-affiliated school. From the spring of 1856 on, they made their paper the medium for airing such an idea. Specifically, their plan, they said, was to establish a "school to educate young Brethren for school-teachers."[2] They stressed, "We think it is not only right that the church should encourage such institutions in which our youth may acquire useful knowledge, but we think it is her duty—a duty she owes to her God, to herself, and to the rising generation, to encourage and build up such institutions."[3] The kind of institution they had in mind would

> be under the influence of spiritually minded brethren. We would want religious teachers—teachers who would have a regard to the religious as well as to the intellectual improvement of students,—consequently the students would have religious counsel administered to them. We would have the Bible daily used. . . . We would have the students to board in a religious family. . . . In short, we would have the school to resemble a pious family, under such rules as would discountenance whatever is evil, and encourage whatever is good.[4]

But Annual Conference moved with caution, dismissing the Kurtz-Quinter proposition in 1857 with the terse answer, "It is conforming to the world. The Apostle Paul says, 'Knowledge puffeth up but charity edifieth.' " Yet the two men would not let the matter rest, plying the pages of the *Gospel Visitor* with cogent arguments for their project. The question came up again at Annual Conference the next year, and this time the church elders relented, modifying their former stand. They decided: "Concerning the school proposed in the *Gospel Visitor,* we think we have no right to interfere with an individual enterprise so long as there is no departure from Gospel principles." With that statement, a new era in Brethren educational history began.

The implication of the 1858 decision was clear—the proposed school was not to be church controlled. Annual Conference had only indirectly sanctioned private schools to be conducted by Brethren educators. Nevertheless, an important hurdle was cleared, and from

1860 to the close of the century Brethren schools mushroomed in profusion. Meanwhile, Kurtz and Quinter, in 1861, opened a school in New Vienna, Ohio.

Early Educational Activities in Middle Pennsylvania

BLOOMING GROVE SCHOOL

The "Wilderness" mentality did not apply to at least one Brethren community before 1850: the Blooming Grove settlement near Williamsport, then included in Middle District.[5] Here from the start education and religion were combined. Soon after settling Blooming Grove in 1805, the Brethren colonists put up a hut to serve them as church and school.

In 1828 a larger meetinghouse, a hewn log structure, replaced the old one. One description says that inside, it

> was arranged with the desks along the walls and the pupils facing the same, with the little children around tables in the middle of the room. The boys occupied one side and the girls the opposite. The teacher's desk was at the rear of the room. It was warmed by a ten plate stove.[6]

Then curriculum and discipline are described:

> The teachers were extremely severe in their discipline, often unreasonably exacting, and cruel with the rod. The smallest children had a little primer from which they learned their letters, and the simplest combinations. They were then promoted to the "spelling class," then to the "Psalm class," then to the "Testament class," finally to the "Bible class," after which their education was completed. The teacher would set them "sums to do," and write them "copies" on foolscap paper, to be laboriously imitated with a goose quill pen.[7]

The school term lasted the three winter months, and many pupils walked four miles to and from their homes.

Blooming Grove's first teacher and cofounder was Dr. Conrad Haller. A bachelor with a German university degree, he spoke five languages. "As a teacher he was of the old type," the 1925 district history says of his pedagogy. "His discipline measured up to the standard quite common for that day—to catch a child playing meant to give it a flogging."

Apparently, Haller's successors continued to perpetuate a high-quality school after his death in 1828. Years later, in the 1860s, when the state enforced the public school system in that area the people protested. They argued that the education gained under their teachers was superior to that of the state system. One time after this, so the story goes, the local grade school had a poor teacher. Defiantly, the residents withdrew their children and set up classes in a shop on a nearby farm.

Despite passion of this kind for what is best in learning, the Blooming Grove Brethren played no part in the church's educational awakening. Geographically isolated, they remained completely out of touch with the rest of the Brotherhood. Moreover, by the time the school issue was being bandied about at Conference, the community had started to break up, eventually passing into oblivion.

BUFFALO MILLS SCHOOL

In Henry Holsinger's opinion the man who actually cut the first turf for the Brethren school dream in the 1850s was Jacob Miller of Bedford County. He opened his school in the fall of 1852, almost five years before Kurtz and Quinter first raised their cry for such a move. Born February 18, 1828, the young educator was frail in health and physique and ill-suited for farm work. His understanding father, Andrew Miller, the second minister in the Wills Creek congregation, a churchless group that became defunct soon after the Civil War, steered him toward a teaching career.

As a teenager Jacob studied in Bedford, some ten miles from home, under Thomas A. Harris, said to have been a Catholic. In 1845, at age seventeen, he took a position in a public school near Schellsburg, where he stayed on for two years. From 1847 to 1852 he taught a select school in New Enterprise, boarded free by local Brethren as a way to keep him there. During this time he was baptized by James Quinter and called to the ministry.

The summer of 1852, Miller—ambitious, brainy, and sociable—was set to head West, but his father was able to change his mind. He then built a schoolhouse (36' x 50') on family property at Buffalo Mills in Wills Creek Valley. That fall he opened an elementary school with about forty students. Several of them hailed from distant places, rooming and boarding with the family. The school was coeducational, but the girls all came from the local area. Though not intended for Brethren, it enrolled a solid core from the church, proving that times were changing.

It was an auspicious beginning. But tragedy struck before the close of the second term. In May 1853 the idolized teacher, only twenty-five years old, died unexpectedly. The school did not survive his untimely death.

Pedagogically, Miller advocated the lancastrian system, a controversial approach that used advanced students as teaching assistants. Solomon Sharp, himself a pioneer Brethren educator, once said that Miller "revolutionized the methods of common-school teaching in his part of the State and became exceedingly popular."[8] This appraisal of the model schoolman was shared by his former scholars. One of them told his daughter, Mrs. Emma Replogle, who was one of Jacob Zuck's first student-assistants at Juniata College, that her father "had a more systematic mode of instructions than the old-styled teachers at that time, and a number of young men became more proficient in teaching than those of the common schools of that day under his system of teaching. . . . Young men became interested in him and his school."[9]

Henry Holsinger, who later failed in a similar project, once exclaimed in wonderment about the Buffalo Mills school and its teacher: "What a work! What a life! Without the aid of the press, without a bit of advertising, to build up a school and get students from other counties right at his own home and in his own congregation! What a personality!"[10] Jacob Miller, however, did not provide post-common school training; his teaching was confined to the elementary grades.

KISHACOQUILLAS SEMINARY

In the decade after Miller's abortive venture came the mounting agitation in the Brotherhood for a Brethren high school to prepare teachers. Thus in 1866 two schools got underway, Kishacoquillas Seminary in Middle Pennsylvania and the Kurtz-Quinter academy at New Vienna, Ohio (referred to in chapter 6). According to Dr. Floyd Mallott, the New Vienna Academy was designedly Brethren; Kishacoquillas was only incidentally so.[11] Nevertheless, the District had been sounded out beforehand, and the response guaranteed a steady flow of Brethren students.

Kishacoquillas Seminary was located in Big Valley about ten miles from Lewistown (the brick building still stands, in good shape). Its owner and headmaster was Solomon Z. Sharp, a Mennonite-turned-Dunker. Sharp was born near Allensville December 21, 1839, and grew up on a farm. From the time he was twelve he had his mind set on being a schoolteacher. In 1855, unmarried and aged twenty, he took his first teaching job, and soon after was made principal at McVeytown. He became a member of the Spring Run congregation in 1860, and in 1862 was elected to the ministry, the same year he married.

Years afterward Sharp recalled that when he joined the church there were only three Brethren with a college education: Lewis Kimmel of Armstrong County, Oliver W. Miller, a native of West Virginia, and Henry Kurtz. The District educator himself became the fourth, receiving three degrees from Millersville State Normal School by 1868 and, in 1875, an M.A. from Washington and Jefferson College.

In 1860, then, with a teaching degree in hand, Sharp was, said he of himself, "prepared to take the principalship of any normal school or seminary." Meanwhile, his reputation in the District had spread. He came to know a wide circle of Brethren young people with teaching aspirations in Juniata, Mifflin, Huntingdon, and Bedford counties eager for academy-level study. With the promise of their patronage and with money borrowed from his brothers, he bought and took over Kishacoquillas Seminary, a defunct Presbyterian plant on April 1, 1861. This was six months before Quinter launched New Vienna Academy that fall.

Kishacoquillas Seminary prospered five years under Sharp's management. Coeducational, it aimed to prepare its students to teach or to qualify for sophomore standing in college. Thus it was the first school among the Brethren to offer a curriculum that included college studies. It also marked the birth of Brethren interest in the liberal arts, offering course work in the classics (Latin, Greek, Hebrew), higher mathematics, advanced sciences, music and oil painting, and German, along with regular English subjects.

The District Brethren did not renege on their promise to patronize the Seminary. Its student body included a batch of names with a familiar Brethren ring—Amich, Bashore, Bolinger, Brumbaugh, Custer, Hagey, Hanawalt, Myers, Smith, Snowberger, Spanogle, Swigart, Rush, and Zuck. John B. Brumbaugh, the future publisher and cofounder of Juniata College, studied there for a time under Sharp. And quite often District ministers held services in the Seminary chapel.

Unlike its sister institution in Ohio, Kishacoquillas made it safely through the inflationary Civil War years. (Quinter's school closed in 1864, plagued by money problems and church opposition.) It was a struggle, but the Seminary emerged in the black, contrary to what the 1925 history says. It was his wife's broken health, not financial problems, that caused Sharp to sell the school. He sold it to Martin Mohler, brother of John M. Mohler, the noted Lewistown evangelist. However, Brethren like William J. Swigart and Jacob H. Brumbaugh still continued to attend Kishacoquillas until Juniata College was founded a decade afterward.

Sharp left the District shortly after selling the Seminary. He went on the serve as president of three Brethren colleges before the turn of the century (Ashland, McPherson, Plattsburg). He also gained recognition in the broader academic world. A geologist of some repute, he won membership in state and national scientific societies. In terms of formal education he had no peers in the church before the 1890s. An active churchman, he towered over most men in those salad days of Brethren higher education.

Agitation for a "Brethren" School after the Civil War

Meanwhile, the first serious attempt to establish a Brethren college took place in 1870 in Indiana. The Northern district of that state sanctioned the purchase of Salem College, located in the small community of Bourbon. Salem College was to be controlled by its home district, a provision that aroused considerable opposition in the Brotherhood. Its articles of incorporation contained a clause that read: "Said trustees and their officers were and are to be elected and directed by their religious body, from time to time according to the usages of said religious society." In reaction, Middle Pennsylvania took the following stand at its 1870 District Meeting: "We oppose the establishment of a college or high school by our church; but take no exceptions to an individual enterprise." This, of course, had been Annual Conference's official position since 1858, reiterated by it in 1871. Nevertheless, the college opened in December 1870. But it was a premature step, and four years later it failed, at great financial loss to the sponsoring Brethren.

By now the antieducationists were stirred up. These reactionary elders looked upon Brethren schools as an innovation that would lead only to grief. Some argued that schools would make church members "proud." Others feared that they would prepare ministers who would defect to other denominations. And there were those who linked schools with the coming of a paid ministry, an even worse prospect.

Joining the fray on the educationists' side, meanwhile, were two new voices—the Brumbaugh brothers, Henry and John. Their paper, the *Pilgrim*, almost from its 1870 debut, supported higher education. In one editorial after another they promoted the school idea. Henry argued in 1871 that "a good liberal education" could not be obtained in the public schools.[12] By *liberal* he meant education in a religious milieu. He cited his own case. For this kind of training he had to go to Cassville Seminary, located in a village south of Huntingdon and run by a Methodist minister, when he would have preferred being taught by Brethren. Therefore, he editorialized in

1872, "We are, and ever were, in favor of having our children educated in Brethren's schools, not in name only, but in substance."

At the time Henry Brumbaugh wrote this, he and his brother John, along with Henry Holsinger, were pushing to locate a school in Pennsylvania financed on a joint stock basis. The three men first got together on the project in March 1871 in Marklesburg, and then held a second meeting in October with some of the District elders. They discussed a number of possible locations for the school: Berlin, Tyrone, Mount Union, McVeytown, and Martinsburg, inspecting the last three places in 1872. Holsinger pressed for Berlin, where he was then publishing, and the Brumbaughs favored Martinsburg, where they currently had plans to move. Henry and John Brumbaugh argued that the latter place was near a railroad, was set in a stronghold of Brethrenism, and had available the building and grounds of the Juniata Collegiate Institute, then for sale.

From 1871 to 1874 this clique of erstwhile schoolteachers (now joined by George Brumbaugh) conferred periodically on the subject, relying on the *Pilgrim* and Quinter's paper for publicity. Finally, to test the extent of support, they called a meeting of interested Pennsylvanians for March 16, 1874, at the Martinsburg Church. Middle District was well represented, and prominent elders like James Sell and Graybill Myers spoke out forcefully in favor of a school in the Keystone State. But a real difference of opinion surfaced. Henry Brumbaugh told of one bearded elder at the meeting who addressed him and his collaborators in all candor: "Well, Brethren, I love you but I don't love your cause."[13]

Several potential school sites were nominated, but the list was finally narrowed down to three: Huntingdon, Martinsburg, and Berlin. The Brumbaughs had dropped their advocacy of Martinsburg to boost Huntingdon, where they had relocated their business in 1873. But that railroad town, despite the advantages of basic public utilities (waterworks and gaslights), had as yet no organized church, and so it was ruled out. Martinsburg was likewise vetoed after the delegates decided to locate the school at the place which pledged the most money. The best the Cove people could do on the spur of the moment was to raise only a few thousand dollars.

This left Berlin, whose supporters came up with thirty thousand dollars in pledges. The plan that was eventually adopted, at Holsinger's urging, was to subscribe $100,000 before starting the school. Solomon Sharp came from Tennessee, where he was teaching at Maryville College, to help Holsinger in the early stages of the financial drive. Middle and Western Pennsylvania were intensively canvassed, as were parts of Ohio. Jacob Zuck, a teacher in Maryland, was slated to head the Berlin High School, as it was to be called. But the projected amount was never subscribed (the most Holsinger got was $60,000), and the campaign was given up. Then the Brumbaughs stepped in.

They had never been fully in sympathy with Holsinger's rather grandiose notion that the Brethren must have a $100,000 in hand before beginning a school. True, Henry Brumbaugh had once editorially advised that nothing should be attempted until the facilities were adequate if the Brethren hoped to compete with secular schools. But he and his brothers thought this could be realized on a more modest scale. Furthermore, the Brumbaughs considered it presumptuous and tactically unwise to use the word *college* for a church institution just yet. They suggested adopting simply the name *Brethren School.* Meanwhile, without any fanfare, Lewis Kimmel began his Plum Creek Normal School in 1874 near Elderton, Armstrong County.

Behind the scenes there was another member of the Brumbaugh clan fighting for a school—Dr. Andrew B. Brumbaugh, cousin of Henry and John. He was the first man in the church to earn a medical degree. It was he who had enticed his publisher relatives to Huntingdon in 1873. Dr. Brumbaugh, who had practiced medicine there since 1866 (the year he got his M.D. degree from the University of Pennsylvania Medical School), was sold on his hometown for a school site. In November 1872 he took Henry Holsinger on a buggy ride up the hill on which J. C. Blair Hospital now stands. The doctor thought that knoll the ideal place for a school. So did Holsinger, who afterward wrote in his paper's column, "Editor's Diary":

> Before we leave Huntingdon, we must not forget to mention the beautiful site for a College. About one mile west of town, is an elevation which appears to have been especially thrown up for a location for some public institution. The scenery is grand beyond description. At a distance can be seen the mountains and hills, dressed in their coats of many colors, overlooking the tallest steeples that rise from the town at the base. If a Normal School should be wanted in that section of country, that Normal Hill is the finest location in our knowledge.[14]

Not long after, Dr. Brumbaugh bought two corner lots in the town's west end. He wrote in his diary that he had purchased the land "for a mission school or church" and "had taken Graybill Myers, Solomon Sharp and others over the ground and urged that *"this was the place."* On the knoll or wherever, for the Brumbaugh family there *had* to be a Brethren school in Huntingdon. Henry was already having dreams, as he shyly confessed a few years later to David

Emmert, Juniata's first art teacher, "in which he saw the school full-fledged and a large body of students marching down one of the main streets."

Then in June 1875 the Huntingdon Brethren renovated a room in the *Pilgrim* Building as a place for regular worship (not until 1878, however, did they formally separate from the James Creek congregation). Strategically, so far as the school issue was concerned, this was an astute maneuver. No longer could the county seat be disqualified as unsuitable for lack of proper Brethren environment, as some antischoolers had argued. The Brumbaugh junta was ready to make its move.

9

Juniata College: The First Permanent Brethren-founded School

Middle Pennsylvania Gets a Brethren College

The Brumbaugh dream of a Huntingdon school came true in the spring of 1876. One day in March the two *Pilgrim* brothers, Henry and John, and their physician cousin, Andrew, got together, presumably at John's bidding. He had received a letter that excited him. The main purpose of the conference was to discuss the education movement in the church, a subject John's letter dealt with. In analyzing the state of affairs they sensed rightly that the Berlin endowment fund was doomed to fail. They also pondered over the problems Lewis Kimmel was then having trying to raise scholarship money for Plum Creek in the District of Western Pennsylvania. Then, rather paradoxically in view of the odds against the idea, the three men decided to start a school right there in Huntingdon. John was asked to write Jacob Zuck, the young man Henry Holsinger had hoped would head the Berlin High School and who had sent the catalytic letter, inviting him to be the teacher.

There is no mystery why Zuck was tapped for the job. John Brumbaugh and he had struck up a close friendship in 1872 at Millersville State Normal School. Zuck, John's senior by a year and a half, had returned for the spring session to take science courses (he had graduated a couple years before), but also taught several classes and acted as a residence hall adviser. John took a fancy to him (they were two of about eight Brethren students there), and afterwards the two of them continued to keep in touch through letters and occasional visits.

Zuck, the most dominant spirit in the formative years of Juniata College, provides an interesting biographical study.[1] He was born at

Clay Lick, Franklin County, October 27, 1846, the second in a family of six sons and five daughters. A fall when he was two years old injured his hip, leaving him permanently lame. Never of robust health, he was excused from farm work and encouraged to get a public school education. Joining the Welsh Run Church in 1860, he enrolled at Millersville in 1865 and five years later completed the normal course. His first teaching position was in Schuylkill County, situated in the heartland of the anthracite coal fields, then famous for its Molly Maguire terrorism. The fall of 1872 he was made principal of the Waynesboro grammar school. Then during 1873 and 1874 he studied science at Ohio National University, Lebanon, Ohio. The next year he taught high school at Medina in Northern Ohio. In 1875 he came back East, to an elementary school position near Boonesboro, Maryland. All the while, he was writing eloquent articles for Brethren papers, especially the *Pilgrim,* warning that the church must educate or else it would perish.

On New Year's Day 1876 Zuck was passing through Huntingdon by train. He stopped off to pay his friend John Brumbaugh a surprise visit. Zuck stayed overnight, and as the two comrades reminisced their talk turned to the plight of education in the church. The young visitor said, "I am sorry, for there is surely a pressing need for a revival of educational work among our people."[2] Then he went on to remark that the "revival could only be brought about by hard work and sacrifice on the part of the friends of education," obviously an oblique criticism of what Holsinger was trying to do by starting out first-class.

At this point in the conversation Brumbaugh responded, "All is quiet now, and no effort is being made to start a school anywhere. Let us quietly start one right here. There are a few vacant rooms in the Pilgrim Building that could be used for this purpose." Zuck looked at his friend in surprise and replied that "he had no money and that the income from the students he might get would not pay his boarding." To this the youngest of the Brumbaugh trio retorted, "Do it on a small scale. You can board at least six months in my home without any charge. We will not let you suffer."

"I shall never forget how he looked me squarely in the eyes," John Brumbaugh later recalled, "and said, 'Do you mean it?' I affirmed my sincerity and that ended our conversation on the subject, for I felt the apparent absurdity of such a proposition and supposed he did also."

But in about two months John Brumbaugh received a letter in which Zuck confessed that the school proposition kept "ringing in his ears." He wrote, "I cannot see through the project financially, but am sure the Lord will supply our need. I feel sure we need a school, and if you brethren are in sympathy and will stand by my work, I am willing to try it." It was this letter that brought the Brumbaughs together for their historic March meeting.

John Brumbaugh answered and assured Jacob Zuck that Henry and the doctor were anxious to cooperate. He reminded him how all three of them had supported the Berlin cause and had worked to get Huntingdon selected. However, Zuck was advised, if he wished confirmation on the position of the other two men, to write them personally (which he did). The prospective teacher was also told that Henry would provide him a room in the *Pilgrim* Building, John would offer free board, and Dr. Andrew would recruit students and furnish basic equipment. Several letters were exchanged, and Zuck spelled out the nonsectarian policy that should guide the school. Then he resigned his job in early April, prematurely ending the school year there.

So precipitately did the founders act that little public notice was given prior to the opening of what they at first chose to call the Huntingdon Normal Select School. The initial announcement was brief, carried by the *Pilgrim* on March 28. But fuller information followed in the April 4th edition, emphasizing the existence of an active church and indicating that students would room and board with members. "The design of the school," this latest announcement explained, "is not to teach religion but to educate; therefore in principle it will not be sectarian." Graduates, it continued, would be prepared "for teaching," "for life," or "for entering college."

Mindful of the antischool element among their readers, the Brumbaughs were careful to make it clear that the new undertaking was not linked to their publishing business. It was strictly a "private enterprise" on Zuck's part, they stressed, and would in no way financially obligate the church. All they asked for was the "patronage of Brethren and friends."

Jacob Zuck arrived in Huntingdon four days before classes were scheduled to begin—April 17. Only three students, instead of the expected fifteen or twenty, greeted him on opening day. All were from the local area—two girls and a boy, Gaius M. Brumbaugh, the doctor's fourteen-year-old son. Zuck met with them in a little second-story room (14' × 16') of the *Pilgrim* Building. It was a "very discouraging" beginning, Henry Brumbaugh had to admit. But before the term ended, ten more were added to the roll, and the founders were heartened.

The Formative Years: 1876–1879

The nation's economy was still reeling from the effects of the 1873 depression when Zuck, a man of average height and slight build, brown eyes, hair, and beard, started teaching that "experimental" term. Henry Brumbaugh lamented in the January 4 *Pilgrim* that while 1876, as America's centennial, should be hailed with special interest, the country was mired "in a financial depression that it has been our lot seldom to experience." Little wonder Zuck betrayed a trace of pessimism the day before his school opened. He said to John Brumbaugh, "I must confess I cannot see the way to success in this enterprise, but I do believe it is right, and I believe God will show us the way as we go onward."

Zuck's first year was not an easy one, causing Henry Brumbaugh to marvel at his perseverance. Yet there were some grounds for optimism. After a disastrous summer teachers' term, fifteen matriculants were on hand in September. The winter term doubled in size, and the spring of 1877 found forty-five in attendance. A few of the new students in April came from Plum Creek, where Lewis Kimmel had decided to discontinue his work. Kimmel helped to augment Zuck's paltry library collection with a gift of fifty books.

Between 1877 and 1879 the Normal School went through three critical periods that tested its durability. The first one began when the three Brumbaughs and Zuck met several times in January and early February 1877 to reckon with its future. They decided to continue on, organize it as a joint stock company, and put up a new building. The James Creek congregation, upon their petition, granted approval for such a plan in February. That same month Zuck moved his students a block away to the more commodious Burchinell House, 1224 Washington Street.

Six temporary trustees were now authorized to solicit funds by selling stock, at one hundred dollars a share, to "brethren and others friendly to the cause." Zuck put his facile pen to work in the local newspapers over the next several months. In a series of articles he called upon the townspeople to donate a tract of land for the projected building. Shrewdly, he reminded the local merchants that the school officials foresaw not too far ahead a student body of some three to five hundred. If the school should stay on in Huntingdon, he noted (Ashland College in Ohio, later to be taken over by the Progressive Brethren, was getting underway right then, and there was talk of merging the two schools there), they would stand to benefit annually anywhere from $100,000 to $150,000 in student business. He also played upon a theme remarkably reminiscent of the current affirmative action policy in higher education. While conceding that his school was designed to meet a denominational need, he stressed that it was also committed to educating all applicants, "regardless of creed, sex, or social distinctions."

Ten months later Zuck and the Brumbaughs finally got action. In December they took their case to the newly formed Huntingdon Board of Trade, which eventually agreed to organize and lead a community drive. During the month of March 1878 the merchants raised $3,400 to purchase a block of sixteen lots on the west end slopes. The trustees received the deed for this three-acre plot on April 25, and on May 6 ground was broken for Founders Hall.

The generosity of the town fathers was a crucial vote of confidence in what Zuck was doing and the first crisis passed; had they failed to act, it is quite clear that he would have left. But, even so, it could all have gone for nothing. At the very time the Board of Trade was debating whether or not to get involved, the school was closed for an indeterminate period. A smallpox epidemic, which broke out during Christmas recess, had swept through the borough. The first diagnosed case had occurred next door to the Burchinell House. Returning students in January were met with the odor of disinfectant everywhere. Then the wife of a married student died from smallpox, throwing Zuck's little band into deep melancholy. The situation worsened, and the borough fathers then banned all public gatherings. On January 31 the school was forced to suspend classes.

What followed had all the makings of a calamity. Students—fifty-seven of them—and teachers—four counting Zuck—scattered, most to distant homes, a few girls to emergency quarters in town, and three plucky Ohioans, who refused to leave the area, to a mountain forge near Marklesburg. Some of those closest to the school despaired and gave it little chance to bounce back. As the students were leaving, John Brumbaugh said to Zuck, "Well, if there is no hope at all, I suppose we must stop." But the doughty thirty-two-year-old bachelor replied defiantly, "Stop! No!" And then, in words that soon proved prophetic, he went on, "We commenced this work as an experiment and nothing less than death will stop me, and if I should be stricken and die, I hope some others will have the courage to take up the work and continue it."[3]

After the epidemic had run its course, no one was sure how many students would return. Jacob H. Brumbaugh and Phoebe Weakly, two of the teachers, resumed classes on a tentative basis late in February (Zuck did not come back until March 28). The extent of demoralization caused by the interruption, everyone realized, would not become fully known until the school officially reconvened in April. To the amazement of all, the spring term began with an increase in enrolment, not an attrition, with sixty-nine reporting for classes. That summer the teachers' session had thirty-six more than the previous year. The second crisis had passed.

The academic year 1878–79 got underway with high expectations and was filled with signs of growth. It started off with sixty students and ended up in the spring with 109. In November the school got its first charter and a new name, a more impressive one: Brethren's Normal College. Then in April came the excitement of moving into Founders Hall (not yet completed) in time for the spring term. This was followed by the dedication of the new building on the rainy afternoon of April 14. Now all were looking ahead to July, when the first class would graduate.

But in May the College community was dealt a stunning blow by Jacob Zuck's sudden death. It now had to face its third crisis in two years. Ironically, Founders Hall, where Zuck roomed, was probably his undoing—the dampness caused by still-drying plaster and the strain from extra stairs aggravated his deformed hip. Fatigued, he caught a cold that quickly developed into pneumonia. He was carried in a chair to John Brumbaugh's house four days before he died, May 11, at age thirty-three.

At first dismay, confusion, and paralyzing sorrow gripped Zuck's students and colleagues. Could the still struggling school survive the calamity of its founder's death? As Zuck's dear friend, David Emmert, who had stood a deathbed vigil, wrote, "To take up the thread of his thought and develop the enterprise which he had merely begun was no small task."

Despair soon gave way to hope. At the funeral service James Quinter spoke on the text, "The Lord will prepare a sacrifice." He said, "Someone will take up this work where Professor Zuck laid it down. The seed sown in faith and watered with tears cannot fail of the harvest." In the reorganization of the work that followed, Quinter's faith was vindicated, and the third crisis passed. The College's roots were struck deep.

The Transition Years: 1879–1893

Administrative readjustments after Zuck's death came at the Trustee Board meeting in July. The trustees created the new position of president. James Quinter, publishing partner of John and Henry Brumbaugh, was given the nod. The presidency, however, was essentially titular, carrying only ceremonial duties. But the choice of Quinter was deliberate and crucial. At sixty-three he was the most revered churchman in the Brotherhood, the one man, it was felt, who could salve the wounds higher education had inflicted upon the Brethren. At the same time, Jacob H. Brumbaugh, who had been Zuck's right-hand man, was installed as principal (the head administrative office).

Brother of Dr. Andrew, he held the principalship fourteen years (with one break, 1881–1883), until the presidency in 1893 was made the chief academic post. He had studied at Kishacoquillas Seminary and in 1874 had graduated from Millersville. For the next three years he was principal of the Millersburg public schools. Brumbaugh, at age twenty-six, joined Zuck for the 1877 summer teachers' session and remained on. His principalship brought stability on campus in the critical years after Zuck's death while Quinter mended fences with the Brotherhood at large.

Jacob H. Brumbaugh was representative of a unique core of men who served the college as "teacher-trustee" in those transition years. Others who served in this dual capacity were William J. Swigart, David Emmert, William Beery, Joseph Saylor, Martin G. Brumbaugh, I. Harvey Brumbaugh, and J. Allen Myers. Jacob Brumbaugh was a trustee for fifty-one years and was vice president of the board 1894–1934. Equally remarkable were William J. Swigart's sixty-one years as a trustee, forty of them as treasurer (1880–1920). Both Brumbaugh and Swigart, a church elder and well-known pulpiteer, were birthright Brethren, born and bred in the District. These teacher-trustees spent the day teaching and the night wrestling with the problems of administration and finance.

During the transitional period the enrolment steadily increased to nearly two hundred for the spring term. The fall and winter terms averaged somewhat less. The student body was predominantly Brethren, but in 1885, for instance, six denominations were represented and eleven states. Almost all students pursued the normal English course. The administration and curriculum, for the most part, were patterned after the state normal schools.

Debt free by 1884, the Normal School lost its first president four years later. James Quinter died May 19, 1888, while giving a public prayer at Annual Conference, North Manchester, Indiana. In July the trustees named Henry Brumbaugh to succeed him. Brumbaugh had been serving as Board chairman since 1878, a position he held for forty years until his death in 1919. He was president for five years.

During that time Ladies Hall (later named Brumbaugh Hall) was erected in 1890, and a new discipline was added to the curriculum. The College catalogue for 1888 announced the creation of a Bible department. It stated:

> The Normal College, from the beginning, aimed to be strictly religious, both in influence and practice. But of late years we have been impressed with the necessity of making religious teaching a part of the school work. And to this end we now announce the Bible Department.

The purpose of the department was to permit students "to attain a religious and Biblical education that will enable them to become efficient laborers in the different departments of church work." Biblical studies were Henry Brumbaugh's bailiwick initially, but afterward he was joined by his brother, John, and William Swigart.

In 1890 President Brumbaugh also helped to inaugurate the winter Bible terms. These institutes, usually scheduled for a period of three weeks, attracted Brethren from all parts of the East. As many as seventy or more adults would spend the time in residence. The Bible term continued until 1925 and provided a unique experience in adult education within the Brotherhood.

Meanwhile, some elders had become uneasy about what was being taught at the five Brethren colleges then in existence: Huntingdon, Daleville, Bridgewater, Mount Morris, and McPherson (ten more were started by 1900). They urged Annual Conference to take measures to monitor them in some way. Thus in 1890 Standing Committee was authorized to assign to each college an advisory board, made up of three area elders. Their task was "to watch over the moral and religious influences of the schools." It was further stipulated that all Brethren faculty members "should conform to the order of the Brotherhood in their personal appearance." Each year, then, three District elders visited the Huntingdon campus. James Sell acted as chairman of the advisory board for about twenty years, until the practice was finally given up.

In May 1893, with a school endowment of six thousand dollars, the fifty-seven-year-old president stepped aside. He was replaced by Martin G. Brumbaugh, who went on to become one of the College's most illustrious sons. The latter's inauguration bore out a presentiment of David Emmert's mother. On the evening of Jacob Zuck's funeral, Emmert's visiting mother witnessed Martin Brumbaugh's baptism in the Juniata River. As she watched she said to Emmert, "That boy [he was seventeen] may some day fill Professor Zuck's place." She clung to her intuition, the son claimed, till her dying day, although she did not live to see it happen.

The College Comes of Age: 1893–1930

Martin Grove Brumbaugh was born April 14, 1862, on a farm in Woodcock Valley. After a public school education he entered the College in 1878, showing up in the company of the three "Forge orphans" after the smallpox epidemic. He graduated in 1882 with two degrees. At age twenty-two he began six years as superintendent of schools in Huntingdon County, the youngest superintendent ever in the state. He grew a beard to make himself look older. For three years (1889–1891) he taught natural science and pedagogy at his alma mater. After a year of graduate study at Harvard, he earned his M.A. degree at the University of Pennsylvania in 1893. Meanwhile, the Huntingdon congregation had made him a lay preacher. With these credentials the youthful educator, only thirty-one years old, took over the presidency.

"M.G.," as he was called by his friends, put in two terms as head of the College (1893–1911 and 1924–1930). Most of his first term, however, he was an absentee president. During that time he furthered his education and held academic posts elsewhere. In 1894 he became the first member of the Church of the Brethren to earn a Ph.D.—from the University of Pennsylvania. The following year that Ivy League school created a chair of pedagogy and named him its first occupant. He taught there nine years, taking a two-year leave (1900–1902) while Commissioner of Education in Puerto Rico—all the time still officially president.

The chronic absence of its chief administrator handicapped the College, and so the trustees tried to work out a solution. They still wanted to capitalize on his growing reputation and hold on to him, even if on a nominal basis. Thus in 1896 they created the office of vice president, elevated I. Harvey Brumbaugh to fill it and named him acting president. This administrative arrangement lasted until 1911, when Martin G. Brumbaugh resigned and second cousin Harvey moved up.

The College's fourth president was born March 10, 1870, the only son of Henry B. Brumbaugh. Destined for an academic career, he graduated from Juniata with a teaching degree, and in 1892 earned his B.A. at Haverford. After a short stretch teaching the classics back home, he got another bachelor's degree from Harvard in 1895. He spent part of the next year studying in Germany, and then, at age twenty-six, came back to be acting president. His scholarly training was rounded out in 1899 with an M.A. from Harvard.

I. Harvey Brumbaugh's thirteen-year presidential tenure (1911–1924) was the longest in the College's history until that of Dr. Calvert

N. Ellis following World War II. It was he who chose the Latin words for Juniata's motto: "Veritas Liberat" (The Truth Sets Free). While president he often said that it was his intention to run "a right little, tight little college." An ordained minister, he resigned to give Martin G. Brumbaugh, his sixty-two-year-old cigar-smoking relative, a second turn as president. (He continued to teach, however, until his death in 1937.)

By then M. G. Brumbaugh was a famous man in his native state. For nine years (1906–1915) he had been Philadelphia's popular school superintendent. Then during World War I he had been elected governor on the Republican ticket. This was a significant achievement in several respects. No other Brethren has ever held a gubernatorial office, and he was the second and last clergyman in Pennsylvania to do so. Moreover, he was the only college president and Ph.D. holder to become the Keystone State's chief executive. Ineligible to succeed himself in 1918, he left politics to lecture on peace and public playgrounds until persuaded to return to the College in 1924. He turned down presidential offers from three prominent schools, including Penn State, in making his decision.

It was his loyalty to the church and the College that drew him back. He once dedicated a published series of lectures on the Book of Ruth "To the Church of the Brethren and Juniata College—the Church and School I love." Dr. Charles C. Ellis, on whom he had a profound influence, wrote of M. G. Brumbaugh: "He had been bred in a Dunker home, he knew the history of his people as few have ever known it, and the allurement of high honor and worldly recognition never weaned him away." On his death the Brotherhood's Educational Board paid tribute to "his loyalty and devotion to the faith and ideals of the church and to her interests and program." Author of many books, officer of state and international Sunday School associations, popular preacher and teacher, he was, as we saw in the introduction, the pioneer historian of the Church of the Brethren.

The presidencies of these two Brumbaugh cousins, which spanned three decades, mark an important era in the growth and history of the College. After 1894, when its name was changed to Juniata College, the institution began to take on a different character.* This change in name denoted its new status as a college of arts and sciences, the result of state accreditation gained largely through the

---

*The name change came in deference to a ruling of Annual Conference against use of *Brethren* in naming a school. Place names—like that of a town—were recommended. Thus all the existing Brethren-founded schools except Juniata are so denominated. *Juniata* means "beautiful," an Indian word for the nearby river.

influence of its youthful president. Rechartered in 1896 as a legal college, Juniata graduated its first B. A. candidate the next year: Daniel C. Reber, who later became president of Elizabethtown College. Thus Juniata became the first full-fledged Brethren-backed institution of higher education (the B. S. degree was not available until 1920). Further recognition came in 1922, under I. Harvey Brumbaugh, when the Middle States Association, the regional accrediting agency, put Juniata on its list, again a Brethren first.

This was not only the period when Juniata became a full-fledged college, but also the heyday of the Academy. The Academy was started in January 1899 and offered a four-year college preparatory course. By the early 1920s it enrolled over one hundred students. A large number of its graduates, as was intended, continued their study at Juniata. Ordinarily, the College faculty also taught in the Academy. But the Middle States Association looked with disfavor upon this policy, and so in 1924, for this and other reasons, it was decided to abolish the preparatory school.

From the mid-1890s to 1930 the student body increased to over five hundred, and these years produced a major transformation of the campus. Its bounds were expanded sevenfold—to more than twenty-three acres. In addition to Founders and Brumbaugh Halls the campus complex came to consist of Students Hall (1895), Oneida Hall (1898), the Infirmary (1900), the Gymnasium (1901), Carnegie Library (1907), a personal gift of Andrew Carnegie, Science Hall (1916), and Cloister (1928). Also, part of the campus was converted into an athletic field in 1899 and a grandstand erected on it in 1919. The physical layout of the College remained much the same after the Brumbaugh era until the reconstruction period of Calvert Ellis.

It was during the time of the Brumbaughs that the College came into possession of the Cassel collection, which is described in the introduction. M. G. Brumbaugh, as we saw there, personally bought the collection and donated it to the College in 1899. It has proved to be a treasure trove for church and social historians.

Midway during the period under survey, the curriculum was expanded to include a School of Theology. Largely the handiwork of Charles C. Ellis, it operated from 1918 to 1924. It was theologically more conservative than its Chicago rival, Bethany Bible School, which had been founded thirteen years earlier. The School of Theology evolved out of the Bible department, which from 1906 to 1918 was called the Bible School. (Incidentally, in 1906 Mary S. Geiger, a Philadelphia trustee [1895–1917], endowed a chair in Bible, making Juniata the first Brethren college with an endowment specifically for the promotion of biblical studies.) Beginning in 1897 the College offered a Bachelor of Sacred Literature degree, but this degree was withdrawn in 1916. Meanwhile, a three-year bachelor of divinity course, with two years of college work prerequisite for entrance, was set up in 1908. But it produced only two graduates. The School of Theology, however, thanks to Dr. Ellis's promotional efforts, was more successful. It turned out ten B.D.'s in its seven-year life span. The School's demise came about when the church took over Bethany in 1925 and requested that the denomination have only one seminary.

During the pre-1930 period, Juniata's charter was revised two other times after 1896, one of the changes being somewhat revolutionary for a Brethren college but reflecting the school's basic nonsectarian stance. The original charter specified that all the trustees (fifteen) had to be Brethren, live near the College, and be elected by the stockholders. These provisions were abrogated in 1908. The institution ceased being a joint stock corporation, and its control was vested in a self-perpetuating board (still fifteen), regardless of church affiliation. Another charter revision in 1923 increased the number on the board to twenty-one. It is interesting to note, however, that a non-Brethren was not elected trustee until 1939.

By 1930, when M. G. Brumbaugh died, Juniata had come of age. It enjoyed an endowment fund approaching $800,000, not a large fund, perhaps, compared with that of much older schools then, but by far the biggest among the seven Brethren colleges (Daleville had not yet merged with Bridgewater). The enrolment, as mentioned earlier, totaled over five hundred, the faculty numbered about forty, and the summer sessions, although showing a decline since the mid-twenties, were still well attended. In enrolment, Juniata ranked twenty-second among the fifty-three accredited Pennsylvania colleges. But the Great Depression was at hand, and small colleges like Juniata faced a rocky road ahead.

The Ellis Era: 1930–1968

The man who for thirteen years (1930–1943) guided Juniata during the hard Depression and early World War II years was Charles C. Ellis, called by Dr. John Baker, a long-time Juniata trustee, "one of the most beloved and inspirational leaders that any college ever had." He was born July 21, 1874, in Washington, D.C. Of Methodist parentage, he became a Brethren as a boy in Baltimore. He attended public school there, and when thirteen years old entered the Normal College. He completed the Normal course in

1890, at age sixteen. In 1898 he became Juniata College's second B.A. graduate. He went on to Illinois Wesleyan University for an M.A. in 1903 and the next year a Ph.D., making him the fourth church member to earn that degree. In 1907 he obtained another doctorate from the University of Pennsylvania. A divinity degree from Temple University in 1920 ended his impressively extensive formal academic training. The previous year, the Huntingdon congregation had inducted him into the ministry.

Between 1890 and 1894 Dr. Ellis was a public school teacher. After receiving his B.A. degree, he taught English at Juniata in 1898–99 and 1900–1901. His permanent association with the College began in 1907 when he became head of the department of education. Made vice president in 1917, he was long ripe for the top post by 1930.

When Ellis assumed the presidency he declared, "I have placed on the desk in the President's office the picture of Arnold of Rugby inscribed with the words which I adopted on my assumption of this responsibility: 'God grant that I labor with entire confidence in Him and with none in myself without Him.' " This philosophical outlook typified his whole life, and to him the church and its interests were of vital importance. He served the District in many capacities, including that of moderator. At the Brotherhood level, he was chairman of the General Education Board from 1931 to 1941, and three times he was moderator of Annual Conference—1935, 1944, 1950. He was also a director of Bethany Biblical Seminary (as it was then called). Known as the "boy orator" in his youth, Ellis had a wide ministry as a preacher.

Juniata's fifth president was a noted author and a lifelong contributor to religious publications. From 1919 to 1930 he wrote a column for the *Sunday School Times* titled "This Week's Teaching Principle." He frequently submitted articles to the *Gospel Messenger,* and he published three books on religious and devotional subjects. He also wrote *Juniata College: The History of Seventy Years* (1876–1946).

In that book Dr. Ellis characterized his own administration as a time of "strengthening" the faculty and consolidating the College's "varied interests." Under him admission standards were stiffened, and the quality of the educational program improved. In 1938 a faculty committee, headed by his son, Calvert, devised an innovative curriculum that introduced required courses in general education and comprehensive examinations for seniors. It attracted national notice and became a model for curricular revisions at many liberal arts colleges, including Harvard. Other academic gains included recognition by the Association of American Universities in 1940 and accreditation by the American Chemical Society in 1942.

One of the College's most ambitious programs during the Great Depression was extension education, which led to establishing a branch school in Altoona. Records show that extension work began in that city in 1929. But in 1933 it was decided to open a center there in response to demand for a greater variety of course offerings. The center had a resident director and employed several full-time instructors. It was closed in 1939, but in the six years it existed it enrolled over five hundred students.

It was during the C. C. Ellis years that the charter was overhauled once again. The trustee board was reconstituted and its electoral process modified. Beginning in 1940 the limit on the number of board members was raised from twenty-one to thirty. But, more important, provisions were made for the special election of certain trustees. Each supporting church district of Pennsylvania—Western, Middle, Southeastern—was authorized to elect one trustee. Additionally, the Alumni Council was given three seats on the board. These changes, still effective today, permit the six special trustees to serve for three years, but as such they cannot succeed themselves. As Dr. Ellis wrote in his history, "This arrangement not only brings to the board a more direct representation from the churches and the alumni, but the rotation gives a larger group the opportunity of this service and closer contact with the college."

Mainly because of Oscar R. Myers, the College's treasurer, Juniata made it through the 1930s in fair shape, although salaries had to be pared and cutbacks made in the faculty. Never once, though, did the faculty and staff miss a payday. A year and a half after Pearl Harbor the operating budget was $243,000, but by then the endowment had atrophied to less than $643,000. After the construction of Oller Hall in 1940, total assets amounted to just under two million dollars.

During the thirties the enrolment never fell below 426. But the military draft in 1940, followed by the outbreak of war with Japan in 1941, eroded the male population on campus. In 1943, when Dr. Ellis retired, the number of students had dwindled to 377.

When the trustees met in Harrisburg in June of that year to choose a replacement, there were some who feared the meeting would be a stormy one. The trustees were not of one mind on a lot of issues, especially on College regulations. But on one thing they did concur: the new leader must be a dedicated churchman who knew and respected Juniata's past. They found such a man in Calvert Ellis, the retiring president's thirty-nine-year-old son.

Calvert N. Ellis was born on April 16, 1904, in Zion City, Illinois.

A graduate of the Academy (1919) and Princeton Preparatory School, he received the B.A. degree from Juniata in 1923, the year after being called to the ministry by the Huntingdon church. Pursuing graduate studies over the next nine years, he received a Th.B. at Princeton Theological Seminary (1927), an M.A. from Princeton University (1927), and a Ph.D. from Yale (1932). During this time span he also taught in the Lewistown High School and at Wilson College in Chambersburg. In 1932 he joined the faculty of his alma mater and taught religion and philosophy. He had been secretary of the Trustee Board for six years prior to being elected president.

Though a busy administrator and a national leader in the world of higher education, Calvert Ellis proved to be the kind of active churchman the trustees had hoped for. He made himself available to District and Regional programs and accepted a host of invitations to preach in churches all over the Brotherhood. He was the 1948 moderator of Annual Conference and for nine years was chairman of the General Brotherhood Board. He also found time to submit occasional articles to the *Gospel Messenger*.

Dr. Ellis piloted Juniata for a quarter of a century (1943–1968), the longest presidential tenure in the College's history. His time in office coincided with the dynamic postwar decades and the unprecedented upsurge of higher education that attended them. Dr. John Baker put Calvert Ellis's twenty-five years as president in sharp historical focus when he wrote:

> Dr. Ellis' administration covered many of the most crucial years in the history of American education. One world war and several smaller wars; too few students, too many students; Sputnik, with the upgrading of all education; changing social mores; restlessness among faculty and students; faculty shortages; inflation with its attendant financial problems; government aid and involvement and a host of other issues beset him and all other college presidents. These were indeed exacting times and any president who succeeded in guiding his institution through this era successfully merited high praise.[4]

Calvert Ellis was equal to the challenge and changed Juniata from a little-known college to one of national academic distinction. But in the process, Dr. Baker said, "He and his advisors preserved the best of Juniata's past without limiting in any way the entry of the College into the demanding revolutionary world of the 1950s and 1960s."

One of Ellis's controlling goals as president was to preserve Juniata as a small college. In the *Alumni Bulletin* for summer 1945, he wrote, "only so can we maintain the associations and personal relations so distinctive of our campus. Here each student is an

individual person whose development is our main concern."
"Small," however, was interpreted in relative terms, and while
Juniata's student body under him grew from 249 to twelve hundred,
it was a controlled growth. Seen now in retrospect, this was a wise
policy and prevented the College from overexpanding during the
student "boom" of the 1960s. Many small colleges failed to act so
deliberately and met with financial chaos when the "boom" abruptly
ended in the early seventies.

The College's financial state improved dramatically between 1943
and 1968, despite the problems created by American involvement in
Korea and then Vietnam, and the institution operated annually
without a loss except for one year. When Ellis retired, the operating
budget amounted to $3,180,000. To ensure financial stability,
Juniata's business-minded president worked to strengthen the
Board of Trustees, recruiting some of its key personnel from the
District. Their record of support became exceptional for a small
college. Exceptional support also came from the alumni and the
churches of the three Pennsylvania districts identified with Juniata.
Alumni giving in those years won two citations from the American
Alumni Council. Through the generosity of its supporters and
through sound investments, the College was able to enlarge
significantly its endowment funds, the symbol of a solid institution.
By 1968 these funds exceeded two million dollars, a twenty-five-year
gain of nearly a million and a half.

The biggest financial thrust of Calvert Ellis's presidency was the
ten-year $5,350,000 development program initiated in 1961. As a
result of this campaign and earlier lesser ones, the Juniata campus
underwent a phenomenal reconstruction. Nine main buildings were
erected under Dr. Ellis's leadership. The first one was the Memorial
Physical Education Building in 1951. After that, five residence halls
went up: for women, Maude Lesher Hall (1957) and South Hall
(1962); for men, Sherwood Hall (1961), North Hall (1965), and
Tussey-Terrace Hall (1966). Three academic buildings completed
the expanded campus complex: Beeghly Library (1963), Brumbaugh Science Center (1965), and Good Hall (1965). In addition, the
College acquired a number of other buildings, which were remodeled and converted to a variety of uses: Faculty Club (1946), I.
Harvey Brumbaugh House (1947), Swigart Hall (1950), N. J. Brumbaugh House (1953), Emmert House (1956), and the College Manse
(1964). These renovated dwellings along with the new and other
existing structures dotted a main campus occupying fifty-five acres.

Federal loans made possible the dormitories, but funds for the
rest of the College's energetic expansion program in the fifties and
sixties, both for building and academic purposes, had to come from

Good Hall, the main academic classroom building, honoring Juniata's only million-dollar donor, J. Omar Good, a Philadelphia Brethren alumnus.

other sources. Three foundations made substantial grants for two of the academic buildings. The Longwood Foundation made a "challenge gift" toward the Science Center, while the Kresge Foundation and the L. A. Beeghly Foundation provided resources for the library. Several industries, foundations, and federal agencies awarded grants to Juniata to aid its instructional and curricular development. Among them were: Danforth Foundation, W. K. Kellogg Foundation, National Institutes of Health, Atomic Energy Commission, National Science Foundation, Research Corporation, and Du Pont Company.

These grants for academic purposes bore testimony to the first-rate undergraduate training Juniata College provided. In the mid-fifties the Ford Foundation made a nationwide survey to learn which educational institutions had the best record in producing "young American scholars of promise." The study concluded that fifty of the nation's colleges and universities produced such scholars. Juniata was ranked forty-third and was one of only four in Pennsylvania in the national listing. Another study of 198 liberal arts colleges revealed that Juniata ranked eleventh nationally and fourth of twenty-eight in the East in the production of graduates who later obtained the doctor's degree. Honors came from other quarters too. Six graduates during Calvert Ellis's time were awarded Fulbright Scholarships to study abroad, and three other graduates were recipients of the nationally coveted Root-Tilden scholarships from the New York University School of Law.

In building Juniata's scholarly reputation Ellis had the valued help of Dr. Morley Mays, a 1937 alumnus, whom he appointed dean of the College in 1948. An ordained minister, Mays, who was promoted to Vice President for Academic Affairs in 1963, was a respected leader and prominent preacher in the District. Under him the full-time faculty increased to seventy-nine, of whom forty-six percent held earned doctorates. He left Juniata in 1966 to become president of Elizabethtown College.

Not only did Calvert Ellis show interest in faculty development, but for twenty-five years he demonstrated a remarkable capacity for understanding student attitudes. A former Juniatian editorialized in the Huntingdon *Daily News* the last week Ellis was in office: "We often remember, in this day of student dissent and demonstrations, how the student problems of that post–Korean War period were often settled through the active participation and understanding of the president." In the mid-sixties he offered no resistance to student petitions to be represented on faculty standing committees, and Juniata took this step long before most colleges and universities were making headlines for similar moves. As chairman of the Association of American Colleges in 1968, he urged on his fellow presidents the view that students have the right to know the procedures under which the colleges operate. It was this same concern for student welfare that led him in 1963 to create the position of Minister to Students. Juniata was the first Brethren college to provide a full-time campus ministry.

In August 1968, at summer commencement exercises, Dr. Ellis conferred his 3,004th and final bachelor degree, the last official act of his twenty-five-year presidential career. In that period of time he not only led Juniata to its eminence in the world of liberal arts colleges, but, as one national educator said, "helped mold the fabric of a whole sector of American higher education."[5]

Moving into Juniata's Second Century

Finding Calvert Ellis's replacement, the trustees admitted, would not be easy. For the first time in the College's history, a faculty committee participated in the presidential search. Among the trustees a worthy successor was found in Dr. John N. Stauffer, who brought to the office an impressive set of credentials; at age fifty-two he was a tested administrator. He had spent twenty-one years in administration at Wittenberg University, Springfield, Ohio, as Dean of Students (1947–1957), Dean of the College (1957–1963), and President (1963–1968). A Lutheran, he became the first non-Brethren president of Juniata, his alma mater, and the first layman.

Born in Palmyra, Pennsylvania, he graduated in the class of '36 and earned his master's (1942) and doctor's (1964) degrees at the Pennsylvania State University. His five-year presidency at Wittenberg was notable for a number of major accomplishments, but what most impressed the trustees was his expertise in budgeting and financial control procedures.

As Juniata's president, Dr. Stauffer brought about marked improvement in these areas, completely revamping the budget structure and budgetary controls. Meanwhile, the current operation budget increased forty-three percent, from $3,600,000 to $5,100,000 under his guidance.

In the area of fund raising Stauffer inherited the Margin of Difference campaign, which had been launched on Founders Day 1968. This was a capital funds drive geared to raise at least $10.1 million for endowment and certain essential buildings by 1976, the College's Centennial Year. That goal was not only met, but exceeded by several thousand dollars. Under Stauffer there was an endowment growth of ninety-four percent, from $2,800,000 to $5,500,000. The Charles A. Dana Foundation made a one-to-one $250,000 matching grant in 1972 for endowment purposes, the income of which goes toward the salaries of five full professors. Juniata is one of only four Pennsylvania colleges with a Dana endowment.

Especially noteworthy has been the continuing giving performance of the alumni, the percentage of contributors increasing from thirty-five to forty-six percent during the Stauffer administration (the ACC cited Juniata a third time). In May 1969 Juniata announced a one million dollar bequest from the estate of alumnus J. Omar Good, a Philadelphia Brethren. It remains the largest single gift received by the College. The new academic building (formerly old Science Hall) was named Good Hall by way of recognition.

Some of the capital funds from the Margin of Difference program have gone toward the expansion of the physical plant. The College Center, named Ellis Hall in honor of the two former presidents, was completed in 1969. East Houses, two residences for more than two hundred students, were erected the next year. But in 1970 the trustees saw fit to raze Oneida, Brumbaugh, and Student Halls. Architectural consultants and engineers had declared the buildings unsafe for future use and indicated that the cost would be prohibitive to restore or remodel them. About this time the College acquired one hundred and seventy acres of undeveloped land near the main campus which is called the Baker-Henry Nature Preserve. There has also been the acquisition of a 365-acre field station at the new Raystown Dam, located just a few miles from Huntingdon. Total assets in 1975 came to $22,300,000, an advance of forty-two percent from the time President Stauffer took over.

Just as significant was the progress made in the academic program during the Stauffer years. When Stauffer took over the presidential reins he called for educational reform. A task force of seven faculty members and two students was appointed in 1969 and charged with redesigning the curriculum. Their work culminated in a newly conceived plan for general education and greater student autonomy, which was implemented in September 1971. The new program was built upon the assumption that to be human is to be reflective, interpretive, and decision-making, and professors were urged to make their courses more value-centered and thus humanize the educational process. The curriculum was supported by substantial grants from the National Endowment for the Humanities totaling $268,895, and, though recently revised, it is still basically in effect.

In March 1975 John Stauffer unexpectedly announced his resignation, upon the advice of his cardiologist. His seven-year presidency had kept Juniata in sound fiscal condition, and the College had been able to maintain a stable enrolment of between eleven and twelve hundred full-time students against national trends. He earned a reputation as one of Juniata's most progressive presidents, certainly as the most student-oriented.

At the time of Stauffer's resignation the Centennial year was almost upon the College. Plans for its celebration were well under way. The Margin of Difference campaign was building to a climax. The reins of leadership needed to be picked up quickly and surely.

The man who took them up was Frederick M. Binder, fifty-five, neither an alumnus (he graduated from Ursinus College) nor a Brethren (he is Episcopalian). A layman, he had headed two colleges: Hartwick (1959–1969) in Oneonta, New York, and Whittier (1970–1975) in California.

Binder is a native of New Jersey and got his master's and doctor's degrees in American economic history at Penn. He was the first Fulbright lecturer in American history appointed to Yugoslavia. He has published two books, *Coal Age Empire* and *The Serbian Assignment,* a spy novel. As a young administrator, his "hero" had been Calvert Ellis; Juniata's traditions and history, therefore, were not unfamiliar to him.

Juniata's eighth president continues in the tradition of executive excellence on College Hill. Under his leadership alumni giving has steadily risen. In 1979 well over half the alumni (fifty-two percent) made gifts, ranking Juniata, on this score, among the top one percent of all colleges and universities in the nation. That fall Founders Hall underwent a major renovation in an effort to salvage the century-old building, the lone relic of the College's genesis. The fall of 1979 was also when the Humanities complex along Sixteenth Street—a series of remodeled Victorian-era houses and a newly constructed central unit—became available, providing classrooms and faculty offices. In 1980 the trustees launched a $13,000,000 campaign for the eighties, the immediate objective being a Sports/ Recreation Center. Most encouraging, in the face of gloomy forecasts about the future of higher education in America, the new decade began with the largest entering class in Juniata's history.

Juniata College and the Brethren Today

Historically, as this chapter has illustrated, Juniata's ties to the Church of the Brethren have never been legal ones. The original charter did not place ownership of the College in any arm of the church. However, the 1878 charter did specify that all the trustees had to belong to the denomination. This provision, we saw, has been amended periodically until now the charter contains no clause at all with respect to Brethren representation on the Trustee Board, unlike the charters of the other five Brethren-founded colleges. (True, the charter does specify that the three supporting church districts be represented on the Board, but technically this is at the sufferance of the co-opted members and under certain constraints.) Moreover, Juniata is unique among Brethren colleges in that its charter contains no dissolution clause that provides, in the event the School closes its doors, for the assets from its sales to go to some agency of the church. This is important because the eligibility of private schools to receive government funds in recent years has depended upon the degree of control exercised by religious bodies. Therefore, of late the officials of the College have preferred to speak of the College as "free-standing" or "independent," rather than "church-related," as once was the case.

Despite this new terminology, there is no attempt to ignore the College's religious heritage. The College has always maintained a close liaison with the Pennsylvania church districts within its sphere of influence. Faculty and administrators used to appear regularly in church pulpits, often as interim pastors, and many times served as congregational elders. This is still true today, though on a lesser scale. What professors and presidents once did in representing the College to local churches, student deputation groups are now doing.

The real problem for Juniata, so far as its ties to the various constituent districts are concerned, is the erosion of a Brethren population on campus in recent years (about four percent belonged to the denomination in 1980). To remedy this predicament, there is now, since 1969, the Church-College Relations Council, which has a varied representation of twenty-seven members. It holds high among its objectives recruitment of Brethren students and fostering regular dialogue between church and College. In 1969 the Alexander Mack Scholarship Fund was established specifically to aid youth of the church. All financial support from local congregations goes into this fund.

Some members of the Church-College Relations Committee from Middle District. *Row 1:* **B. Baugher, M. S. Over, E. A. Cherry, C. N. Pheasant.** *Row 2:* **H. B. Brumbaugh, D. W. Detwiler, G. Kensinger, M. C. Good, R. D. Wilson.**

The fact must be faced that the high cost of private education has prompted Brethren young people generally to enrol in lower-tuition public colleges and universities. For example, in 1960 there were 1,155 Brethren students in the denomination's six colleges; in 1975 the number had declined to 919, out of a total enrolment of 5,684 for that year. Hence Juniata does not suffer alone among its fellow Brethren colleges in struggling with competition of this kind. Its student body, of course, remains basically Protestant—though, curiously, Roman Catholic enrolment is high (almost twenty percent).

The picture is different with respect to the faculty, about a quarter of whom are Brethren. Many, though, do not have a Brethren background but have entered the denomination by choosing to affiliate with Stone Church. But like their predecessors, these men and women are committed to preserving Juniata as a Christian liberal arts college of high quality.

Brethren are also clearly visible among the trustees, but are generally absent among administrators and staffers. "Still," declared President Binder on the occasion of his investiture, "we have been, we are, and we shall continue . . . [to be] concerned with moral and cultural values," rooted as Juniata is, he emphasized, "in the tradition of the church."

What has emerged in America, we must keep in mind, is perforce a new definition of a religious college. It is no longer one with required religion courses and mandatory chapel, and headed by the clergy. As a report of the Middle States Association of Colleges and Secondary Schools noted recently in the case of another Brethren school: "A religious college is one where the person is central, where the person develops through choosing between intellectual options, where living and learning are not separate, where the person becomes truly a person in the name of God."[6] That is precisely the image of Juniata College that Frederick Binder was projecting for the future in his 1975 presidential address.

10
Fundamentalism and the Church of the Brethren

Rise of Fundamentalism in the United States

One of the divisive influences at work among Protestant American churches in this century has been the fundamentalist-modernist controversy. The fundamentalist movement had been foreshadowed by periodic Bible conferences in the late nineteenth century that emphasized the literal acceptance of every biblical idea. Out of these conferences had come the promulgation of the "Five Points," destined to be accepted as the *sine qua non* of fundamentalism: the infallibility of the Bible, the deity of Jesus, His virgin birth, substitutionary blood atonement, resurrection, and premillennial Second Coming. This hard core of fundamentalist doctrine was given further currency with the appearance of *The Fundamentals: A Testimony to the Truth* (1910–1914), a set of twelve small pamphlets published and widely circulated through the generosity of two wealthy Los Angeles brothers, Lyman and Milton Stewart. Eventually, three million copies were distributed throughout the English-speaking world.

The principal cause for the rise of the fundamentalist controversy was the basic incompatibility that many Americans saw between their authoritative faith and the progress made in science and theology after the Civil War. That part of the church which maintained contact with prevalent cultural ideas was labeled modernist. Modernism was especially hospitable to the new findings of science, accepting as final Charles Darwin's theory of evolution, with all its implications about the origin and nature of man. It was also an exponent of higher criticism, the critical study of the Bible by methods of historical and literary analysis that regarded the Scriptures as human documents capable of error. Thus modernists were inclined to look lightly upon belief in the supernatural, and rejected out of hand biblical stories of natural and biological miracles *per se.* To those who held to the "older view" of the Bible, modernism threatened to destroy Christendom entirely. They were persuaded that it degraded the central figure of Christianity—Jesus Christ—by making him a mere man. During the 1920s fundamentalists and modernists collided violently.

The Fosdick Case

Two events attracted the attention of the public mind to this conflict. The first was the furor directed against the famed Harry Emerson Fosdick, a liberal Baptist then preaching regularly for the First Presbyterian Church, New York City. In May 1922 he gave a sermon entitled "Shall the Fundamentalists Win?" It was a plea for tolerance, and was prompted by a desire to cool the issue. He wanted to counter the threat of an impending split in the nation's churches. But the well-intentioned effort backfired and produced an explosion of ill will. The fundamentalists were convinced that coexistence meant denial of the faith, and pressed at once for intramural purges.

In Fosdick's case the attack was launched by Clarence McCartney, a leading Presbyterian preacher in Philadelphia. He was backed by William Jennings Bryan, three-time Democratic presidential candidate and Wilson's Secretary of State, who was a leading figure in the church's General Assembly. The object was to bring Fosdick to trial for heresy and to force him, a Baptist, either to unite with the Presbyterians or vacate his pulpit. He chose to do the latter, and subsequently became the pastor of New York's Riverside Church, where John D. Rockefeller habitually worshiped. Long after, he remained the despised symbol of undisguised modernism to the fundamentalists.

The Scopes Trial

The other event was the sensational Scopes trial in 1925, one of the most widely publicized legal cases in modern American history. Fundamentalists had mounted several state-level campaigns, beginning in the 1920s, to outlaw the teaching of evolution in the public schools and were moderately successful in the South and Southwest. John T. Scopes, a teacher in the public schools of Dayton, Tennessee, was charged with violating the antievolution law in that state. Scopes was defended by a distinguished array of legal talent headed by the freethinking Clarence Darrow, greatest criminal lawyer of his generation. William Jennings Bryan, self-appointed spokesman for religious conservatives, assisted the prosecution. The state's brief was that if it was unlawful to teach religion in public schools, it was equally unlawful, under the guise of science, to teach ideas hostile to religion. Because of the blatant bias of the judge and jury, Scopes's conviction was a foregone conclusion (the Tennessee Supreme Court later set aside the mandatory one-hundred-dollar fine on a technicality). The "monkey trial" was a memorable event, deadly serious for some but a good show for others. It exemplified, however, a deep cleavage among Protestants still not resolved today.

In the end the Dayton spectacle dealt the fundamentalists a cruel blow. Bryan—their "peerless leader"—went through a devastating experience. He made the mistake of taking the stand himself. Darrow, the agnostic, subjected him to a long and grueling cross-examination on his religious beliefs. The "great Commoner" was annihilated by Darrow's courtroom performance. This put-down, many historians conjecture, hastened Bryan's death, which occurred five days after the trial. It was an inopportune loss for the fundamentalists and deprived them of their most eloquent and notable apologist. There remained no public figure of his stature to mobilize the "true believers," well represented in all denominations, into a fighting unit.

Latter-day Fundamentalism

During the 1920s the leaderless fundamentalists grew so hostile that they became what one historian described as "almost stereotypically rude types." Their rhetoric was abusive and their tactics divisive, leading to repeated fissures even within their own ranks. The Bible colleges and seminaries they started gloried in a manifest antiintellectualism.

A distinction needs to be drawn, however, between fundamentalist theology, which conservatives of all denominational brands could accept, and the fundamentalistic spirit, which was self-righteous, vituperative, intolerant, ill-mannered. It was this persecutive mentality that inhibited their usefulness and alienated the rest of Protestantism. Until World War II, therefore, militant fundamentalism declined as a united force in American society, preserving itself primarily through the formation of independent Bible churches.

With the mid-1940s the fundamentalists began to regroup and show signs of new life. The National Association of Evangelicals was formed in 1942 to consolidate the more moderate fundamentalistic groups. Another organization that spearheaded the recovery of fundamentalism was Youth for Christ, founded in 1943, which sponsored mass rallies for young people and members of the armed forces. Out of it came an outstanding new revival preacher, Billy Graham. This resurgence of strength among the biblical literalists was undergirded by a coterie of young theologians, like Carl F. H. Henry, Edward J. Carnell, and Cornelius Van Til, whose goal was to provide a more rational and philosophical defense of their faith. They also manifested an interest in social ethics quite unknown to many of their compatriots.

More militant than these advocates of what is usually termed *cooperative Protestantism,* was a small and extremely conservative group led by Carl McIntire. He was a dissident Presbyterian minister who broke away to establish the Bible Presbyterian Church. One of his favorite targets was the Federal Council of Churches (since 1950 renamed National Council of Churches), organized in 1908, which he denounced for its "soul-destroying modernism" and alleged communistic tendencies. Basic to the Federal Council's program was its social gospel creed. Thus the Council spoke frequently on behalf of its affiliated churches concerning social problems, particularly that of race relations. McIntire, noted for his acidic polemics and racist associations, opposed social Christianity. He drew the radical wing of fundamentalism into the American Council of Christian Churches, founded by him in 1941 as a counterpoise to the social activism of liberal Protestantism.

Fundamentalism, of course, is still deeply entrenched in the American way, as the 1980 presidential campaign illustrated, although it no longer captures the headlines it did in the 1920s. Its influence, as we saw, permeated all of Protestantism, and even the Brethren could not escape its sway. Fundamentalism, however, in affirming the "Five Points," virtually demanded a creed as a test of orthodoxy. This, of course, was diametrically opposed to the non-creedal heritage of the Brethren, which made the New Testament the basis of faith.

Fundamentalism and Juniata College

Dr. Herbert Hogan, former academic dean and professor of history at LaVerne University, argues convincingly that fundamentalism, particularly as expressed in *The Fundamentals,* had held a strong attraction for many Brethren in the past.[1] The pamphlets themselves were given rave reviews by the *Gospel Messenger* editors, including Henry Brumbaugh, and other leaders at the Brotherhood level.[2] Hogan suggests that there were several reasons why some

Brethren were favorably disposed toward the movement. For one thing, certain social and cultural historians contend that fundamentalism can best be understood as a facet of the rural-urban conflict. They point out that it won its most cordial hearing among rural-oriented people, who quarreled with almost every aspect of modern life. In the early decades of this century, the Brethren were still predominantly rural and painfully facing the adjustments to a rapidly expanding urban-industrial society.

Then, too, the Brethren noncreedal position was not necessarily incompatible with biblical literalism. For the most part Brethren theology, aside from its distinctive ordinances and pietistic mores, essentially held to the "fundamentals." In fact, the Brethren's Card, a brief unofficial statement of doctrines and practices first published by the *Gospel Messenger* in the 1890s and carried regularly for several years, illustrated this. The Card declared that the church "firmly accepts and teaches the fundamental evangelical doctrines," and then went on to paraphrase the "Five Points."

Moreover, Brethren thought could, and did, accommodate the doctrine of premillennialism, a basic tenet of fundamentalism that taught that the Second Coming of Christ will occur before the millennium and not after it, as the liberals contended. The *Gospel Messenger* published many articles by Brethren ministers predicting the imminent end of the world. It was Dwight L. Moody, the great urban revivalist of yesteryear, who rescued premillennialism from the obscurity into which it had fallen since the Millerites missed in their calculations on the Second Coming back in 1843. The concept was a pessimistic reaction to the urban-industrial-scientific world. It contrasted with the optimistic world view of the postmillennialists, to whose theological fraternity the social gospel reformers belonged, who thought that the globe would be transformed in preparation for Christ's return and reign.

After World War I, Hogan notes, a new generation of Brethren leaders came on the scene. Of a different stamp from their predecessors, they manifested a hostility to the dogmatism and basic presuppositions of fundamentalism. This attitude was shared by the new editor of the *Gospel Messenger,* Edward Frantz. He took over the paper in 1915 after having studied at the University of Chicago Divinity School, where the theological liberals had set up camp. During the 1920s, when the nation was rocked by acrimonious dispute over evolution, he kept the *Gospel Messenger* curiously muted on the subject.

There were antievolutionists in the church, but they did not gain an open Conference debate until 1929. Even then, Standing Committee voted to return the two queries that came before it criticizing the teaching of evolution in public schools, colleges, and universities. But Conference overruled the recommendation, and referred the queries to the Board of Religious Education and the General Education Board for joint study. Two years later the commission reported, neither condemning the theory of evolution nor specifically upholding the Genesis creation story.[3]

It is Hogan's thesis that, in the period of 1918–1931, "the most articulate expression of fundamentalism within Brethren leadership centered around Huntingdon, Pennsylvania."[4] He identifies Charles C. Ellis, Galen B. Royer, and Tobias T. Myers as the guiding lights. All three were members of the Juniata College faculty, C. C. Ellis doing double duty as vice president also. They made up the core of a School of Theology at the College which was in operation from 1918 to 1924 and founded as a rival to Bethany Bible School in Chicago (see chapter 9). The School of Theology's faculty and course offerings were listed in the regular College catalogue. But that section of the catalogue also contained a credal preamble, which was an expanded version of the "Five Points," setting forth the School's doctrinal base. As Hogan writes, "The men at Huntingdon were interested in preserving the fundamental doctrines of Christianity which go beyond the distinctive Brethren doctrines."[5]

Of the three Juniatians, C. C. Ellis, just emerging as a distinguished and revered Brotherhood leader, enjoyed the widest recognition in fundamentalistic circles outside the denomination. For years after 1919 he was a weekly contributor to the *Sunday School Times*, an influential nonsectarian voice with a fundamentalist bias. His booklet entitled *The Religion of Religious Psychology* was published in 1922 by the Sunday School Times Company, located in Philadelphia. Later it was revised and republished by the Los Angeles Bible Institute (1928). In 1922 he accepted an invitation to become a contributing editor of the *Bible Champion*. This publication was the official organ of the Bible League of North America, a fundamentalistic organization formed in 1902. During the 1920s the League attracted many distinguished contributors to its magazine, which featured scholarly articles contesting new concepts in biology and theology. Dr. Ellis was also invited to teach at Moody Bible Institute during the summer of 1923, and overtures were made to him to join its faculty permanently. This Chicago institution and its West Coast sister, Los Angeles Bible Institute, were educational strongholds of the fundamentalist cause.

Vice President Ellis believed that Brethren colleges should openly become the citadels of theological conservatism. In 1920 he wrote a brief article in defense of this view for the *Gospel Messenger* called "A College Entrance Examination."[6] In it he raised the question, "Does the college, with all its individual instructors, hold and teach the following":

> 1. The unique and infallible inspiration of the Bible (by this is meant inspiration different in kind as well as in degree from that of every other book in the world) and every part of the entire Bible equally inspired and infallibly accurate and correct, both in matters of fact as well as of doctrine, in its original or autograph manuscripts.
> 2. The lost condition of all men by nature since the fall of Adam.
> 3. Redemption for men only through the death of Christ, who became man's Savior by becoming man's Substitute, receiving in himself the penalty of man's sin and the necessary and holy wrath of God against sin.
> 4. The deity of Christ, different not in degree, but in kind from any so-called "divinity" that man has.
> 5. The virgin birth of Christ.
> 6. The resurrection of the body of Christ and of all men.

Ellis concluded: "It is not always easy to answer for other individuals, but for the college and for those who are its leaders it ought not to be difficult to answer"—presumably, by publishing similar articles of faith in its catalogue.

Curiously omitted in his six-point checklist was the Second Coming of Christ. But C. C. was a vocal premillenarian, and as such was critical of the social gospel theology, which equated the Kingdom of God with the progressive transformation of society. In his schematized picture of the future, he did not expect to see society transformed toward the shape of the Kingdom; the Second Coming of Christ alone would bring in a new order. For him all human history was a struggle between Satan and Christ. Social ills will never be cured until Christ comes to judge the world, destroy Satan, and institute His reign. Ellis, like all premillennialists, believed that the social gospel washed out all theological concern in favor of sheer action, and thus was a distortion of the full gospel of judgment and redemption. He taught that Christians would do better to occupy themselves saving souls and to wait patiently for Christ to bring in a social order from above, upon His return.

The Juniata professor was understandably unhappy in 1922, therefore, with the appearance of *The Social Message of Christianity*, published by the church's General Education Board. This pamphlet, which dwelt upon social gospel themes, purported to represent the position of the Church of the Brethren. Dr. Ellis wrote a critique of the pamphlet for the *Gospel Messenger*, challenging such a claim.[7] He gave four objections, the last one insisting that the "positions set forth are . . . without adequate Scripture support." He said, "Surely if the Social message of Christianity was so important, we ought to have had much of it in the Acts of the Gospels and in the doctrine of the Epistles." Most of the scriptural references in the pamphlet were taken from Old Testament prophetic books. Therefore, he claimed that the author ignored New Testament evidence that contradicted the idea of the fatherhood of God and the universal brotherhood of man (John 3:3 and 8:44).

Ellis the fundamentalist reminded his readers that he did not stand alone among the Brethren in his opposition to the social gospel heresy. He pointed out:

> The writer happens to know that there are many in our fellowship who do not expect the establishment of the Kingdom by the method that is here set forth, but are "looking for the blessed hope and appearing of the glory of the great God and our Savior Jesus Christ (Titus 2:13)" and they can not but wonder why, when we speak so much of the Kingdom, we should say no word about bringing back the King who alone can set up the Kingdom.

"The Gospel Message," he stated, "is a personal message to men who need to be born again, and no abiding social uplift can come where this is ignored, or where the social by-product is mistaken for the heart of the Gospel." He concluded by citing the Salvation Army and the preaching of Dwight L. Moody and Charles Spurgeon as examples of how "individualistic religion" and a dedication to "real and abiding social service" can be combined in a way more theologically sound.

Middle Pennsylvania stood solidly behind Ellis. Juniata College had "gained a favorable opinion" among many Brethren because of C. C.'s fundamentalist stance, Harry Cassady, the College pastor and money-raiser, told fellow-trustees in 1919. The 1922 District Conference, held at First Church, Altoona, sent a query to Annual Conference petitioning that body to adopt the Brethren's Card as the official doctrinal statement of the church. The Card contained no reference to social and political activism, except to say that the Brethren oppose "violence in industrial controversy." In response to this query and two other related ones, Conference disavowed *The Social Message of Christianity* but took no action on the Brethren's Card.

But C. C. Ellis had the backing of many sectors of Middle Pennsylvania on more than the social issue. The 1921 District

Conference voiced grave concern about the "great apostasy . . .
spreading throughout Christendom." At Twenty-Eighth Street's
urging, the delegates went on record deploring

> That hundreds of false teachers are bringing in "damnable heresies,"
> even denying the Lord that brought them and bringing upon themselves
> swift destruction;
> That the fundamentals of the Christian faith are being considered as
> archaic and are being supplanted by high-sounding phrases such as
> "Find of Science," "Consensus of Scholarship," "New Light from Origi-
> nal Sources," etc.

Then followed a list of "fundamentals." That the Twenty-Eighth
Street congregation should raise alarm about modernist heresies is
not surprising. Their pastor was Benjamin F. Waltz, then a student
at Juniata College's School of Theology.

There was therefore a strong conservative theological element in
Middle District as early as the 1920s. Later, when a more militant
brand emerged within the area in the 1940s, its advocates were
deceived into thinking that C. C. Ellis was their ally. But the popular
educator and preacher was anything but a disaffected Brethren
insurgent. While president of Juniata College (1930–1943), he was
one of the Brotherhood's most revered leaders. He was a classic
example of Harry Emerson Fosdick's observation: "All fundamentalists are conservatives, but not all conservatives are fundamentalists." Dr. Paul M. Robinson, while president of Bethany Theological Seminary, provided the following assessment of his onetime
college teacher:

> While Dr. Ellis might well be called a Fundamentalist so far as his
> beliefs were concerned, he was a great churchman and was regarded as
> sort of a leader of the conservative. As such he gave a kind of leadership
> to the Brotherhood which stood as a rebuke to the fundamentalistic
> spirit, while upholding the fundamentalist theology.[8]

This is clearly substantiated by the counsel given District Elders'
Meeting by C. C. Ellis, then president emeritus, on Armistice Day
1944. He said:

> We are not a credal church. There is none of us who has found anyone
> else who agrees with us in every particular. We cannot expect to have
> 100% agreement on all problems but we must have a tolerant attitude for
> each other. The "Brethren card" is the only place on which there is
> definite unity. In the days of debate with other churches, we debated our
> own distinctive doctrines, not the fundamental doctrines. We must now
> think of the fundamental doctrines because they are not all accepted.

Even the doctrine of God is under fire. We should bring our thoughts together in meetings such as we have here. When we discuss these things together we find that we are not as far apart as we think. Be tolerant enough to give the other man the tolerance we desire for ourselves.[9]

Historically, then, militant fundamentalism has never been a characteristic of the Brethren mentality. But during the 1940s it evoked a strong expression in Middle District, with convulsive consequences. Open rupture was precipitated by Brethren affiliation with the National Council of Churches, inciting far more rancor than the Progressive imbroglio of the early 1880s. Two congregations, ranking among the Brotherhood's largest, were left virtually decimated for a period. The split led to extensive litigation, dragging the church into the courts, a regrettable outcome for the traditionally nonlitigious Brethren. Reverberations were still felt as late as the sixties.

11
Fundamentalism and the Lewistown Schism

Background of Harold Snider

The Lewistown church had been introduced to fundamentalist theology by Herman B. Heisey, who had studied at Juniata during the heyday of Ellis, Royer, and Myers. He earned a Bachelor of Sacred Literature degree in 1911 and pursued divinity studies almost to completion in the School of Theology. Heisey served the congregation twice as pastor—1919 to 1925 and 1935 to 1940. An able, galvanic preacher and one-time missionary to India (1912–1914), he hand picked as his successor in 1940 Harold Snider, around whom the storm of fundamentalism first broke in the District.[1]

Snider was a Waynesboro native who attended business college for a year before taking a position in a furniture store in Hagerstown, Maryland. In 1927 he was licensed to preach and the next year installed into the full ministry. He studied at Gettysburg Seminary, but obtained no degree, and in 1935 was ordained an elder.

While pastor at Martinsburg, West Virginia (1933–1940), he earned a reputation for his independent, fiery, fundamentalist warp. Consequently, the majority of District leaders held him under suspicion when he became a Lewistown candidate. Some time before his election took place, he was interviewed by the District Ministerial Board in the home of Edgar Detwiler. According to Snider, "they put me through an inquisition" and were under instructions to "keep me out of the district."[2] He also accused the board of interfering with the church council that extended him a call, which was given on the strength of a 111 to 10 vote. From the start, therefore, the forty-year-old pastor was not fully accepted by the elder's body. His eldership status was never reconfirmed in the District, and in the annual District booklet each year he was simply listed along with other licensed ministers.

Beginnings of the Breach

It was not long after Snider assumed his duties—December 31, 1940—that there were covert signs of a non-Brethren bias at work in the Shaw Avenue church. The standard *Brethren Hymnal* was dropped and an outside hymnal adopted. Likewise, Sunday School literature prepared by Elgin was changed to that of the Union Gospel Press, a nondenominational publishing house.

A more overt sign was his open challenge of Brethren pacifism, branded by him as "unscriptural and unthinking." In 1941 he wrote an editorial for the Lewistown *Sentinel* in which he defended the country's war preparedness program and took some digs at conscientious objectors. The following year Snider published a book titled *Does the Bible Sanction War?*, explaining why he was not a pacifist. He drew upon 150 Scripture verses in an attempt to disprove the Brethren teaching that "all war is sin." He made a distinction between "aggressive" war and "defensive" war, contending that only the former was proscribed by the Bible. He took the position that he was speaking for the Brotherhood, since the great preponderance of Brethren boys chose to enter military service rather than become C.O.'s.

Spurning Brotherhood-sponsored youth programs, Snider became wrapped up in the Youth for Christ movement. He was instrumental in organizing a Christian Laymen's Association in Lewistown to promote it. Youth for Christ services were held in his own church, to which nationally known fundamentalist speakers were invited. He was very critical of fellow-clergymen who entertained doubts about this kind of mass evangelism. He found it a "good and wholesome thing" because, he said, it made no

> mention of the unscriptural world brotherhood, nor does it make an issue of the race question. Social service must take a secondary place to the work of giving the gospel of Christ to the lost. It [Youth for Christ] teaches youth to stand off from current evils such as movies, dancing, cards, smoking, petting, etc., in fact it stresses the new-birth in such a positive manner its converts have no desire for these evils.[3]

In his opinion the movement was of no less moment than the Great Awakening of colonial days.

It was an Annual Conference decision in 1941, however, that transformed Snider's ministry into an all-out crusade against "modernism" and culminated in his alienation from the church some half dozen years later. That year the Conference at LaVerne, California, authorized constituent membership in the Federal

Council of Churches of Christ in America—"out of a desire to share in the larger fellowship of the Protestant world and to be a more effective comrade of other Christian groups in those movements for peace and world reconciliation to which we all in Christ owe a common loyalty."

The Federal Council had been formed, as we saw in chapter 10, in 1908, to enable the nation's churches by common action to deal more effectively with the problems of an industrial society. Theological conservatives had always been wary of the Council because of the liberalism of its leadership and its social gospel creed. Thus Brethren conservatives did not let the decision go unchallenged. Many of them, like Snider, were also disturbed that the question was not raised through the regular query method, but came as a recommendation from the Council of Boards.

At the 1942 Conference in Asheville, North Carolina, a large conservative bloc (Snider was one of the kingpins) carried the matter to the convention floor and asked the church to reconsider membership in the Federal Council. The query that put reconsideration on the agenda had originated in Middle Pennsylvania. Three papers on the subject had been presented at the Roaring Spring District Conference that May and were taken up together. It was decided to pass on to Conference the one submitted by the Martinsburg Memorial Church.[4] The delegates at Asheville, however, sustained the action of 1941 by a substantial margin, after a boisterous debate.

The fight was now on for the anti-Council minority in the Brotherhood. It was intensified early in 1943 by an open letter defending Conference's reaffirmation of Federal Council membership, written by Dr. Paul H. Bowman, president of Bridgewater College and the 1942 moderator. Bowman referred to some pamphlets he had received that were vehement in their denunciation of the Federal Council. He described them as "based on shabby evidence" and "born of prejudice and bitterness," and cautioned all Brethren ministers and churches against "anonymous propaganda."[5]

Harold Snider countered with an open letter of his own, but published it in the November 18, 1943, issue of the *Christian Beacon*, a fundamentalist magazine edited by Carl McIntire at Collingswood, New Jersey. In the letter "to all Brethren," he charged:

> Instead of defending the faith which we print in our doctrinal statement our leaders at Elgin have sought every means possible to supplant it with a milky "Social Gospel" which has fully culminated in the hobby of the Federal Council, namely: "The Universal Fatherhood of God and Brotherhood of Man," and this in complete defiance of the Word of God in John 8:44 which tells us ". . . ye are of your father the devil."[6]

This edition of the *Beacon,* which also carried a letter of Snider's to Bowman, stressing his own premillennial faith, was mailed to every Brethren minister and elder. In all, 2,800 received copies in this way, the expense absorbed by Lewistown friends of McIntire.

The following spring, Snider published a forty-two-page booklet called "Modernism: The Federal Council, and the Church of the Brethren." Privately financed, it too was sent without charge to all Brethren ministers. A total of five thousand copies were printed and distributed free. The booklet professed to expose the false claims of the Federal Council and to demonstrate how it and the leaders of modernism repudiated the "fundamentals." Because of its social creed, he declared, "it is anti-American, and is honey-combed with communism and many un-American doctrines." He quoted—out of context—from the published works of noted churchmen, such as Harry Emerson Fosdick, George A. Buttrick, Bishop Francis McConnell, and Henry Sloane Coffin, to illustrate their "blasphemous" theology. He charged that "Elgin—like the Federal Council—doesn't want fundamentalists" and that the LaVerne Conference amounted to a *coup d'état.* The booklet concluded with a battery of twenty-seven questions about the Federal Council and Brethren leadership at Elgin that really amounted to a checklist of indictments against those two bodies. The last question summarized his main thesis:

> After bringing evidence to prove that the Federal Council is not helping the cause of Christianity but rather is aiding mightily in destroying the Bible, which is the cornerstone of the TRUE church, and helping with its ungodly literature to destroy even the morals of our youth, we ask this: HOW LONG ARE TRUE BRETHREN GOING TO STAY IN THE FEDERAL COUNCIL?

The booklet caused quite a stir, enough so that Standing Committee granted Snider a private hearing when Conference convened in 1944 at Huntingdon. Duly impressed, that body proceeded to introduce a query that began by confessing that the church had affiliated with the Federal Council without adequate study, and then went on to recommend the appointment of a committee to research the facts about the Council and report the next year. The query passed, and an investigating committee of five was created, with C. C. Ellis as chairman.

Meanwhile, the Lewistown pastor was anxious that the Brethren be kept abreast of the Federal Council controversy, and at the urging of friends began to publish a monthly paper for that purpose. The first edition appeared in January 1945 under the caption *Gospel Trumpet* and signified in an explanatory subtitle: "A Brethren

Paper Protesting *Membership in the Federal Council*." But in April the name was changed to *Brethren Fundamentalist,* which its editor deemed a more "descriptive" term.[7] At first distributed free, it was put on a subscription basis beginning in 1946, at a yearly rate of fifty cents.

Snider contended that a protest paper had been "virtually forced into existence," since the *Gospel Messenger* failed to carry the whole truth to the Brotherhood about the Federal Council. He charged: "It is all too clear that certain ones known as 'fundamentalists' do not have the right of expression through the columns of the *Messenger* enjoyed by others who choose to extol the social gospel and modernism."[8] His paper, he promised, would shun "editorials and articles savoring of the social gospel, pacifism and politics," and place more emphasis on the "pungent themes of fundamentalism" and evangelism. At the end of the first year some 25,000 copies had been sent out, and in January 1946 Snider expanded the paper from four to eight pages.

Anti–Federal Council Sentiment: Brotherhood and District

The study committee on the Federal Council had in the meantime reported to the 1945 North Manchester Conference. Its analysis of the Council and of the church's attitude toward affiliation was a keen disappointment to Snider—which he made very plain in several blunt speeches on the Conference floor. The report acknowledged that there were pockets of firm resistance in the Brotherhood, but concluded that the prevalent sentiment was favorable. Therefore it urged "that the Church of the Brethren continue its cooperation with the Federal Council of Churches of Christ in America until the Holy Spirit leads otherwise." Harold Snider wrote C. C. Ellis, the committee chairman, criticizing him for not bringing "a more evenly balanced report," which, in his judgment, was nothing more than a "poorly veiled slap at all who have raised a voice of objection to this unholy union." According to Snider, Ellis wrote back and accused him of "reading into the report that which did not exist."[9]

By this time the retired college president had fallen from Snider's good graces. The Lewistown pastor felt, upon his arrival in the District, that "a more or less attitude of intimacy" had quickly sprung up between the two of them. Ellis filled his pulpit twice in 1943, and the congregation had put Juniata College in its budget. In 1951 Snider wrote an editorial upon learning of Ellis's death. He said that when the Federal Council issue arose, "many of us had . . . considered that Dr. Ellis was the logical man in the brotherhood to head up the fundamentalist movement."[10] But he noticed that in 1944, when Ellis was moderator, he (Snider) was given "a cold reception." "I could not believe . . . I would not believe," the anti-Council foe went on, "that he sympathized with the modernist crowd in the church . . . yet the years that followed proved that was the case. My idol was dethroned." He continued in the 1951 editorial:

> The Annual Conference of 1945 [North Manchester] proved conclusively that Dr. Ellis was on the side of the Federal Council, and he was willing to serve as delegate to that Bible-scoffing group of so-called "church men."
> Many of the true students of the Word in the Church of the Brethren were dumfounded. They—like me—had considered Dr. Ellis should be the one to help promote the opposition to the modernistic Federal Council.
> It was all too disappointing.

One notable church conservative who did not prove a disappointment to the opposition forces was the inimical I. N. H. Beahm, whose idiosyncratic behavior and wit were legendary among the Brethren. The ex–college administrator published a nineteen-page booklet titled *Twenty Reasons on the Council* at his own expense in 1945. At that time the octogenarian, who paid an unsolicited visit to Lewistown as a would-be conciliator, was moderator of the Eastern Virginia District. His support of Harold Snider and the *Brethren Fundamentalist* was acknowledged in *Twenty Reasons*.

On the West Coast Snider's most vocal stalwart was Fred A. Flora, pastor of the First Church in Los Angeles and coeditor of the *Brethren Fundamentalist*. Three years later, in June 1948, he would resign as a Brethren minister but refuse to sever his pastoral relations with First Church.

As for Middle Pennsylvania, other pastors besides Snider openly opposed the Federal Council. One was Herman Heisey, whose congregation, Altoona's First Church, went on record ratifying his stand. But he was antagonistic toward the Snider approach. A member of Standing Committee in 1945, he told his colleagues, "I have no crow to pick with our church. We [at Altoona] do not follow the editor of the paper. We've had our own views at Altoona before him."[11] In 1947 Heisey wrote a letter to the Federal Council's general secretary repudiating all personal relationship with that organization.[12] Another critic of the Council was Henry F. Kulp, pastor of the Twenty-Eighth Street church, where Heisey was moderator. He openly approved of Snider's demagoguery, and became himself a District gadfly and schismatic. Both Heisey and

Kulp helped found, in 1947, the Blair County Fundamental Ministers' Association. Heisey was elected its first president.

By 1945, therefore, the Brotherhood was under considerable strain because of its Federal Council connections, and Middle Pennsylvania was the hotbed of discontent. Tempers flared at Conference when C. C. Ellis gave his report. Snider was particularly upset by some remarks by Dr. Vernon Schwalm, president of Manchester College, who referred to the Snider faction as "vicious, unchristian, and ungentlemanly."[13] Displaying anger, the Shaw Avenue minister responded in kind. In the interest of harmony, Standing Committee asked the elders of the District to counsel with Snider and request him to cease publication of his paper.

District Elders Get Involved

Accordingly, a committee of three—Harry H. Nye, chairman, Edgar Detwiler, and John Roland—interviewed him in his home on October 18. The meeting lasted from 2:30 to 5:00 P.M. The charges against him were as follows:

> That he failed to heed the statement of Standing Committee (*Gospel Messenger,* June 30, 1945) in regard to publication of articles affecting the disunity of the church; that he failed to discontinue the publication of articles on items closed for discussion by virtue of a strong majority vote by Annual Conference; that he published a paper in competition with the *Gospel Messenger* and circulated its copies only among a sympathizing group, thus endangering a church division (precedents of 1882 and 1926); that he offered outright thrusts against our church leaders in pamphlets circulated and also in non-Brethren journals beyond the bounds of the brotherhood; that he failed to protect the peace and unity of the church as the ordination vows would convey; and that he took an adverse stand against the peace principles of our church.[14]

Professor Nye, of Juniata's history department, conducted the parley with exceptional tact. It was suggested that there was no longer any need for a "minority" paper because a Brotherhood committee was available to interpret the Federal Council or any other issues to local congregations. Snider was urged to put his obvious writing talents to work on biblically centered articles for the *Gospel Messenger.* The Lewistown pastor, however, responded that he felt "divinely commissioned and led by continued prayer to uphold his present position." But he did assure the committee that he had no intention of separating the Lewistown church from the Brotherhood. The session adjourned with the visiting elders hopeful that they had forestalled an impending follow-up visit by a

Conference delegation. They were uneasy, though, about Snider's "marked and sustained controversial temperament."

But the publication of the *Brethren Fundamentalist* continued, with frequent attacks upon the Church of the Brethren and its leadership. Snider grew abusive, leveling personal attacks at clerical peers, both in editorials and from the pulpit—tactics reminiscent of Henry Holsinger. He denounced them as "false," "apostate," "corrupt," and "unworthy of the support and respect of local congregations." Levi K. Ziegler, secretary of the Eastern Region, remarked in a letter dated February 28, 1947, "The thing that bothers me is that he makes some statements which anyone can recognize on the surface as untruth. [But] gullible readers accepting everything they read as truth are misled."[15]

The Showdown

The first real indication that Snider's dissidence had turned schismatic occurred in January 1948. On the twentieth of that month, Earle W. Strauser, later a District pastor but then a lay minister, was notified that he was no longer Lewistown's presiding elder, because the official board had declared that position vacant. Moreover, Strauser was told, the Shaw Avenue congregation was now independent from the Church of the Brethren and was prepared to file papers of incorporation.

Matters had obviously got out of hand, and on April 10 Levi Ziegler met with Snider in Lewistown to ascertain the gravity of the situation. The estranged pastor was urged to attend the pending District Conference and to arrange for delegates from his church. Ziegler recorded Snider's response in his diary:

> He assured me that he did not expect to attend and that his church would not send delegates. I tried to point out that such action would be a mistake, that it would widen the breach already existing between himself and the leadership of the church, and lessen the processes of reconciliation. He said that neither he nor his people were wanted in the Conference because they had been treated indifferently. When I raised with him the desirability of cooperation on his part in an effort to resolve the differences existing, he said it was "too late."[16]

Indeed, it *was* "too late" for reconciliation. Six days later the pastor was visited by a committee of elders—Dr. Tobias F. Henry of Huntingdon, Mahlon J. Weaver of Bellwood, and Perry L. Huffaker from McVeytown (C. C. Ellis and Edgar M. Detwiler were also on the committee). Chairman Henry, professor of sociology at Juniata, handed Snider a letter containing the following indictments:

First, publishing incorrect statements.

Second, opposing by publication and preaching the historic peace position of the Church of the Brethren, thereby repudiating your ministerial obligation to "live in harmony with the doctrines, principles, and practices of the Church of the Brethren," and to "maintain the honor of the Church."

Third, refusing to hear the Church as represented by the Elders of Middle Pennsylvania and the Standing Committee of Annual Conference.

Fourth, attempting to incorporate the Lewistown Church of the Brethren in the name of another denomination.[17]

The conclave lasted nearly three and a half hours, and ended with little promise of reconciliation. Snider was invited to meet with the committee on the twenty-seventh at the Hotel Huntingdon to answer the charges against him.

Snider Faction Defects

The scheduled hearing, however, never took place. On Monday the nineteenth the congregation, which had grown from five hundred to eight hundred under Snider's ministry, met in special council. It upheld the January decision to apply for articles of incorporation. By unanimous vote (230 to 0), council also renewed the pastor's contract for an indeterminate period. With this show of confidence, Snider promptly apprised the District Ministerial Board of his resignation from the Church of the Brethren. His letter of April 20, announcing this coup, read in part:

Inasmuch as the trend toward regimentation in the present leadership leads to the "unfrocking" of ministers who are not pacifistic and who do not approve our relationship with . . . the Federal Council, I am respectfully resigning my ministry of more than 20 years in the Church of the Brethren to take effect as of this date. . . .
P.S. This in no way is to be interpreted as a resignation from my pastoral duties in the Lewistown church. I shall continue in this relationship just as long as they desire it.[18]

Snider gave public notice of this communication to the Board through the local press and the *Brethren Fundamentalist*. It was his letter of resignation from a denomination, rather than from a charge, that provided the model for the Reverend Fred Flora of Los Angeles when he followed suit there several weeks afterward. It also inspired Samuel J. Steinberger, after eighteen years in the lay ministry at Lewistown, to renounce his own Brethren ordination.

A rebellion on their hands, the District elders' body met in emergency session on May 1 at Martinsburg. Their first act was to strip Snider of his ministerial status, which was, of course, gratuitous in light of his already publicized resignation. The crucial problem facing them was how to handle his usurpation of the Lewistown pulpit. They authorized a stern letter advising the expelled minister, "[You] are expected to discontinue your activities in the [Lewistown Church] as of May 20th, 1948; and further, you are hereby notified to vacate the parsonage not later than August 1st, 1948."[19] When he failed to comply by May 20, Henry, speaking for the elders, sent a registered letter, dated May 26, warning that the District would "take such action as may be necessary to enforce your compliance." The trustees of the Lewistown church, now called the Calvary Independent Church of the Brethren, responded on the twenty-eighth, stating pointedly:

> Inasmuch as you did not seem to understand our letter [of May 8], we now repeat the gist of it, viz: that we do not recognize any authority outside of our local congregation: that the title of the church property rests in our hands, and that we have given Rev. Snider full authority to reside in the parsonage and function in the pulpit of the church building.[20]

The Shaw Avenue congregation had declared its independence on April 26, two days after Snider gave notice of his resignation. At that time church council withdrew the application for articles of incorporation (the congregation had already been incorporated since May 17, 1917, a fact that Snider and his followers apparently were ignorant of). Instead, it declared the congregation "sovereignly independent" according to the constitution and bylaws adopted May 4, 1942, "and will recognize no authority outside this congregation." On May 2 the local constitution was amended to change the church's name to Calvary Independent Church of the Brethren. The amendment clause was also rewritten to provide that the constitution could not be altered except by *unanimous* consent of council members present. This made Lewistown's declaration of independence practically irrevocable.

Two weeks later, church council met again and declared that all members of the congregation who held any office in the District must resign immediately. The next night, May 17, a service of ordination was conducted for Snider, the examining committee made up exclusively of ministers of independent churches.

The District Goes to Court and Wins

With these developments, the nonschismatic remnant at Lewistown met in July in the Burnham church and reorganized. The

Brethren Fundamentalist gave the impression that this was a small minority of only forty-seven. The court record, however, lists the names of seventy-one persons who signed a petition to restrain Snider from dedicating the Shaw Avenue property under a new name on Sunday, October 31. It was this maneuver by the rump group that initiated legal proceedings.

A preliminary injunction was issued by William W. Uttley, president judge of the Mifflin County Court of Common Pleas, on October 27, 1948. He scheduled a hearing for December 13–15, and then disqualified himself since he had represented the Lewistown members when they incorporated back in 1917. He called in another jurist, W. C. Sheely of Gettysburg, president judge of the Fifty-first Judicial District, consisting of Adams and Fulton counties, to preside over the case. The case was a bill in equity, "with the simple issue, whether, when there is a division within a congregation or church organization affiliated with a church body, the majority of that group may divert the church property to the support of doctrines contrary to the faith and doctrines of the Church of the Brethren."[21]

The three-day hearing got underway with a record crowd on hand—some three hundred, mostly congregational members representing both sides. Attorney Paul E. Fetterolf, along with Frank E. Hahn, Jr., of Philadelphia, were retained as counsel for the plaintiff, while Paul S. Lehman, assisted by James E. Bennett of New York City, served as attorneys for the Snider group. Because of several delays, however, the court trial was not concluded until February 26, 1949. Over 150,000 words of testimony were taken. A long wait ensued until Judge Sheely handed down his decision on March 9, 1950, more than sixteen months after the legal battle began. The judge's verdict ruled in favor of the minority group, "a stunning blow" to the optimistic Sniderites upon whom the costs of the suit were placed. They immediately procured a stay order, allowing them to occupy both the church and the parsonage pending an appeal to the State Supreme Court.

The final phase of the legal battle began on July 17, when the Calvary Church followed up its stay order petition and voted (115 to 64) to appeal the lower court decision. But the following spring, on March 19, 1951, the State Supreme Court delivered a decree upholding the original findings of Judge Sheely. Snider was ordered to cease preaching and vacate the Shaw Avenue facilities within thirty days. After two and a half years of litigation, all real and church property at last reverted back to the First Church of the Brethren of Lewistown.

Background of Henry F. Kulp

At the western end of the District, fundamentalism of the Lewistown sort contributed to a similar congregational split and another legal bout, the two taking place almost concurrently.[1] Harold Snider's counterpart there was Henry F. Kulp. Kulp came to Altoona from Brooklyn, New York, with no college or seminary training, and on December 4, 1945, assumed the pastorate of the Twenty-Eighth Street church. He became the congregation's third full-time minister and was given a three-year contract.

Statistically, outstanding progress was made over the next three and a half years. Sunday evening services attracted overflow crowds and midweek prayer meetings averaged between 200 and 250 regularly. The annual budget more than trebled. The church went on the air weekly, broadcasting both morning and evening Sunday services, and Kulp developed into a popular radio personality.

Tensions Develop at Twenty-Eighth Street Church

But soon after Kulp's contract was renewed for another term, in October 1948, the young pastor openly refused to cooperate with District and Brotherhood programs. Apparently, he had taken a cue from the rebellion then being staged at Lewistown under Harold Snider. Charles L. Cox of Claysburg, who was a member of Standing Committee and a few months later elected the local church's moderator, grew alarmed. He sensed trouble early, and soon after becoming moderator called the official board together on several occasions in an attempt to head off another incident like the Lewistown one.

On March 30, 1949, he wrote to Edgar Detwiler, District moderator, and briefed him on the situation:

Since accepting the Eldership of the 28th Street Church around the first of the year I have attended a number of Official Board meetings. At the first meeting I discovered the Board about equally divided, a part of them wanting to remain loyal to the Church of the Brethren, its institutions and program with the exception of the Federal Council, the majority being opposed to affiliation. The other half of the Board, led and apparently influenced by the pastor, was opposed to and very critical of the Brethren program and institutions.

The specific charges brought out and discussed at the various meetings are these: Criticism of Juniata College and the discouraging of any young people to attend this school. Criticism of Camp Harmony and refusal to cooperate in sending any young people there, but rather encouraging them to go to an independent camp at Williamsburg, though the pastor confessed he had never spent any time at Camp Harmony, therefore making the criticism unjust. Opposition to the Brethren Service program and open opposition to sending any money through that particular channel. Criticism of Bethany and its teachers. Open criticism, even from the pulpit, of church leaders, especially "the outfit at Elgin," and finally criticism of the Missionary program of the Brotherhood.[2]

Cox went on to mention other problems, such as Kulp's refusal to participate in union services sponsored by the Altoona Ministerium. Rather, he chose to be in league with the Blair County Fundamental Ministers' Association.

Cox described the political infighting that was taking place, so that the official board could be enlarged and loaded against the Brethren loyalists. A special board meeting was then called the last week of March to consider inviting the Committee of Five, appointed the previous year to deal with any trouble like this in the churches of Middle Pennsylvania. When a roll call vote by the board was taken, it ended in a tie. By prior agreement Cox, as elder, was permitted to cast the tie-breaking vote, which he did—in favor of a visit from the elders' committee.

DISTRICT SENDS ITS COMMITTEE OF FIVE

Before involving the Committee of Five, however, Moderator Detwiler decided to appoint what he called an Advisory Committee. This committee, consisting of Haddon Q. Rhodes of Roaring Spring, George Q. Showalter of Duncansville, and Paul R. Yoder, a Juniata physics professor, was instructed to investigate and counsel. It met with the Twenty-Eighth Street official board on April 5, but made no headway toward reconciliation. The committee then asked for the assistance of the permanent Committee of Five. Henry Kulp was notified by letter on April 11 that the joint committee was prepared to file four charges against him. These were:

1. Failure to be loyal to the specific emphases of the New Testament as interpreted by the Church of the Brethren.
2. Fomenting and participating in strife in the church.
3. Disseminating doctrines contrary to the beliefs and practices of the Church of the Brethren.
4. Insubordination and failure to comply with the doctrines and practices of the Church of the Brethren.[3]

The letter informed Kulp that he would be given an opportunity to defend himself at a closed meeting with the two committees at the Twenty-Eighth Street church on Thursday, April 14 at 2:00 P.M.

Kulp would have nothing to do with a closed hearing, and on April 14 he wrote to each member of the two committees questioning the propriety of the proceedings against him. He contended that the District elders were in violation of the procedures for disciplining ministers adopted by the 1947 Annual Conference. He noted in particular:

1. The committee of three was appointed by the moderator alone and not by the officers of the district elders' body.
2. The committee of three had no authority to appoint additional members or to form a joint committee with the permanent committee of five.
3. It was the committee's function to investigate and counsel on charges filed not by the committee itself but by somebody else and that they should not hear and determine the charges which they themselves had preferred.
4. He should be furnished with a statement of the specific offenses alleged against him in order to prepare a defense.[4]

Technically, the Altoona pastor had cause to plead irregularities on two scores. First, the charges against him were couched in generalities. Second, his case had not been reviewed by the elders' body as a whole before accusations were made by its two subcommittees. On these dual counts the elders' body had, in fact, deviated from the step-by-step *modus operandi* on ministerial discipline spelled out by the 1947 Conference at Orlando, Florida.

Kulp did acquiesce, however, in an open council session, at which time he promised to respond to the general charges. Thus on Friday evening, April 15, a special council convened at Twenty-Eighth Street. But when the visiting elders began to press Kulp to answer specific questions on existing conditions in his congregation, the session degenerated into mass confusion.

Shortly afterward, on the nineteenth, the 1949 District Conference opened at Martinsburg. The following day the joint committee reported on the latest developments at Twenty-Eighth Street to the elders' body. That assemblage unanimously agreed, after hearing the report, that the council meeting of the fifteenth had been in a state of disorder. This was evidenced by:

1. Irreverence in God's house as shown by applause, confusion and noisy demonstration.
2. Failure to observe parliamentary procedure in speaking without addressing the chair and interrupting speakers who were granted the floor.
3. Disrespect to the presiding Elder.
4. Attempting to replace the presiding Elder and illegally recognizing one of their own number as moderator contrary to the constitution of the 28th Street Church of the Brethren.[5]

The elders refused to recognize any action taken at that council, which meant that the church's delegates to District Conference, elected on the fifteenth, could not be seated.

Kulp Suspended by District Action and Appeals to Standing Committee

Then on the twenty-first the elders adopted a resolution suspending Kulp's ministry. This suspension was to take effect May 5, unless before that date he and his church were brought back into Brethren fellowship. The controversial pastor was advised of this action by letter, sent the twenty-second. On the twenty-fifth he wrote H. Q. Rhodes and invited the joint committee to meet with him and his church officers on the twenty-eighth. Such a meeting was held but without results. Another closed session was held on Tuesday, May 3 at which Rhodes, as chairman of the joint committee, reminded Kulp that his suspension would become effective on the fifth. But the Altoona pastor stood his ground, and in a letter dated May 5 Rhodes wrote him saying his suspension was now in force and that "it is illegal for you to officiate in any capacity" within the Twenty-Eighth Street church.

Kulp immediately appealed his suspension to the moderator of Annual Conference, a right guaranteed by the Orlando Conference. Thus his appeal was placed on the agenda of Standing Committee when Conference convened at Ocean Grove, New Jersey in mid-June. Kulp's case came up on Tuesday evening, June 14. His appeal statement was accompanied by supporting resolutions from Juniata Park and First Church of Altoona. But action was deferred until the next day, when the committee planned to go into executive session and admit the elders' committee from Middle Pennsylvania.

Standing Committee reconvened at 2:00 P.M. on Wednesday.

Moderator Paul Bowman instructed Kulp that the committee was not a court, but functioned in giving advice and counsel to local churches and districts in dealing with difficulties. The suspended minister made his statement, which was followed by a period of questions and discussion. After a brief recess protests against the elders' treatment of Kulp were heard from representatives of Juniata Park, First, and Twenty-Eighth Street churches. Additional statements were then taken from Charles Cox and H. Atlee Brumbaugh, a Twenty-Eighth Street deacon and one-time Altoona mayor, who supported Kulp's suspension. The session adjourned after Standing Committee voted appreciation for the "fine spirit" displayed by all who testified.

Then Friday evening the seventeenth, Standing Committee met to consider the Middle District elders' report on the disciplining of Kulp.[6] Tobias Henry, himself a member of Standing Committee who had represented his home district in the Lewistown case, spoke first for the elders' body. He pointed out that Twenty-Eighth Street was planning to erect a new church, and that the Kulp faction was anxious to arrange the deed so that the property would have no connection with the Church of the Brethren. The Juniata professor stressed that if Standing Committee did not intervene, since the District elders had failed to resolve the problem, then the loyalists at Twenty-Eighth Street intended to move their membership to Hollidaysburg or elsewhere. H. Q. Rhodes spoke next and observed that six of the ten deacons were loyalists. Even so, he urged, the church will go independent if a solution was not soon found. Paul Yoder followed and observed, "This situation is tied up with the Lewistown situation and is spreading rapidly to Morrisons Cove where we have one of our strongest churches." He noted that Twenty-Eighth Street contributed to the General Brotherhood budget only because the treasurer, J. Quinter Replogle, was a loyal Brethren. Mahlon Weaver, of Western Pennsylvania, then spoke up and recalled that Henry Kulp once announced that "if it's a matter of having a Brethren minister in my pulpit or having a vacation, I'll have no vacation."

After much discussion, Henry presented the argument that the District elders had followed the procedures outlined by the Orlando Conference. He then submitted two requests:

> 1. If you feel that our procedure has been according to Annual Conference ruling, will you take some action confirming the procedure followed by the Elders of Middle Pennsylvania?
> 2. Will you appoint a committee for counsel with these Elders of Middle Pennsylvania and all parties concerned in the problem?

A subcommittee was appointed to draw up a proposed answer on the Twenty-Eighth Street situation.

The subcommittee reported the next morning. As finally adopted, its report read:

> The Standing Committee desires to express deep regret and sorrow concerning the situation which has arisen among the Brethren in the Altoona area. And now after hearing the appeal of Brother Henry Kulp and also the report of the committee of Elders of Middle Pennsylvania the Standing Committee adopts the following:
>
> *First.* We deeply appreciate the expression of those appearing before the Standing Committee in their desire for reconciliation and harmony which expressions we accept as being honest and sincere.
>
> *Second.* We believe that the elders from the district of Middle Pennsylvania acted in all good faith within their rights in revoking the ministry of Brother Henry Kulp, but that his ministry may be restored upon his reconciliation with the elders of the district and upon his compliance with the program and spirit of the Church of the Brethren.
>
> *Third.* Since much confusion and misunderstanding is revealed in the churches involved in this situation, we recommend the appointment of a committee of three elders who may be of assistance in clarifying and establishing better understanding.[7]

The special committee of three to counsel with Kulp was then elected and was constituted of C. H. Bonsack, I. S. Long, and J. H. Moore. William M. Beahm, Conference clerk, was instructed to send a copy of the above resolution to the elders' body. On June 23 he also wrote Kulp informing him that his appeal had been considered and that the special committee of three would be getting in touch with him soon.

On Friday, July 9, Bonsack and Moore met with Henry Kulp in his home. They urged him to apologize and cooperate with the Brotherhood program. Kulp maintained there was nothing for which he needed to apologize and refused to pledge his support.

By this time Harold Snider was praising Kulp in the *Brethren Fundamentalist* as "an out-and-out fundamentalist." Said Snider:

> He preaches the whole Word of God, lives a separated, consecrated life, and ministers faithfully to his people. . . . Pastor Kulp dared to expose some irregularities in the leadership of the denomination; he had the temerity to criticize some of the programs of the brotherhood. In the opinion of the present leadership of the denomination, this constitutes the unpardonable sin.[8]

Meanwhile, on Thursday afternoon, July 7, the elders' body had convened at Martinsburg to give further consideration to Kulp's ministerial status. In a letter dated July 8, Lewis S. Knepper, clerk of elders' body, wrote Kulp of its unanimous decision:

We reaffirm our former action of April 21, 1949, in suspending the ministry of Brother Henry F. Kulp of Altoona, Pa., and today take action to revoke his ministry permanently on July 13, 1949, unless Brother Kulp presents in writing to the Committee in charge prior to that date, a satisfactory statement of assurance of his willingness to bring his congregation into fellowship with the District and the Brotherhood Program.[9]

On July 12 Kulp wrote Knepper acknowledging that he and his congregation were obligated to conform to the requirements of the denomination in order to remain in good standing. But he gave no indication that he would take any steps toward conformity. Consequently, H. Q. Rhodes, chairman of the elders' committee, replied: "We consider it [Kulp's letter of the 12th] unsatisfactory as an answer to the letter of the Elders' Body to you under date of July 8, 1949. Therefore, you are hereby notified that your ministry in the Church of the Brethren is permanently revoked as of this date."[10] A follow-up letter from Rhodes, dated the fourteenth informed Kulp that Levi K. Ziegler, Eastern Region Secretary, had been secured as the interim pastor of Twenty-Eighth Street. Ziegler was to assume his duties Sunday morning the seventeenth.

District Appoints Interim Pastor

Friday forenoon, the fifteenth, Ziegler received a phone call from Robert Good, a church trustee. The prominent Altoona businessman warned Ziegler that if he came on Sunday, someone would present his name and that of Kulp's to the congregation for a vote on who should take charge of the service. Kulp was on another line listening to the conversation.

Ziegler arrived at the church about 10:00 A.M. and sought out Kulp. The two ministers and some other persons went to the church kitchen for a brief conference. This is Ziegler's account of that parley:

After all were assembled I addressed them: "Brethren, you know that I have been named temporary pastor by the Elders' Committee of Middle Pennsylvania and have been sent to take charge of the service today. I hope for your respect and cooperation. I am prepared to take charge today." Kulp answered: "So am I." I said to Kulp: "Do you mean to say that you are denying me the privilege of taking charge of the services?" Kulp replied: "My Brethren will decide that." R. B. Replogle then said that they expected to take a congregational vote on whether Kulp or I should be in charge of the services. I remarked that Kulp would give the answers today. Kulp reiterated: "My Brethren will decide." I then remarked that if they denied me the privilege of conducting the services it would be considered by the Elders' Committee as a challenge to their authority and would be illegal, and further, that any meeting in which business would be transacted when not presided over by a member of the Elders' Committee would be illegal. I read to the group a statement to this effect from the Elders. R. B. Replogle tried to get me to consent to a congregational vote. I assured them that I would have no part in such a procedure as that, and that, having been warned, anything that they did which was illegal, they would be fully responsible for.

Kulp said repeatedly that my being there today was entirely out of order, as had been the entire procedure of the Elders in dealing with the 28th Street Church situation. A. L. Rhodes said that he knew why I was there. He said that because I am Regional Secretary I had to do as the Elders told me because my bread and butter depended on that and that the Elders had made a goat of me. I spoke out against both accusations without any uncertainty.

A final attempt was made to get me to consent to their voting on who should conduct the services today. Kulp said I should just go ahead and take charge of the services if I didn't mind being booed, hissed, interrupted, etc. I said that I was not there "to fight my way in." I said that I wanted it clearly understood that I would have nothing to do with what I considered illegal on their part, and that I was through as of right then with the whole morning's affair.[11]

The confrontation in the church kitchen lasted about fifteen minutes, and Ziegler left. He did not return for the evening service.

The Altoona *Mirror,* meanwhile, had carried two separate notices about services on the seventeenth. One announcement reported that Levi K. Ziegler, temporary pastor, would conduct morning worship at 10:30. The other newspaper notice read "Come to Church by Radio," identifying Kulp as the pastor, and had the morning service scheduled for 10:45 over station WVAM. Ziegler's mother wrote him next day about the radio broadcast:

Yesterday the 28th Street Church in broadcasting their morning service *announced* that Levi K. Ziegler would read the Scripture lesson and have prayer—there was a pause—then *someone* read and prayed—but David's mother-in-law [Dr. Wieand, a Bethany Seminary professor] said it wasn't Levi Ziegler's voice. It was she who heard the broadcast. Then there was a long organ number—seemingly prolonged and then Kulp preached.[12]

The following Friday evening, July 22, a council was held at the church, attended by the elders' committee and the three elders from Standing Committee. Unfortunately, the two groups of elders had not previously discussed what tactics to take in handling the meeting, which led to considerable confusion. Charles Bonsack wrote afterwards that this lack of coordination "weakened our position to offer conciliating explanations. I think I was never more embarrassed in my life." He went on to say:

One of my friends here asked if I didn't feel a little mad at times. I said, "I might if I knew who to get mad at." We are all to blame a little; but I do pray God may yet have glory out of it.[13]

Either at this council or at another one around this time, the Twenty-Eighth Street members, so it was said, gave Kulp their moral backing by a vote of 26 to 3.

Lay members of surrounding congregations continued to express an interest in developments at Twenty-Eighth Street. Late in July officials of three congregations—First Church, Juniata Park, and Riggles Gap—met in First Church and framed another protest to the District elders that was then forwarded to Annual Conference. A committee of five men—two each from First Church and Juniata Park, and one from Riggles Gap—drafted the statement and then met with the District elders' committee. They requested a meeting with the Twenty-Eighth Street loyalists, referred to in the *Fundamentalist* as the "minority," but the elders refused to approve such a meeting.

District Goes to Court Again

Faced with Kulp's intransigence, the District elders served him with a court injunction at noon on Saturday, July 23, 1949. Kulp was enjoined from occupying both the parsonage and the pulpit until further order of the court. Meanwhile, the District elders, Brotherhood Moderator Paul Bowman, and Levi K. Ziegler were being bombarded with letters and cards from I. N. H. Beahm, deploring drastic action. Uninvited, he hitched a ride from Richmond, Virginia, to Altoona on a goodwill visit just before the court intervened. In a letter to Paul Bowman dictated soon after his arrival, he wrote:

I am impressed that this is not only a strong Brethren city, but perhaps the church attendance for the Brethren is the best of any city in the Brotherhood. I have already found out that it goes far beyond the church attendance we have in Roanoke, Virginia [where he then lived]. Also the Brethren here seem to be very active in other ways and especially in their contributions to the cause of the church. I am seeing the church houses and visiting the several groups of particular interest, and I am in position to give a pretty good diagnosis of the situation.[14]

He attended the protest meetings called by the surrounding churches and was impressed with their sincerity and intense interest in the Kulp case. He wrote, "I am also actually surprised to find the people with so much general Bible information, and they certainly seem to want fair play." In a postscript written from York, Pennsylvania, he commented:

I further repeat that the unfrocking of Brother Snider and the unfrocking of Brother Kulp is a law-like slap in the face of free speech. I am not trying to justify either Snider or Kulp. I am speaking of the disciplinary work of the case in each instance and there is no New Testament teaching that will justify the procedure used at Lewistown and Altoona on the question of the unfrocking. We tried that at a certain place in Virginia to stop a woman from talking and it certainly increased her every capacity in loquacity.[15]

He concluded, referring to himself in the third person, as he sometimes did:

Bro. Beahm is certainly convinced that the eldership of Middle Pennsylvania, regardless of whatever might have been their spirit and attitude, were completely justified and loyal to the Church of the Brethren in their assuming to discipline at Lewistown and at Altoona as were the Brethren concerning the First Church in Los Angeles. But on the other hand they were at the same time disloyal to the New Testament as I have shown from the '47 minutes. . . . There is no New Testament authority whatever for what the church laid down at Orlando on this point.

Five days after I. N. H. Beahm wrote Moderator Bowman, Eastern Region Secretary Ziegler was once again denied access to the pulpit. He arrived on Sunday the twenty-fourth prepared to broadcast the morning service if necessary. But he was taken to the Men's Class room, along with loyalists H. Atlee Brumbaugh and C. C. Brumbaugh, where some twenty-five or thirty men were gathered. Ziegler announced that the elders had filed an equity suit the previous day that placed Kulp under a temporary injunction. The men then tried to pressure him into consenting to a congregational vote on whether or not he should be allowed to conduct the two worship services for the day. It was made clear to him that he would be voted down and that the laymen of the church would then take charge. The interim pastor later recounted:

I said to them that if the laymen would prevent me from officiating and preaching, and if they would carry through their other plans for conducting the services, they would have to assume full responsibility for their doing this. Several asked, "Is that a threat?" Some said, "That *is* a threat." "No," I said, "that is not a threat, but simply a statement of fact in the order of things."[16]

As he had done the week before, Ziegler left after the confrontation and did not return for the evening service.

The Judge Hears the Case

According to the restraining order of July 23, the injunction against Kulp and six laymen was to be in force for only five days, until a hearing could be conducted by the president judge of Blair County, George G. Patterson. Consequently, on Thursday the twenty-eighth both factions appeared before the judge and their attorneys at the Court House in Hollidaysburg. Kulp and the other defendants—R. B. Replogle, A. L. Rhodes, Edgar Fogelman, Robert Good, Willard T. Stuckey, and E. P. Miller—were represented by James W. Nelson, Samuel H. Jubelier, and Robert D. Campbell. Legal counsel for the District was provided by attorneys Robert C. Haberstroh and Park H. Loose.

Judge Patterson, according to Ziegler, "was in a mood to compromise and in an effort to give a chance for reconciliation directed that the original injunction be annulled."[17] He then proceeded to construct a modified version of it, removing all but one of the five restraints. Under a special injunction, Kulp was denied control of church property. Pending final disposition of the litigation, all monies were to be turned over to the church treasurer, J. Quinter Replogle. But Kulp was permitted continued use of the property and parsonage and could conduct services and hold meetings, and the church was ordered to pay his salary as under contract. For the time being, however, each faction in the church was to designate the minister in charge on alternate Sundays.

The judge further established a committee of reconciliation. It was to consist of three members, each faction naming one and the judge the third. This committee was to be made up of members from outside Blair County and was to report to the judge. The day-long hearing was then adjourned, with Judge Patterson expressing the hope that the church would be reconciled and a settlement reached in advance of the final court decree.

The Kulp faction, however, held an "indignation" meeting soon after the court session, objecting to the decree. Consequently, on Monday, August 1, Judge Patterson called a special hearing for further arguments on the issue. It was reported to Ziegler, who was not present, that the judge got angry and reinstated the original injunction. Another hearing was set for later in the week, Friday the fifth, when witnesses were presented, and the proceedings took on the appearance of a full-fledged court trial. Ziegler was saddened by the direction the whole situation was going, and wrote to Rufus Bucher, pastor at Mechanic Grove, Pennsylvania:

One wonders what will be next. We all need to be in prayer that the will of God might be done.

We cannot prevent people from believing what they want to believe, but there ought to be a resource within the church by which we could make a withdrawal of those who do not want to be Brethren, easy. We have not found the way. The loyal Brethren long to worship and work in peace and quietness.[18]

On Sunday evening the seventh, five of the loyal deacons formulated a letter to Robert Good, offering to try to iron out the church's problems. They proposed buying a lot Mr. Good owned and which he wanted the congregation to have when it built the projected new structure. They also indicated a willingness to arbitrate that part of the building fund collected since the coming of Kulp. A copy of the letter was delivered to Judge Patterson, requesting that he appoint the arbitrator.

I. N. H. Beahm, kept abreast of the Altoona troubles through the running accounts provided by the *Brethren Fundamentalist,* dashed off repeated notes to Levi Ziegler caviling the treatment of Kulp. On August 30 he wrote, "The awful case of Brethrenism seems to grow worse. Too tragic for me! Primarily I lay it to '41 Am. and to '47 Am. We should repent in sackcloth and ashes and go in reverse action."[19]

The final hearing of oral arguments on the preliminary injunction took place the morning of October 25. Attorneys for the defendants developed their case around three points: first, the revocation of Kulp's ministerial license was improper; second, the plaintiffs' bill of complaint was too vague; third, the bill failed to show that the elders had exhausted all remedies to settle the problem. The plaintiffs' counsel argued, on the other hand, that the District elders had followed all the rules and regulations of the denomination in dismissing the pastor.

Judge Patterson rendered his decision on December 12. He dismissed the objections of the defense against the suit in equity and ordered the special injunction of July 23 to remain in force. The defendants were compelled to make answer to the charges within a period of thirty days. Both the plaintiffs and defendants immediately filed briefs in support of their respective causes. Meanwhile, Levi Ziegler received a card from I. N. H. Beahm, written on Christmas day, declaring: "The good name of our people is at stake. Call both cases [Altoona and Lewistown] out of court at once! 'Peace on earth.' "[20]

The legal dispute, however, was allowed to fester for another five months before the court was ready to take action. By that time Judge Patterson had removed himself from the case and was replaced by

George G. Griffith of Cambria County. Judge Griffith opened hearings on the dragged-out suit on Tuesday morning, May 23, 1950. Testimony was taken for two days. At the conclusion of the first day's hearing, Judge Griffith expressed some doubts about whether the elders had complied in all respects with the denomination's procedure of counseling and disciplining in the ouster of Kulp. He suggested that the plaintiffs retrace their steps and follow precisely their church's basic law. Further hearing was deferred until sometime in August.

Standing Committee Rejects Kulp's Appeal

By that time Standing Committee for 1950 had received the report of the special committee of three appointed to consult with Kulp. In a session on Thursday, June 15, this report came up for discussion. Tobias Henry observed that "our appointing a committee left the matter as equivocal unless . . . we affirm last year's action. . . ."[21] A confirmatory resolution was passed (80 for, 0 against, 4 abstentions), and William M. Beahm, the clerk, was authorized to send an interpreting letter to Henry Kulp defending Standing Committee's position. The resolution was brief—one sentence—and simply stated that "the Standing Committee of the Church of the Brethren rejects the appeal of Bro. Kulp and confirms the action of the elders of Middle Pennsylvania in revoking his ministry." Kulp was notified by letter of Standing Committee's action.

Judge Rules against District

The ouster suit was resumed August 5 and entailed three full days of testimony. A key witness was William M. Beahm, dean of Bethany Theological Seminary and writing clerk of Annual Conference since 1942. He testified about Standing Committee's connection with the year-long church feud. On the afternoon of August 8 the plaintiffs rested their case. The defendants then moved for the dismissal of the bill. Final arguments were held several weeks later—on October 31—at which time the opposing attorneys filed their briefs.

Three weeks after that—on Monday, November 22—Judge Griffith handed down a decree dismissing the equity suit. The costs were placed on the plaintiffs, and the decree was to be entered as final unless exceptions were filed within ten days. The judge wrote in his opinion that it was not the function of the court to determine the guilt or innocence of Kulp. He conceded that it could well be that the Altoona minister and his codefendants were guilty of "disloyalty, insubordination and the dissemination of doctrine contrary to those of the Church of the Brethren." Furthermore, the visiting jurist stated, the procedure for defrocking a pastor as outlined in the minutes of the 1947 Orlando Conference was "in no wise in conflict with the laws of this Commonwealth."

Judge Griffith reviewed each of the seven steps constituting the method of handling cases of discipline involving any ordained minister or elder. He noted that "it is apparent that unless the ministry of the defendant, Henry F. Kulp, was properly revoked in accordance with the church laws, the bill must be dismissed." He then proceeded to cite six violations of the church code. His argument revolved around three points: (1) that the charges against Kulp lacked specificity, requiring him to answer broad complaints; (2) that the elders' subcommittee did not conduct an impartial inquest, failing to "gather carefully and impartially all the facts relevant to the case"; and (3) that the District elders' body invested the subcommittee with undue authority in passing final judgment on Kulp's guilt, the jurisdiction of which resided solely with the elders' body corporately. In summation, the visiting jurist wrote that "an examination of the records brings us to the conclusion that the organic rules and forms of proceeding prescribed by the ecclesiastical body of the Church of the Brethren have not been followed."[22]

One of the most frequent spectators of the struggle taking place in the Blair County Court House those months in 1950 had been Harold Snider, who diligently sat through "cool days, warm days, and sweltering days" of testimony. The whole scenario was characterized in his paper as "THE QUINTESSENCE OF SUPER-HYPOCRISY."[23] He insisted that the elders had taken him and Kulp to court simply because they "would not bow to the silly pacifism of the church." He warned in bold print—"CHURCH OF THE BRETHREN LEADERS: YOU HAD BETTER GET OUT OF COURT AND BACK TO THE PRAYER BENCH BEFORE GOD VISITS YOU IN JUDGMENT!"

District Reinstitutes Suspension Proceedings against Kulp

The District elders had no stomach for further legal action if it could be avoided. But they were committed to salvaging what they could of the Twenty-Eighth Street congregation. Consequently, within a month after Judge Griffith's court decision, the elders' body moved to reinstitute an investigation of Kulp's ministry. This time they were prepared to follow scrupulously the church's regulations. On December 14 five loyalist members filed charges against their pastor with the moderator of elders body, Everett's Stewart

Kauffman. The officers of elders' body met three times to study the list of complaints. At the third meeting, December 28, they decided to become a committee of inquiry and counseling. Stewart Kauffman assumed the chairmanship, and the other members were Alvin S. Cox (Lewistown), Isaac Wareham (Everett), Millard Wilson (Martinsburg), and Elmer Ebersole (New Paris). The next day Kulp was mailed a copy of the charges and informed that he was under investigation again.

Over the next several months the committee counseled with representatives of both sides on fourteen different occasions. Patiently the elders solicited Kulp's cooperation in working out a solution. But the disaffected pastor took the position that no elder from Middle Pennsylvania could take part in the inquest because of the widespread bias against him among the District leaders. He now became unavailable and incommunicado. The elders had no recourse but to revoke his ministry, an action taken at a special session in Huntingdon on April 7.

About two weeks prior to this, the deacon board at Twenty-Eighth Street had come to a fateful conclusion. In conference with the elders' committee, they decided that the two factions in the congregation could not be reconciled. By unanimous vote, they recommended that the two groups separate peacefully. The elders' committee was invited to provide counsel in bringing about this separation.

Kulp Faction Relocates

On this basis the committee conferred four times with the deacons. The contending factions agreed that, in separating, there could be no division of property. This provision, they concurred, would not apply to the disposition of the church treasury (about twenty-six thousand dollars). But it was the financial question that led to a deadlock in negotiations. The majority group rejected a proposal by the elders' committee that the money be divided in half, with the understanding that the Kulp element vacate in thirty days. There appeared to be no promise of a quick solution to this impasse. Beginning in September the loyalists and irreconcilables held separate worship services on Sunday in the Twenty-Eighth Street church. The Kulp majority assembled at the customary hours in the morning and evening, leaving the sanctuary to the loyalists during the afternoon. Levi Ziegler, at the bidding of elders' body, took over as minister for the minority group, which then reorganized as a separate congregation.

Soon after this *modus vivendi* was worked out, the loyal minority turned to the District for recognition. They petitioned District Conference, held at New Enterprise in October 1951, asking that their group be approved as the Twenty-Eighth Street Church of the Brethren. These members had signed a declaration of faith and loyalty card. Their petition became the first item of business. It was granted without a dissenting vote, and their delegates were promptly seated. At least one element of the congregation had now been brought officially into "order."

The way was thus cleared for the loyalists to pursue a course of action that eventually enabled them to regain control of the church property. On Thursday, November 8, the official board of the faction now recognized by the District—J. Quinter Replogle, George Rhodes, H. Atlee Brumbaugh, Clarence Brumbaugh—visited Kulp and asked him to vacate the pulpit. He declined, contending that he was still pastor in spite of the fact that the elders' body had removed his license.

Then on Tuesday, November 13, the loyalists held a special council and authorized the trustees to secure the church doors with padlocks. This was done the next morning. Thus the group supporting Kulp found itself locked out when it arrived for prayer meeting that evening. They removed the locks, and the loyalists then called the police to have the church repadlocked.

The next day, Thursday, November 15, Kulp announced that his group had "decided to end the quarrel . . . by forming its own corporate body and building a new church." His congregational allies made no further attempt to use the sanctuary, and services for the immediate future were scheduled in the Howard Avenue armory. The Kulp party left without making any claims on their share of the treasury. A separation had finally taken place, leaving a faithful core of sixty-four members to pick up the pieces and carry on.

Import of Lewistown-Altoona Court Cases

The Lewistown and Altoona courts cases were not unique in the history of the denomination. The Brethren had gone to law before in a time of intramural strife. During 1882 and 1883 the Old Order schism bred a rash of law suits. Several congregations resorted to legal action against the seceders in Miami and Stark counties, Ohio. The Old Order movement was also fought in the courts of Cedar County, Iowa, and Franklin County, Pennsylvania. In none of these cases, however, was there intent to fight for the custody of duly incorporated church property; there were other legal issues involved. Interestingly, every court decision went against the plaintiffs.

But in the Lewistown equity case we saw that the Church of the Brethren—as plaintiff—did win. The judicial ruling in that instance set legal precedent for the Brotherhood, which thereafter safeguarded congregational proprietorial rights. The Altoona decision, though upholding the dissidents on the question of due process, did not counteract the Lewistown decree on property title. Thus both cases represented a defeat for the fundamentalist insurgents in the District, a development that, for the moment at least, probably kept other borderline churches from going independent. Certainly, there were two or three congregations in Middle Pennsylvania that could easily have fallen into the Snider-Kulp camp had the courts taken a different stand.

More Rumbles over Ecumenism

Fundamentalism and especially the issue of interdenominational cooperation did not finally fade away as a source of contention in the District after 1950. Opposition to the Federal Council of Churches was still well entrenched among certain congregations, as it was in some areas of the Brotherhood. The controversy was kept alive, reopening debate among the Brethren, by new developments in ecumenism. As a result of a series of international conferences, the World Council of Churches was formed in Amsterdam in 1948. The rather dormant Federal Council was altered and reconstituted as a subbody of the WCC. In 1950 it took the name National Council of Churches of Christ in the United States.

The main item of business at Annual Conference that year, held in Grand Rapids, Michigan, was the ecumenical question. The most vocal opposition against joining the two ecumenical organizations came from Eastern districts. Nevertheless, after a prolonged discussion the ecumenists carried the day easily. But for the next few years efforts were made, as earlier with the Federal Council, to force Annual Conference to reconsider its relationships with the WCC and NCC.

Then somewhat belatedly, after opposition had begun to subside, the Smithfield congregation raised the issue locally. It submitted a query at the 1963 District Conference registering "conscientious objection" to all ecumenical involvement, and called upon the denomination to sever its ties with the WCC and NCC. It was decided that the District Board would make a study of the matter for a year. Assistance was invited from members of the Smithfield church and any others who had an interest in this study. A committee of five from within the Board was appointed for this purpose: Stewart Kauffman, Harold Bowser, Charles Heltzel, Joseph Mason, Berkey Knavel, and Bernard King, ex officio. This committee was to make its report at the next District Conference.

It soon became obvious to the committee that opponents of the WCC and NCC were not fully informed and could not substantiate their objections with facts. In reporting to the 1964 District Conference, it confessed that "the purpose of the year's study has gone completely awry." The committee's statement went on to say:

> Far from reaching agreement as to the facts about the councils of churches, many of those participating in the study became emotionally and irrationally involved. The cause of Christ is not furthered by an undertaking that produces harsh words, suspicion, accusations, and recriminations. In such an atmosphere the Holy Spirit cannot have his way, to say nothing of the failure to get at the facts honestly and without feeling. It has become apparent that the problem was not as simple as an objective inquiry into the facts. It is painfully clear that persons of differing mood, temperament, and commitment find it difficult to compose their differences. Therefore, the District Board recommends that the study be discontinued and that it be relieved of any further responsibility in connection with the query.

It was recommended and passed, however, that the 1965 District delegates to Standing Committee relay the "conscientious objection" raised by the Smithfield query to that body. This was done, and Standing Committee responded with a communication commending the District Board for the way it handled the Smithfield query.

There was talk at the time that the Smithfield church was at the brink of declaring its independence, so strained had relations grown during the course of the year-long dialogue. But its members and leaders were too steeped in Brethren tradition to let that happen. Nevertheless, the congregation has become withdrawn, and ever since the mid-1960s the Smithfield people have chosen to remain aloof from all District and Brotherhood programs.

Fundamentalism and Secession at Riggles Gap

Since 1950 four congregations in Middle District have been shaken by discord over fundamentalism and the related issue of ecumenism. What happened in three of them—Dunnings Creek, Maitland, and Juniata—is briefly told in their congregational sketches. In the fourth church, Riggles Gap, there developed a situation that threatened to take on the legal dimensions of the

Lewistown-Altoona disputes. But, in the end, the District stopped short of court action, though losing a whole congregation.

The Brethren of Riggles Gap, a valley community a short distance northeast of Altoona, were churched in 1916, the result of mission work by Juniata Park's pastor, Joseph W. Wilt. The congregation remained under Juniata's oversight until 1949 when it gained independent status. There was slow but steady growth, and in 1965 the congregation erected a new brick structure with a seating capacity of 260. Their pastor then was Norman C. Waite, a local ministerial recruit. By this time, however, the Smithfield query had provoked some of the leaders and members at Riggles Gap to call for congregational separation from the denomination. Ever since the Snider-Kulp troubles of the late 1940s, there had been a strong fundamentalist leaning, with accompanying hostility to the WCC and NCC, among the Brethren of the Gap community. Their unhappiness came to a head in the mid-1960s when Norman Waite, who had no seminary training, became pastor. At that time they articulated their grievances against the Brotherhood as threefold: (1) the failure of the 1966 Annual Conference to rally behind anticommunist crusades and to call for meeting sovietism with "hatred and retaliation"; (2) the use of curricula that accepted "higher criticism"; and (3) continued denominational affiliation with the WCC and NCC.

The final break came in November 1966 when the congregation voted to withdraw from the District and the Brotherhood. The members, some eighty-five of them, having incorporated in 1965, took the name Riggles Gap Bible Church. District Secretary Bernard King met with representatives of the congregation at Bellwood in December, but reconciliation was out of the question.

The name change received approval by Blair County courts in March 1967. District leaders, of course, made every conciliatory effort possible to prevent this secession. The Church of the Brethren could legally have retained title to the Riggles Gap property, as it had at Lewistown and Twenty-Eighth Street, but its officers were, as District Moderator Guy Fern wrote in a letter to the congregation, "more interested in people then in buildings." Hence they decided not to contest the will of the congregation and its pastor, who was reordained by a group of independent ministers.

13
Middle District:
Its Structure and
the Great Commission

Evolution of the District and Its Administration

The congregation was the first policymaking unit among the Brethren of colonial America. The next step in church polity came in 1742 with the first Annual Conference, some two decades after the first members arrived in Germantown. Since Civil War days there has been a third arm of government: the district. This plan was proposed in 1856 to lessen the volume of business coming to Annual Conference. Only the problems that could not be resolved at yearly area meetings, so the query posited, were to be referred to Annual Conference.

Several churches—in Virginia and Indiana—proceeded to align themselves into fellowships before the Brotherhood took formal action on the query. That occurred in 1866 when a republican form of polity was spelled out. The deliberative bodies of both the district and the Annual Conference were to be comprised of duly elected delegates, thus instituting a new approach to governance for the Brethren.

An advance step in representative government was taken two years later. A Conference action of 1868 empowered each district to elect from among one of its own elders a member of Standing Committee, then the agenda-setting body of Annual Conference empowered to act for the Brotherhood between Conferences. This gave the districts more governmental dignity, but their authority was limited, and so they were slow in evolving into administrative agencies of consequence.

The first district conference in Pennsylvania took place in 1860 when the churches east of the Susquehanna River met in common council. But the first district to organize formally in the State was

296

Middle Pennsylvania's own, in the following year. It was convoked by Elder Graybill Myers, whose old friend and noted historian, James Sell, always insisted that it was Myers who thought up this idea of polity and spread it among the Brethren while on preaching tours "throughout the Brotherhood." Whatever the case, he placed a "hearty invitation" in the *Gospel Visitor* of April 1861 to all the churches between the Susquehanna River and the Allegheny Mountains, urging them to send delegates to "a general council meeting" at the Aughwick church on May 9, 1861. Daniel M. Holsinger, a descendant of Alexander Mack whose son, Henry, provoked the schism of 1882, was moderator of this historic session. How many congregations were represented was never reported, but the next year there were delegates from nine churches. Thus Middle District came into existence five years before Annual Conference gave its approval to the system.

Middle District originally embraced sixteen counties and parts of nine others. According to the *Christian Family Companion,* the number of congregations in those counties in 1866 totaled twenty-one.[1] Ten years later there were twenty-six churches in the District.

But by then some elders like George S. Myers, from Morrisons Cove and later a key researcher for the 1925 history, were pressing for a division of the District. The church papers carried articles on this question as early as 1874, stressing logistic problems related to

District Board, 1979–80. *Row 1:* M. C. Good, L. D. Fisher, E. A. Cherry, P. Over, J. Keiper. *Row 2:* D. G. Lynn, W. E. Fether, L. Sollenberger, E. Metzler, G. H. Snyder. *Row 3:* R. Boose, M. L. Hall, E. D. Rowland, S. Hoover, R. Landrum.

the District's mountainous terrain and expansive boundaries. The subject of division was not allowed to die, though there was strong opposition to it. In 1889 a query from Duncansville actually got to District floor, only to be denied. But the supporters of separation finally prevailed in 1892, by a vote of 19 to 9. Southern District thus went its separate way, leaving fifteen churches in Central Pennsylvania's five-county area. These congregations had a combined membership of approximately 2,500.

A more compact District better fostered what many have thought to be the essential purpose of such a unit in the Brotherhood organization: to maintain fellowship among the churches of a geographical region by face-to-face contacts. Equally important, the district as such enables the local church and the Brotherhood to keep in better touch with each other.

One district organization, the elders' meeting, is of unrecorded origin in the Brotherhood. In Middle Pennsylvania the first mention of such a get-together appears in the District minutes for 1897. The elders' body, until recently, exercised great authority, especially on matters of ministerial discipline. More will be said about the eldership in later pages.

For nearly a century only elders could preside at district meetings, a prerogative that had been theirs at the congregational and Annual Conference levels from the first. In 1957, however, ordained ministers became eligible for the office. Then a decision of Annual Conference opened the moderatorships, at all levels, to lay persons. Dan West, of Brethren Service fame, was the first layman elected moderator of Annual Conference, in 1966. Middle Pennsylvania's

District Board Officers, 1979–80. M. C. Good, G. Fern, R. Landrum, G. Etzweiler.

first lay moderator was Ray Sollenberger of Everett, who wielded the gavel in 1971. Appropriately, the first woman to fill the post was his wife, Elaine, at the 1975 District Conference. The duties of District moderator, whose chief function in the past was simply to preside, have grown along with the expansion of the District's organizational structure. In 1968 the name alternate moderator was dropped and replaced by moderator-elect, an office with specific duties. One of the purposes for this was to provide a more orderly transition in the moderatorship each year, in the manner of Annual Conference.

Lloyd Sollenberger, a layman from Everett and District Moderator for 1981.

Not until 1941, a dozen years after being first petitioned, did Middle District draft a constitution and set of bylaws. The District Board, with a chairperson elected by its members from among themselves, came about in 1950, the result of a reorganization. The constitution was revamped several times over the next two decades, mostly to conform to changing Brotherhood models. Its last overhaul, again in response to an Annual Conference action, was in 1968. Since then, much of the Board's work is done through four commissions: Ministry, Nurture, Stewards, Witness.

Meanwhile, in 1949 the time of District Conference was changed from the spring to the fall. Then in 1955 a charter incorporating the District Board got court approval.

By that time the governmental structure of the Church of the Brethren had moved, so it was complained, another step closer to what some critics called presbyterianism. First, in 1947 the General Brotherhood Board was created, to be a central administrative body of twenty-three members. Then, that same year, Annual Conference put its stamp on the region as an organizational unit of the denomination. Beginning in 1932 the Brotherhood had been divided, on an informal basis, into five regional areas: Eastern, Southeastern, Central, Western, and Pacific Coast. But the regional program was of little consequence until its ratification in 1947. Church historian Floyd Mallott, however, did not think that these developments spelled presbyterianism. He rather characterized Brethren polity as "conciliarism." The church, he wrote, "acts through a series of councils and assemblies."[2]

The general purpose of the regional setup was to provide a more efficient link between the Brotherhood and the districts. In Pennsylvania, the Regional Board began to function on September 1, 1947, Middle District's first two representatives being Dorsey I. Pepple and Perry L. Huffaker. The Board employed Levi K. Ziegler as Regional Secretary, and from 1949 to 1951 David K. Hanawalt, a product of Central Pennsylvania and later an area pastor, held the title of Associate Executive Secretary. Ziegler was succeeded by Stewart B. Kauffman (1953–1955), himself a District pastor, once before and once after his Regional Office stint. There followed Harold Z. Bomberger (1955–1960) and Roy S. Forney, during whose tenure the regional program was phased out, in September 1964.

By then, 1960, Middle District had entered its own field program. The subject of a fieldman first came up at Elders' Meeting in 1950, and for the next nine years was regularly discussed and studied. There was even some thought of aligning in such a venture with Western Pennsylvania, which in 1958 took the step for itself. One of the strongest arguments for an executive secretary held that only a full-time professional could carry out the kind of program the District needed to obtain its goals. Finally, in 1959 District Conference voted to employ a field worker, but not by much of a margin: 65 to 44. Opponents of the idea were afraid the added cost would place too much of a strain on the budget. At that time there were forty-eight districts in the Brotherhood, thirty-two with less than five thousand members. The count on Middle Pennsylvania in 1959 came to 12,349.

Clyde L. Carter, in his late thirties, became the District's first secretary, in September 1960. A native Californian, he was a graduate of LaVerne University and Bethany Theological Seminary and held a master's degree from Penn State. He was an ex-missionary (India) and came to his District post after a seven-year pastorate at Johnstown's Walnut Grove church. His wife was the former Eleanor Snare of the Stonerstown congregation. They moved into a house on Oneida Street in Huntingdon, not far from the District Office on the Juniata College campus that the District had purchased for a parsonage. Everyone was shocked by Carter's unexpected death, only three months after his arrival. The parsonage was sold to his widow and three sons.

The search for a new fieldman brought Bernard N. King, from the pastorate of the Bridgewater church in Virginia, to Middle District in August of 1961. He had been educated at Juniata College, Bethany, and the Divinity School of Boston University, and had enjoyed a distinguished pastoral career. His qualifications were further enhanced by experience as a member of Standing Committee, the General Brotherhood Board, and several regional boards. The Kings took occupancy of a new District-built parsonage on Cassady Avenue, one block from the high school and within a few minutes' walk of the District Office. The programmatic progress Middle Pennsylvania made in the next half dozen years clearly vindicated the decision to employ an executive secretary.

Joseph Mason succeeded Bernard King in 1967, moving to Huntingdon from the Bedford church where he had served six years. Prior to that he had pastored churches in Virginia, his home state, and West Virginia. He was an alumnus of Bridgewater College and Bethany, from which he later received the Doctor of Ministry degree—in 1977. The District Board served as his supervisory committee during his three-year course of study, benefiting in return from the insights and expertise he had gained from his doctoral training.

In 1969 the Board decided to relocate the District Office and moved it from Founders Hall on Juniata's campus into a mobile home located outside Huntingdon along the Route 22 bypass. Then in 1972 the house trailer was placed at its present site in Huntingdon—on Mount Vernon Avenue, two blocks from the State Correctional Institution. Two years later the District parsonage was sold to the Masons. The proceeds from the sale went into Morrisons Cove Home Notes and toward paying off certain debts.

Accepting a call from Ohio's Southern District, Joe Mason left the District in the fall of 1979. He was replaced by Monroe C. Good of Baltimore, who began his duties in April of 1980. In the interim Administrative Assistant Miriam Williamson and June Peters attended to office chores and mailings.

Present District Office.

The incumbent District Secretary, a native of Lancaster County, studied at Elizabethtown College, Eastern Baptist Seminary, and Bethany. From 1952 to 1964 the Goods were missionaries in Africa. Upon their return Monroe became pastor of the Dundalk congregation in Baltimore, where he was active in community youth and drug-abuse programs. Three times he was elected to Standing Committee, and he has held numerous district-level positions. The Goods bought a home north of Huntingdon on Route 26, near the Valley Rural Electric Co-op headquarters.

Before the day of District secretaries, there existed for almost a

The two most recent District Executives, Joseph Mason and Monroe Good.

quarter century a little subscription paper, published quarterly, called the *District Echo*. It began in January 1928, sponsored by the Sunday School Board, and, often twenty or more pages in length, continued until 1952. Its editor for two decades was Lewis S. Knepper of Huntingdon, a one-time pastor and schoolteacher who became alumni secretary at Juniata College in 1926. The *District Echo*, printed in Huntingdon, was a well-conceived magazine, filled with news about Board work, adult and youth activities, special conferences, and latest congregational developments. Beginning in 1934 it was issued cooperatively with Western District, Tobias F. Henry, then at Roxbury, assisting as coeditor for several years. Even during the Depression the *District Echo* had an average mailing list of 3,500.

Since the time of Bernard King, the *District News,* a xeroxed multipage newssheet has been the "house organ." It is sent automatically each month to anyone holding a District office or whose name appears on the local church annual reports. There is also the monthly *Memo to Pastors*.

In summary, Middle District, like most of the other twenty-four districts making up the Brotherhood today, has become much more institutionalized with the passing of time. In form it has moved from a loosely organized council to that of a corporation, so to speak, legally chartered and acting through a board and committees. By the same token, the government of the Church of the Brethren has changed from a congregational type to one more subject to district legislation and Brotherhood decisions. The office of district secretary represents the latest stage in this shift toward a more centralized church polity.

The Changing Ministry

Not only has church polity been modified, but the position of the ministry has radically altered. It has changed from a free to a professional status, from a part-time calling to a full-time career. Originally, there were three degrees to the office of minister. The first degree was marked by a congregational call—the election—and conferred the right to preach. Advancement to second degree involved another local election, permitting the individual to officiate at baptisms, communions, marriages, and funerals. The third degree meant ordination as elder, the highest pastoral office, making the recipient eligible to oversee one or more congregations (sometimes the word *bishop* was used in earlier days instead of *elder*). All ministers, of whatever degree, were elected for life. Often in con-

Ministers. *Row 1:* R. D. Hoover, R. E. Miller, C. R. Arndt, Jr., M. R. Reeves, L. A. Weaver. *Row 2:* R. Page, G. D. Ebersole, C. H. Shoenberger, Jr., R. Z. Ebersole, G. D. Crumrine.

Ministers. *Row 1:* W. E. Coldren, J. R. Gottshall, R. Boose, M. Olivieri, C. D. Clark. *Row 2:* N. Cain, J. D. Brown, R. C. Myers, L. Lockett, C. Bush.

Ministers. *Row 1:* E. Harper, E. D. Rowland, K. W. Crosby, R. G. Bright, G. S. Fern. *Row 2:* C. Heltzel, L. G. Bowman, C. Hall, M. L. Hall, G. H. Snyder.

Ministers. *Row 1:* C. N. Pheasant, L. D. Bloom, E. M. Weyant, A. Spaeth, H. Spaeth. *Row 2:* H. E. Schimpf, W. E. Fether, H. M. Kenepp, W. K. Roop, R. L. Landrum.

gregations there was a plurality of ministers, with several sharing parish responsibilities. Hence the need for the long preachers' bench.

The "free" ministry meant that preachers and elders, whose livelihood depended on some other occupation, got no regular income for their pastoral care. Sometimes, though, expenses were reimbursed, and this was commonly designated a "supported" ministry. For decades, however, it was forbidden to make a livelihood in the ministry. As late as 1890 Annual Conference ruled that "stipulated salaries are again condemned" in regular ministerial work. But there were those in Middle District, like James Sell, who argued emphatically at that time that Altoona and city churches could not survive without a paid ministry.[3] The Brethren clergy, insisted Sell, was in a "transition period" and would soon become professionalized by necessity.[4]

The first paid pastor in the denomination was Tobias T. Myers, then of Philadelphia's First Church, in 1897. Later he came to Juniata College, where for twenty-two years he taught in the Bible Department. He, of course, was a strong proponent of a salaried ministry, as were all the men associated with the College. But Tyrone, not Huntingdon, initiated the practice in Middle District—when Walter S. Long became the pastor there in 1897.

Not until the First World War did the Church of the Brethren formally recognize the pastoral ministry. From 1911 to 1917 Annual Conference engaged in earnest debate on the subject. At Wichita, Kansas, in the latter year, Conference adopted a long "Ministerial Report" that spelled out a whole new pastoral system. It established two degrees in the ministry (ordained and elder), permitted "reasonable" financial support, and authorized district ministerial boards. In 1919 it was further stipulated that the pastoral year begin September 1. Then in 1922 came the licensing system for aspiring ministers and authorization for the permanent licensing of women, who, as we shall see, were excluded from ordination for another three decades. There was no pension plan for salaried pastors until 1943, and only in the early 1950s did clergymen became eligible for Social Security coverage.

Brethren ministers of the past were not only unpaid but also of limited schooling. The fear of a trained ministry, as we saw in chapter 8, was one reason the early Brethren opposed higher education. An educated clergy would lead directly to "commercializing" the Gospel, the warning went, producing "preachers-for-hire." The Brumbaughs, in starting their Huntingdon school in 1876, were insistent that if there was the slightest chance their

Ministers. *Row 1:* J. D. Keiper, R. R. Baugher, R. E. Hill, D. Webster, K. O. Holder-read. *Row 2:* H. H. Salyards, M. C. Good.

educational undertaking would breed a professional clergy, they would call it off at once. But in another two decades they had changed their tune and were in the forefront of those singing the praises of a trained ministry.

In 1898 the Huntingdon Brethren sold District Conference on authorizing a three-year "Ministerial Preparatory Course," complete with examinations and diploma. A committee was appointed to draw up a reading course and consisted of three men from the College—Henry B. Brumbaugh, John B. Brumbaugh, William J. Swigart—in addition to James A. Sell and John B. Fluck of Snake Spring. The novel idea later got kudos in the *Gospel Messenger.*

The demand for a trained ministry increased with time, hastened along by a better-educated laity. Moreover, most of the Brethren colleges had strong Bible departments, and then in 1905 Bethany Bible School, the forerunner of the denomination's seminary today, was founded to provide theological training. In 1959 Annual Conference suggested minimum educational qualifications for ministerial licensees and provided a three-year reading course for non-seminary persons curiously like that of Middle District's in 1898. In 1979 thirty-two men and women in Central Pennsylvania were enrolled in the course, which is supervised by the District Ministry Commission. Executive Secretary Joseph Mason gave the following profile of the District's pastoral force in 1979:

> The twenty-nine pastors employed in Middle Pennsylvania District during the current year have an average age of 48.3 years. The age range is

26 to 66 years ... [and they] have already contributed 494 years of service in the pastoral ministry. ...

Pastors' educational preparation includes fourteen with seminary degrees, three of whom have earned doctorates. Five are college graduates, several of whom have masters degrees or their equivalent. Four pastors have had some college or Bible school training in addition to a high school diploma.[5]

Other statistics in his report revealed that there were seventy-seven ordained ministers, active and emeriti, in the District, thirteen licentiates, and nine lay speakers.

Among the ordained is Emerita Madolin Boorse Taylor of Alum Bank, who was licensed in 1923 by her home church (Coventry, in the Southeastern District) while a student at Juniata College. Frequently in the late 1920s she preached three times every Sunday morning in the Dunnings Creek congregation, which she joined after her marriage to Joseph E. Taylor. In 1928 Middle District granted her a permanent license, and the minutes of that year indicate four licensed women but do not name them. The 1929 minutes, which for the first time include a ministerial listing, again fail to mention any other woman besides Madolin Taylor, although Bertha Longenecker, at Bethany Seminary, is named as a "licentiate." At any rate, since the 1920s the ministry in Central Pennsylvania has not lacked for femininity. Not until 1952 did Annual Conference, however, grant women equal rights with men in the ministry—in other words, ordination. Seven years later, Madolin Taylor, still at Dunnings Creek, became Middle District's first ordained female. To date, she has been the only one.

Madolin B. Taylor, now in her eighties, as she looked while teaching school at Chestnut Ridge.

Four early elders of the Dunnings Creek congregation: Levi Rogers, Abraham Fyock, George H. Miller, Thomas B. Mickle.

Not only the ministry as such, but the eldership has undergone change. As the role of the salaried pastor became more central in congregational life, the importance of the elder correspondingly decreased in importance. In the beginning the office of elder or bishop, as noted earlier in this chapter, was preeminent among the Brethren. During colonial times, it took on the dimensions of patriarchalism; "the bishop," writes one historian, "was a father to the brotherhood around him."[6]

No less in district affairs than in congregational, the elders, as a body, exercised great authority. But a changing ministry and the rise of lay leadership combined to call the position into question. After several years of study and debate, Annual Conference voted to phase out the eldership in 1967, agreeing that the denomination had moved "beyond the patriarchal concept of church government to a more democratic one." However, Conference action permitted the eldership to continue as a local church office where so favored, and those who had been ordained for life had the privilege of retaining that status. Today there are but two stages to the set-apart ministry: licensed and ordained.

Home Missions and Church Extension

Organized home missions work in Middle Pennsylvania began in 1880 when District Conference elected James A. Sell and John M. Mohler, then of Dry Valley, as "missionaries for one year." It was just such a plan for district-sponsored church extension, especially in towns and cities, that Annual Conference recommended for the Brotherhood in 1884. But it applied with equal force to planting the church in the prairies of the Plains States and farther west, where colonizing bands of Brethren were attracted by railroad literature and realtors' circulars. Evangelizing and churching the Far West was a major concern of the Brethren in the forty years after the Civil War.

In 1886 the Middle District adopted a more efficient program, creating a Mission Board, one of whose original members was John B. Brumbaugh of Juniata College. Brumbaugh would give twenty-six dedicated years to the Board, longer than anyone else. Churches in communities like Tyrone, Bellwood, Stonerstown, Hollidaysburg, and Riddlesburg got their start as "mission points" during his long tenure. George S. Myers, the historian, was a seventeen-year veteran of the Mission Board and never accepted one cent for compensation, not even for expenses. Board members like him and Brumbaugh frequently filled "mission" pulpits.

By 1935 the Mission Board had expended $90,000 for, among other things, ministerial support and subsidizing the erection of new church buildings. Fifteen years later, in the immediate post–World War II decade, the District was still paying out $2,200 a year to assist needy congregations, some of them long established. Indeed, Middle District as we know it today is nothing but the latest stage in the missionary work begun one hundred years ago. The churches at Bedford and State College stand as the most recent testimony to the District's ongoing home mission concern.

Foreign Missions

Middle Pennsylvania, with a good record in church extension, was just as ready to commend a worldwide ministry, though the 1925 history is strangely silent on this subject. The story of foreign missions in the history of the Church of the Brethren began late. The 1880s have been called the "Great Century of Protestant Missions," but the denomination did not get deeply involved in missionizing non-Christian countries until the early decades of the twentieth century. Prior to the Civil War, as earlier chapters have shown, the Brethren tended to be sectarian, committed to preserving their German life and language from any inroad by American culture.

But by 1850 the church began to change; there surfaced interest and agitation for publications, schools, and home missionary work. Until the end of World War I, church extension was primarily the product of land purchase and colonization, although Brethren were no longer strangers in towns and cities. Even in Chicago the straight coat and bonnet could be seen by 1885, the year city work began there. Since the Second World War, home mission churches have been almost exclusively established in cities.

BEGINNING OF BRETHREN MISSIONS

The first Brethren preacher sent abroad was Christian Hope, a Dane, who began a mission church in his homeland in 1876. Later the work spread to Sweden. The Scandinavian mission, from 1929 to 1934, was headed by Glen E. and Lois Detweiler Norris. The Norrises, whose son Wilfred is a Juniata College physics professor, twice served in Middle District pastorates—at Twenty-Eighth Street, Altoona (1935–1945) and Williamsburg (1959–60). In 1947, however, the denomination recalled its missionaries from the Scandinavian Peninsula and phased out its support.

Four years after Christian Hope sailed to Denmark, Annual Conference established the Foreign and Domestic Mission Board, its sole overseas responsibility being the Danish church. Middle Pennsylvania's illustrious citizen, James Quinter, was named to the Board and became its treasurer. This board was replaced in 1884 by the General Church Erection and Missionary Committee, which, with a sum of $8.69 on hand, ushered the denomination into a new era in the missionary movement.* The Brotherhood goal in 1884 was the grand total of one penny per member in support.

There soon followed mission activity in India (1894), Asia Minor (1895), and Europe (1899). Daniel L. Miller, for twenty-six years a Committee officer, sounded the watchword for the Brethren: "The Church that is not a missionary church is a dead church." In 1894 he began publishing, in the name of his Committee, the *Missionary Visitor,* which for the next thirty-six years, except for a brief interval (1896–1902), championed the cause of foreign missions. From 1884 to the outbreak of World War II, it can be said, this cause was "the great first work of the church."

Among Brethren youth the Student Volunteer Movement, which flourished at every one of the Brethren colleges, inspired many to volunteer for overseas church work. This organization took its rise in 1888 and exerted profound influence upon idealistic American collegians. Its slogan was "The evangelization of the world in this generation"; for three decades it attracted the very ablest men and women. When the United States entered the First World War, there were scores of its recruits on Brethren campuses pledged to a missionary career. The impact of SVM on the nation's rising generation has no parallel in history, expect perhaps the Peace Corps in the 1960s and early 1970s.

The enthusiasm for missions upon the part of students at Juniata

---

*The name of the Brotherhood's chief mission committee has undergone numerous changes. Today the World Ministries Commission supervises overseas mission programs.

College in that age, therefore, was not untypical. By 1919 twenty-six Juniatians had dedicated themselves to the foreign field. The College administration solidly put its stamp of approval on SVM's goal of all-out world salvation, a goal that Juniata, it was strongly felt, had a duty to further. The moral and educational call of the times, the stockholders heard President Martin G. Brumbaugh say in 1900, was to "meet the mission need." Echoed teacher-trustee William J. Swigart on the same occasion: "The mission work is a product of the schools. We need the men and women properly educated."

DISTRICT SUPPORT

One of the students most responsible for organizing Juniata's first Volunteer Mission Band was Jesse B. Emmert, in 1898. Waynesboro born and reared, he graduated two years later, at age twenty-nine. But in 1901, while still a student, he held the position of District Sunday School Secretary. At District Conference that year he recommended that the forty-two Sunday Schools of Middle District support a missionary in India. Wilbur B. Stover, who pioneered the work in India, was present and heartily endorsed the suggestion. The minutes of the meeting report that it was then decided to poll the Sunday Schools of the District. Within a week thirty had responded favorably; twenty-five of them, unsolicited, plumped for sending their secretary himself.

The matter came up for a final decision at New Enterprise the next District Conference and carried unanimously. What happened after the vote was taken is described by an eyewitness in the following way:

> Now that the decision to appoint and support a missionary on the foreign field had been made, the question, "Whom shall we appoint?" at once faced the Conference and called for a decision. A hush of deeply solemn silence fell upon all present. The question which came along centuries ago to Isaiah now took this form to each one there assembled. "*Whom* shall *we* send and *who* will go for *us*?" No one spoke. The stillness was so impressive as to be eloquent. From each silent throat this question of solemn import seemed to well forth again and again. Instinctively all faces and minds turned to Jesse, for thus was he addressed by all. He was glad and ready to say, "Here am I; send me."[7]

The fall of 1902, then, Emmert set sail for India, there to marry Gertrude Rowland, a Juniata alumna and fellow-SVMer, and there, with his wife, to labor until 1919, all the while supported by the Sunday Schools of Middle Pennsylvania.

Meanwhile, the Huntingdon Brethren had assumed in addition

the sponsorship of Mary N. Quinter and Jacob M. Blough. The church there, because of its close association with the College, became the congregational home of many future missionaries during their student days. For that reason the person who wrote the Huntingdon sketch in the 1925 history took great pride in calling attention to the church's "blessed missionary record." Said the writer, "Missions, both home and foreign, have always been a large factor in the church life of the Huntingdon congregation."

Mary N. Quinter, like the Bloughs, was a 1903 appointee to India. She was the daughter of James Quinter and a charter member at Huntingdon, so that it was natural for the congregation to support her. "Sister Mamie," as she was affectionately known, died in 1914 on the field. Jacob M. Blough, who with Jesse Emmert and John M. Pittenger* started Juniata's Student Volunteer Band, spent forty-six years in India. All that time he was sponsored by the congregation and the College jointly.

Missionary zeal was evident in other congregations, too, in the early decades of this century. First Church, Altoona, became Herman B. Heisey's patron in 1912, when he and his wife left his Stonerstown charge for India. Failing health, however, compelled their return in 1914, and in subsequent years Heisey put in ministerial stints at Lewistown and his host church in Altoona.

First Church in 1914 next took on Ida Himmelsbaugh, born non-Brethren and reared near Mattawana, Mifflin County. While living in Altoona as a young woman, she was baptized in 1896 by Joseph W. Wilt. Later at Juniata she was an early recruit to the Volunteer Mission Band. Her missionary service as a nurse in India began in 1908 and lasted till 1923, when she resigned because of poor health.

About that time, and for similar reasons, the Jesse Emmerts terminated their work in India. For a few years—until 1928—the District's Sunday Schools, while searching for another candidate, did not collectively subsidize any one missionary, though funds continued to be earmarked for "Worldwide Missions." Four hundred and seventy-five dollars went toward that cause in 1927 from Middle Pennsylvania.

But the Sunday Schools' most ambitious mission project of the 1920s was a home for missionaries on furlough. This was the pet dream of Ardie E. Wilt, son of Joseph, who, though a layman, shared his father's zeal for the spread of Christianity. An Altoona

---

*Pittenger was in India from 1904 to 1919. After returning to America, he took over, at the request of the District Mission Board, the pastorate of the Beech Run Church (1928–1940).

businessman and Juniata College trustee (1914–1959), he would give all his adult life to local and State Sunday School activities. His plea for a furlough-retreat, says the 1925 history, could be capsulized in these words: "Our missionaries come home for a year or two to rest; but they have no home. Let us build one at Huntingdon and give these worthy ones a home free of rent—a good home."

The decision to go ahead on his idea came at the Spring Run convention in August of 1924. The building committee for the Mission Home, as it came to be called, was Ardie Wilt, Benjamin F. Waltz, and Galen B. Royer. Costing twenty thousand dollars, the structure, completed in 1925, was built on a corner lot, donated by the College, at Washington and Eighteenth streets. The two-story residence was divided into four-room apartments, two on each floor. Then the Depression hit, and the District asked the College to assume half the indebtedness. This it did, getting in return permission to use the apartments, when not occupied by returnee-missionaries, for married students and faculty. Today the Mission Home belongs to the College, which recently converted it into a dormitory.

The 1920s not only saw a Mission Home erected, but were a time when several congregations began to emulate Huntingdon and Altoona in backing individual missionaries on their own. New Enterprise started it off in 1919, when the people there chose Sara Replogle, born and raised in that vicinity. Then followed Woodbury (1922), Albright (1924), Everett (1924), and Carson Valley (1926), each backing a different person. All the support, however, went to missionaries on the Indian field.

This policy changed in 1928, when the Sunday Schools resumed combined support and decided upon Mrs. Bertha Robertson, stationed at Garkida, Nigeria. The African field had opened up in 1922, under H. Stover Kulp, who had been New Enterprise's first salaried pastor (1918–19), and Albert D. Helser. Then in 1933 Mrs. Martha Neiderhiser Parker, serving in China, became the District's missionary. The Brethren had established their first station in China in 1908. In 1933 six hundred dollars was raised for Nurse Parker.

The young people of Middle Pennsylvania were no less mission-minded in those days of the BYPD (Brethren Young People's Department). They began contributing toward the partial support of Annetta Mow in 1928. But when she could not return to India in 1934, the District BYPD opted for Nigerian missionary William M. Beahm. In 1939, after the Beahms did not go back to Africa, the youth selected Mrs. Pauline Garst Kinzie on the Indian field.

Middle Pennsylvania, then, from local congregation to District program, proved itself deeply mission-conscious once the Brethren as a denomination began to emerge from their sectarian shell in the mid-nineteenth century and to respond more positively to the Great Commission.

Oddly, though, only a handful of individuals with roots deep in Middle District have been recruited for the mission field. As we have seen, early in this century there was Mary Quinter, Sara Replogle, and Ida Himmelsbaugh—all women. Joseph W. Swigart of Maitland was commissioned to go to India in 1904 but died a few weeks before sailing.

Since then, there have been only V. Grace Clapper, Dr. Paul S. Hoover, Eleanor Snare Weaver, and Beverly Laird Minnich.* Grace Clapper grew up in the Snake Spring congregation, where her father was a bishop. She went to China in 1917, after attending Juniata and Bethany, and, but for a three-year interlude, continued to work there until interned by the Japanese in 1941 and later sent home in a prisoner-of-war exchange. Dr. Hoover was born in Tyrone, grew up in Johnstown, and then returned to Central Pennsylvania after graduating from Juniata College. While teaching high school, he was licensed to the ministry by New Enterprise in 1937. After medical school he and his wife served one term in India (1951–1956). From Stonerstown there was Eleanor Snare, who with her first husband, the late Clyde L. Carter, also put in one term on the Indian field right after World War II (1946–1951). Bellwood's Beverly Laird and her husband, Dale Minnich, spent four years (1966–1970) with their three children in Ecuador, where work in that nominally Roman Catholic country began in 1943 by a group of wartime Brethren Service men.

Since World War II, however, the picture of foreign missions has changed drastically. The communist takeover in China in 1949–50 put an end to all missionary activity in that Oriental country. At the same time, the postwar rise of nationalism among so-called Third World peoples in opposition to Western colonial politics forced the churches of Europe and America to rethink their missionary attitude.

For the Brethren, as with other denominations, this has led to a strategy called "partnership missions," whereby evangelistic Christendom works within the programs and structures of existing national churches. Annual Conference defined this new approach in 1955, indicating that the prevailing pattern for Brethren missions in

---

*Not included are those who within the last decade have gone abroad as quasi-missionaries, under the employ of foreign governments, or those who in the past were commissioned by other denominations, of which there have been several.

the years ahead would be one of building indigenous churches, not only "self-supporting, self-propagating, and self-governing," but also, insofar as Christian principles permit, identified with the culture of the countries where they are located.[8]

The 1955 action also called for encouraging the native churches to "affiliate with the over-all Protestant church in their respective areas. . . ." Thus in 1970 Nigerian Brethren united with the Church of Christ in the Sudan and the Indian Brethren the same year joined the Church of North India; in Ecuador the Brethren congregations since 1965 have belonged to the United Evangelical Church of Ecuador, while in Indonesia, Guatemala, Puerto Rico, Haiti, and the République du Niger there are other forms of ecumenical coopera- tion.

Since 1970 it is no longer the practice for congregations to designate individual missionaries in supporting overseas evangelism. The Brotherhood's World Ministries Commission now continues its mission commitment largely through financial aid to national churches, to special programs (like Lafiya, in Nigeria), and by recruiting professional or skilled personnel employed by foreign governments. Nevertheless, as late as the mid-1960s Curryville, Carson Valley, Albright, Martinsburg, Pine Glen, and First Church, Altoona, were still budgeting funds for some special missionary in a foreign country.

14

Middle District
and the Call to Servanthood

The Brethren Become Politically Aware

Until well into the present century, the Brethren posture on society in general and the state in particular was dictated by the church's Anabaptist heritage. Chapter 1, in part, deals with this heritage and shows how it induced the Brethren to withdraw and become an in-group. This was in sharp contrast to the Quakers, it is there pointed out, who, though sharing many Anabaptist ideals, like pacifism, have historically rejected separatism. With time, however, the Brethren shifted ideological grounds, almost unwittingly, to take a more Quaker-like position on the redeemability of society.

In the denomination's formative period, nevertheless, a separatist mentality prevailed, reinforced by the persecution of its members during the American War of Independence. It is true that the Brethren accepted and supported the laws of the state, since, according to the New Testament, rulers and governments are ordained of God. Thus when laws, such as military conscription, violated their conscientious beliefs, they did not try to avoid the penalties attached to violations. They did, however, petition for exemptions to be written into the law. But, with few exceptions, the Brethren preferred to be left alone, to remain a separate community, to look after their own affairs. They put a literal interpretation on the Scripture when it says to be "*in* the world but not *of* the world." Accordingly, they were forbidden to go to court, to participate in elections, or to hold political office.

It was the temperance movement in the late nineteenth century that caused the Brethren to rethink their policy of separation from society. The church took no part in the prohibition movement that swept over most states in the decades prior to the Civil War. In fact, Annual Conference, arguing that the Brethren have always disapproved of intemperance, saw no point in 1842 to signing pledges and therefore advised members not "to meddle with the proceeding and excitement of the world on this subject." After the war the prohibition cause quickly revived in the United States, but Annual Conference in 1867 thought it unnecessary to belong to temperance societies. However, a reformer's outlook was taking hold in many parts of the Brotherhood.

In Middle Pennsylvania, for example, Henry Holsinger's *Christian Family Companion* in the late 1860s and early 1870s became a forum on the temperance question for District members. By the 1880s Brice Sell of Leamersville had emerged as one of the Brotherhood's best-known temperance lecturers. But while sympathizing with the foes of strong drink, he could not endorse their political action. A favorite weapon of drys, short of total statewide or nationwide prohibition, was local option. This was an election in which communities could vote to close up saloons within their area. Brice Sell and his brother James, another temperance spokesman, faced a dilemma, typifying the predicament of many contemporary Brethren. Wrote James Sell in the *Christian Family Companion* in 1873, "no license" was an effective political tactic, but, lamented he, there was the danger inherent in the very act of voting.[1] That was the reason, he went on, he had never voted for a "political figure" up to that time.

In 1889 Annual Conference, for the last time, advised against "taking part in the public agitation" on prohibition. Nineteen years later, in 1908, the denomination reversed its position, and Annual Conference urged the Brethren at all levels—Brotherhood, district, local congregation—to "organize and maintain aggressive movements toward counteracting and stamping out the evil of intemperance." Middle Pennsylvania, at the instigation of First Church, Altoona, had already anticipated such a change in Brotherhood policy and appointed a temperance committee the previous year. In fact, it was an Altoona query that motivated Annual Conference to create a similar committee for the denomination in 1908, when it issued the call for "aggressive" action.

In 1913, for the first time, the Women's Christian Temperance Union and other "outside" antidrink groups officially gained admission to Brethren churches. That was the year the Anti-Saloon League, as a political machine of Protestant churches, adopted its policy of seeking national prohibition. It was a Leamersville query, in 1918, that prompted Annual Conference to take the ultimate political step: petitioning both the Congress and the President to stop the export of grains that might be used to manufacture alcohol in other countries. In another year, the Brethren rejoiced with other drys in the ratification of the Eighteenth Amendment, which for the next fourteen years constitutionally banned the sale and use of intoxicants in the United States.

By 1920 there were other signs that Brethren views of the state had changed. It was no longer taboo to vote or to run for political office. In the early days, at least in Middle Pennsylvania, church members were sometimes elected township road supervisors or to look after the poor; later a few were appointed to postmaster. But not all congregations were so open-minded about public service. Aughwick Brethren twice in the 1860s forbade members to attend political meetings. And in 1877 a council ruling prohibited anyone to "electioneer" for a township office. And sometimes, as in the case of Elder George Brumbaugh, the first resident minister in Woodcock Valley, who in 1822 was named tax collector, the Brethren chose to pay a fine rather than accept their turn in filling a local political position, even if it was one for which they did not electioneer. At any rate, no one in the Brotherhood had ever held a high public post until the early 1900s. That distinction first went to Middle District's Martin G. Brumbaugh, who courageously committed his life to public service when many Brethren felt it was wrong to do so.

His political career began while he was president of Juniata College. A political appointee, he served as the first Commissioner of Education in Puerto Rico (1900–1902). Then, still an absentee college head until 1911, he spent nine years (1906–1915) as Superintendent of the Philadelphia Public Schools. His reputation attracted the notice of certain state Republicans, who saw in him the makings of a governor. And so they tapped him to be the party's candidate for the gubernatorial race in 1914.

This was something of a daring decision for the Brethren educator, then in his early fifties. Only two years before, Annual Conference had reaffirmed the idea that a Christian's citizenship was in heaven and that "the church of Jesus Christ is no part of this world system." On this basis, the Brethren were advised: (1) "not to allow themselves to become entangled in politics"; (2) neither to vote nor accept an office of any kind unless they are convinced that by so doing they can "more completely fill their mission in the world"; (3) to accept no office, the duties of which might "require the use of physical force or might compromise, in any way, the nonresistant principles of the Gospel of Christ."

Almost everyone at Juniata College, however, hailed with pleasure his entrance into politics. Some saw the White House at the end of the road for him. To them it was certain that he would be the

Republican answer to the Democrat's Woodrow Wilson, then the president and also an educator and a deeply religious man.

But others had misgivings, among them Charles C. Ellis, who tried to talk Brumbaugh out of his candidacy. He feared that his friend would get "mixed up" in "gang" politics. Brumbaugh insisted, however, that he would not be controlled by party bosses, that he was an "Independent Republican." He saw himself as a Progressive, of the Theodore Roosevelt ilk, out to reform politics.

But there was another reason M. G. Brumbaugh wanted to be governor, according to Tobias F. Henry, long a District educator and pastor, who heard it from C. C. Ellis. And that was, by the candidate's own confession, to bring the Brethren into public notice. He felt that he had been dealt a golden opportunity to put the principles of his church to work in the political arena. He believed that he was fulfilling the second proviso in the 1912 Annual Conference proclamation.

On the campaign trail Brumbaugh pledged himself to a thoroughly progressive platform, which included the ballot for women. He lashed out at "bossism" in tough language. No less a political hot potato for him was the prohibition issue. The ties between the Republican Party and the liquor traffic had long been close, and so the Anti-Saloon League, skeptical that Brumbaugh was his own man, refused to support him. Undaunted, and defying party leaders, who counseled silence on the wet-dry debate, Brumbaugh came out for local option rather than "blanket prohibition" as the practical solution to the problem.

The election in November 1914 gave him a majority of nearly a half-million votes. This was one of the largest margins for a gubernatorial candidate before woman's suffrage. On inauguration day in January 1915, in keeping with Brethren teaching, he "affirmed" instead of taking the "oath."

While historians today do not assess his administration as outstanding, they do rate it as successful. And none fail to laud him for his character and high sense of public calling. There was significant social legislation during his four years (1915–1919) in the governor's chair, such as a Child Labor Law, a Workman's Compensation Law, and an act establishing the Direct Inheritance Tax. However, local option—his answer to the liquor problem—failed of acceptance in the Legislature.

Ironically, Governor Brumbaugh, a man of strong peace principles, was called upon to preside over the Commonwealth during World War I. Many Brethren criticized him when he mobilized the Pennsylvania National Guard, which went to France as the

Twenty-Eighth Division and took part in some of the chief campaigns in the last months of the war. They felt that he had breached the peace stand of the Brethren.

Though Annual Conference of 1915 commended him "for the high ground on all moral issues" he had taken in the early months of his governorship, not all the Brethren were so complimentary later on in his administration. Henry C. Early, a prominent church elder who would be elected moderator of Annual Conference six times (including the year 1915), wrote to a friend in 1916:

> The feeling of the general brotherhood as to Brother Brumbaugh serving his state as governor is much divided. There is dissatisfaction and there is pleasure among the members with his position. Some of the conservative members and congregations are displeased with his being governor of the state.[2]

Daniel L. Miller, the publisher, was unhappy when M. G. sent the militia to quell a Pittsburgh riot in 1916. In a letter to D. L. Lepley of Connellsville, Pennsylvania, he wrote, "This is a clear violation of the teaching of the Gospel." He further observed, "The clipping you sent me shows that the Governor is busy even on the Lord's day. If he uses that holy day for political work he is certainly in the wrong. . . ."[3]

The year 1916, when Daniel Miller was voicing his displeasure about M.G., propelled the Governor into the presidential limelight briefly. He was one of eleven candidates nominated at the Republican Convention in Chicago that June. He received twenty-nine votes on the first ballot as a favorite son, although in the meantime he had pledged his support to Theodore Roosevelt. Charles Evans Hughes became the party's banner-bearer, but he lost the election to Woodrow Wilson, the incumbent.

Martin G. Brumbaugh, the last minister to be chief executive of Pennsylvania, did much to help the Brethren appreciate the political process, especially as a means of effecting social reform by legislative action. Within a few years of his death, in 1930, Annual Conference was urging church leaders and pastors to speak out on the social problems of the day. The denomination was told that Brethren ideals—peace, temperance, the spiritual life, brotherhood—must be applied to domestic and world crises. In 1965 Ralph Smeltzer, then Director of Peace and Social Action for the Church of the Brethren, wrote, "Our Christian faith teaches that God is concerned about all aspects of life. Some political decisions affect life so extensively and deeply, we believe that God is concerned about an action in the political realm."[4]

Since World War II the Brethren have made their presence strongly felt in the halls of government. Men like Ernest Lefever and Luke E. Ebersole have given the church a new understanding of how religion can impact the political scene. They paved the way for a Brethren lobby in the nation's capital that works in cooperation with other denominations. The first Brethren representative in Washington was Miss Ruth Early, who began her work in January 1962. Thousands of Brethren youth and adults have attended the popular church-sponsored Washington seminars, instituted in 1955, on behalf of Christian citizenship and government. Closer home, since 1970 Middle Pennsylvania has had a Legislative Representative, appointed by the Witness Commission, whose responsibility it is to alert the churches of relevant legislation before lawmakers in Harrisburg and Washington.

But Kermit Eby, ex–labor leader and for many years a professor at the University of Chicago, always argued against church lobbies and for the involvement of Christian men and women at primary decision-making levels. He said in 1950, ". . . more Brethren . . . should be in Congress making the decisions and fewer Brethren . . . should be operating through churches as pressure groups."[5] However, few have heeded his advice. There have been no governors since Martin G. Brumbaugh, no congressmen, no federal or state judges. A few Brethren have held state cabinet posts or been elected to a state legislature, and some, as Altoonans know, have become mayors or police chiefs. The highest-ranking Brethren politically was Dr. Andrew W. Cordier, who was the executive assistant to the first two secretaries-general of the United Nations and undersecretary for General Assembly affairs.

Witnessing for Peace

Though the Brethren had been a peace society from the time of their origins, it was not until World War I that they formulated a reasoned statement of their historic pacifist position. The church had been severely tested during the Civil War, but its pronouncements at that time (1864 and 1865) were typically concise and firm, set forth in a sentence or two and providing no rationale. At the time of the Spanish American War (1898), all the church had to say was, "Since we are inclined to peace and a defenseless state, it would in no wise be proper nor allowable for Brethren to learn war." So in the fifty years after 1865 there was no emphasis on pacifism as a denominational principle.

That half century was devoted primarily to evangelism and expansion. As a result, thousands of new converts, many with no German background or understanding of the Pietist-Anabaptist heritage, presented something of a problem. This was one reason for the change of name in 1908 from German Baptist Brethren to Church of the Brethren. Denominational leaders failed to understand the significance of this infusion of new blood and neglected to stress the traditional tenets of the church. Appreciation of its stand on war and peace suffered accordingly.

The outbreak of World War I aroused a greater concern about peace education and resulted in the appointment of a Peace Committee. Still, the church was unprepared when the United States entered the war in 1917. It had no peace program beyond its general statement of opposition to war on the basis of the teachings of Jesus. The immediate problem now was what to do about the draft law of May 18, 1917, which exempted Brethren from combatant service only, not conscription.

In the Civil War the draft laws, both North and South, provided exemption from military duty for conscientious objectors. Southerners could pay a fine of five hundred dollars, while Northerners had three options: be fined, hire a substitute, or do alternative service (usually as a hospital aide). How widely exemptions were used is not known. But hundreds of Brethren no doubt followed the example of Henry B. Brumbaugh, the District's pioneer publisher and educator, who, in mid-September 1862, traveled from his Raystown Branch farm to Huntingdon to pay his exemption fine.

The draft law of 1917, however, allowing no exemptions, found the leadership of the church confused about a proper policy for the denomination to follow. Some, pleased at the active interest in politics shown recently by the Brethren, argued for noncombatant service. Others urged those of draft age to refuse induction altogether. Meanwhile, some Brethren men went straight into the armed forces. Local churches were generally tolerant toward them; very few were disciplined. Most male members went into noncombatant service, but several hundred, however, once inducted, refused to bear arms, drill, or submit to any kind of camp control. They were placed in detention camps and later either furloughed to farms or sent to prison.

No man in the Brotherhood was more involved in working out a compromise with the government, or more influential in articulating the peace position of the church, than William J. Swigart of Juniata College. He had been a member of the Peace Committee since 1916 and during the war became chairman of the Central Service Committee, which represented the Brethren on all matters of the draft.

As chairman of the CSC, he had charge of all camp visitation and interviews with the War Department. The *Gospel Messenger* carried numerous articles written by him on the draft and the treatment of CO's in detention camps.

Despite anti–M. G. Brumbaugh sentiment upon the part of conservative Brethren, the Governor was another son of Middle Pennsylvania whose peace witness was well-known within the Brotherhood. In the early years of the century, he had been a frequent lecturer at the Quaker-sponsored Annual Lake Mohonk Conferences on International Arbitration in New York. And in 1904 the *Echo,* then the campus paper for Juniata College, envisioned him one day on the Hague Tribunal, where he could work "to make the principles of our Brotherhood a powerful factor in world peace." Though he did mobilize the Pennsylvania National Guard, his critics ignored the fact that he had sent a telegram to one of the state's senators protesting Congress's declaration of war in April 1917.

Juniata College, the next year, refused to participate in a War Department program that made cooperating institutions a place for combined military and collegiate training. The involvement of military personnel as instructors and the presence of uniformed men—the symbol of war—were unthinkable to the trustees. They knew full well that their decision would be costly in terms of male students.

Eventually, the draft law was modified to permit conscientious objectors, already inducted, to be furloughed to farms, but no solution was reached for those who refused all army service. Most important, the war produced the Goshen Memorial of January 1918, which one historian calls the "most magnificent" statement of the Brethren peace position ever formulated.[6] The memorial, however, which urged Brethren not to drill or wear a uniform, produced a panic among church leaders when the government threatened to prosecute them for treason under the provisions of the Espionage Act of 1917. When the Brethren agreed to withdraw it from circulation, the case was dropped.

World War I, then, prompted the Brethren to reappraise their peace position. As one church scholar has written:

> Many Brethren leaders were disillusioned regarding noncombatant service. There was a general feeling of dissatisfaction regarding the church's war record. The church saw that its teaching program on peace had been a failure. Some of the strongest peace leaders of the church came out of disillusioning war experiences. The denomination was committed toward more co-operation with other churches in peace work.[7]

In the postwar years there was a marked increase in peace education and in the exercise of pressure politics. M. G. Brumbaugh spent much of the period after leaving Harrisburg, and before returning to Juniata College in 1924 for a second round as president, in traveling the lecture circuit championing a Congressional bill to introduce physical education into the nation's public schools. He saw this measure as a proper substitute for making universal military training a part of high school curriculums. He and William Swigart kept *Gospel Messenger* readers informed about the Congressional mood on a selective service act through repeated articles during the early 1920s.

The half dozen years after 1928 were a time when many nations of the world called for disarmament and the renunciation of the war. The Church of the Brethren applauded the general peace movement of that era through frequent Conference resolutions. And so did Middle Pennsylvania. Leonard R. Holsinger, head of the District Peace Division, urged members to write Washington in 1928 in support of those churchmen, feminists, and liberal pacifists calling for naval reduction. District leaders sent a telegram to Senator David A. Reed appealing that he would use his influence toward this end. In 1930 the District memorialized President Hoover on the Naval Disarmament Conference, then in progress. The years 1931 and 1932 saw continued petitioning in behalf of international efforts at outlawing war.

By the 1930s it was evident that the Church of the Brethren had moved dramatically away from the separatism of its Anabaptist heritage. In chapter 1 the pacifism of the Brethren was identified as *vocational,* a personal, perfectionistic love ethic that is indifferent to the needs of the social order. The pacifism of the Quakers, on the other hand, was termed *activistic,* since it seeks to create, by political means and social action, a more peaceful society, even a world in which force is not used. The Anabaptists believed that the social order could not be Christianized, the Quakers that it could. Thus a decade before World War II, both the Brethren and the Mennonites had been virtually "Quakerized"—attitudinally, that is, toward society.

In terms of opposition to war, this meant philosophically that the basis of the church's position was now ethical as well as biblical, which a special resolution of Annual Conference in 1932 for the first time enunciated. Rufus D. Bowman, in his classic study *The Church of the Brethren and War,* observed in regard to that resolution:

> The peace teachings of Christ are applied to the state as much as to the church. *The whole war system is considered to be wrong.* The church's

opposition to war is both "religious and ethical." And the ethical note is significant. For more than two hundred years the Brethren opposed war because the Bible said it was wrong. "Thus saith the Lord" was enough for them. Now other reasons for wrongness are appearing. The "social gospel" emphasis with its optimism for the building of a better world is increasingly gripping the church.[8]

The church—and the government—had learned much from the experiences of World War I, and so when the government enacted a Selective Service law in 1940, after war erupted in Europe, the Brethren joined with the other historic peace groups—the Schwenkfelders, Mennonites, and Friends—in forming the National Service Board for Religious Objectors. With offices in Washington, D.C., this organization acted as a liaison with the government in matters relating to conscientious objectors and issued a monthly paper, *The Reporter.*

The historic peace churches lobbied, as soon as there was talk about a peacetime draft, against such a law; failing in that, they pressed for a provision that exempted CO's from any type of military service. Moreover, to demonstrate their patriotism, they argued for a program of alternative civilian service. As a result, through an Executive Order by President Franklin D. Roosevelt in February 1941, Civilian Public Service camps came into existence, to provide an honorable substitute for those opposed to entering the armed forces. These camps were devoted primarily to soil and forest conservation projects, although there were other opportunities to engage in civilian work of national importance.

Again, this compromise with the state illustrated that the Brethren had largely abandoned their separatist past. Rufus Bowman pointed out in this connection, "Although the Brethren oppose conscription, when it comes they prefer to render creative service to the state in harmony with conscience, rather than being obstructionists and doing nothing!"[9]

From 1941 to March 1947 some twelve thousand CO's, nearly seven thousand of whom belonged to the historic peace churches, worked in CPS camps and units. Of this number, the Church of the Brethren accounted for 1,368. How many of these were from Middle Pennsylvania cannot be determined, but there is no evidence to indicate that there were more than a few. However, the District youth in 1941 went on record exhorting "the young men of the draft to give their testimony by accepting assignment to our church camps."

There were eleven camps plus several smaller units supervised by the Church of the Brethren, which, in all, spent $1,250,000 to maintain its part of Civilian Public Service operations between 1941 and 1946. Hundreds of essential items were contributed by local congregations through district organizations. In 1942 Middle District adopted a CPS camp near Kane, Pennsylvania, in McKean County, to help regularly with certain basic supplies. The previous year, Wilfred N. Stauffer had been elected to a three-year term as District Director of Civilian Service. Under his leadership the churches, especially Women's Work, donated bed clothing, knitted articles, towels, canned fruits and vegetables, among many other necessities, and transported them to Camp Kane each year.

Meanwhile, as in World War I, there was no military unit at Juniata College, an expedient many small liberal arts schools felt necessary for survival. The War Department had approached the administration as early as 1939 for permission to set up a flight school on College Hill. But the authorities still felt bound by the Brethren peace position and said no to that tender and to later ones. It cost the College dearly, of course, in terms of enrolment and finances. Of the two hundred and forty-nine students who enrolled the fall of 1943, only sixty-five were men—the lowest male population among colleges of similar size in the state. When the war ended, President Calvert Ellis immediately announced a scholarship of one hundred and fifty dollars to each man from Civilian Public Service who wished to study at Juniata.

The years since 1945 have been a history of constant world tension: Arab-Jew flare-ups in the Middle East, Cold War shoot-outs in Korea and Vietnam, and now the Persian Gulf crisis. Over it all has loomed the specter of nuclear destruction. Then there has been the persistent problem of the draft, which for most of the past several decades, from 1948 to 1974, was a fact of life for the nation's youth. Twice, in 1947 and 1948, Middle District declared its opposition to universal conscription and the militarization of the United States. After a visit by Ora Huston, Brotherhood Peace Counselor, Ralph Ebersole was appointed draft counselor during 1963–64 to work with District young men. Someone filled this position until April 1974, when the draft ended. However, continued Brethren witness against war and all forms of militarism was promoted in the District by a Director of Peace Education. The revival of draft registration in the summer of 1980, many feel, once again makes the need for individual counseling a work of first order.

Earlier, under pre-1980 draft provisions, conscientious objectors were given special consideration. The 1948 law exempted them altogether; later, the Korean War brought changes in the law, one of them making CO's draftable but eligible for alternative service. By then, for draftees who belonged to the church, Brethren Volunteer Service was available. BVS was a product of the 1948 Annual Conference, when youth leaders like Don Snider called for some trailblazing kind of peace witness for those confronted by a peace-time draft, especially those who did not wish to be exempted but wanted to show their love of country in another, nonmilitary way.

By the 1970s over three thousand persons, youth and adults, had served in some way in the program. (In 1951 it was expanded to include adults.) BVS has offered a broad range of ministries, both at home and overseas. Some of its features were copied when President John Kennedy established the Peace Corps in the early sixties. Nearly every congregation in Middle Pennsylvania can name individuals who have given a period of time to BVS, either as an alternative to the draft or as a witness to their faith. BVS in 1980 is still going strong, with nearly two hundred volunteers serving in the USA and overseas.

Despite the church's historic peace stand, it should be noted in conclusion, the dogma is less evident among the rank and file. Writes Roger E. Sappington, a history professor at Bridgewater College, ". . . for every Brethren young man who has served as a conscientious objector since 1940, at least three others have become a part of the military service."[10] At the grassroots, then, the Brethren are no longer disposed to a protesting witness against war as they were before World War II. Instead, they are more ready to favor service, relief, and rehabilitation. Observed Donald Royer, a sociologist who studied Brethren beliefs about war and peace in the 1950s, that as a result of this attitudinal shift "there has come something we may not have anticipated. . . . An increasing number of Brethren are saying that in the case of war they would increase their giving to Brethren Service, but they would also buy war bonds and work in defense factories if needed."[11]

Later, during the Vietnam War, when Annual Conference (1970) passed a paper commending the position of nonviolent noncooperation with the draft system, there was much unhappiness in the local church. In 1973–74 Donald Hoover, entrusted with draft counseling, reported to the District Board, ". . . a few opportunities have presented themselves to encourage young men to register as Conscientious Objectors. Yet the truth of the matter is many of our youth are not choosing this view. . . ." Nor has the church's official position against taxes for military expenditures and recruitment by the armed forces on Brethren college campuses been greeted with any more enthusiasm. Likewise, Conference's adoption of a paper in 1973 favoring "unconditional amnesty" for draft dodgers who fled the country and for army deserters was just as unpopular.

Service, Relief, and Rehabilitation

World War II and its aftermath further intensified the "Quakerizing" of Brethren social outlook, especially with respect to relief and reconstruction in war-wasted countries. Before 1940 the Brethren had shown some interest in alleviating world suffering, but nothing was done on a large scale. Between 1918 and 1921 a Relief and Reconstruction Committee raised a substantial amount of money to help the Armenians and Syrians. Brethren aid was also forthcoming during the civil war in Spain and after the Japanese invasion of China, both late-thirties events. In each instance there was close cooperation with the American Friends Service Committee and the Mennonites.

Meanwhile, in 1939 Brethren Service as we know it today had its inception.* It found its charter in Matthew 25: 35–40: feeding the hungry; sheltering the stranger; clothing the naked; visiting prisoners and the sick. In 1941 the Brethren Service Committee became the agency responsible for administering the denomination's Civilian Public Service program. Renamed Brethren Service Commission in 1947, it gave the church's peace witness, through postwar relief and rehabilitation, a global outreach. During the late forties and early fifties, writes Donald Durnbaugh, "It is fair to say that the Brethren Service interest displaced missions as the chief focus of the denomination although support still ran high for the latter."[12] During those years, the homes of most members prominently displayed the familiar wooden Brethren Service cup, the receptacle for daily offerings.

Brethren Service embraced a variety of programs in Asia, Africa, Europe, South America, and the United States. Some of its projects won interdenominational cooperation and even that of the United Nations Relief and Rehabilitation Administration. Eventually, New Windsor, Maryland, the site of a former Brethren college, became the center of a vast relief operation, which it still is today. Since the 1950s the humanitarian concern of the church has remained vital, though programs have been reduced and there is more collabora-

---

*This name, scholars are quick to notice, is obviously borrowed from the Quakers.

tion with ecumenical agencies. Today the World Ministries Commission, a creation of the seventies, is responsible for alerting the church to the needs of suffering people around the world, no matter what the cause of their suffering—war or natural disaster. This name change is suggestive of the recent deemphasis on a strictly denominational, self-interested approach to alleviating the misery of humanity.

Middle Pennsylvanians built a solid record of support for Brethren Service over the years. Clarence Rosenberger was one of the original "seagoing cowboys," having helped to organize, in 1945, the first "Heifers for Relief" shipment to Europe as the *Zona Gale*'s

Koontz-Waterside members round up heifers for shipment abroad.

crew chief. The Heifer Project was still alive in the District in the mid-1960s, by which time the Brotherhood had sent over one thousand shiploads of livestock and poultry to seventy-four countries. Over Christmas holidays in 1970, Elwood Hunter, then a James Creek member, sailed as a latter-day cowboy on a heifer shipment to Liberia. More recently—in 1974 and 1975—the Koontz-Waterside congregation, with a helping hand from members at Snake Spring and New Enterprise, shipped off twenty-three heifers, seventeen to Tanzania and the rest to an Indian reservation out West.

Other examples of humanitarian concern abound: the backing of the men's, women's, and youth groups for specific projects; Juniata College's giving a job to George Dolnikowski, now a professor there, in 1950 under the Displaced Persons Act; the Roaring Spring church hosting Egon Borgmann from Germany for a year (1953–54) through the Student Exchange Program, begun in 1949; the congregations sponsoring European families in the District under the Refugee Resettlement Act of 1954, and now families from Southeast Asia; the District giving special recognition to those in Brethren Volunteer Service, whose ages range from high school or college graduates like Cathy and Yvonne Hoover, young women from Carson Valley, to the Edgar Kiracofes of Juniata College, who spent a couple of their retirement years in the mid-1960s at Castener, Puerto Rico; taking ghetto black children into District homes through the summer "fresh air" program (e.g., forty-four in 1964) sponsored by Baltimore's Pilot House.

In Search of Domestic Social Justice

The seventies brought a different social-action emphasis on the part of the Church of the Brethren. This came about once the denomination saw that the "genius of the Brethren," in the words of the late relief worker Dan West, for coming up with imaginative ways of ministering to the needs of the world had found expression in ecumenical and secular organizations, like Church World Service and the International Voluntary Services Agency. The emphasis now is less international in aspect, though, to be sure, there is still a sensitivity to world problems—hunger, for example, or refugees. But the Brotherhood is now more inclined to concentrate on domestic crises: the rights of minority groups, criminal justice reform, ecology, alcoholism and drug addiction, the shortage of low-cost housing, disaster relief.

The minority question, of course, is a carry-over from the sixties, which were a decade of widespread racial tension and violence. An estimated 350 people died and more than 12,000 were reported injured in that turbulent period. Major riots erupted in some of the largest cities in mid-decade, amid cries of "Burn, baby, burn!" by rampaging blacks. Forty-one riots rumbled through the country from coast to coast in 1967, the most serious occurring in Detroit, where sixty-three people died.

The nation's intensifying problem of racism was early reflected in Annual Conference business. In 1963 Conference passed a paper entitled "The Time Is Now," calling for action to "heal our racial brokenness." Each congregation was urged to "affirm by specific council action" the Brotherhood policy of extending membership to anyone, regardless of racial or ethnic background. In fact, the theme of Annual Conference between 1962–1965 was: "To Heal the Broken."

Curiously, however, though the Brethren have had a long-standing interest in the welfare of American blacks—the church adamantly opposed slavery—their ministry to that race has been largely ineffectual. Bridgewater College's Roger Sappington writes: ". . . it proved to be very difficult for the Negroes to fit into the Brethren cultural pattern of separatism, and very few Negroes have become members of the church."[13] The church, on the other hand, has had more success in working with Mexican-Americans and other migrant folk.

In 1969 Annual Conference set up a program called "The Fund for the Americas," the Brotherhood's response to the Kerner Commission report (1968), which was a much-heralded study, authorized by President Lyndon Johnson, of the causes and cures of rioting. The report attributed much of the trouble to white racism and stressed that "police brutality" and the "double standard of justice" were perennial complaints in the riot-torn cities.

There was opposition to the fund throughout the denomination, although a few churches in Middle Pennsylvania did contribute to it. The purpose of the Fund for the Americas was to assist blacks and other minority groups in economic development and community organization. But the program came under fire because many Brethren believed, with some justification, that part of the money ended up in the coffers of black militants. And so, generally speaking, local congregational giving to the Fund was disappointing to church leaders.

The Brethren witness on civil rights and racial harmony prompted a number of ministers and lay persons to participate in public demonstrations throughout the United States during the sixties. There was some sympathy for this kind of testimony in Middle Pennsylvania, although, because the District is predominantly rural, its population of blacks and other minorities is minuscule. Juniata College was a source of occasional civil rights agitation, and in March 1965 a few students and professors drove to Alabama to take part in the Selma-to-Montgomery march, while a larger contingent, sixty-four in all, joined a demonstration in Washington, D.C., a few days before.

District pastors were not identified with these rallies, but Jay E. Gibble of the Twenty-Eighth Street church participated in the Altoona Sympathy March for the Alabama demonstrators. In the *Tower Times*, the parish paper, he gave his reasons for doing so:

1. The local "march" was approved and endorsed by the Blair County Ministerial Association.
2. Clergymen from the three major faiths—Catholic, Jewish, and Protestant—participated.
3. The pastor has a deep conviction that equal justice, now being denied to some, must be awarded to all.
4. The church can no longer remain silent; to do so is to endure sudden death for the church. As a leading clergyman said, "The Civil Rights cause has now become a matter of survival for the church."

The very fact that the young Altoona pastor felt compelled to give a public explanation of his behavior indicated that there was much resistance among Middle Pennsylvania Brethren to civil rights agitation of this kind.

As for other social issues of more recent concern, the District has been far from indifferent. Since 1969, when Richard Grumbling was elected a trustee of the Pennsylvania Council on Alcohol problems, there is an annual report to District Conference each year on that agency's work. The Carson Valley church, under the leadership of its pastor, Eugene Miller, recently formed the Blair County Ministries, with official District backing, which has acquired property and intends to erect a drug and alcohol rehabilitation facility, primarily for paroled prisoners. District programs for alcoholics and addicts, through detoxification centers and halfway houses, became a Brotherhood challenge in 1975. Earlier, it was a query from the Everett church in 1971 that set Annual Conference to thinking about environmental conditions, in the United States and the world, and the need for strict, enforceable legislation against pollution, both industrial and private. A paper in 1974 exhorted Brethren to promote and take pride in conservation and clean environment.

Criminal injustice became an Annual Conference concern in 1974, and since then the District has been quite active in educating its membership on the dehumanizing effects of imprisonment and the need for more efforts toward prisoner reconciliation. Two churches, Carson Valley and State College, have been providing ministries at the Blair County Jail and the Rockview State Prison, respectively, for the last few years, and very recently similar programs have been introduced at two other county jails in Middle Pennsylvania (Mifflin and Centre).

In 1975 the District, through the efforts of Ralph Z. Ebersole, organized the District Disaster Response Network, a Brotherhood priority for 1974–75. Each congregation was asked to appoint a Disaster Response person or team. Since then the District has responded to a number of emergencies, locally and afar. Twenty-one workers, from twelve congregations, went to Canton, Mississippi, in 1976 to rebuild and repair tornado-damaged homes, and that December four men were sent to the Big Thompson Canyon flood area, north of Denver, Colorado, to put in a week's work. In the summer and fall of 1977 the disastrous Johnstown flood, caused by prolonged rains, brought a tremendous response from the District: large sums of money, many truckloads of emergency supplies, and several thousand hours of volunteer labor in search and rescue, cooking, mudding out, repairing and rebuilding damaged homes—all in collaboration, of course, with other relief agencies. Since then workers, financial help, and material supplies have gone to places in North Carolina, Massachusetts, and Mississippi. The network, still coordinated by the Ebersoles, has also become instrumental in helping to resettle the "Boat People"—those Vietnamese who, in 1975 after the fall of Saigon, took to the sea by the thousands to flee the communist takeover and to search for freedom.

Care for the Young and Old

CHILD RESCUE WORK

In 1812 Annual Conference first went on record stating that it was the duty of the church to care for orphans and for the children of widows in desperate straits. A statement in 1870 endorsed the idea of Brethren orphanages, but there was none in operation until the mid-1880s, when the Middle District of Indiana established two homes for children. Annual Conference recommended in 1910 that each state district organize a "Children's Aid Society," and two years later created an Orphanage Committee at the Brotherhood level. In 1917 the denomination adopted the term "Child Rescue Work" for its ministry to parentless children.

Walter S. Long, pastor at First Church, Altoona, sparked the movement for a Brethren orphanage in Middle Pennsylvania in 1915 by calling for an investigation into the matter. (An unacted-upon query on this subject had come before District Conference as early as 1873.) And so in 1917 District Conference authorized a "detention home" in Martinsburg, to be supervised by the trustees of the home for the aging already in existence there. Its purpose, said the 1925 history, was "to provide for orphans and other children of need of the Church of the Brethren, also for other children within, or apart from this District where there is room and means to make it possible and practical to care for them."

Not until 1923, however, was a building purchased; it cost, along with its twenty-seven acres of land, $7,800. In the meantime, children were placed with foster Brethren families. But the debt on the orphanage was too heavy for the District to bear, and so it was necessary to dispose of the property during 1928–29, at a deficit of two thousand dollars that was met by a bond issue for that amount. An assessment was placed upon the churches at the same time. Homeless or needy children were now referred to other orphanages or placed with foster families. Child Rescue Work ceased altogether in 1950, this kind of service by then having been covered by state and federal Public Assistance programs. By court decree, official dissolution came in October 1954.

MORRISONS COVE HOME

According to its Minute Book, the Duncansville congregation (now Carson Valley), in council session in May 3, 1879, raised the following question: "Are we justifiable in sending our poor to the county alms house, if we see that they are properly cared for?" This was probably in response to advice given by Annual Conference in 1862, 1870, and 1875 to the effect that local congregations should take care of their own poor, especially elderly widows, rather than letting them become public wards. The matter came before District Conference ten days later in the form of a query, the answer to which merely stated, not "if it can be possibly avoided." There was no mention of a home at this time, and the 1925 history is in error in attributing the idea to a Duncansville petition.

That honor goes to Huntingdon, whose query in 1880 read: "Resolved, that we . . . favor the establishing of a 'Home' somewhere in the East, for the benefit of the poor and infirm of our fraternity." This was still while Southern Pennsylvania was part of the District, but the proposal got no support. The Huntingdon Brethren would not let the subject die, especially Henry and John Brumbaugh, who had the pages of the *Gospel Messenger* at their command. By the mid-eighties interest was building, and soon the Brethren began vying for the home's location, especially those at Huntingdon and James Creek.

A petition from the Lewistown church in 1891 finally won District acceptance to move ahead on such a project. However, there was a temporary delay until the question of dividing the District was settled. That was taken care of the following year, and in 1894 the District purchased a property in Shirleysburg, which the Aughwick congregation had brought to the attention of the committee investigating possible sites. The price of the large brick house, which stood on slightly more than two acres of land, was two thousand dollars, a sum toward which the District oversubscribed by a substantial amount. It took the name Rockview Old Folks Home and reported six inmates in 1895.

By 1900 there were fourteen wards in the now outgrown facility. Plans to enlarge were scrapped in 1901, when it was decided to investigate the possibility of relocating the home. This was then found advisable, and so a new site was picked in Martinsburg, the Shirleysburg property sold (for a profit) in 1902, and construction on a new home begun that summer. Total costs connected with putting up the Martinsburg building amounted to $7,823.12, leaving an indebtedness of $2,923.76. The structure, equipped to handle seventeen "guests," was dedicated on August 12, 1903, as the Morrisons Cove Home for the Aged and Infirm. Brick-veneered, it was two stories high with dimensions of 32' × 64'. The Home was open to people of all faiths, though the Brethren were given preference, as had been true at Rockview. This nonsectariarian policy was not always a popular one, especially later during the Depression years.

From the early 1900s to the end of World War I, there was a series of remodeling and expansion projects. In 1912 a second building, identical in size and architecture, went up as an annex at a cost of something over four thousand dollars. A wing, costing $6,667.50, was added in 1936 on the north side, enabling the Home to accommodate forty-three residents. Four years later the double porches on the east side were enclosed. And in 1945 the Home purchased, for $4,800, an adjacent property on South Market Street, later converting the dwelling on it into the administrator's residence.

The 1950s brought further improvements. During 1955 twelve rooms in the women's section were remodeled and extensive renovations carried out in other parts of the Home. A seven-year Improvement Fund assessed upon District churches, plus a $15,000 bequest, allowed, in 1958, the erection of the Cherry-Forney Addition, which raised the guest population to fifty-three. The new one-story unit, costing approximately sixty thousand dollars, was named in honor of Charles J. Cherry, a prominent Lewistown layman, who was a staunch loyalist there during the postwar fundamentalist crisis, and chairman of the Trustee Board at the time of his fatal auto accident in 1955, and Emanuel Forney of Everett, from whose estate came the $15,000 legacy.

The decade of the fifties ushered in a Women's Auxiliary, organized by the District Women's Work in late 1956 and reporting a membership of over one thousand within a year's time. Over the next decade the Auxiliary contributed close to $25,000 to improvement and building programs at the Home.

The sixties, therefore, marked a time of continued construction. The most ambitious undertaking of that decade was the Brumbaugh-Detwiler wing. Because of stricter state and federal regulations, it became necessary to modernize the infirmary, a request for which the District gave its approval in 1964. This two-story north-side unit, completed in 1967, provided a twenty-three-bed infirmary with the latest equipment, plus two apartments and eight guest rooms in addition to other facilities. It cost $288,796.08, and honored Clarence D. Brumbaugh, a well-known Altoona layman, and Edgar M. Detwiler, the beloved pastor from New Enterprise. At that time the Home's population was eighty-six. During the year 1968–69 a dwelling across the street from the Home's front entrance was purchased for twenty thousand dollars and remodeled into the administrator's house, the property also providing additional parking space for Home visitors.

State and federal codes forced the Home into another major remodeling effort within the last decade, even though the Home, in 1973, had a No. 1 Class rating, the highest possible for institutions caring for the aging. The seventies began with the purchase of the adjoining Keagy property ($10,200) to the south, which provided a new access to the Home and permitted the trustees to look at future expansion in a different light. The expansion program, begun in 1973, was completed in 1975 in two phases, for a cost in excess of one million dollars, $855,000 of which was raised by five-year notes. The first phase involved the construction of a kitchen, a dining-

Aerial view of the Home in 1980.

Administrators and some Home trustees. *Seated:* N. French, M. Dean, M. L. Hall. *Standing:* R. M. Delk (Administrator), R. C. Over, C. R. Wareham, G. D. Crumrine (Assistant Administrator).

room, a lounge, and storage areas. Phase II entailed a forty-eight-bed nursing wing. This increased the total bed capacity to 141, to meet three levels of care: residential, intermediate, skilled.

In January 1974 the Board of Trustees voted to change the corporate name to Morrisons Cove Home and accordingly rewrote the bylaws, which the District ratified in 1976. There are plans someday to build independent living cottages on nearby property, recently purchased, but that will have to wait. Rampant inflation, minimum wage laws, and the problem of conformity to state and federal regulations keep the Home in financial straits and work against holding charges and fees to a minimum. During the fiscal year of 1978–79 it operated at a loss of $95,290. In 1977–78 the Home received its largest bequest ever—$78,000—from the will of Mrs. Mary E. Mountain, formerly of Loysburg.

Since its 1903 opening the Home had by 1977 served 809 individuals. That year seventy-seven percent of the residents/patients were Brethren, while forty-three percent of the population was on public assistance, unable to pay the full rate. In September 1978 there were 131 residents, forty-seven requiring skilled nursing care. The fall of 1979, the Home's balance sheet showed an appraised value, for property, plant, and equipment, of $2,205,054.18.

The Home, which for a long time has kept the District informed through the "Open Window," now a bimonthly sheet, is staffed by men and women of deep humanitarian sympathies. Said the trustees' report to the District in 1973: "We constantly hope the Home never becomes an institution, but always a 'HOME.' "

Fifteen men have been in charge of the Martinsburg institution since its beginning: Joseph Gates, Isaac Metzker, Elmer Snoberger, George Davis, Isaac Showalter, Jacob S. Showalter, William Royer, John Snoberger, George Batzel, H. Will Hanawalt, Paul A. Stayer, Levi K. Ziegler, Arthur R. Teeter, Charles H. Heltzel, and Ralph M. Delk.

An Enlarging Concept of Christian Education

THE SUNDAY SCHOOL MOVEMENT

At one time the District Sunday Schools, as a district organization, exercised great influence in Middle Pennsylvania. Their great promotion of missions, for example, was discussed in an earlier chapter. But the Sunday School, in its institutional form, came late to the Brethren.

Only in 1857, seventy-seven years after Englishman Robert Raikes began to tutor loafing children on Sundays in his hometown, did Annual Conference put its imprimatur on "Sabbath-schools." Clover Creek was not only the first congregation to start a Sunday School in Middle Pennsylvania (1865), but was one of the earliest in the whole Brotherhood. A few churches before that had participated in union Sunday Schools; still, to many Brethren, until after the Civil War, Sunday Schools were a form of worldliness. The Sunday School issue was part of the reason for the three-way denominational split in 1881–1883.

Gradually, the movement won general acceptance, and by 1876 the church began to publish its own educational material. Holsinger and the Brumbaughs, it was noted in another chapter, pioneered in the field of children's magazines and newspapers, portions of which were designed as study guides. During the early 1870s the *Christian Family Companion* and then later the *Primitive Christian,* both as weeklies, ran Sunday School lessons in each issue. Thus from the start Middle Pennsylvania stood at the forefront of agitation in support of the Sunday School idea. Indeed, the Districtwide Sunday School Convention held October 21, 1876, at James Creek might well have been the first of its kind in the Brotherhood. These conventions were held annually for the five decades thereafter, and in 1898 the position of Field Secretary was created to give Sunday School work systematic direction in those ante–District Board days.

Further centralization took place in 1923, when a constitutional change put supervision of the work in the hands of a five-member Sunday School Board, though the office of Field Secretary was retained on a part-time basis till 1928. That was the year the *District Echo,* a quarterly publication, made its appearance through the instigation of the Board.* By then training conferences for teachers were beginning to get District attention, especially through the promotion of Charles C. Ellis. Meanwhile, the mid-1920s introduced Middle Pennsylvania to a new facet of religious education: Vacation Bible School. In 1939 the Sunday School Board became the Board of Christian Education, whose functions were broadened to include "all the educational interests of the Church of the Brethren in the District." Then, in 1954, the Sunday School Convention passed into history, the same year the District commission system went into effect.

The 1920s were the heyday of the Sunday School, both for the Brethren and other Protestant bodies. That was the decade Brethren enrolment peaked—at 139,915.[14] Sunday Schools are still very much a part of the American religious scene, of course, and remain the normative Protestant pattern of religious education, especially for children. But for several decades now the institution has been in decline and attendance figures reflect a steady downward trend.

In Middle District, for example, thirty-eight churches in 1923 reported a membership of 6,816 and an average Sunday School attendance of 4,756. Statistics for 1976 show that fifty-four congregations, totaling 11,283 members, can count on only 5,393 to be present at church school each week (77,967 for the denomination at large). Proportionately, therefore, Sunday School rolls have failed to keep pace with the gains in membership over the last half century. Even as early as the thirties, the editor of the *District Echo* found himself wondering why the Sunday School had seemed to reach a plateau. The latest tally, when it comes out, will no doubt give an even gloomier picture of arrested growth.

Adult and Youth Fellowships

The women's aid movement in the Brotherhood got its start when Ella Snavely of Huntingdon suggested in 1884, through the *Gospel Messenger,* that the female members of the church hold a meeting of their own the next year at Annual Conference, scheduled for Mexico, Pennsylvania. They did get together, giving rise to several

---

*Prior to that, news items about Middle Pennsylvania appeared in the *District Herald,* which Walter J. Hamilton edited and published in Western District for eight years.

local groups. The earliest one on record was at First Church, Altoona, organized on July 21, 1885. Its prime mover was Eliza Freet, a maiden lady who rallied her sister-members to undertake money-raising projects to reduce the church's lingering debt. The Huntingdon women were next, in September, followed soon after by one at Mount Morris, Illinois. This idea spread, the women calling their organizations by a variety of names: Mission Band, Sisters' Benevolent Society, Dorcas Sisters, Willing Workers. Their immediate energies were given to raising funds for the Danish mission.

But the new movement received a setback at the Annual Conference of 1886. There had been sharp criticism of what the women were up to from the beginning. As Altoona's Ada C. Sell wrote in the *District Echo* (November 1935) about the role of women in the church then:

> [They] were weaker vessels and should remain silent partners. It was altogether unseemly for sisters to sit on the rostrum and publicly take part in a meeting. The Brethren were also opposed to a separate organization. Cooperation was the thing, and to achieve it the sisters and brothers should labor together for the cause of missions.

And so women's societies were denied Annual Conference's sanction, forcing them to continue their work in a quiet way.*

Not until 1895 did Conference repeal its decision and give the green light to local guilds. By 1910, fifteen years later, the women were ready for a national organization. Thus came into existence the Sisters' Aid Society. But its official recognition by Annual Conference as an independent body came later, in 1917. In another three years there were 441 societies with 8,563 members.

By that time the women of Middle Pennsylvania were occasionally getting together at District Conference for informal discussion. Their first public program at District Conference took place in 1924 when twenty-two Sisters' Aid Societies reported 419 members. In all, up to that time, they had contributed $3,881.76 to District activities, especially mission work. In keeping with Brotherhood action, the Sisters' Aid Society in Middle Pennsylvania became Women's Work after 1929, and since 1959, Women's Fellowship.

District women have engaged in a dynamic ministry, one that has historically centered on relief and missions. But they have also fostered a variety of other causes like camping, the Morrisons Cove

---

*Only in 1891 were women permitted to lead or speak in social meetings. In 1899 they gained the right to represent a congregation at district conference. But they could not be licensed to the ministry until 1922, or be ordained until 1958.

Home, peace, temperance, home and family life, and scholarships and loans for college-age youth, a topic treated in a later section. Over the years they have raised thousands of dollars for their ministries through various projects. One of these projects, since the 1940s, has been the annual banquet, a popular inspirational and rallylike fund-producing event.

The men of the Church of the Brethren were much later in organizing than the women. It was at the Hershey Annual Conference in 1927 that the Men's Work Organization was formed. Its purpose was to stimulate "the interest of laymen everywhere in the general program of the church . . . creating thereby in them a consciousness of their united possibilities for the Kingdom and training them for full and consecrated service."

For Middle Pennsylvania, the first recorded District "Men's Meeting" took place in 1932, on April 12 during District Conference, which the Minutes describe as "very enthusiastic" and "with a full attendance." The Minutes for 1933 speak of men's groups in Claysburg, Roaring Spring, and Bellwood, but there is no general information on what the situation was in other churches. Since 1933 there has regularly appeared a report on men's work in the District each year. D. M. Sell, R. B. Stambaugh, Paul B. Stayer, H. A. Brumbaugh, and E. O. Kinsel were among the layment most active in the early days of the movement.

In the early 1950s the men instituted an annual banquet for themselves, a practice discontinued in 1971. The Men's Retreat is the event that calls them together each winter today, for a weekend of Bible study at Camp Blue Diamond. In the last four and a half decades, District men have been closely allied with Brethren Service programs, projects at the Morrisons Cove Home, Camp Harmony, Camp Blue Diamond, and ministerial scholarships.

In the 1940s the men's and women's groups began to sponsor joint meetings. For several years after 1944 they convened at District Conference for a Laymen's Conference. Then in September 1956 they inaugurated the Annual Men's-Women's Fellowship Banquet, later called Adult Banquet, then Fall Festival, and still an ongoing tradition.

Curiously, the youth of the Brotherhood had organized nationally long before the men. A petition in 1904 passed Annual Conference granting young people of the various churches the right to hold meetings on Sunday evenings and through the week. This developed into the Christian Workers Society of the denomination, but it failed to meet the needs of the younger generation. However, right after World War I the youth movement took new hold, soon giving birth to the Brethren Young People's Department (BYPD). This title held until 1948, when it was voted to call the BYPD the Church of the Brethren Youth Fellowship (CBYF). Across the Brotherhood there sprang up in the 1920s district and local youth cabinets to direct Brethren young people in study, worship, service, and recreation.

In Middle District the formation of a BYPD resulted from the efforts of the Sunday School Board. At the Twenty-Sixth Sunday School Convention, August 23–25, 1921, Galen B. Royer spoke on the theme "Organizing the Young People." On that occasion Grace B. Stayer (later Mrs. Foster B. Statler) was named superintendent of a yet-to-be-organized BYPD. She and Galen Royer soon after called the youth of Morrisons Cove together at a Sunday afternoon meeting in the Williamsburg church to help them organize. The District was divided into six Circuits, each with its own officers. In 1923 an Inter-Circuit Council took shape to coordinate activities and provide Districtwide fellowship. From 1921 on there have been annual rallies, banquets, and other kinds of social gatherings.

One of the earliest interests of the BYPD was to establish a camping program for the youth of Middle Pennsylvania. Another primary concern was foreign missions, which led to the partial support of a missionary, discussed in another chapter, by 1928. The all-time high in missionary giving by District youngsters was in 1944 when $1,009.86 was sent to Elgin. Since then the youth have been engaged in activities just as worthwhile—promoting BVS, conducting recreational laboratories, and participating in Brethren Youth Seminars at Washington and the United Nations, work camps in America and abroad, interracial camps, peace caravans, and various relief and rehabilitation projects. For several years they have also sponsored a "Surprise Day" at the Morrisons Cove Home, a time of visitation and gift-giving.

Today the youth of Middle Pennsylvania have no newsletter. But when the *District Echo,* a paper they helped to finance, held forth (1928–1952), there were regular articles concerning their activities. In 1953 "Dunker Doings," published bimonthly, became the organ of the District youth, which it continued to be into the 1960s.

CAMPING

The camping movement in the Church of the Brethren dates from the mid-1920s. In order to provide permanent places for young people's conferences, three camp sites were established— Camp Harmony (Pennsylvania), Camp Bethel (Virginia), and Camp

Mack (Indiana). Soon camping became a popular summertime activity throughout the Brotherhood. By 1939 there were twenty-nine church-owned or church-operated camps in thirteen states and Canada.

Camp Harmony, in Somerset County, was chartered in March 1924 to be a training school for the eight state districts of Pennsylvania and Maryland. Middle Pennsylvania, which in 1923 turned down an invitation to become co-owner of Camp Harmony with Western Pennsylvania, was closely associated with its camping program from the beginning. In 1936, for example, there were 497 young campers, of whom 159 came from the District. By then the District was also providing leadership by individuals like Roscoe Wareham and Wilma Stern, both of Martinsburg. Then, in December 1944, Middle Pennsylvania entered into a joint relationship with Camp Harmony, but there were no legal transactions and no changes in charter. By 1958 Middle District was sending almost half of all the campers enrolled and providing over a third of the financial support.

Meanwhile, however, there had developed dissatisfaction with the jointure, primarily because of the camp's inconvenient location and limited space. And so at the District Board meeting on May 8, 1959, the Camp Committee recommended that Middle Pennsylvania look forward to the time when it could operate its own camping program. This recommendation came in response to a query from Upper Claar at District Conference the previous fall, requesting the appointment of a committee "to study the needs, the possibilities, and the location of a camp in Middle District."

The Camp Harmony Study led to a proposal, endorsed by District Conference in 1959, that, until a camp site could be acquired, Middle Pennsylvania look to renting the vacated Boy Scout Camp at Blue Knob State Park, near Pavia. This plan finally cleared District Conference in 1960, Ralph Ebersole was appointed camp manager, and the first camping season (seven weeks) for the Brethren on Central Pennsylvania soil took place in the summer of 1961. The site and facilities were leased on a yearly basis from the Pennsylvania Department of Forests and Waters for the next five summers. In the meantime, all ties with Camp Harmony were amicably severed.

A first-year attendance by over five hundred campers only reinforced the cries for a District-owned camp. The search committee, made up of the Christian Education Commission, Stewardship and Finance Commission, and the Camp Committee, considered six properties, four of them in Morrisons Cove. The clearest choice was the Blue Diamond Lake Property in West Township, Huntingdon

County. It was a 238-acre tract, surrounded by the Rothrock State Forest, and included three cottages and a lakelet formed by a dammed-up mountain stream. Nestled in the famous Diamond Valley, it was located seven miles northwest of Petersburg. A special District Conference on May 29, 1963, authorized its purchase for $25,000.

A Master Plan Study won District acceptance in another special Conference the next May, and on October 14, 1964, in regular annual session, the District gave its go-ahead to a first-phase development program costing $89,000. Over 100,000-board feet of

Dining hall–lodge complex.

lumber were harvested from the camp site by the men of the District in the following months. A sawmill, still in operation, was built to process the felled timber. The first use of the grounds came in August 1965, when a youth work camp was held. The summer of 1966 saw Blue Diamond ready for the first resident season, Nancy Faus serving as program director.

The next three years brought further developments as part of Phase I. Dedication day for the dining hall, shower house, thirteen tents and hogans was Sunday, October 30, 1966. In 1968 District Conference approved the building of a Resident Manager's house and the hiring of a full-time manager. Ralph Ebersole began his duties as the first camp manager in February 1969. That year the District certified Phase II of Camp development.

Over the past decade the status of Camp Blue Diamond has

changed and its physical resources and programming have been vastly expanded. In 1972 the camp was removed from the District budget and made responsible for raising all its own monies for program and development. A temporary tent-trailer family campground was set up that year—the summer of Hurricane Agnes, which did extensive damage to the Camp—and a permanent one constructed in 1974. Ralph Ebersole resigned in 1976 and was replaced by Nelson Wenner (1976–1980), a minister of the United Church of Christ. A new program, "pastor-in-residence," began in 1977, bringing Brethren clergy into a week of involvement at the camp as "friends" and resource leaders. Two buildings, the dining hall–kitchen complex and the Hemlock Cloister Retreat Center, are winterized and provide year-round accommodations for a variety of uses.

The churches of Middle Pennsylvania have contributed liberally in time, personnel, and finances to Camp Blue Diamond. A number of congregations have provided the funds for particular buildings, while others have chosen to make undesignated donations. For the fiscal year 1978, District churches raised from among their members $15,982.51, about one-fourth of the Camp's income. Individuals have also been generous in their financial support, through bequests, annuities, and other kinds of stewardship. But, like the Morrisons Cove Home, the Camp is hard hit by inflation; in 1978 it reported an operating loss in excess of ten thousand dollars. Its total assets, as of December 1978, amounted to $313,496.41.

Ever since 1963 the style of the Camp has been guided by the

Campers in front of a typical shelter.

District Conference's statement that year on a philosophy of camping. It said:

The ever increasing recognition of the significant role of the small group (house-church) in the vitality and life of the church is adding support to the experience and convictions of our church camp leaders that the small, intimate group, living together 24 hours a day for a period of time, has real validity. These experiences have and are offering unlimited opportunities to learn more about God and his gifts to man, man and his relationship and responsibility to God, and man and his awareness of his fellowman.

But, good as this philosophy is, the interest in church camping seems to be slowly dropping off. There has been a constant decline in the number of resident summer campers from the very start. For the 1979 season there were 309 campers altogether, forty-seven less than the summer before and 194 below the turnout for the first year at Blue Knob in 1961.

HIGHER EDUCATION

Juniata College is a child of Middle Pennsylvania Brethren, and it is only natural that the ties between the District and the institution should always have been close and cordial. As Charles C. Ellis wrote in 1947, from the College's perspective:

The men who have built Juniata were so intimately connected with the work of the Church of the Brethren that the two cannot be divorced. From the beginning the brethren who have carried the work of the college have also been intimately connected not only with the program of the local church but also with the larger work in the Middle District of Pennsylvania. They have served in the district offices and on district committees, and have represented the district on Standing Committee of Annual Conference.[15]

Observed he in conclusion, "[That] there has been the finest fellowship between them and the elders and ministers and churches of the district and the contribution of the Middle District of Pennsylvania to the progress of the brotherhood through the years is well recognized."

By the same token, the educator-churchman would be quick to admit, the College has done well by the District. It has sent hundreds of students, and from among its members have come some of the most loyal and generous trustees, capable professors, administrators, and staff personnel, and since the 1940s its organizations and churches have been a regular source of financial support. Long before 1940 there had always been individuals from Central Pennsylvania on Juniata's patrons' list, and as early as 1932 the elders and ministers had established a pre-ministerial Student Loan Service, which, however, was applicable to all Brethren schools. (This was a loan that was canceled after the recipient served the church for a stated period of time.) Then in 1940, during C. C. Ellis's presidency, the charter of Juniata was amended to provide for the election of a College trustee from each of the three supporting church districts of Pennsylvania. Since that time Middle District has shown much more of an official interest in the College's well-being.

The men's and women's groups soon after 1940 became very actively involved. The women began a student loan program of their own in 1942 that lasted until 1952, when it was discontinued at the College's suggestion and replaced by a scholarship for Brethren coeds, preferably from Middle Pennsylvania (ended in the late 1960s). Earlier, in 1948, they had set up a cash prize, to be awarded at commencement each year to "a worthy Brethren girl . . . who has contributed most to the spiritual welfare of the College" (also dropped in the sixties). The men, in the meantime, had started up a ministerial scholarship independent of the one by the elders in 1942, and it is still on the books.

In 1961 there went into operation a new policy on the 1932 Student Loan Service fund. The elders and ministers terminated this loan program at that time and called for a general District fund, a proposal that was adopted. In 1971 the policy was changed again to permit loans to those attending non-Brethren colleges. It was further extended in 1979 to include seminarians and graduate students preparing for any kind of church-related vocation.

The District today is linked to Juniata College in two other important financial ways. Since 1969 the Brethren of Atlantic Northeast, Middle, and Western districts contribute to the Alexander Mack Scholarship Fund, which affords grants-in-aid— preferentially, of course—to members of the denomination. There is also the Church of the Brethren Annual Support Fund Scholarship Fund, established in 1976 on the 100th anniversary of Juniata's founding, which is provided by contributions from individuals and churches. Pecuniary help from it goes to needy Brethren students.

Over the years the president of Juniata has presented a written report at each District Conference, a practice begun by C. C. Ellis in 1939. For a time (1961–1967), while Clarence H. Rosenberger was Director of Church Relations, he prepared the annual statement for the president. It was Calvert Ellis, upon succeeding his father, who began reporting District giving to the College in 1945. The District had, in 1944, for the first time made a specific commitment to Juniata: five thousand dollars. This was in response to the College's appeal for ten thousand dollars from its three constituent districts. Individual churches were urged to put the College in their budgets, which is still Juniata's main source of revenue from the District. For 1978–79 contributions from twenty-eight congregations totaled $16,011.75.

Conclusion
The District of Middle Pennsylvania
in Perspective

Today's Church of the Brethren is divided into twenty-four districts that include 1,179 congregations with an aggregate membership of 178,157. This is strictly a domestic count, since the denomination no longer makes any claim upon those overseas churches born of the missionary movement but now indigenously supported, propagated, and governed. Five hundred and thirty-eight congregations have full-time pastors, while 183 rely on a part-time ministry. There are 147 yoked parishes. The number of worshipers, overall, on a Sunday morning averages 95,156.

Middle Pennsylvania's membership, for its fifty-four congregations, is 11,283, good enough for a sixth-place rank among the Brotherhood's twenty-four districts. Of this membership, half (5,948) will be in attendance at Sunday worship each week—also a sixth-place standing. In the number of churches, however, the District slips to a tie for the ninth spot. Fifteen of the District's pastors are part-time, and, at Hollidaysburg, there is a pastoral team (husband-and-wife), for which there are no Brotherhood statistics for comparison purposes. There are six yoked parishes, which include both city (2) and country churches (10). In 1976 the Brotherhood reported fourteen affiliated/federated congregations, two of them located in Middle Pennsylvania (State College University Baptist and Brethren and Black Valley Federated).* The educational qualifications of District pastors are very sound—certainly as good as the denominational average—with two men holding earned doctorates and others in the process of getting theirs.

Middle Pennsylvania was one of the first two or three districts to

---

*In affiliated churches members hold membership in the local congregation without regard to denomination. Federated churches have joined programs and shared leadership, but retain separate denominational identities.

form in the Brotherhood, toward the end of the Civil War. Geographically, it is an isolated region carved up into long narrow valleys by a series of parallel mountain ranges, whose wilderness terrain first became a haven for pioneering Brethren in the last years of the Revolutionary War. These early backsettlers were among the very first white men to hack out farms and colonize the territory, enduring perilous conditions, toilsome challenges, and the loneliness of isolation to a degree experienced by very few of their fellow religionists who had earlier migrated south or later moved west.

As districts go, we saw above, Middle Pennsylvania holds its own in terms of membership, but its growth in the beginning was very gradual. By 1901, 118 years after the Revolution, the membership still barely exceeded 2,700 for the District's twenty-two congregations. New Enterprise had the most members then, 282; in fact, nearly half the District's constituency was concentrated in Morrisons Cove at that time. The church rolls reached an all-time high in the late fifties and early sixties, when the Church of the Brethren Yearbook showed a membership that hovered around 12,500. There has been a gradual decline in the past two decades, a trend generally reflected as well in Brotherhood statistics. The five districts with a larger head count than Middle Pennsylvania, it should be said, either have greater territorial boundaries or embrace highly populated urban areas.

Though Middle District was one of the first to promote and establish town churches, it has remained essentially rural-oriented. Its largest congregations are town-based, but the bulk of its membership is identified with country churches, which outnumber borough congregations by a three-to-one ratio. The socioeconomic status of the Brethren of Central Pennsylvania is solidly middle-class, with, of course, a strong contingent of farmers, as well as a good complement of blue-collar workers and office employees, a sizable number in business for themselves, and a disproportionately large phalanx of educators.

In playing the game of "firsts," the District can more than hold its own. The denomination's first two weekly papers had their origins here, and for a time in the last quarter of the nineteenth century Central Pennsylvania represented the very hub of Brethren journalism and publishing. Men like Henry R. Holsinger, the Brumbaugh brothers, and James Quinter stand among the most illustrious pioneers in the history of Brethren publications. Moreover, in Kenneth I. Morse, born and reared in Altoona, the District had a native son who put in twenty-one years (1950–1971) as editor of the

Gospel Messenger (it was during his career, in 1965, that the name was shortened to *Messenger*). It was his difficult lot to be editor during the explosive decade of the sixties, but he courageously grappled with the issues of the time: civil rights, campus unrest, the Vietnam War.

The first Brethren-operated elementary schools and one of the two earliest academies in the church took their rise in the District. And, of course, in Juniata College the District can point to the oldest existing Brethren-founded institution of higher learning. It has graduated scores of eminent churchmen and churchwomen down through the years. Most notable of these alumni have been Charles and Calvert Ellis, father and son. Four times the moderatorship of Annual Conference went to the two of them, and both held numerous other high positions in Brotherhood circles. Three other graduates have been elected moderator, and two have become president of Bethany Theological Seminary, including the incumbent, Warren F. Groff. (The Ellises were the only resident members from Middle Pennsylvania to wield the moderator's gavel.)

Other "firsts" or avant-garde involvement include such things as initiating town missions, holding regular districtwide ministerial conclaves, organizing women's groups in local congregations, starting Sunday Schools, accepting the salaried pastorate, and supporting political action. In William J. Swigart and Martin G. Brumbaugh the denomination had two of the most articulate spokesmen for the peace position during and after the First World War. In all other areas of programmatic development within the Brotherhood, Middle Pennsylvania, if not in the vanguard, at least has been ready to fall in line once the Brotherhood has committed itself to a position or course of action. Furthermore, a quick survey of Annual Conference Minutes reveals that some seventy queries have originated with this District since 1861, very few of which could be considered reactionary.

Sometimes, though, the churches of Middle Pennsylvania fell in step only haltingly. It was not mentioned before, but the unified budget system, for example, did not win quick acceptance after its introduction following World War II. Indeed, only in 1955 did the District itself adopt a budget. It took a few years for the Self-Allocation Program, which did away with assessments and encouraged each congregation to set its own outreach goals for the Brotherhood Fund, to take hold after this stewardship strategy became the practice in 1960. Today the statistics on Partners in Mission, since 1971 the new name for self-allocation whereby budgets are projected on a biennial basis, show Middle Pennsylvania's giving still significantly below the per capita average for the Brotherhood: $12.86 vs. $11.64. That puts it fourteenth among the twenty-four districts on the stewardship score. Some congregations have in the past turned to professional fund-raising organizations to help challenge them to do better, although this is no longer very common.

The most unhappy case of opposition to the Brotherhood program in Middle District was the fundamentalist unrest following the Second World War, when the denomination affiliated with the National Council of Churches of Christ in America. A conservative, biblically oriented theology had been strongly entrenched in the District from the time the School of Theology at Juniata College came into existence in 1918. But the fundamentalism taught there was not anti-Brethren in thrust, though its spokesmen were not exactly pleased with what they perceived to be the more liberal posture taken by Bethany dons. The late 1940s and early 1950s turned the District into a battleground—theologically and legally; no other sector of the Brotherhood was so profoundly agitated by fundamentalist rancor. In fact, the controversy was almost entirely confined to this District. In the end, the loss—as far as head count goes—was not devastating, but two congregations were split asunder. Another pair later seceded, each as a body, and elsewhere in the District there have been other individual or small-group desertions to independent "Bible Churches."

The District, therefore, provides an interesting study in contrasts—at times, especially in an earlier age, out in front of the rest of the denomination, then again sometimes stubbornly resisting change. As in other districts, moreover, there has always been a difference of opinion among individual members on what now seem to have been quaint concerns: dress, legal services, picnics, parades, women's hats, dancing, or moustaches. Likewise, the Brethren of Middle Pennsylvania have never been of one mind on the draft or military service, despite the church's heritage and the pronouncements emanating from Brotherhood and District conferences.

Now we are in the 1980s, and as was the case two hundred years ago, the challenges that confront the Brethren of Central Pennsylvania are considerable but not insurmountable. I have noted above the decline in church membership and attendance, which is really a national phenomenon in Protestantism. The old doctrines and the old forms no longer seem to sustain America's younger generations; it appears that they have lost curiosity about the Protestant heritage. The sixties bred a suspicion of religious institutions among them, and a "youth culture" emerged which, though sensitive to spiritual values, took little interest in such things as parishes, Sunday Schools, or foreign missions.

Then, too, Protestant officials now worry about what friend and foe alike call the "electronic church"—the use of television for mass evangelism—and the influence it has come to have within the past decade. They see a two-fold threat in this product of the seventies: members and money are leaving local congregations, and TV viewers are getting a simplistic, distorted Christian message. Whether this is so remains to be seen, but it is true, as Kermon Thomasson editorially observed in the *Messenger* (February 1980), "The society we live in and its ways of communicating with, reaching and attracting people produce too much competition for the methods Brethren traditionally have used for evangelization."

We are a shrinking denomination and a shrinking District. Annual Conference in 1979 assigned a committee to come up "with specific recommendations for dealing with the problem of diminishing membership" in the Church of the Brethren. However, as Julie Andrews sings in the movie *The Sound of Music*, "Strength doesn't lie in numbers." A drop in numbers, as Thomasson rightly observes, does not necessarily mean that the Brethren cannot speak out in a strong voice. The men and woman at Schwarzenau that day in 1708 seemed to understand this.

Notes

Notes to Introduction

1. Martin G. Brumbaugh, *A History of the German Baptist Brethren in Europe and America* (Mount Morris, Ill.: Brethren Publishing House, 1899), pp. xvi f.
2. *Gospel Messenger,* April 12, 1930, p. 235.
3. David M. Adams, *A Brief History of Claar Congregation* (Cleona, Pa.: Holzapfel Publishing Co., 1908). This booklet is preserved in the archival collection of Juniata College's L. A. Beeghly Library.

Notes to Chapter 1

1. Floyd E. Mallott, *Studies in Brethren History* (Elgin, Ill.: Brethren Publishing House, 1954), p. 25.
2. Donald F. Durnbaugh, ed., *The Church of the Brethren: Past and Present* (Elgin, Ill.: The Brethren Press, 1971), p. 9.
3. Edward L. Long, Jr., *War and Conscience in America* (Philadelphia: The Westminster Press, 1968), p. 61. I have drawn heavily upon this work in defining the basic positions of vocational pacifism, the viewpoint of the Anabaptists, and activistic pacifism, the stand the Brethren most nearly represent today.
4. Ibid., p. 67.
5. Durnbaugh, *The Church of the Brethren,* p. 11.
6. Ibid., p. 14.
7. Martin G. Brumbaugh, *A History of the German Baptist Brethren in Europe and America* (Mount Morris, Ill.: Brethren Publishing House, 1899), p. 45.
8. Donald F. Durnbaugh, ed. and trans., *European Origins of the Brethren* (Elgin, Ill.: The Brethren Press, 1958), p. 292.
9. See ibid.
10. Mallott, *Studies in Brethren History,* p. 37.
11. Ibid., p. 41.
12. Durnbaugh, *European Origins,* p. 216.
13. Ibid., p. 214.
14. Ibid., p. 107.
15. Ibid., p. 292.
16. Ibid., pp. 130, 131.
17. See ibid., pp. 190–97; 199–201; 268–75.
18. Durnbaugh, *The Church of the Brethren,* p. 78.
19. Durnbaugh, *European Origins,* p. 202.
20. Mallott, *Studies in Brethren History,* p. 41.
21. Paul W. Wallace, *Pennsylvania: Seed of a Nation* (New York: Harper and Row, 1962), p. xii.
22. Durnbaugh, *European Origins,* p. 202.
23. Donald F. Durnbaugh, ed. and trans., *The Brethren in Colonial America* (Elgin, Ill.: The Brethren Press, 1967), pp. 39–41.
24. Durnbaugh, *European Origins,* p. 309.

25. Ibid.

26. Ibid., p. 311.

27. Brumbaugh, *A History of the German Baptist Brethren,* pp. 178 f.

28. Wallace, *Pennsylvania: Seed of a Nation,* p. 140.

29. Morgan Edwards, *Towards a History of the Baptists in Pennsylvania, Both British and German* (Philadelphia: Printed by Joseph Crukshank and Isaac Collins, 1770), 1:90.

Notes to Chapter 2

1. My primary source on existing roads in the 1790s is the *U.S. Census, 1790: Pennsylvania* (Washington, D.C.: Government Printing Office, 1808). The map accompanying this volume, showing the road system in 1796, is at variance with accounts of road building in some of the local histories.

2. Solon J. and Elizabeth Hawthorn Buck, *The Planting of Civilization in Western Pennsylvania* (Pittsburgh, Pa.: University of Pittsburgh Press, 1939), p. 218.

3. John W. Jordan, *A History of the Juniata Valley and Its People* (New York: Lewis Historical Publishing Co., 1913), 1:87.

4. J. Simpson Africa, *History of Huntingdon and Blair Counties* (Philadelphia: Louis H. Everts, 1883), pp. 61, 245.

5. Uriah J. Jones, *History of the Early Settlement of the Juniata Valley* (Harrisburg, Pa.: The Telegraph Press, 1940), p. 193.

6. Ibid., p. 194.

7. Ibid., p. 375.

8. Galen B. Royer, ed., *A History of the Church of the Brethren in the Middle District of Pennsylvania* (Prepared and published under the supervision of the District Conference through its Home Mission Board, 1925), p. 21. Hereafter cited as the 1925 *History of the Church.*

9. Pearl E. T. Hanawalt, *Hahnewald: "Cock of the Woods."* Privately printed, n.d., pp. 158–61.

10. Jones, *History of the Juniata Valley,* p. 193; the 1925 *History of the Church,* p. 20.

11. Jones, *History of the Juniata Valley,* p. 196.

12. Jesse C. Sell, *Twentieth Century History of Altoona and Blair County* (Chicago: Richmond-Arnold Publishing Co., 1911), p. 421.

13. Jones, *History of the Juniata Valley,* pp. 199 f.

14. Sell, *History of Altoona and Blair County,* p. 421.

15. The 1925 *History of the Church,* p. 23.

16. Emma A. M. Replogle, *Indian Eve and Her Descendants* (Huntingdon, Pa.: J. L. Rupert, 1911), pp. 7 f.

Notes to Chapter 3

1. Galen B. Royer, ed., *A History of the Church of the Brethren in the Middle District of Pennsylvania* (Prepared and published under the supervision of the District Conference through its Home Mission Board, 1925), p. 19.

2. Gaius M. Brumbaugh, *Genealogy of the Brumbach Families* (New York: Frederick H. Hitchcock, 1913), p. 157.

3. Ibid., p. 406.

4. Gaius M. Brumbaugh and John G. Fouse, *Genealogy of the Descendants of Theobald Fouse (Fauss)* (Baltimore, Md.: Waverly Press, 1914), p. 6.

5. Ibid., p. 10.

6. Ibid., p. 5.

7. Most of my genealogical data on the Brumbaughs comes from the monumental volume published by Gaius Brumbaugh in 1913.

8. J. Maurice Henry, *History of the Church of the Brethren in Maryland* (Elgin, Ill.: Brethren Publishing House, 1936) pp. 33, 34.

9. See Freeman Ankrum, *Alexander Mack the Tunker and Descendants* (Scottsdale, Pa.: The Herald Press, 1943), p. 116.

10. See Lawrence W. Shultz, ed., *Paul Family Record, 1763–1963* (Winona Lake, Ind.: Light and Life Press, 1963), pp. 13–14.

11. See Brumbaugh, *Genealogy of the Brumbach Families*, p. 49.

12. George Ernest Long, Jr., and Margaret W. Long, *John Long of Lancaster County, Pennsylvania* (New Orleans, La.: Polyanthos, Inc., 1974), p. 14.

13. For this section I have supplemented data in the 1925 history with information from Pearl E. T. Hanawalt, *Hahnewald: "Cock of the Woods"* (Privately printed, n.d.) and John W. Jordan, *A History of the Juniata Valley and Its People*, vol. 1 (New York: Lewis Historical Publishing Co., 1913).

14. *Primitive Christian*, August 14, 1877, p. 502.

Notes to Chapter 4

1. Published at Lewisburg, Pa. in 1882.

2. *Pilgrim*, October 14, 1873, p. 326.

3. Donald F. Durnbaugh, "Brethren Beginnings in Middle Pennsylvania, Prepared in Recognition of One Hundred Years of District Organization" (1961), p. 4.

4. Ibid., p. 8.

5. Ibid.

6. Ibid.

7. *Pilgrim*, October 29, 1872, p. 351.

8. The Minute Book for 1864–1904 and the Financial Record Book (1847–1910) are both preserved in the Archives of Juniata College's Beeghly Library as part of the Middle District collections.

9. *Gospel Messenger*, September 26, 1893, p. 604.

10. Ibid., October 4, 1887, p. 609.

11. *Christian Family Companion*, October 22, 1872, p. 665.

12. *Gospel Messenger*, November 26, 1895, p. 763.

13. *Primitive Christian and Pilgrim*, June 12, 1877, p. 360.

14. *Christian Family Companion*, December 12, 1877, p. 786.

15. *Gospel Messenger*, September 20, 1924, p. 605.

16. See David M. Adams, *A Brief History of Claar Congregation* (Cleona, Pa.: Holzapfel Publishing Co., 1908), in Juniata College's Beeghly Library.

17. See n. 16.

18. *Gospel Messenger*, July 2, 1898, p. 411.

Notes to Chapter 5

1. *Christian Family Companion*, July 8, 1873, p. 428.

2. Ibid., April 21, 1874, p. 310.

3. *Gospel Messenger*, September 4, 1883, p. 129.

4. *The Pilgrim*, August 5, 1873, p. 241.

5. *Gospel Messenger*, July 28, 1906, p. 473.

6. *The Pilgrim*, December 5, 1872, p. 390.

7. "Stone Church Fiftieth Anniversary Booklet," December 11, 1960.
8. "Stone Church Dedication Souvenir," December 11, 1910.
9. Ibid.
10. *Gospel Messenger*, October 29, 1895, p. 701.

Notes to Chapter 6

1. Of the abundant literature on Sauer, his times, and the Sauer family press, the general reader will find three works by Brethren scholars especially helpful: Martin G. Brumbaugh, *A History of the German Baptist Brethren in Europe and America* (Mount Morris, Ill.: Brethren Publishing House, 1899); Donald F. Durnbaugh, ed. and trans., *The Brethren in Colonial America* (Elgin, Ill.: The Brethren Press, 1967); John S. Flory, *Literary Activity of the German Baptist Brethren in the Eighteenth Century* (Elgin, Ill.: Brethren Publishing House, 1908). Equally valuable but not so available is another study by a Brethren writer: Anna K. Oller, "Christopher Sauer, Colonial Printer," Ph.D. diss., University of Michigan, 1963. I have relied heavily on these works in dealing with the Sauer era.
2. Flory, *Literary Activity,* p. 264.
3. There is no book-length study of Kurtz, except for a fictionalized account by Harry A. Brandt, *Meet Henry Kurtz* (Elgin, Ill.: Brethren Publishing House, 1941). A number of biographical sketches appear in Brethren publications. The most scholarly treatment of Kurtz's life and publishing activity, which throws new light on his communitarian involvement, is Donald F. Durnbaugh's article, "Henry Kurtz: Man of the Book," *Ohio History* 76, no. 3 (Summer 1967): 115–31. This article has been reprinted in *Brethren Life and Thought* 16, no. 2 (Spring 1971): 103–21. It has provided much of the data used in my brief sketch of Kurtz.
4. There are two copies of this scarce magazine in the Archives of the Beeghly Library, Juniata College.
5. Durnbaugh, "Henry Kurtz: Man of the Book," p. 126.
6. A brief biographical sketch of Holsinger, which is not altogether accurate, appears in the 1925 district history, pp. 445 f. Random personal data can be found in his *History of the Tunkers and the Brethren Church* (Oakland, Cal.: Pacific Press Publishing Co., 1901), the *Christian Family Companion,* and the *Gospel Messenger.* See also Freeman Ankrum, *Alexander Mack the Tunker and Descendants* (Scottdale, Pa.: The Herald Press, 1943), pp. 197–201; J. H. Moore, *Some Brethren Pathfinders* (Elgin, Ill.: Brethren Publishing House, 1929), pp. 324–31.
7. Most of my information on Holsinger at Tyrone is gleaned from the *Christian Family Companion.*
8. Holsinger related these stories to John B. Brumbaugh, who worked for a time in his shop and later was co-founder of the *Pilgrim.* See *Gospel Messenger* 45 (August 4, 1906): 482.
9. Holsinger published the *Herald* for a year and a half, from May 1863, to November 1864, not for only six months as reported in the two local histories cited above. It should also be noted that Holsinger, together with J. H. Holmes, revived the *Herald* for a second time in August 1867. They added C. & W. Jones as a third partner in 1868. The following year Jones bought out the partnership and became the sole owner. There are no known extant copies of the *Herald.*
10. *Brethren's Almanac* (1874), p. 15; *Christian Family Companion* 9 (December 16, 1873): 791.
11. Holsinger, *History of the Tunkers,* p. 473.
12. Ibid., p. 477.
13. *Christian Family Companion* 7 (May 16, 1871): 321.
14. Moore, *Brethren Pathfinders,* p. 326.
15. *Christian Family Companion* 5 (January 26, 1869): 61.
16. *Gospel Messenger* 64 (May 25, 1915): 342.
17. Ibid.

18. Ibid., 26 (April 24, 1888): 6.

19. *Pilgrim* 5 (May 11, 1875): 228 f.

20. She is one of the few women given biographical recognition in the 1925 history. See pp. 407 f.

21. Moore, *Brethren Pathfinders,* p. 231.

22. *Minutes of the Annual Meetings of the Church of the Brethren* (1882), Art. 21, p. 412.

Notes to Chapter 7

1. J. H. Moore, *Some Brethren Pathfinders* (Elgin, Ill.: Brethren Publishing House, 1929), p. 324.

2. Freeman Ankrum, *Alexander Mack, the Tunker and Descendants* (Scottdale, Pa.: Herald Press, 1943), p. 198.

3. Ibid., p. 199.

4. Moore, *Brethren Pathfinders,* p. 328.

5. Letter dated December 10, 1881, in Henry R. Holsinger, *History of the Tunkers and the Brethren Church* (Oakland, Cal.: Pacific Press Publishing Co., 1901), pp. 403 f.

6. Holsinger's account of the committee's visit is given in his history, pp. 501–14.

7. See Carson Valley "Church Record," August 26, 1882, a manuscript journal of council minutes, 1871–1883, on file in the Middle District Historical Collections, Beeghly Library, Juniata College.

8. Holsinger, *History of the Tunkers,* pp. 792 f.

9. *Primitive Christian* 8 (June 19, 1883): 392.

10. Aughwick "Minute Book," September 11, 1880; January 1, 1881.

11. Moore, *Brethren Pathfinders,* p. 337.

12. Ibid., p. 338.

13. Ibid.

Notes to Chapter 8

1. John S. Flory, *Flashlights from History: A Brief Study in Social Development* (Elgin, Ill.: Brethren Publishing House, 1932), pp. 130, 147. Not all Brethren historians share the view that the membership was poorly educated during the "Wilderness Period." See Auburn Archie Boyers, "Changing Conceptions of Education in the Church of the Brethren," Ph. D. diss., University of Pittsburgh, 1969, pp. 53 f. Also, S. Z. Sharp, *The Educational History of the Church of the Brethren* (Elgin, Ill.: Brethren Publishing House, 1923), p. 41.

2. *Gospel Visitor* 6 (March 1856): 76.

3. Ibid., 6 (September, 1856): 249.

4. Ibid., 6: 250.

5. Besides the material in the 1925 History on Blooming Grove (pp. 268–73), there is an article by Russell Wieder Gilbert, "Blooming Grove, the Dunker Settlement of Central Pennsylvania," *Pennsylvania History* 20, no. 1 (January 1953): 23–39. The basic source on the colony is Joseph H. McMinn, *Blooming Grove* (Williamsport, Pa.: Scholl Brothers, 1901).

6. McMinn, *Blooming Grove,* p. 74.

7. Ibid.

8. *Two Centuries of the Church of the Brethren: Bicentennial Addresses* (Elgin, Ill.: Brethren Publishing House, 1908), p. 315.

9. Galen B. Royer, ed. *A History of the Church of the Brethren in the Middle District of Pennsylvania* (Prepared and published under the supervision of the District Conference through its Home Mission Board, 1925), p. 295.

10. Ibid., p. 296.

11. Floyd E. Mallott, *Studies in Brethren History* (Elgin, Ill.: Brethren Publishing House, 1954), pp. 198 f.

12. *Pilgrim* 2 (March 7, 1871): 106.

13. *Pilgrim* 5 (July 28, 1874): 236.

14. *Christian Family Companion* 8 (November 5, 1872): 696.

Notes to Chapter 9

1. For an extended biographical sketch of Zuck, see Earl C. Kaylor, Jr., *Truth Sets Free: A Centennial History of Juniata College, 1876–1976* (Cranbury, N.J.: A. S. Barnes and Co., Inc., 1977), chap. 2.

2. This account is taken from a Founder's Day speech by John B. Brumbaugh, printed in the *Gospel Messenger* 47 (May 16, 1908): 317 f.

3. *Gospel Messenger* 47 (May 16, 1908): 318.

4. *Juniata College Alumni Bulletin* 67 (Spring 1968): 2.

5. Ibid., p. 3.

6. Elmer Q. Gleim, *Change and Challenge: A History of the Church of the Brethren in the Southern District of Pennsylvania, 1940–1972* (Harrisburg, Pa.: Triangle Press, 1973), p. 98.

Notes to Chapter 10

1. Herbert Hogan, "Fundamentalism in the Church of the Brethren, 1900–1931," *Brethren Life and Thought* 5, no. 1 (Winter 1960): 25–36.

2. See H. B. Brumbaugh, "Fundamentals," *Gospel Messenger* 50 (February 4, 1911): 73.

3. *Minutes of the Annual Conference of the Church of the Brethren* (1931), pp. 81–83.

4. Hogan, "Fundamentalism in the Church of the Brethren," p. 32.

5. Ibid.

6. *Gospel Messenger* 69 (September 11, 1920): 542.

7. Ibid., 71 (March 25, 1922): 180.

8. Letter from Paul M. Robinson to Herbert Hogan, quoted in Hogan, "Fundamentalism in the Church of the Brethren," p. 36n.

9. Mimeographed minutes in the Middle District Historical Collection.

Notes to Chapter 11

1. There is an article on the Lewistown problem by Kenneth L. Gibble, "Brethren in Conflict: A Study of the Lewistown Split of 1948," *Brethren Life and Thought* 15, no. 3 (Summer 1970): 125–35. In my own investigation of the split, I have received invaluable help from James A. Hamilton, a former student of mine and a Lewistown resident. He organized for me the vast amount of legal and periodical literature related to the controversy.

2. *Brethren Fundamentalist* 7, no. 7 (July 1951): 4.

3. Ibid., 11, no. 41 (April 1946): 7.

4. *Minutes of the District Conference* (1942), p. 17, and *Minutes of the Annual Conference* (1942), p. 174.

5. This letter is published in its entirety in *Modernism: The Federal Council and the Church of the Brethren,* a forty-page pamphlet written by Harold Snider in 1944. It is deposited in the files of the Lewistown Church, Middle District Historical Collections.

6. Ibid., p. 26.

7. The Middle District Historial Collections contain sixty-five editions of Snider's paper. These are found in the files of the Lewistown Church.

8. *Gospel Trumpet,* January 30, 1945, p. 1.

9. *Brethren Fundamentalist* 1, no. 5 (May 15, 1945): 1.

10. Ibid., 6, no. 8 (August 1950): 1.

11. Manuscript record of 1945 Standing Committee minutes by William M. Beahm, Conference clerk, in the author's private library.

12. The full text of the letter is printed in *Brethren Fundamentalist* 4, no. 1 (January, 1948): 6.

13. This is reported in *Elders Committee of the Church of the Brethren vs. Brethren Fundamentalist,* a forty-page transcript of the October 18, 1945, hearing at the home of Harold Snider. This transcript was found among the papers of I. N. H. Beahm and now belongs to this writer's private library.

14. *Report of Committee on Harold Snider Interview,* "Admonitions Necessary," p. 1.

15. Letter to fellow regional secretaries in the Lewistown files.

16. Taken from excerpted entries deposited in the Lewistown files.

17. The full text of this document appears in the *Brethren Fundamentalist* 4, no. 5 (May 1948): 1.

18. The letter in its entirety is given in ibid.

19. This letter, dated May 4, appears in ibid., p. 7.

20. See full text, ibid.

21. *Gospel Messenger* 100, no. 22 (June 2, 1952): 14.

Notes to Chapter 12

1. I am indebted to a former student of mine, Paul C. Keely, who researched the material on the Twenty-Eighth Street church and organized it in a way that greatly facilitated my own study of the split and the preparation of this chapter.

2. Letter from Charles L. Cox to Edgar M. Detwiler, March 30, 1949. Plaintiff Exhibit 1, Court Case No. 1571, Equity Docket 1949, in the files of the Twenty-Eighth Street church, Middle District Historical Collections.

3. This letter constituted Plaintiffs Exhibit 2, ibid.

4. Altoona *Mirror,* November 27, 1950, p. 8.

5. *Minutes of the District Conference* (1949), p. 4.

6. The account of Kulp's hearing before Standing Committee is taken from the manuscript record of 1949 committee minutes by William M. Beahm, Conference clerk, in the author's private library.

7. Ibid. Unpaged typewritten insert.

8. *Brethren Fundamentalist* 5, no. 6 (June 1949): 1.

9. Plaintiffs Exhibit 4, Court Case No. 1571, Equity Docket 1949.

10. Plaintiffs Exhibit 5, ibid.

11. A typewritten report of this confrontation, in the Twenty-Eighth Street files.

12. Letter dated July 18, 1949, in the Twenty-Eighth Street files.

13. Charles D. Bonsack to Levi K. Ziegler, July 25, 1949. This letter is in the Twenty-Eighth Street files.

14. Letter dated July 19, 1949, in the Twenty-Eighth Street files.

15. Ibid.

16. A typewritten account of this encounter in the Twenty-Eighth Street files.

17. Letter from Levi K. Ziegler to Rufus P. Bucher, August 2, 1949, in the Twenty-Eighth Street files.

18. Ibid.

19. Postal card to Levi Ziegler, in the Twenty-Eighth Street files.

20. In the Twenty-Eighth Street files.

21. Manuscript record of 1950 committee minutes by William M. Beahm, Conference clerk, in the author's private library.

22. Altoona *Mirror,* November 22, 1950, a clipping in the Twenty-Eighth Street files.

23. *Brethren Fundamentalist* 7, no. 5 (May 1951): 1.

Notes to Chapter 13

1. *Christian Family Companion,* August 14, 1866, p. 254.

2. Floyd E. Mallott, *Studies in Brethren History* (Elgin, Ill.: Brethren Publishing House, 1954), p. 185.

3. *Gospel Messenger,* October 30, 1897, p. 700.

4. Ibid., February 22, 1908, p. 115.

5. *District Directory and Conference Minutes* (1979), p. 33.

6. Mallott, *Studies in Brethren History,* p. 167.

7. *District Echo* (May 1933), p. 2. The Record Book of the Sunday Schools of Middle District from 1899 to 1902, which gives a firsthand account of these proceedings and subsequent correspondence with the Brotherhood's General Missionary and Tract Committee, is located in the District Library at Juniata College.

8. "Report on the Foreign Mission Program and Policy," *Conference Minutes . . . Annual Conference of the Church of the Brethren* (1955), p. 67.

Notes to Chapter 14

1. *Christian Family Companion,* February 18, 1873, p. 109.

2. Quoted in Elmer Q. Gleim, *From These Roots: A History of the North Atlantic District, Church of the Brethren* (Lancaster, Pa.: Forry and Hacker, 1975), p. 75.

3. Ibid.

4. *Gospel Messenger,* January 21, 1965, pp. 16 f.

5. Quoted in Gleim, *From These Roots,* p. 141.

6. Floyd E. Mallott, *Studies in Brethren History* (Elgin, Ill.: Brethren Publishing House, 1954), p. 272.

7. Rufus D. Bowman, *The Church of the Brethren and War, 1708–1941* (Elgin, Ill.: Brethren Publishing House, 1944), p. 230.

8. Ibid., p. 238.

9. Ibid., p. 318.

10. Donald F. Durnbaugh, ed., *The Church of the Brethren: Past and Present* (Elgin, Ill.: The Brethren Press, 1971), pp. 98 f.

11. *Gospel Messenger,* February 27, 1954, p. 10.

12. Durnbaugh, *The Church of the Brethren,* p. 34.

13. Ibid., p. 106.

14. Mallott, *Studies in Brethren History,* p. 223.

15. Charles C. Ellis, *Juniata College: The History of Seventy Years, 1876–1946,* (Elgin, Ill.: Brethren Publishing House, 1947), p. 152.

Works Cited

Adams, David M. *A Brief History of Claar Congregation*. Cleona, Pa.: Holzapfel Publishing Co., 1908.

Africa, J. Simpson. *History of Huntingdon and Blair Counties*. Philadelphia: Louis H. Everts, 1883.

Altoona *Mirror*. November 22, 1950.

Ankrum, Freeman. *Alexander Mack the Tunker and Descendants*. Scottdale, Pa.: The Herald Press, 1943.

Aughwick "Financial Record Book." 1847–1910.

Bowman, Rufus D. *The Church of the Brethren and War, 1708–1941*. Elgin, Ill.: Brethren Publishing House, 1944.

Boyers, Auburn Archie. *"Changing Conceptions of Education in the Church of the Brethren."* Ph. D. dissertation, University of Pittsburgh, 1969.

Brandt, Harry A. *Meet Henry Kurtz*. Elgin, Ill.: Brethren Publishing House, 1941.

Brethren's Almanac. 1874.

Brethren Fundamentalist. 1945–51.

Brumbaugh, Gaius M. *Genealogy of the Brumbach Families*. New York: Frederick H. Hitchcock, 1913.

Brumbaugh, Gaius M., and Fouse, John G. *Genealogy of the Descendants of Theobald Fouse (Fauss)*. Baltimore, Md.: Waverly Press, 1914.

Brumbaugh, Henry B. "Diary." 1855–1916.

Brumbaugh, Martin Grove. *A History of the German Baptist Brethren in Europe and America*. Mount Morris, Ill.: Brethren Publishing House, 1899.

Buck, Solon J., and Elizabeth Hawthorne. *The Planting of Civilization in Western Pennsylvania*. Pittsburgh, Pa.: University of Pittsburgh Press, 1939.

Carson Valley. "Church Record." 1871–83.

Christian Family Companion. 1864–75.

District Echo. 1928–52.

Durnbaugh, Donald F. "Brethren Beginnings in Middle Pennsylvania. Prepared in Recognition of One Hundred Years of District Organization." 1961.

———, ed. and trans. *European Origins of the Brethren*. Elgin, Ill.: The Brethren Press, 1958.

———. "Henry Kurtz, Man of the Book." *Brethren Life and Thought* 16, no. 2 (Spring 1971).

———. "Henry Kurtz: Man of the Book." *Ohio History* 76, no. 3 (Summer 1967).

———, ed. and trans. *The Brethren in Colonial America*. Elgin, Ill.: The Brethren Press, 1967.

———, ed. *The Church of the Brethren: Past and Present*. Elgin, Ill.: The Brethren Press, 1971.

Edwards, Morgan. *Towards a History of the Baptists in Pennsylvania, Both British and German*, vol. I. Philadelphia: Printed by Joseph Crukshank and Isaac Collins, 1770.

Ellis, Charles C. *Juniata College: The History of Seventy Years, 1876–1946*. Elgin, Ill.: The Brethren Publishing House, 1947.

Flory, John S. *Flashlights from History: A Study in Social Development*. Elgin, Ill.: Brethren Publishing House, 1932.

———. *Literary Activity of the German Baptist Brethren in the Eighteenth Century*. Elgin, Ill.: Brethren Publishing House, 1908.

Garber, Ora W., comp. and ed. *Minutes of the Annual Conferences of the Church of the Brethren, 1945–1954*. Elgin, Ill.: Brethren Publishing House, 1956.

Gibble, Kenneth L. "Brethren in Conflict: A Study of the Lewistown Split of 1948." *Brethren Life and Thought* 15, no. 3 (Summer 1970).

Gilbert, Russell Wieder. "Blooming Grove, the Dunker Settlement of Central Pennsylvania," *Pennsylvania History* 20, no. 1 (January 1953).

Gleim, Elmer Q. *Change and Challenge: A History of the Southern District of Pennsylvania, 1940–1972*. Harrisburg, Pa.: Triangle Press, 1973.

———. *From These Roots: A History of North Atlantic District, Church of the Brethren*. Lancaster, Pa.: Forry and Hacker, 1975.

Gospel Messenger. 1884–1964.

Gospel Trumpet. January 30, 1945.

Gospel Visitor. 1851–73.

Hanawalt, Pearl E. T. *Hahnewald: "Cock of the Woods."* Privately printed, n.d.

Hartsough, H. L.; Miller, J. E.; and Garber, Ora W.; eds. *Minutes of the Annual Conference of the Church of the Brethren, 1923–1944*. Elgin, Ill.: Brethren Publishing House, 1946.

Heads of Families at the First Census of the United States Taken in the Year 1790, Pennsylvania. Washington, D.C.: Government Printing Office, 1808.

Henry, J. Maurice. *History of the Church of the Brethren in Maryland*. Elgin, Ill.: Brethren Publishing House, 1936.

Hogan, Herbert. "Fundamentalism in the Church of the Brethren, 1900–1931." *Brethren Life and Thought* 5, no. 1 (Winter 1960).

Holsinger, Henry R. *History of the Tunkers and the Brethren Church*. Oakland, Calif.: Pacific Press Publishing Co., 1901.

Jones, Uriah J. *History of the Early Settlement of the Juniata Valley*. Harrisburg, Pa.: The Telegraph Press, 1940.

Jordan, John W. *A History of the Juniata Valley and Its People*. Vol. I. New York: Lewis Historical Publishing Co., 1913.

Juniata College Alumni Bulletin 67 (Spring 1968).

Kaylor Earl C., Jr. *Truth Sets Free: A Centennial History of Juniata College, 1876–1976.* Cranbury, N.J.: A. S. Barnes and Co., Inc., 1977.

Long, Edward L. *War and Conscience in America.* Philadelphia: The Westminster Press, 1968.

Long, George Ernest, Jr., and Long, Margaret W. *John Long of Lancaster County, Pennsylvania.* New Orleans, La.: Polyanthos, Inc., 1974.

Mallott, Floyd E. *Studies in Brethren History.* Elgin, Ill.: Brethren Publishing House, 1954.

McMinn, Joseph H. *Blooming Grove.* Williamsport, Pa.: Scholl Brothers, 1901.

Messenger. 1965–80.

Minutes of the District Conference of Middle Pennsylvania, 1868–1979.

Moore, J. H. *Some Brethren Pathfinders.* Elgin, Ill.: Brethren Publishing House, 1929.

Oller, Anna K. "Christopher Sauer, Colonial Printer." Ph. D. dissertation, University of Michigan, 1963.

Pilgrim. 1870–76.

Primitive Christian. 1876; 1880–84.

Primitive Christian and Pilgrim. 1877–79.

Replogle, Emma A. M. *Indian Eve and Her Descendants.* Huntingdon, Pa.: J. L. Rupert, 1911.

Royer, Galen B., ed. *A History of the Church of the Brethren in the Middle District of Pennsylvania.* Prepared and published under the supervision of the District Conference through its Home Mission Board, 1925.

Sell, Jesse C. *Twentieth Century History of Altoona and Blair County.* Chicago: Richmond-Arnold Publishing Co., 1911.

Sharp, Solomon Z. *The Educational History of the Church of the Brethren.* Elgin, Ill.: Brethren Publishing House, 1923.

Shultz, Lawrence W., ed. *Paul Family Record, 1763–1963.* Winona Lake, Ind.: Light and Life Press, 1963.

Snider, Harold. "Modernism: The Federal Council and the Church of the Brethren." Pamphlet. 1944.

"Stone Church Dedication Souvenir." December 11, 1910.

"Stone Church Fiftieth Anniversary Booklet." December 11, 1960.

Two Centuries of the Church of the Brethren: Bicentennial Addresses. Elgin, Ill.: Brethren Publishing House, 1908.

Wallace, Paul W. *Pennsylvania: Seed of a Nation.* New York: Harper and Row, 1962.

Winger, Otto; Longenecker, J. H.; and Studebaker, George L.; eds. *Revised Minutes of the Annual Meetings of the Church of the Brethren from 1778 to 1922.* Elgin, Ill.: Brethren Publishing House, 1922.

Index of Personal Names

General Index